DEGREES OF FREEDOM

A.S. Byatt's *Possession* won the Booker Prize and the Irish Times/Aer Lingus International Fiction Prize in 1990. Her other fiction includes *The Shadow of the Sun, The Game, The Virgin in the Garden, Angels and Insects* and *The Matisse Stories*. She was educated in York and at Newnham College, Cambridge, and taught at University College London before becoming a full-time writer. She was appointed a C.B.E. in 1990.

BY A. S. BYATT

Fiction
The Shadow of the Sun
The Game
The Virgin in the Garden
Still Life
Sugar And Other Stories
Possession: A Romance
Angels & Insects
The Matisse Stories
The Djinn in the
Nightingale's Eye

Criticism
Unruly Times: Wordsworth and Coleridge
Passions of the Mind: Selected Writings

A. S. Byatt

DEGREES OF FREEDOM

The Early Novels of Iris Murdoch

VINTAGE

Published by Vintage 1994

6 8 10 9 7 5

First published in Great Britain by
Chatto & Windus Ltd., 1965

This edition first published in Great Britain by Vintage 1994

Vintage
Random House, 20 Vauxhall Bridge Road, London SW1V 2SA

Random House Australia (Pty) Limited
20 Alfred Street, Milsons Point, Sydney,
New South Wales 2061, Australia

Random House New Zealand Limited
18 Poland Road, Glenfield,
Auckland 10, New Zealand

Random House (Pty) Limited
Isle of Houghton, Corner of Boundary Road & Carse O'Gowrie,
Houghton 2198, South Africa

Random House UK Limited Reg. No. 954009

A CIP catalogue record for this book
is available from the British Library

ISBN 9780099302247

Printed and bound in Great Britain by
CPI Antony Rowe, Chippenham, Wiltshire

CONTENTS

v

ACKNOWLEDGEMENTS

Degrees of Freedom
I am very grateful to Iris Murdoch for reading the original volume in typescript and for many helpful suggestions for further reading and thought.
First published by Chatto & Windus, 1965.

The Time of the Angels
A lecture on *The Time of the Angels*, 1971.

The Nice and the Good
A review of *The Nice and the Good* (Chatto & Windus), *New Statesman*, 1968.

Bruno's Dream
A review of *Bruno's Dream* (Chatto & Windus), *New Statesman*, 1969.

The Black Prince
A British Council pamphlet, first published by The British Council, Printing and Publishing Department, London, 1977. Reproduced with the kind permission of the British Council.

Henry and Cato
A review of *Henry and Cato* (Chatto & Windus), *Daily Express*, 1976.

The Sea, The Sea
A review of *The Sea, The Sea* (Chatto & Windus), *Books and Bookmen*, 1978.

Nuns and Soldiers
A review of *Nuns and Soldiers* (Chatto & Windus), *New Statesman*, 1980.

The Good Apprentice
A review of *The Good Apprentice* (Chatto & Windus), *Vogue*, September 1985.

The Book and the Brotherhood
A review of *The Book and the Brotherhood* (Chatto & Windus), *Independent*, 1987.

The Writer and her Work
An edited text of a British Council pamphlet: 'Iris Murdoch', Writers and their Work, no. 257, published by the Longman Group for the British Council, 1976, reproduced with the kind permission of the British Council, and its 'Postscript', 1986, reproduced with the kind permission of Scribners, USA.

The Religion of Fiction
A review of *Angels and Insects*: Two Novellas by A. S. Byatt, by Michael Levenson, *The New Republic*, USA, August 2, 1993. Reprinted by permission of *The New Republic*, © 1993, *The New Republic*, Inc.

An essay, 'The Achievements of Iris Murdoch', has not been included here because it overlaps with other material in this volume.

FOREWORD TO THE VINTAGE EDITION

DEGREES OF FREEDOM was first published in 1965, when I had published one novel, and was thinking very hard about how to write novels and why I wanted to write them. The book was, as I said in my final chapter, written out of a passionate curiosity about how Iris Murdoch's novels *worked*, what the ideas were behind them, how the ideas related to the forms she chose, how her world was put together. It was a writer's curiosity about techniques that started me on the work. When I had finished it I had developed a deep admiration for Murdoch's wisdom, her understanding of the way philosophical, political, aesthetic and narrative thought worked (or failed to work). It is not too much to say that I was morally changed, for the better, I think. And I had learned a great deal about both writing and thinking.

I am happy to see the book reprinted after all this time. I have not tried to update the text of the original book, but have added (also unchanged) various articles and reviews I have written about Murdoch's work since 1965, and find it interesting to see how my attitudes to some of the novels and aesthetic preoccupations have changed over time. I now value *A Severed Head* more than I did at the time of writing, for instance, and both Murdoch's preoccupation and my own with nineteenth century realism, and the nature of realism in general have changed over time, and differently. It is partly for this reason that I was happy to have permission to include Michael Levenson's essay, *The Religion of Fiction*, which was in fact a review of a fiction of my own, but took some of the ideas in this book further than I might have done myself and in a direction which surprised and excited me.

The various later essays and pamphlets were written for

different audiences; the two British Council pamphlets, for instance, were written with foreign readers in mind, and have explanatory footnotes about things which British readers may find not to need any explanation. There is inevitably some repetition, for which I apologise; it would have been worse if Lynn Knight, to whose editorial skill I owe a great deal, had not excised some of the redundant repeated quotations.

The nature of criticism has changed a great deal since I wrote *Degrees of Freedom*. Critics have become very professional, politicised and relatively powerful, and writers have lost authority. As this happens, what writers write about writing seems almost to be a genre of its own, almost the only place where the kind of delighted reading I did when I first discovered Irish Murdoch can, in public, go on. Iris Murdoch herself has the breadth and depth which come from being a writer not confined by a narrowly 'literary' background; she expects novels to engage other ways of thinking and other ways of living in the world. My own background is narrowly literary, and my reading of Murdoch was one way out of that narrowness. I never wanted to be thought of as a literary critic, and want that still less now. *Degrees of Freedom* tried to *read* Iris Murdoch as best it could; and I hope it can be seen, not as a book about my writing, but as a writer's book about writing, a book by a writer reading.

That said, I must record that on rereading my book I have been occasionally dismayed by its sometimes solemn, almost Leavisite insistence on making severe judgments of tone and texture, a function both of the journalism and of the serious criticism of the time when I was writing. I had remembered my feeling about the novels as almost too enthusiastic, but the text sometimes contradicts that feeling. And this leads me to think that criticism written very close to the publication of important books is almost always too cautiously critical, too carping, even when admiring. Reviewers hedge their bets, and can seem absurdly censorious in retrospect. This book is not entirely free of that tone of voice.

A footnote. *Degrees of Freedom* was commissioned by Cecil Day Lewis, then my editor and also Irish Murdoch's editor. It did not occur to me to ask Iris Murdoch any questions whilst I was writing the book – I read what I could find, and made my own bibliography. When the book was finished, Day Lewis, much to my alarm, sent it to Iris Murdoch, who was generally kind, pointed out that I should have read Simone Weil, and said that she disagreed with some points of emphasis. I felt, rightly or wrongly, that there was a decorum that prevented me from asking questions, which I look back on ruefully as a kind of paradisal innocence, now that I receive almost weekly requests for bibliographies and explanations and ideas from students of both Murdoch's writings and my own.

DEGREES OF FREEDOM

I

INTRODUCTION

IN AN ARTICLE, *Against Dryness* (*Encounter*, No. 88, Jan. 1961), Iris Murdoch wrote: 'We need to be enabled to think in terms of degrees of freedom, and to picture, in a non-metaphysical, non-totalitarian, and non-religious sense, the transcendence of reality.'[1]

This article is concerned with defining and criticizing the idea of 'dryness' in literature and in life. In literature, Miss Murdoch says, we associate 'dryness' with the symbolist movement, with 'writers such as T. E. Hulme and T. S. Eliot, with Paul Valéry, with Wittgenstein'. It is an ideal, as she sees it, which admires the work of art in so far as it is whole and complete, containing its own terms of reference, not depending upon any resonance outside itself for its statement. The practitioners of 'dry' art admire myth and symbol, precision and coherence; they would, theoretically, be more excited by an interpretation of one of Shakespeare's plays which offered them a beautifully plotted, 'containing' framework of themes and recurrent symbols, than by one which placed its main emphasis on Shakespeare's skill in reproducing the accidental, the idiosyncratic happenings of life, or his power to arouse in the audience an immediate emotional attachment to Falstaff.

Miss Murdoch defines this literary 'dryness' as 'smallness, clearness, self-containedness' and offers as a particular example of it the 'crystalline'* novel of the twentieth century,

* The novels of William Golding are obvious examples of the 'crystalline'.

3

which she describes as a 'small-quasi-allegorical object portraying the human condition and not containing "characters" in the nineteenth-century sense'. The alternative to the crystalline novel is the journalistic story, 'a large, shapeless quasi-documentary object... telling with pale conventional characters some straightforward story enlivened with empirical facts'.

Neither of these literary forms, Miss Murdoch considers, engages with the problem she is setting out to present to us, the fact that we have, as she sees it, 'been left with far too shallow and flimsy an idea of human personality'. She describes a 'dry' view of the human personality, which she instances particularly in the work of Stuart Hampshire and of Sartre, which produces a picture of man as a 'lonely, self-contained individual', who is seen as the analogue of the literary self-contained symbol.

Of the man in Stuart Hampshire's *Thought and Action* Miss Murdoch writes:

> He is rational and totally free except in so far as in the most ordinary law-court and commonsensical sense his degree of awareness may vary. He is morally speaking monarch of all he surveys and totally responsible for all his actions. Nothing transcends him ... His inner life is resolved into his acts and choices and his beliefs, which are also acts, since a belief can only be identified through its expression. His moral arguments are references to empirical facts backed up by decisions ... His rationality expresses itself in awareness of the facts, whether about the world or about himself. The virtue which is fundamental to him is sincerity.[2]

Sartre's picture of man, Miss Murdoch argues, is essentially the same.

> Again, the individual is pictured as solitary and totally free. There is no transcendent reality, there are no degrees of freedom. On the one hand there is the mass of psychological desires and social habits and prejudices, on the other hand there is the will. Certain dramas, more Hegelian in character, are of course enacted within the soul; but the isolation of the will remains. Hence *angoisse*. Hence too, the special anti-

4

bourgeois flavour of Sartre's philosophy which makes it appeal to many intellectuals: the ordinary traditional picture of society and the virtues lies under suspicion of *mauvaise foi*. Again, the only real virtue is sincerity.[3]

Against what she calls 'this facile idea of sincerity', Miss Murdoch would put the 'hard idea of truth'; that is, in her terms, we should see man, as we no longer do, 'against a background of values, of realities, which transcend him'. The concept of sincerity is 'self-centred', the concept of truth 'other-centred'.[4]

The aspect of this transcendent reality upon which, both in terms of liberal morals, and of the art of the novel, Miss Murdoch lays most emphasis, is what she calls the 'opacity of persons'. The pursuit of sincerity as opposed to truth leads, as she sees it, to what she calls fantasy, and it opposes to imagination a process which leads to myth-making, to a dry and facile ordering of experience into false and easily comprehended wholes whilst, as Miss Murdoch insists, 'Reality is not a given whole'. She writes:

> We are not isolated free choosers, monarchs of all we survey, but benighted creatures sunk in a reality whose nature we are constantly and overwhelmingly tempted to deform by fantasy.[5]

We need, she says, 'a respect for the contingent', for imagination as opposed to fantasy, and an essential part of the concept of the contingent is seen to be an awareness of 'the real impenetrable human person'. 'Real people are destructive of myth, contingency is destructive of fantasy, and opens the way for imagination.' Imagination, a quality Miss Murdoch exemplifies in Shakespeare and the Russians, 'those great masters of the contingent', is an attempt to apprehend truth, and Miss Murdoch suggests that the novel, to return to its imaginative power, must pit against 'the consolations of form, the clear crystalline work, the simplified fantasy-myth', 'the now so unfashionable naturalistic idea of character'.[6]

This idea of character, that is, is the literary equivalent

of the moral idea of the real impenetrable human person, 'substantial, impenetrable, individual, indefinable and valuable'. And this individual human person lives in a world where there are degrees of freedom, he is 'free and separate' but 'related to a rich and complicated world from which as a moral being he has much to learn'.[7]

All Miss Murdoch's novels can in an important sense be seen as studies of the 'degrees of freedom' available to individuals, and it is from this point of view that I have approached them in the following pages.

The kinds of freedom studied vary, and the style and matter of the novels also vary greatly, but there is, I would maintain, a surprisingly constant unity of theme underlying the ideas of all the seven novels we have so far. Between the first two novels, *Under the Net* and *The Flight from the Enchanter*, and the third, *The Sandcastle*, there is a break – not only a stylistic attempt to move from fantasy-myth to depiction of character, but a break in subject-matter. The first two books have a social dimension, an emphasis on the possibilities of man's freedom in society at large and mechanized, an interest in work, in the sense of jobs, which is not importantly present in the later novels, which are more concerned with freedom within personal relationships, with Jamesian studies of one person's power over, or modification of another person – although both ideas are of course present in most of the novels. *The Flight from the Enchanter* is certainly concerned with one individual's power over another within relationships as well as socially, and the problem of freedom in work, or how work limits freedom, recurs both in the organization of the community in *The Bell*, and in Mor's struggles with his job and the Labour party, or even Rain Carter's painting, in *The Sandcastle*. And the problem which Jake Donaghue encounters from time to time in *Under the Net*, the problem of economic freedom, of whether he can accept large sums of dishonourably earned money in order to live free of economic necessity, also, in a different form, besets Randall in *An Unofficial Rose*, who buys a kind of freedom with the money obtained from the sale of his father's Tintoretto.

But the general idea with which I want to begin the study of the freedom of the characters in the novels is that this freedom is worked out, very broadly speaking, in terms of a constant – and, in the nature of things, incomplete and unresolved – interaction of their own attempts to act, or to order their experience (a process which constantly degenerates into 'deforming' reality by fantasy) with the transcendent 'reality'. This reality is seen in part as that fundamental, indefinable stuff of existence to which in her book on Sartre, Miss Murdoch refers in these terms:

> What *does* exist is brute and nameless, it escapes from the scheme of relations in which we imagine it to be rigidly enclosed, it escapes from language and science, it is more and other than our descriptions of it.[8]

But Miss Murdoch's concept of incomprehensible reality does not exactly coincide with Sartre's 'contingent over-abundance of the world'. It contains an element which Sartre would ignore, dividing, as Miss Murdoch says he does, the world between the 'swooning abundance of existence' and the reason and will of the isolated human individual. This element can be located in her criticism of Sartre as a novelist. She writes:

> Sartre has an impatience, which is fatal to a novelist proper, with the *stuff* of human life. He has, on the one hand, a lively interest, often slightly morbid, in the details of contemporary living, and on the other a passionate desire to analyse, to build intellectually pleasing schemes and patterns. But the feature which might enable these two talents to fuse into the work of a great novelist is absent, namely an apprehension of the absurd irreducible uniqueness of people and of their relations with each other.[9]

Miss Murdoch believes, that is, in a respect for people as they are, and not, as she says of Sartre's man in another context, 'stripped and made anonymous by extremity'[10], which leads her to set a higher value upon those social and moral ideas and habits which do in fact exist and affect people, a respect for something that G. S. Fraser has excellently isolated when he entitled his article on her work *The Solidity of the Normal*.[11] The normal also forms part of the ultimately mysterious transcendent reality, in a way which is illuminated by a remark of Miss Murdoch's husband, John Bayley, who, discussing the 'normal' virtue of Henry James's Maggie Verver, says that she is human in the way in which 'to be human is to be virtually unknown' and comments that 'the conventional and the mysterious are closely allied, are indeed one and the same thing'.[12] I think that 'normal' is a better word for what Miss Murdoch wishes us to take into account than 'conventional', and I do not, even so, want to suggest that normality is *ipso facto* something desirable in Miss Murdoch's world; only that it is one of the aspects of the stuff of human life which contributes to the opacity of persons, to the mystery of freedom in relation to reality.

2

UNDER THE NET

G. S. FRASER has written: '*Under the Net*, Miss Murdoch's first novel, as its very title suggests, presents an image of the private will, of various private wills, at odds with the "social spirit" and the "needs of external co-operation"; society is seen as precisely the net which is always coming down to catch us, but which has large or coarse meshes that we can easily escape through, if only later to be caught on other, finer meshes.'[1] Malcolm Bradbury, in an article in the *Critical Quarterly*, Spring 1962, to which I am indebted throughout this chapter, suggested that 'the myth of Mars, Venus and Vulcan is used as a kind of scaffolding'[2] for *Under the Net*. Mr Bradbury gave several instances of the ingenuity with which this myth has been used – the comparison of the hulking Hugo Belfounder, armaments manufacturer and fireworks maker, to Vulcan, and of Sadie the film star and Anna, her sister, to various aspects of Venus; from the name of the dog, Mr Mars, to the location of Hugo's film studio at Hammersmith. I was very impressed by this argument, and had thought I had found a continuation of the use of this myth of Vulcan's net in this sense in *A Severed Head*, where Martin Lynch-Gibbon sees his wife and her lover, who have 'simply' freed themselves from the reality of her marriage, as Ares and Aphrodite, and Palmer assures Martin, the deceived husband, that he is not Hephaistos. But Miss Murdoch assures me that she had no intention, when writing *Under the Net*, of referring to the myth in this way; and it seems to me that what her intention was, here, is important.

9

Besides its social significance, the net is given a philosophical significance within the novel. The image is used precisely by Hugo, who is shown as having a kind of non-classifying vision of life which sees everything as 'unutterably particular'. Jake, the narrator, says of him:

> With Hugo I felt like a man who, having vaguely thought that all flowers are the same, goes for a walk with a botanist. Only this simile doesn't fit Hugo either, for a botanist not only notices details, he classifies. Hugo only noticed details. He never classified. It was as if his vision were sharpened to the point where even classification was impossible, for each thing was seen as absolutely unique. I had the feeling that I was meeting for the first time an almost completely truthful man.[3]

Hugo, that is, is aware of that aspect of Miss Murdoch's truth or reality which consists of a respect for the contingent, for the way in which things cannot be arranged finally in patterns by the organizing intellect. It is Hugo, or Hugo in the figure of Annandine, as he is presented by Jake in Jake's book, *The Silencer*, who uses the image of the net in a philosophical sense, as a symbol for theorizing, or forming concepts about a situation. Annandine is made to say:

> What I speak of is the real decision as we experience it; and here the movement away from theory and generality is the movement towards truth. All theorizing is flight. We must be ruled by the situation itself and this is unutterably particular. Indeed it is something to which we can never get close enough, however hard we may try as it were to creep under the net.[4]

Here the net is seen, not, as in G. S. Fraser's picture of it, as something which is, initially at least, a trap, through whose meshes one tries to escape, but as something thrown over truth, *underneath* which we must creep in order to get at the precise situation. This is Hugo's view of it; he is a man who represents what Miss Murdoch called in a philosophical article on the subject, the nostalgia for the particular.* Miss Murdoch has said that the image of the net of which she was thinking when she wrote the book was that of Wittgenstein (*Tractatus Logico-Philosophicus*, 6.341). Here Wittgenstein uses the net as a picture of the way in which concepts, ideas, connections of thought, can be used to 'bring the description of the universe to a unified form'. (He instances Newtonian mechanics.)

He writes:

> Let us imagine a white surface with irregular black spots. We now say: Whatever kind of picture these make I can always get as near as I like to its description, if I cover the surface with a sufficiently fine square network and now say of every square that it is white or black. In this way I shall have brought the description of the surface to a unified form. This form is arbitrary, because I could have applied with equal success a net with a triangular or hexagonal mesh. It can happen that the description would have been simpler with the aid of a triangular mesh; that is to say we might have described the surface more accurately with a triangular, and coarser, than with the finer square mesh, or vice versa, and so on.

Wittgenstein writes a little later:

> Laws, like the law of causation, etc., treat of the network and not of what the network describes.

Or, to return to Miss Murdoch's description of reality, 'it is more, and other, than our descriptions of it'.

What is important about the net is that it is *there*, both in the social sense and in the sense in which Tamarus, the figure

---

* This article (*Proceedings of the Aristotelian Society*, 9th June 1952) deals with the idea of the inner life, the mental event, the search for 'a particular and immediate kind of experience [cf. Hugo] which should be independent of our ordinary modes of understanding'. Miss Murdoch concludes, 'We fail to discover this; but what we do discover are those features of experience which inspire the quest – features which analysis has neglected or denied.' In a sense the 'quest' here is Jake's quest, and the conclusion the conclusion of *Under the Net*.

Jake puts against Hugo/Annandine, argues in the dialogue; 'What you say goes against our very nature. We are rational animals in the sense of theory-making animals.' And 'there are theories abroad in the world, political ones for instance, and so we have to deal with them in our thoughts and that at moments of decision too'.[5]

Political theory enters the narrative in the person of Lefty Todd, to whom, in fact, Hugo ultimately surrenders what power and wealth he has, and whom he comes greatly to admire. I will discuss Lefty later; for the moment I want only to suggest that we accept, loosely, the double image of the net, seen first as a series of social patterns, or relationships or traps, within the book, from which the 'private will' seeks to escape, or to liberate others, with the aid of a hairpin, a file, or Belfounder's Domestic Detonators, and secondly as a net of concepts, of ideas, man-made and in one sense at least inevitable, which we use to try to describe truth, and underneath which Hugo and the impulse he represents would try to creep to come at the unutterably particular situation.

It is important to recognize that Hugo's view of truth, however sympathetic we, and Jake, may be to it, is not meant to be the final statement of the book. Jake, when re-reading *The Silencer*, reflects that 'there occurred to me instantly a variety of ways in which the position of Tamarus might be strengthened',[6] and Miss Murdoch herself says 'it is through an enriching and deepening of concepts that moral progress takes place'.[7] And Hugo and what he stands for yield constantly throughout the book to the socially committed Lefty, whose concepts are rigid and absolute.*

The story of the book follows two quests, that for Hugo and that for Anna, whose 'simple' theory of art, and silence in art, since all speech is lies, parallels the lack of concepts, philosophically, of Hugo, the 'silencer'. At the end of the book, Jake, having found and lost both the objects of his search, has found out more about reality and about art, as represented by Anna, and about his own relationship to

---

* This point is excellently made by Malcolm Bradbury.

12

them. He knows much more about his own limitations and his own relationship to these. The novel could be described as a philosophical novel very precisely, since there is clearly a very conscious attempt to pattern the events in Jake's story in terms of ideas of freedom, of philosophical approaches to reality, to what we know and what we cannot know. But it is nevertheless a novel, and not simply a philosophical game.

In her first two books Miss Murdoch's great skill in proliferating precise symbols, complex cross-references, situations, such as traps or mimetic actions which repeat and elaborate each other, fuses her gift for story-telling with her gift for arranging an action around a pattern of ideas, more happily than in some of her later, more deliberately 'real' novels. That is to say, the exploration of the ideas and of the characters, the human behaviour, in the novel here, work *together* – and whereas Hugo is fascinating as a phenomenon and can be 'placed' as the representative of certain intellectual attitudes to experience, Jake, in spite of the fantastic nature of the events through which he moves, is a real character, and cannot be simply 'placed', however much we plot around him.

Jake, it has been remarked, is to a great extent a standard fictional hero of our time. He is an 'outsider', uncommitted politically or emotionally, opposed to formal work, socially classless – he is constantly asking himself, for instance, if he 'belongs to a social class which takes money in situations like this' – but his decisions are ultimately determined by considerations of morals rather than class. He has, that is, a kind of negative freedom. G. S. Fraser says of him that he

> does not have to make himself a bohemian, he is one, and the roots of his restlessness seem to lie more in an inquisitive desire to test out the range of his own adaptability than in any strong hatred of any particular atmosphere or milieu.[8]

When the book opens we are told of him that he has 'shattered nerves' and 'one effect of this is that I can't bear being alone for long'.[9] And it becomes clear from his relationships with the other characters that his detachment is nervous, a kind of instinctive protecting himself from life, rather than a purposive search for 'freedom'. When at the beginning of the book, Magdalen, in whose flat and to a certain extent on whose charity he has been living, announces that she is getting married, he is at first surprised and a little guilty that he has not noticed what was taking place, and even tells her that 'I ought to have looked after you better'. He feels for a moment a 'need' for her, and 'her eyes were troubled' but

> I took a deep breath and followed my rule of never speaking frankly to women in moments of emotion. No good ever comes of this. It is not in my nature to make myself responsible for other people. I find it hard enough to pick my own way along.

And he comments, 'The dangerous moment passed'.[10]

In his description of his early relationship with Anna Quentin the same shying away from a relationship is evident; when he can say that he 'did come near to taking the thing seriously' he comments that that was 'perhaps why I let myself drift away from her in the end'. He elaborates upon this:

> I hate solitude but I am afraid of intimacy. The substance of my life is a private conversation with myself which to turn into a dialogue would be equivalent to self-destruction. The company which I need is the company which a pub or a café will provide. I have never wanted a communion of souls. It's already hard enough to tell the truth to oneself. But communion of souls was Anna's special subject ... She took life intensely and very hard. Whereas I think it is foolish to take life so, as if you were to provoke a dangerous animal which will break your bones in the end in any case.[11]

It is not clear that a communion of souls is a better alternative particularly in view of the disastrous effects of Antonia's belief in such a communion in *A Severed Head*, to Jake's uncommitted and self-contained search for truth, but neither is it the only one. Nor is it in Miss Murdoch's terms possible to find truth without some relationship with other people.

At the beginning of the book, too, Jake's relationship to

his work is made clear, through comments of Magdalen's and through Jake's relationship with Dave Gellman, the philosopher. Magdalen, referring to her bookmaker fiancé, says 'We all live on other people's vices. I do, you do, and you live on worse ones than he does.' Jake comments, 'This was a reference to the sort of books I sometimes translated.'[12] And, referring to his translations of Jean-Pierre Breteuil's 'bad, best-selling stuff', he quotes and accepts a judgment of Dave's: 'Anything rather than original work, as Dave says.'[13] Here too, there is a shying away, a refusal to be committed, to grapple with art, as with relationships; he has reflected on the fact that 'the present age was not one in which it was possible to write an epic' and 'had contrived to stop myself just short of the point at which it would become clear to me that the present age was not one in which it was possible to write a novel'.[14] However, he is not writing a novel.

Driven to some kind of action by being turned out by Madge, Jake goes to visit Dave who lives in what Jake calls 'contingent London'. 'Everywhere west of Earls Court is contingent except for a few places along the river.' Dave on hearing of Jake's homelessness, raises the idea of jobs.

'If I would be you,' said Dave, 'I would take a proper job.' He pointed to the white wall of the hospital which loomed very close outside the window.[15]

Malcolm Bradbury writes of Dave that he 'represents a spare utilitarian view of the world', a view that is not quite fair, since there is a great warmth about him, he has the mystery of his Jewishness, and 'his life is a continual *tour de force* of intimacy' – a description which, coming from the uncommitted Jake at that stage of the book, is vaguely derogatory, but is ultimately at least as much of a reflection upon Jake's isolation as upon Dave.

What Dave dislikes is metaphysics, or at least the metaphysics of his pupils to whom the world is a mystery 'to which it should be reasonably possible to discover a key . . . of the sort that could be contained in a book of some 800 pages',[16] a process to which Miss Murdoch would almost certainly refer as 'deforming the world by fantasy'. Dave's relation with contingency is in one sense akin to Hugo's in that he objects to metaphysics and to Jake's 'artistic' uses of language; but in another it is opposed. He can afford, Jake says, to live in contingent London, because he is 'professionally concerned with the central knot of being (though he would hate to hear me use that phrase) and not with the loose ends that most of us have to play with'.[17]

And also, unlike Hugo, his emphasis is not upon the unutterably particular situation. Like certain later clerical and military characters, also attached, as he is, to orthodox forms of religion – I think particularly of James Tayper Pace in *The Bell*, and of the clergymen in *The Sandcastle* and *An Unofficial Rose*, he believes that

> Human beings have to live by clear practical rules and not by the vague illumination of lofty notions which may seem to condone all kinds of extravagance.[18]

Like James Tayper Pace he turns out to have been, in practice, much more right than the ordinary liberal reader is likely to imagine; James's assessment of the effect of his actions on Toby is much better than the much more 'imaginative' Michael's, and Dave's advice, here, turns out to be what Jake ultimately follows – although at this stage we accept Jake's protests at their face value, and when Dave says that Jake is 'too much the incorrigible artist' we think we see where Jake's values, Jake's freedom, differ from Dave's own. And Jake is perhaps searching for something that not so much Dave's utilitarianism, as his 'peculiar brand of linguistic analysis' is opposed to.

Miss Murdoch herself is, like Jake the artist, like Dave's pupils, constantly 'tempted' towards metaphysics, and when Jake says 'Hegel says that Truth is a great word and the thing is greater still. With Dave we never seemed to get past the word'[19] one feels that it is to be seen as genuine artist's frustration with the linguistic philosopher's approach to reality. And when Jake swims symbolically with Lefty and Finn, alive in the river, the fact that Dave sits isolated and contemplates them is perhaps symbolically also connected to this.

However, Dave's prescriptions for Jake contain much of Miss Murdoch's own values.

> I looked at the wall of the hospital. 'To save my soul,' I said. 'Not therefore,' said Dave scornfully. 'Always you are thinking of your soul. Precisely it is not to think of your soul but to think of other people.'[20]

Dave's remarks are not only utilitarian; they are also directed at Jake's own unproductive situation.

> Society should take you by the neck and shake you and make you do a sensible job. Then in your evenings you would have the possibility to write a great book.[21]

During this conversation Jake says, à propos of nothing in particular, 'I can't help my psychology. After all, freedom is only an idea.' I imagine that this is ironically directed at Dave who cannot get past the word in the case of truth, but what does seem clear here is that Jake's problem is more complex than not being able to help his psychology; he does not believe that freedom is only an idea, and it matters to him in terms of freedom what he shall do and where he shall go.

If Jake's attitudes to personal relations become clear through the two women, and his attitude to his work is preliminarily illuminated by Dave, we discover something further about his attitude to Miss Murdoch's truth in his relationship with Finn who 'isn't exactly my servant'. Finn, like Hugo, like Dave, is according to Jake, 'truthful'. 'He never tells lies, he never exaggerates.' Jake sees him as 'an inhabitant of my universe and cannot conceive that he has one containing me; and this arrangement seems restful for both of us'.[22]

He ascribes this to Finn's lack of an 'inner life', which he connects with his truthfulness – Jake himself has 'a complex one and highly differentiated . . . aspects have always been my trouble'.[23] Finn on the other hand is apt to 'make objective statements when these are the last thing one wants like a bright light on one's headache'.

Here we have the first hint of Jake's trouble – a liking for 'aspects', a dislike for objective statements, a belief in his own inner life, and a lack of respect for Finn, whom he automatically treats as an inhabitant of his own universe; this is elaborated in the passage in which Jake tells us that Finn talks a lot to Dave about religion and 'is always saying that he will go back to Ireland to be in a country which really has religion, but he never goes'. Jake obviously does not take this in Finn seriously, brushing it aside with 'I prefer it when Finn doesn't talk too much' and an elaboration of his own talks with Dave.[24] But at the end of the book it is clear that this need is meaningful to Finn, and that Finn inhabits his own universe; it is his return to Ireland that finishes Jake's isolation. Thus, as in the case of Madge, Jake is seeing what he pleases, and as in the case of his views of Sadie's and Anna's real relationship with Hugo, he is distorting reality to fit his own needs. He says at the end:

> I felt ashamed, ashamed of being parted from Finn, of having known so little about Finn, of having conceived things as I pleased, and not as they were.[25]

Jake then, at the beginning of the book is partly a 'private will' at odds with society; he is also from his own point of view afraid of relationships with people, afraid of, or anxious to avoid, work, both useful and creative, and he has a strong tendency to deform the nature of reality by fantasy. In this context, he says significantly 'I hate contingency. I want everything in my life to have a sufficient reason'.[26] I would remark, in passing, that one of Miss Murdoch's achievements is the skill with which, through the medium of the first person narrative, she persuades the reader to accept, or largely to accept, Jake's 'sufficient reasons', his summing up of events, largely because the convention, which she exploits, allows us to suppose that if the narrator says 'I saw that it was not Sadie that Hugo loved, but Anna', this is in fact the case;

thus the force of her revelations that what the other 'truthful' characters said was in fact true is all the greater.

The action of the story is partly Jake's quest for Hugo, his 'destiny', and partly his quest for Anna. It is complicated by the aesthetic, financial and political aspects of the situation in which he finds himself. His only final acquisition during the events related is the company of the dog Mars, whom he releases from a cage, and with whom he develops a relationship of some warmth. Mars is, although he is ageing, a symbol, like the dogs in *The Sandcastle*, *The Bell* and *The Unicorn*, for a kind of natural vital energy which Jake had lacked. Mars has in some ways much in common with Anna, to whom we must now turn. Anna has a naturalness, heavy brown hair which is, like Mr Mars, showing signs of natural ageing, which are emphasized at some length; she has streaks of grey, 'a sort of wrecked look which was infinitely touching' – compared with Sadie she is like a 'sweet blackbird' as opposed to 'some sort of rather dangerous tropical fish'.[27] Anna and Sadie are the first of a series of contrasts of 'natural' and 'artificial' women, who seem to combine the human and aesthetic functions of the objects of desire for her male characters.

Anna is first seen in a romanticized version of Sartre's 'gluey' stuff of life, or maybe, here, primarily stuff of art, since we are in the Mime Theatre, a refinement of art to its purest elements.

> The contents of the room had a sort of strange cohesion and homogeneity, and they seemed to adhere to the walls like the contents of a half-empty jam jar. Yet here was every kind of thing. It was like a vast toy shop that had been hit by a bomb.[28]

In this room Jake sleeps in a bearskin; later, on the Embankment, he sleeps with Mars whose 'body was radiantly warm from nose to tail'. In both cases there is a sense of warmth and life. It is significant, too, that when Madge in Paris offers Jake large sums of money for doing nothing, remarking 'But isn't that what you've always wanted?' it is the thought of

Mars growing old, that 'he would do no more work. He would not swim flooded rivers any more, or scramble over high fences, or fight with bears in lonely places', which crystallizes Jake's resolution to 'live my own life'.[29] Thus the release of Mars releases something in Jake, which impels him towards a 'real' decision about leading his own life.

His relationship with Anna is one of 'love' although he has been reluctant to tie himself down because 'love' would make too many demands on him. Malcolm Bradbury sees Anna, with her 'archaic coils of hair', her romantic surroundings and her singing, as 'an order of life from which Jake feels separated and which he yet feels the necessity to pursue';[30] she is seen as pure art, divorced from social distortions, divorced as far as possible from the distorting effects of speech. Her theories of art resemble those of Hugo, although they are not identical, and it is not her 'philosophy of silence' that Jake finds attractive in her or pursues – indeed he finds this so antipathetic that he immediately supposes her to be 'in the grip of a theory' (which she is) and supposes the Mime Theatre to be Hugo's idea.

In fact, the theatre has been created by Hugo to please Anna, who is in love with him. He tells Jake that the theatre was 'all Anna's idea. I just joined in. She had some sort of general theory about it, but I never understood properly what it was.' Here there is an irony; Anna's 'general theory' which Hugo does not understand, is her attempt to reproduce in her art his respect for the unutterably particular, the simply true, the fact or experience uncorrupted by ideas or personal feelings. Jake tells him this; Anna's theory, he insists, was 'just what was yours. It was you reflected in Anna, just as that dialogue [*The Silencer*] was you reflected in me.' Hugo significantly and consistently says 'I don't recognize the reflections'.[31] Hugo would not; he is interested only in the particular, but both Anna and Jake, who are artists (Jake with a strong streak of the philosopher), whilst recognizing the deep need for Hugo's particular vision, his sense that things are unknowable and unclassifiable, not to be patterned, are nevertheless driven by their own nature to form patterns and theories with that vision.

These contrasted needs recur throughout Miss Murdoch's work, reappearing, as I hope to show, even in Hannah Crean-Smith's attempt in *The Unicorn* to live a life of religious suffering that shall not be a myth or an object of patterned thought to herself or to others – an attempt, like Anna's 'philosophy of silence', doomed to become, at least partially a theory, or a myth, an imprisoning net, in itself.

Anna's philosophy of silence in art contains an element that reappears in Miss Murdoch's religious characters; the attempt to expunge from the experience the corrupting elements, not of generality, or theory, but of the self, one's own desires, one's personal appeal and feelings. Hugo's brush with art has been an attempt to make a moment of simple uncorrupted beauty in his fireworks, real because they were ephemera, 'a spurt of beauty of which in a moment nothing more was left'.[32] He gave them up in disgust when society, the newspapers, enclosed them in a net of concepts, talked about them as 'art'. Anna's mime is an attempt to produce the same purity and simplicity of experience, but her emphasis is on the expunging of the self; she sees her singing as 'the exploitation of charm to seduce people' – a process in which Sadie, of course, engages quite naturally.

Of the mime she says, 'Only very simple things can be said without falsehood', to which Jake, quite properly, retorts, 'What I saw in that theatre wasn't simple.'[33]

And what Anna is doing is not simple, even her theory of simplicity is not simple. Indeed her whole setting is one of great mystery, great cohesive complexity, and it is this mystery and warmth of Anna which attracts Jake to such an extent that he ignores what Anna says in his pursuit of what, to him, she represents.

The relationship of Anna and her view of art to Jake's freedom becomes clearest, perhaps, if we examine her relation to Miss Murdoch's study of Sartre's *La Nausée*. I have already quoted, in my introduction, a passage from this study, concerning the nature of existence: 'What *does* exist is brute and nameless. . . .'* And Miss Murdoch, describing Sartre's sense of the contrast between this indefinable stuff of existence and the world which reason and consciousness, reflection, find desirable as a habitation, quotes *La Nausée*:

> I understood that there was no middle way between non-existence and this swooning abundance. What exists at all must exist to this point, to the point of mouldering, of bulging, of obscenity. In another world, circles and melodies retain their pure and rigid contours. But existence is a degeneration.[34]

Anna, in *Under the Net*, is surely related to the world where 'circles and melodies retain their pure and rigid contours'. The last scene in *Under the Net* where Jake, in Mrs Tinckham's shop, hears Anna on the wireless, singing 'an old French love song' is surely a deliberate parallel of the final scene in *La Nausée* which Miss Murdoch describes in these terms:

> Roquentin, who has abandoned his book on Rollebon, decides to leave. He sits in the café and listens for the last time to his favorite gramophone record: a Negress singing *Some of these days*. Often before, while listening to this melody, he has been struck by its pure, untouched, rigorous necessity. The notes follow one another, inevitably, away in another world. Like the circle, they do not exist. They *are*. The melody says: you must be like me. You must suffer in rhythm. I too, I want to *be*, thinks Roquentin. He thinks of the Jew who wrote the song, the Negress who sings it. Then he has another revelation. These two are *saved*, washed of the sin of existing. Why should he not be saved too? He will create something, a novel perhaps, which shall be beautiful and hard as steel, and will make people ashamed of their superfluity. Writing it, that will be a stale, day to day task. But once it is complete, behind him, he will be thought of by others as now he thinks of the Jew and the Negress.[35]

I have quoted this at such length, because it is obviously *in toto* relevant to the position of Jake at the end of the book; Jake too, wants to *be*, and Jake too is about to abandon his

* p. 7.

22

mechanical translating, which corresponds to Roquentin's book on Rollebon. But it is the differences which are illuminating, at least in terms of Miss Murdoch's concept of freedom.

The first point I want to make concerns the nature of the 'other world' of which Anna and the Negress's song are symbols. Here is Anna's song:

> The words came slowly, gilded by her utterance. They turned over in the air slowly and then fell; and the splendour of the husky gold filled the shop, transforming the cats into leopards and Mrs. Tinckham into an aged Circe.[36]

This with its richness, its transforming magic, its warmth, bears the same relation to the 'pure, untouched rigorous necessity' of the Sartre song, as the brightly coloured 'glueyness' in Anna's room in the Mime theatre does to the 'bulging obscenity' of Sartre's existence. Anna's theory, in her days of silence, corresponds more closely to Sartre's song than her singing. Miss Murdoch's comment that 'Sartre sees our dividedness and yearning sometimes as a flaw and a lack, sometimes as a rather dry mystery, not a rich one like Marcel's or a vivid one like Berdyaev's'[37] is apposite. We have already seen what 'dryness' entails. Anna is in one sense an object of dividedness and yearning, but she is a 'rich' and 'vivid' mystery.

The other point to be made in connection with this scene is to quote Miss Murdoch's criticism of Sartre's idea of freedom in connection with it. À propos of Roquentin she remarks:

> He observes, with a fury which echoes the *belle haine* of his author, the pretentious trappings of the bourgeois Sunday. These trappings, these ideas of law and right, hide the nakedness of reality, of existence.[38]

Miss Murdoch goes on immediately to ask 'But could one ever do without the trappings?' and to comment, not, it appears, with entire agreement, 'To be outside society, to have lost one's human dignity, often appears to Sartre to have a positive value.' She remarks that Roquentin is a Platonist, and sees his salvation in art – in the 'purity, clarity and necessity' of the finished product, that is, not in the writing. (Jake is not the last of her heroes who is tempted in the same direction.) This need for 'form' Miss Murdoch regards as dangerous in the extreme; in several places she refers to form as 'consolatory', and here she clearly connects Sartre's demand of the reason to make comprehensible patterns of our experience, with the dangerous aspects of our need to see life through arranged concepts, or artistic wholes. From this point of view, then, Anna's philosophy of silence, in so far as it is based on Hugo's respect for the particular experience, is opposed to Roquentin's need for necessity – which indeed Miss Murdoch criticizes in the Sartre book. 'Any such sense of necessity must be illusory for reasons that Roquentin has been offering all through the book.'

If she finds Roquentin's solution inadequate, if she finds both his aesthetic and his social attitude inadequate as definitions of 'freedom', she offers us a pointer again towards the real problem with which, according to her, Sartre does not come to grips: the solidity of what I have called the 'normal' as opposed to the unutterably particular, or nakedly existing aspects of reality. She compares Roquentin with Kafka's K, who 'persists in believing that there is sense in the ordinary business of human communication'.[39] Roquentin no longer looks for sense except in melodies and mathematical figures. 'He is unmoved by the fact that these are man-made fictions;' it is their pure form that rescues them from absurdity. Roquentin's plight appears to be a philosopher's plight, whilst K's is that of everyman. We do not in fact resign ourselves to finding the everyday world a senseless place – but in so far as we find it harder and harder to make sense of certain aspects of it, we recognize K's dilemma as our own.'[40]

At the end of the book, Jake does not possess Anna, either in her aspect of a rich mystery, or in so far as she represents a richer version of the artistic solution which Roquentin finds, or, indeed, as a loved woman. One of the things suggested by examining the references to *La Nausée* is that to find freedom in exterior 'forms', in 'another world', without paying attention to the 'ordinary business of human communication', is illusory at least for non-philosophers; this problem recurs more starkly in the case of Randall in *An Unofficial Rose*, and with Max Lejour in *The Unicorn*. Jake's human communication with Anna has been very inadequate, and perhaps for him she will always remain the gilding enchantment of the song on the radio – although, since this is the first of a series of broadcasts, we are to suppose that the enchantment will remain, as it were, available. Communication, at the end of the book, appears to be more possible with Sadie, who is certainly involved in this world, is 'intelligent' and 'will *keep*'. But before discussing the terms of Jake's final enlightenment it is necessary to turn precisely to this world, to the social dimension, the political net, the theme of money, and Lefty Todd.

'The world of *The Concept of Mind*,' Miss Murdoch remarks, in a discussion of the nature of language in the Sartre book, 'is the world in which people play cricket, cook cakes, make simple decisions, remember their childhood and go to the circus; not the world in which they commit sins, fall in love, say prayers, or join the Communist Party'.[41] The complex and serious activities of committing sins, falling in love and saying prayers are better discussed in terms of other novels, particularly *The Bell*; in *Under the Net*, if we do not have the Communist Party, we have the NISP, which is certainly out to make a revolution. And it is to be taken seriously. It is the NISP that takes over, first the Mime theatre, from which Jake escapes in the back of a van amongst the wreckage of Anna's things, now 'but a soiled and broken chaos', and then Hugo's flat, deserted by Hugo, 'disintegrating into a number of black pieces' which turn out to be starlings that spatter the room as the Hugo-like figure of Polyphemus was spattered. Jake takes from the Revolution a large bundle of one-pound notes but cannot bring himself to take Anna's 'beautiful' letters to Hugo.

These he leaves, and as he walks past the house, having

'escaped' through a skylight, 'they were already carrying out the Renoirs'. Anna's world, and Hugo's world, that is, are open to invasion by the NISP, Hugo's Renoirs have the warmth and mystery of Anna.

And it is not fanciful to point out, I think, that in the scene in Paris, where Jake last sees and pursues Anna, the visionary scene where the woods are full of lovers, and a spent Belfounder rocket is thrown into Anna's reflection by Jake, the event which is being celebrated by the crowds that separate Jake from Anna is another political liberation, achieved by a Revolution; the Fall of the Bastille.

Against the world of the NISP, the Revolution, and Hugo, who gives constantly to it, being a curious combination of pacifist, capitalist and craftsman, is set the world of big business, the film corporations, the buying and selling of Mars, Sammy, Magdalen, and ultimately Sadie. Hollywood is constantly present in the book; Anna is feared to have given in and gone there, although finally she remains in Paris, Magdalen is corrupted by big money in films and becomes even more artificial than she initially was as a typist imitating a film star; she attempts to corrupt Jake by the same means. Jake's moments of decision are indeed often seen in terms of films, and the various film corporations, Bounty Belfounder, Phantasifilms, and the new company founded by Madge's allies in Paris make excellent symbols both for art at the mercy of social and economic forces, and for capitalism and the more extreme irrationality of large sums of money not equitably administered.

In this sense they represent the social 'net' at the other extreme from the NISP – Jake is trapped by Sadie, Mars is caged by Sammy, having been a property of something which is surely meaningfully called *Phantasi*films. And they represent one aspect of the union of the aesthetic not only with the social aspect of reality but the mechanical; something which is perhaps best seen in the splendid and extremely funny scene in the Bounty Belfounder studio – 'situated in a suburb of Southern London where contingency reaches the point of nausea'.[42]

What takes place in this studio is in many ways the climax of the social as opposed to the personal events. Jake gains entry by tricking the 'local Cerberi', referring to himself as a 'professional Unauthorized Person'. What is taking place inside the studio is the filming of the conspiracy of Catiline, in which Sadie is to play the wife of Catiline 'whom Sallust says no good man ever praised except for her beauty, and whom Cicero believed to be not only Catiline's wife but also his daughter'. The film repudiates the latter insinuation 'whether prompted by research or by the exigencies of the script . . . by presenting Orestilla as a woman with a heart of gold and moderate reformist principles'. This is Sadie's world, as opposed to Anna's, a world where there is at least a suggestion that truth is more than inevitably corrupted and deformed by 'the necessities of the script'.[43]

The contrast is reinforced by pieces of description which deliberately recall the very different scene in Anna's Mime theatre. In Anna's theatre Jake felt himself watched by the mysterious 'eyes' of the stuffed snake, the masks, the dolls; the light is dim, and comes from a lamp 'buried under a covering of gauzy materials'. In the film studio there is the 'brilliantly white radiance of the arc lamps making the buildings stand out in a relief more violent than that of nature', and the mysterious eyes are replaced by machinery; 'in between, mounted on steel stilts, and poised on cranes, were the innumerable cameras, all eyes'. And, whereas Jake slept alone in the Mime Theatre, here there is 'a crowd of nearly a thousand men in perfectly motionless silence'.

In this light, Jake sees Hugo – for the first time in the actual narrative. Hugo without 'aspects'.

> In the many-angled radiance he cast no shadow and in the whiteness of the light he looked strangely pale as if his flesh were covered with chalk.[44]

In this book, the action moves between two cities, real London, with its bells and pubs, Dave's contingent mansions, and the Thames in which Jake swims with Lefty and Finn, and Paris, which is seen much more romantically, although it contains Madge's offer of money without work, because it is where Anna is last seen, the home of Acis and Galatea, and the lovers in the Tuileries. In the film studio there is a third city, the Eternal City of Rome, made of plastic and Essex board. And it is here that the NISP is seen in action. The figure whom Jake took for 'Catiline inflaming the Roman plebs' turns out to be Lefty, haranguing the film workers. 'And that, comrades, is the only way to get rid of the capitalist system. I don't say it's the only way, but I do say it's the best way.' By this speech Hugo is spell-bound.

The fall of the Eternal City is not achieved, however, by the NISP. Jake, using Judo, captures and imprisons Hugo, in order to tell him that Sadie is double-crossing him, a fact in which Hugo (as film impresario) does not seem interested. At this point fighting breaks out in the meeting; the United Nationalists have come to break it up and are followed by the police. In the struggle, the city sways, people become indistinguishable, and 'the long banner which said SOCIALIST POSSIBILITY rose and fell upon the surge'. Hugo and Jake, incapable of working out which ones are which, join the battle to 'defend the one person whose identity we were sure of': Lefty.

They find themselves trapped by the wall of the city; neither Lefty, nor Jake, who is illegally in possession of Mars, is anxious to be caught by the arms of the law. They are released from this trap by Hugo's production of a Belfounder's Domestic Detonator, which brings down in a splendidly described moment, the whole city, leaving a gap in the wall through which Lefty and Hugo disappear, leaving Jake, who is not quick enough, to escape by persuading Mars to sham dead.

In this scene, city and political activity are by political activity, and by Hugo's action in favour of Lefty, reduced to chaos; at the end of it, one has a sense of everything – film, Rome, socialists, nationalists, capitalists, being reduced to something incomprehensible and muddled. At a later political meeting Hugo is hit on the head by a brick which brings him for the third time into Jake's orbit, in the hospital, from which Jake, this time, releases him.

To this scene in the studio I would apply, loosely, another passage from the Sartre book. Iris Murdoch speaks of Sartre's thinking about the 'reflective revolt' against society.

> There is only the uneasy marginal pursuit of the idea of freedom which seems inevitably to fall into corruption as soon as it takes on the form of a political achievement. This uneasy thinking is dominated by the sense, which few intellectuals can think away, of the historical transitoriness of capitalism in its present form ... Sartre's picture of consciousness as a *totalité détotalisée* may be thought of as a myth of our condition. The spirit seems to have deserted our social fabric and to hang in the air, blowing to and fro on the ideological gales.[45]

I want only to juxtapose these ideas of 'transitoriness of capitalism', 'our deserted social fabric' and the 'ideological gales' with the picture of the fallen pasteboard city, the floating banner of socialist possibility, and Hugo, the capitalist's, lack of belief in his pursuits, or concern with the loss of his asset, Sadie. Hugo, but not Jake, is ready to give to the Revolution, to give way before it: Jake's relation to it is much more peripheral and is seen in terms of the individual, 'the one person whose identity we were sure of', Lefty.

Jake's first meeting with Lefty takes place during the search for Hugo through all the pubs in the city; he is in fact distracted from his search for Hugo by the political conversation he has with Lefty. Lefty says that he has heard of Jake 'that you are a talented man who is too lazy to work, and that you hold left-wing opinions but take no part in politics'.[46]

In conversation Lefty extracts from Jake the admission that he more or less feels it 'hopeless' to fight for socialism, although he is a socialist. When pressed Jake says that

> English socialism is perfectly worthy, but it's not socialism. It's welfare capitalism. It doesn't touch the real curse of capitalism, which is that work is deadly.

This concept of Jake's, the deadliness of work, is important in that it is a valid reason for rootlessness and non-commitment. It is illuminated, perhaps, by comments of the Abbess in *The Bell*, who argues that there are people who can live neither in the world, nor out of it 'and present-day society with its hurried pace and its mechanical and technical structure, offers no home to these unhappy souls'.

> Work as it now is, the Abbess argued with a kind of realism which surprised Michael at the time, can rarely offer satisfaction to the half-contemplative. A few professions, such as teaching or nursing, remain such that they can readily be invested with a spiritual significance. But although it is possible, and indeed demanded of us, that all and any occupation be given a sacramental meaning, this is now for the majority of people almost intolerably difficult... [47]

Jake as an artist, and a seeker for Truth, is a half-contemplative in this sense; his ultimate solution to the work (in terms of jobs) problem is somewhere between that of Rosa, in *The Flight from the Enchanter*, who wants to make of work in the factory 'something simple, hygienic, streamlined, unpretentious and dull', and that of investing nursing with a spiritual significance. But this problem does not concern Lefty, who can certainly, supremely, live 'in the world', and tells Jake 'If you can care at all, you can care absolutely'.

Lefty tells Jake that Marx said that 'consciousness doesn't found being, but social being is the foundation of consciousness'.[48]

This is the statement of an extreme point of view, at least as expounded by Lefty. (Jake says 'We don't yet know what this means.') Lefty argues that what is needed 'is not just to reflect social conditions, but to reflect *on* them – within limits...' Lefty's 'private will' is completely immersed in the 'social spirit' and the 'needs of external cooperation'. Against him, Jake argues from theory to the particular feelings of the particular individual. He attacks Lefty on his own ground, arguing against Lefty's advocacy of reflection *on* social conditions 'what is the use of an intellectual renaissance that doesn't move the people?' And he attempts to move away from the general with his writer's insistence that '*Ideas* occur to *individuals*.'

Here he is with Miss Murdoch's Sartre.

> The Marxists revile Sartre because he describes man as a fundamentally non-social, non-historical individual. But what Sartre wishes to assert is precisely that the individual has an absolute importance and is not to be swallowed up in a historical calculation. Sartre's man is depicted in the moment-to-moment flux of his thoughts and moods, where no consistent pattern either of purposeful activity or of social condition can easily be discerned; at this level freedom seems indeed like randomness, the freedom of indifference.[49]

Miss Murdoch does not, I think, see it as easy, in the way in which it would be easy from this point of view to disentangle what is individual about man from what is historical and social, but she is ultimately with Sartre and Jake when it is a question of asserting the 'absolute importance' of the individual against a 'historical calculation'. Where she leaves Sartre is when she sees him, as in a way she sees Anna, trying to make a pattern from the lack of pattern, to 'create a *total* picture of the broken totality, to describe man's limit from a point beyond that limit'.[50]

In any case the 'freedom of indifference' which is seen as a value here is the freedom that Jake has been struggling for all along. He expresses the uneasy feeling we have that 'being loyal to one's friends and behaving properly to women' is as far as we can go, in our social morality; we are not at all certain that we can save the world or that what we can do will make it any better. As I quoted on p. 29, the idea of freedom 'seems inevitably to fall into corruption as soon as it takes on the form of a political achievement'.

Certainly Lefty's practical use, to which he would put Jake, is as corrupting to Jake's individuality and vision as Madge's offer to make him, for her own ends, a script-writer. He wants Jake to write socialist plays, after 'a scientific analysis of a few recent popular successes' into the framework of which Jake can fit the 'message'. Lefty is, artistically speaking, that is, in Sadie's world rather than Anna's, a world where art and the individual are 'used' to ends other than their own. To a certain extent this is seen as an inevitable process, but not entirely. Lefty represents something – a social force – which exists, and with which Jake must come to terms, but to which he must not submit or he will distort himself and his reality. It is Hugo, without theories, who is practically vulnerable to Lefty's theory of the utilization of consciousness.

But we do not leave Lefty here; he shares in the very *living* episode of the swimming in the Thames; he writes a letter to Jake at the end, recalling this, and ending 'life wasn't entirely a matter of politics, was it?' Jake comments:

> I got a good impression from this letter, and although I doubted whether Lefty really entertained the final sentiment I felt that here I had to do with a man.[51]

It is the fact that Lefty is precisely 'a man', and human, which makes him sympathetic and something to be reckoned with and kept in contact with; whereas the world of script-writing, sinecures, artificial Madge and translating Jean-Pierre Breteuil must be sloughed off altogether. There is some value in the ends to which Lefty would utilize Jake, if there is no personal value, no adequate freedom in it, for Jake as an individual.

We are now, perhaps, in a position to sum up Jake's situation at the end of the book. Malcolm Bradbury remarks that:

> Few things have changed for him; after talk of love he is no nearer to being in it; after much exchange of money . . . he has much the same bank balance as he had in the beginning. But a process of renewal has taken place within him.[52]

Malcolm Bradbury sees this process of renewal as composed particularly of two things – a change from translating to creative work in his own right, and a change from having 'shattered nerves' to being able to encounter life and loneliness.

At the end of the book, Jake is in touch with Sadie, and with Lefty, both of whom are representative of social demands in one form or another. Finn, his servant or body-guard, has left him to his own devices and has returned to Ireland. He decides to take a room on his own, accompanied only by Mars, and to take a job, part-time, in a hospital, following Dave's earlier advice. Of this he writes that it gave him 'a feeling that was almost entirely new to me, that of having *done* something', and comments:

> I could not imagine why I had not thought before of this way of living, which would ensure that no day could pass without *something* having been done, and so keep that feeling of uselessness, which grows in prolonged periods of sterility, away from me forever.[53]

But concurrent with the development of his ability to recognize a need to *do* something, in society, has been a development of his possibility of becoming an artist. The moment of his decision in this context comes in Paris and is made in terms of two shocks; that of Jean-Pierre Breteuil's winning the Prix Goncourt, and that of his own inability to accept Madge's offer – an inability which he sees as a result partly of its incompatibility with the claims of the 'life' repre-sented by Mars, and partly of his own decision not to trans-late any more Breteuil.

Of Breteuil he writes:

> A man whom I had taken on as a business partner had turned out to be a rival in love ... Since it was now impossible to treat with Jean-Pierre cynically, it was impossible to treat with him at all.[54]

Love, here, is connected with 'real' art, which is again con-nected with the mystery of Anna in the succeeding scenes where Jake turns from Jean-Pierre, and Madge to his last pursuit of Anna. But what his new vision of Jean-Pierre reveals is partly that he had been under-estimating Jean-Pierre, by not seeing him as a potentially good writer – again, imposing patterns on a reality too complex for them – and partly that, now 'truth' is apparent to him, and Jean-Pierre's work has the reality of good literature, he cannot take a parasitic living from it, or 'use' it socially in a cynical way.

After Madge's offer, which he dismisses ultimately with 'I must live my own life. And it simply doesn't lie in this direction', he thinks of his refusal in terms of truth and falsehood.

> I had so littered my life already with compromises and half-truths, I could have picked my way through a few more. The twisting halls of falsehood never cease to appal me, but I constantly enter them; possibly because I see them as short corridors which lead out again into the sun: though, perhaps, this is the only *fatal* lie.[55]

His unwillingness to enter these hills of falsehood again is not because they are false, nor, he decides, because of Anna, but because of what has been revealed to him by Jean-Pierre's success.

> All that mattered was a vision I had of my own destiny and which imposed itself upon me as a command ... There was a path which awaited me and which if I failed to take it would lie untrodden forever. This was the substance and all other things were shadows fit only to distract and deceive.[56]

This, with its high language, is the moment at which Jake, as an artist, becomes free, because committed – free from script-writing, half-truths and economic dependence upon them. He says this is 'the real shape of that which before had obscurely compelled me to what had seemed a senseless decision'. But in a world where it was senseless, his freedom was illusory.

Before establishing a way of life which will give scope for action to this new vision of himself, he has to finish his pursuit of Anna and his pursuit of Hugo. The final vision of Anna comes first, in the long chase in Paris, where Anna is seen first against the ephemeral spurts of beauty of the fire-works on the Pont Saint-Michel, and then walking barefoot in the Tuileries; here she is lost, to reappear only as a voice on the wireless. The whole scene has a dream-like quality, and Jake's feelings are those we have in a dream; a feeling of necessity, that Anna is thinking of him, as he is of her, that

> This was a rendezvous. My need of her drew me onward like a physical force. Our embrace would close the circle of the years and begin the golden age.[57]

But, as in dreams, the necessity he feels changes nothing and Anna does not come; he has prevented himself from catching her up when he could, waiting for a 'sign' that she does not give. Malcolm Bradbury sees this loss of Anna as a symbolic loss of a life of 'pure' art.

> We feel that in this moment a certain pattern of life and art has escaped Jake, and when he returns to Dave Gellman and takes a job as a hospital orderly, we feel that he has been driven to an alternative solution, one that unites the aesthetic and the social.[58]

I do not like the idea that Jake has been 'driven' or that anything has 'escaped' Jake, in the sense that it was there to capture. Anna is not a way of life; she is, in so far as she is representative of anything, a 'mystery', an enchantment – the Tuileries where she is seen have 'the dangerous charm of an enchanted garden' – not, one might remark, the last garden in Miss Murdoch's work which is both beautiful, enchanted, unattainable and obscurely 'dangerous'.

It is this quality in Anna that Jake has been pursuing, and this, precisely and inevitably, that he cannot *possess*. He is distorting reality by imposing upon it a dream necessity in which the enchantment of the garden and Anna will end in a rendezvous, an embrace, like that of Acis and Galatea. As I have said, Anna remains only as a song, a broadcast enchantment.

But Anna is not only an object of contemplation; she is a loved woman, who takes life hard, has great skill in human relationships, and with whom both Jake and Hugo are personally concerned. The other side of Jake's freedom, his coming to an awareness of the 'unutterably particular' situation, is made clear in his final conversation with Hugo, when the latter reveals the truth which lies under the net of the distorting fantasies Jake has imposed on it – an Anna, not waiting mysteriously for Jake, but a 'frenzied Maenad' in pursuit of Hugo, a Hugo not in love with Anna, but with Sadie, who is 'keen on' Jake.

> I had no longer any picture of Anna. She faded, like a sorcerer's apparition; and yet somehow her presence remained to me more substantial than ever before. It seemed as if, for the first time, Anna really existed now as a separate being and not as part of myself. To experience this was extremely painful ... When does one ever know a human being? Perhaps only after one has renounced the possibility of knowledge and renounced the desire for it and finally ceased to feel even the need for it. But then what one achieves is no longer knowledge, it is simply a kind of co-existence; and this, too, is one of the guises of love.[59]

What is achieved here is not *knowledge*, it is a way of living, this co-existence, in the world as it is, one's freedom defined by the substantial presence of the other person who inhabits his or her own universe. It is not the same kind of thing as Anna, in the earlier exchange between them, puts against Jake's idea that unsatisfied love is concerned with possession.

'Unsatisfied love is concerned with understanding. Only if it is all, all understanding, can it remain love while being unsatisfied.'[60] Jake's final relation to Anna respects the mystery of her existence, the fact that she is 'a real impenetrable human person' perhaps more – I put this tentatively – than Anna's ideal of understanding respects Hugo, whom she loves. Understanding, in Miss Murdoch's thought, is a good ideal, but one impossible of complete achievement, and we must know this. At least if Jake's actions towards Anna are limited by her nature, he has come to know more of who she is and where he is with regard to her.

This new knowledge comes about through Hugo, and with his revelation about Anna and Sadie Hugo's function in Jake's life comes, at least temporarily, to an end. It is as though

Hugo was Jake's 'destiny' as long as Jake's primary need was precise vision, a sense of the unclassifiable particularity of things, to strip his fantastic net of interpretations and assumptions from his relation to the world. But once this is done, once his romantic fantasy is revealed for what it is, and once he has developed a sense of his öwn 'destiny' as a writer, who *must* presumably use concepts, construct a net of a kind, in art, if not in life, he must move out of Hugo's sphere. Hugo is a craftsman and will become a watch-maker, precise and mechanical. Jake *must* concern himself directly with spiritual (in the Abbess's sense) values. And he is thus freed of his obsession with Hugo's precise vision as an end in itself, the only permissible way of seeing.

Hugo says 'The trouble with you, Jake is that you want to understand everything sympathetically. It can't be done . . . Truth lies in blundering on.' But in fact, once contact with Hugo has *revealed* to Jake the nature of his relationships with the sisters he can do more – a little more – than blunder on.

> He towered in my mind like a monolith: an unshaped and undivided stone which men before history had set up for some human purpose which would remain forever obscure. His very otherness was to be sought not in himself but in myself or Anna. Yet herein he recognized nothing of what he had made. He was a man without claims and without reflections. Why had I pursued him? He had nothing to tell me. To have seen him was enough. He was a sign, a portent, a miracle.[61]

But although seeing him has served its purpose, Jake at last becomes humanly curious about him again; even in these early very patterned novels Miss Murdoch will not allow her characters, or the relations between them, to degenerate into pure symbols.

> Yet no sooner had I thought this than I began to be curious again about him. I pictured him in Nottingham in some small desolate workshop, holding a watch in his enormous hand. I

saw the tiny restless movements of the watch, I saw its many
jewels. Had I finished with Hugo?

The relationship between the individual Hugo and Jake, like
that between the individual Anna and Jake, still exists.

So, Jake is free, although socially and artistically more
defined and in that sense limited, in that his vision is clearer;
he is free of his own net of fantasy; if his love is neither
possession nor understanding it is at least a *real* love, related
to a *real* beloved. He has Mars, and he has a relationship
which he is now free to work out with Sadie, who 'concerned
me' and 'would *keep*' because she had intelligence. He is also
aware of the inexplicable mystery, the wonder of the world
– he is last seen marvelling over the cat with two Siamese
and two tabby kittens.

One feels uneasily that any analytic explanation of the
book weighs it down, adds a portentousness to what is in
fact, light, amusing and rapid. I would plead in extenuation
that this, of all the books, is the most philosophic, the one
where analysis of ideas such as Miss Murdoch herself applies
to Sartre's novels is the most apposite technique of understanding the action, and not illegitimate, since every sentence,
as is not always true in the later books, has a sense of being
carefully written, chosen, 'placed'. The action, as someone
has remarked, has a dream-like inevitability; things happen,
opportunely for the state of mind, or the philosophic
advancement, or the symbolic tidymindedness of character
and reader. Relationships between characters, although they
exist, are worked round ideas, and are in very large part
relationships of ideas. The book is fantasy-myth at its purest,
and excellently cohesive fantasy-myth; but contingency and
the stuff of human life are within the myth *stated* rather than
seen to exist.

The Flight from the Enchanter, the second novel, is also
and obviously fantasy-myth, and its intellectual arrangement
can be stripped and exposed, if we have the skill to do
it, without anything being lost. But the subject-matter, the
characters, at least in part, the theme, are all more those of

the novel proper, as Miss Murdoch sees it, and the patterning is a symbolic patterning of characters and actions, rather than of concepts. It is also concerned with freedom, not as an idea or a state of mind, as in *Under the Net*, but as a *fact*, in relation to a given political and emotional state of affairs. And in this sense, too, it is moving towards a fictional presentation of the reality of the contingent, the accidental, what is.

3

THE FLIGHT FROM THE ENCHANTER

IF THE DOMINANT image in *Under the Net* is one of nets, traps, people locked in or out, that of *The Flight from the Enchanter* is one of pursuit and flight, hunt and capture, enchantment and enslavement. The themes are both political and personal, the war between the sexes, the contrast between youth and age, the problem of the refugee and the state. We have here a proliferation of symbolic naming and imagery: Mischa Fox's surname, the *Artemis*, both suffragette periodical and virgin huntress, Hunter Keepe, ironically named, and the constant references to women in terms of fish, carried even as far as Calvin Blick's 'There are more fish in the sea' when brandishing his 'feelthy pictures' at Rainborough, and the bronze weeping fish in the square of the town where Mischa spent his childhood.

The story centres on the relationships of a group of characters with a dominant 'enchanter' figure, Mischa Fox, a newspaper magnate, who holds power mysteriously in various political and social spheres, exerts a curious sexual attraction over women, and is very rich. We follow the fortunes of three main characters; Rosa Keepe, whom Mischa has loved and who has rejected him, John Rainborough, an ex-civil servant, who works in an organization for the administration of the entry of refugees into the country, and the youthful Annette Cockeyne, who lives with Rosa. At the beginning of the book, Rosa is working in a factory, and is the mistress of two Polish refugee co-workers, Jan and Stefan Lusiewicz, Annette decides to leave her finishing school and enter the school of life, and Rainborough is being pursued, in more ways than one, by his typist, Agnes Casement. The 'plot' is a series of incidents, loosely connected to Mischa's attempt, through Calvin Blick, his henchman, to gain control of the *Artemis*, a periodical edited by Hunter, Rosa's brother, initially suffragette, here something independent, a periodical outside Mischa's newspaper empire, and symbolically, an independent virgin, outside his sexual empire. Various acts of violence are provoked; Rainborough and Rosa are menaced by Miss Casement and the Lusiewiczs; both are ultimately rescued. Annette attempts to 'help' the lonely Mischa, but fails; she is not, however, damaged by her brush with his power as Rosa is. The crisis of the book consists of two suicides, the real one of Nina, the seamstress, a victim of Mischa's power, but for whom Rosa is indirectly responsible, and the comical failure of Annette's attempt to 'end it all'. Rosa, who has contemplated staying with Mischa after all, is driven by Calvin's report of Nina's suicide to return to resume the threads of her London life; Annette returns to her 'free' life with her parents, travelling from country to country. Rainborough, too, cuts free of his social and personal involvement, in SELIB and his engagement to Miss Casement, and accepts the refuge offered by Annette's mother, Marcia Cockeyne. The *Artemis* remains in Rosa's hands, and she is seen at the end of the book to be taking an interest in this survival of her mother's suffragette and socialist faith, which she had earlier avoided. Mischa is last seen, alone but for the watching Calvin, on the Mediterranean shore, near his Italian villa.

The critics generally have seemed to find this a less successful book than *Under the Net*; I think this is possibly because there is at times a slight lack of balance between the sense it imparts of the tragic ways in which people are blind, or at the mercy of a positively evil power, and the two-dimensional game of pure patterning which still persists, less relevantly here in, for instance, Miss Murdoch's picture of Annette and her parents, who rather too obviously 'stand for' something theoretical – eternal youth, the unicorn virgin, in Annette's case – in a world where, however fantastically, real human emotions are involved. To say that this is done deliberately is not to say that it works. The book is nevertheless very complex, and, I find, in many ways more moving and serious than some of the later novels which are not fantastic. And the care with which the parallels are worked out, the apparently inexhaustible invention of situation, are exhilarating.

In this book the characters are not free, and truth is seen as an end so remote that it is hardly to be arrived at at all. What is examined is closer to being degrees of enslavement than degrees of freedom. These can, perhaps, best be seen by drawing a division between the theme of social enslavement and that of personal enslavement, although the two overlap constantly, and the strings are in both cases held by Mischa Fox and his henchman, Calvin Blick. One could put it differently by saying that the book is concerned with the emancipation of the serfs and the emancipation of women, and suggests that neither of these has been, or seems likely to be, achieved in the way that was hoped by the generation of Liberal thinkers who are discussed in *Against Dryness*, the people before the Welfare State, which is criticized by Miss Murdoch for 'removing certain incentives to thinking',[1] the people who are represented in this book by Rosa Keepe's dead mother, militant socialist and suffragette.

These concepts are mentioned in these terms during the brilliantly funny scene at the meeting of the *Artemis* shareholders, where Calvin Blick's attempt to buy the periodical for Mischa Fox is foiled by the arrival of the elderly suffragette shareholders, summoned through Rosa's appeal to Mrs Camilla Wingfield (also symbolically named?). During this scene the following interchange takes place. An old lady says:

> 'Why the very fact that "female emancipation" still has meaning for us proves that it has not yet been achieved.' Calvin . . . said suddenly, 'Would you agree, madam, that the fact that the phrase "emancipation of the serfs" is significant, proves

that the serfs are not yet emancipated?' There was an embarrassed silence. 'Who is that?' asked the woman with the hearing aid, 'Is it Mr Fox?'[2]

The irony of this, of course, is that neither has been achieved, a fact of which Calvin is likely to be sufficiently aware, although he muddles his interlocutor.

I shall consider, first, the emancipation of the serfs. The social scene in the book is dominated by the figure of Mischa Fox, who has certain things in common with Hugo Belfounder; he is, like him, a refugee from a mid-European country, like him a capitalist and very rich, like him in some ways curiously gentle and sensitive about inflicting pain. (Hugo was a pacifist; Mischa is said to weep over what he reads in the newspapers.) But Mischa, to a much greater degree than Hugo, is seen, involuntarily or voluntarily, through Calvin or alone, to exercise an enslaving power, to wield a machine which can automatically, in destroying the 'dark' power of Stefan Lusiewicz, destroy, much more completely, the innocent and bewildered Nina.

There are two social organizations in the book; the factory, where Rosa works, and the offices of SELIB where John Rainborough works. I have already mentioned Rosa's reasons for moving from the 'spiritual' occupation of school-teaching to the factory; her brother, Hunter's, explanation is that it is for what would have been her mother's reason, to be in touch with the People, but her own explanation is that she wants to make of work something 'simple, hygienic, stream-lined, unpretentious and dull'.[3] Rainborough, an opposite case, has left the Civil Service for SELIB in a moment of 'divine discontent' at his own uselessness, and now regrets it; both are now confronted by something they don't understand or see the function of. In both cases we are again confronted by the problem of the half-contemplative in a hurried, mechanical, technical and somehow inimical society.

But if they do not understand their world, there are others who do. In the factory there are the Lusiewicz brothers who graduate out of 'the enslaved group of machine-minders to which Rosa still belonged' into 'the comparative freedom of the technical staff'.[4] In SELIB there is a horde of Amazons, virgin huntresses, headed by Miss Casement, Rainborough's typist, who are promoted often and mysteriously, without the knowledge of their immediate superiors, and are said to be taking charge of the organization. Both the Lusiewicz brothers and Miss Casement are initially subordinate to, and in the case of the Lusiewicz brothers, enchanted by, Rosa and Rainborough; both as they gain social power, gain sexual power and personal destructive power. Both, in the end, uproot their prey from their jobs. These serfs, then, liberate themselves by preying on others, and by understanding how to use Jake Donaghue's 'deadly' and meaningless work.

But there are those who do not understand, and are perpetual serfs; particularly Nina, the dressmaker, who is crushed, as it were, under the pyramid of everyone else's aspirations and desires and selfishnesses, but also the recurrent henchmen – Miss Foy, shapeless, grey and wrinkled, *not* a virgin, Miss Casement's own persecuted typist, even Calvin Blick, who observes 'Mischa did kill me, long ago'. It is the social working of Até, described by Max Lejour in *The Unicorn*, a book whose themes are not so far removed from this, and which shares with it the dominant image of the hunt, and killing of animals and fish, as 'the almost automatic transfer of suffering from one being to another. Power is a form of Até. The victims of power, and any power has its victims, are themselves infected. They have then to pass it on; to use power on others . . .'[5] This is a recurrent idea in Miss Murdoch's work, and we shall meet it again.

It is also prominent in the writings of Simone Weil, by whose work Miss Murdoch says she has been 'much affected and instructed', and whose thought is discussed more fully in connection with *The Unicorn*. Simone Weil instances the way in which, if a hen is wounded, all other hens will *automatically* attack it, as an example of this automatic transfer and remarks:

La nature charnelle de l'homme lui est commune avec l'animal. Les poules se précipitent à coup de bec sur une poule blessée. C'est un phénomène aussi mécanique que la pesanteur.

She continues, with a remark of great insight, which illuminates Miss Murdoch's conception of the character of Nina, her place in the social pattern and the attitudes of the other characters to her.

Tout le mépris, toute la répulsion, toute la haine que notre raison attache au crime, notre sensibilité l'attache au malheur. Excepté ceux dont le Christ occupe tout l'âme, tout le monde méprise plus ou moins les malheureux, quoique presque personne n'en ait conscience.[6]

There are several characters in the book who are described as refugees: the Lusiewicz brothers and Nina, obviously, but also, significantly, Mischa himself, and Annette, the stateless, who calls herself a refugee. The arbitrary nature of social freedom or enslavement is represented by the FPE line – a line drawn through Europe, from the East of which immigration under the SELIB scheme is illegal. Of this line, Hunter Keepe observes 'It would be a sad thing for a man to have his fate decided by where he was born. He didn't choose where he was born.'[7] This echoes the thought of the first paragraph of the book, where Annette, thinking of the passage in the *Inferno* where the Minotaur 'bounded to and fro in pain and frustration' sets the theme immediately by thinking

Why should the poor Minotaur be suffering in hell? It was not the Minotaur's fault that it had been born a monster. It was God's fault.[8]

One of the statements of the book is precisely this; that there *are* monsters, that a man's fate *is* decided, among other things, by where he is born; there is Nina's suicide to prove it.

The FPE line is the weapon that Hunter contemplates using, and Mischa does use, to rid Rosa of the Lusiewicz brothers. It does this, but it also, as the use of power does, destroys Nina accidentally in the process. Nina is completely without freedom. She is dependent upon Mischa for her livelihood, and is used by him for purposes she knows nothing of. Once she loved him, but now she plans an escape to Australia 'where she would live a life of openness and gaiety, respected as a worker and loved as a woman'.[9]

She makes Annette feel automatically that she is a henchman; Annette wants to make of her 'some superior sort of lady's maid', and she subserves Annette's freedom, making her clothes.

> There was no feeling Annette liked so much as the feeling that someone else was making or doing something for her the fruit of which she would soon enjoy. This feeling was perhaps for her *the essence of freedom*. (My italics.)[10]

Nina is stateless, her passport was issued by a Foreign Office which has disappeared from the face of the earth.

> She was without identity in a world where to be without identity is the first and most universal of crimes, the crime which, whatever else it may overlook, every State punishes.[11]

At the moment of her suicide, which takes place because she cannot by nature or in her position know that in fact the SELIB edict would be waived in her case – and, importantly, because Rosa has neglected to explain this to her – she carries the whole weight, the absolute limitation of the 'senseless blackness'. She feels that if it was black and senseless for Christ, it was so for her; if not for him, then not for her. 'For an instant she felt the terrible weight of a God depending on her will. It was too heavy . . .'[12]

She is related to, and illuminates, I think, the more complex figure of Ann in *An Unofficial Rose* (and also Penn, the Australian, whose dream of the free spaces is destroyed in this country). Both are innocent, suffer for others' use or misuse of power, are believing Christians, and feel themselves 'shapeless and awkward'. But whereas Ann has a natural power, and a natural beauty, although faded, Nina has been rendered entirely artificial; she has dyed hair, and is seen as a 'small artificial animal'.

46

Nina, I think, is also related to Hannah Crean-Smith, the central figure of *The Unicorn*. Both suffer, and are, more or less, innocent victims of power – but whereas Hannah makes a conscious attempt to come to terms with the spiritual meaning of suffering, Nina is, one feels, Miss Murdoch's attempt to portray the social effects of Simone Weil's concept of 'malheur' or affliction; she has her moment of apprehension of the spiritual facts involved in her suffering at the moment of her death, but she belongs rather with the afflicted – the slaves, refugees, uprooted, despised – studied by Simone Weil, than with Simone Weil's own spiritual search. One could see the other characters' sense of her as a 'small artificial animal' as a recognition of the effects of affliction described in the following quotation:

> Si le mécanisme n'était pas aveugle, il n'y aurait pas du tout de malheur. Le malheur est avant tout anonyme, il prive ceux qu'il prend de leur personnalité et en fait des choses. Il est indifférent, et c'est le froid de cette indifférence, un froid métallique, qui glace jusqu'au fond même de l'âme tous ceux qu'il touche. Ils ne retrouveront jamais plus la chaleur. Ils ne croiront jamais qu'ils sont quelqu'un.[13]

Simone Weil's book, *L'Enracinement*, is a study of the need of the community to provide a place for people to live and be someone, to have roots and not to be anonymous. (It is concerned precisely with the re-establishment of France after the war.)

Nina is Miss Murdoch's extreme example of the uprooted. As Simone Weil said, defining 'le malheur':

> Le facteur social est essentiel. Il n'y a pas vraiment malheur là où il n'y a pas sous une forme quelconque déchéance sociale ou appréhension d'une telle déchéance.

And many of Simone Weil's examples of affliction are drawn from her sense of the suffering of refugees, people suddenly deprived of home, family, identity, self-respect, as well as food, and the effect of this on them.

Nina's dream, in which she is running through a dark

wood with her sewing-machine, which first produces an end-less stream of cloth, and then turns to savage, with its steel jaws, both it and her, symbolizes the way in which Nina is seen as a victim in two ways. The winding sheet is finally found to be 'a map of all the countries of the world' – in all of which she is stateless. And the sewing-machine monster, impressive in itself, is even more impressive when seen as one of a series of incomprehensible machines which are a means of enslavement. There is Rosa's machine, Kitty, whose song she can never make out; there is the camera and developing machinery in a room like a torture chamber in the basement of Mischa's house, with which Calvin black-mails and terrorizes the other natural victim of the book, Hunter; there is the red M.G. with which Miss Casement finally traps Rainborough into an engagement. Nina is killed by a world in which frontiers and machinery, man-made things, have become incomprehensible, out of hand, and destroy or render savage those who have to do with them.

Nina is balanced by the Lusiewicz brothers, who have brought their old mother, their 'earth', with them, but dance wildly round her, singing *Gaudeamus igitur* (they are aggres-sively on one side in the youth/age battle, too) and declaring that they will 'set fires in her hair'. Their village has been burned by Hitler; at the end Stefan declares that he has buried his mother in the garden, like an old sack. They have a dangerous, rootless freedom; their statelessness is that of the outlaw; only the same kind of rootless power in Mischa Fox can dispose of them.

Nina is also balanced by Annette, who, if we leave Mischa out of question for the moment, completes the picture of the refugees. She is eternally young, and represents the bright side of the *Gaudeamus* theme. She is what Mischa would call the perpetual virgin, although technically she is not one. Her statelessness is a freedom, not an enslavement; she goes from state to state in trains, occasionally wishing to get off and lie down in the grass, or enter little strange hotels, but moving and admiring all the time. She is – and this is import-ant in this book – physically unmarkable; at the beginning

Rosa tells her that she is 'like a little fish ... completely smooth', and, whereas Rosa is marked by her vaccination, and Mrs Wingfield by having chained herself to railings as a suffragette, Annette, although temporarily encased in plaster after being knocked downstairs by Rosa, recovers without a scar. She is, to balance Nina, comically incapable of committing suicide, taking milk of magnesia instead of luminal tablets, when she stages her farewell to the world – significantly with gin and an audience.

Before, however, leaving the social enslavements for the personal, it is worth mentioning the one character who is in this sense neither slave nor master – Peter Saward, the scholar, of whom Hunter says that he is almost a saint and Rainborough comments 'He's a good man, but he'd be the first to tell you not to mistake a scholar for a true ascetic.'

Peter Saward is a fairly successful half-contemplative, we could perhaps say. He is in love with Rosa, and engaged in a fruitless attempt to decipher a Kastanic script, which he finds at the end of the book to have been wasted labour when a bilingual stone is found. But in spite of these two hopeless passions he is a detached man. He is sick of an 'advanced but quiescent tuberculosis', and he provides a place of rest for Mischa outside the action, to fulfil his need to pursue his past, to explain his cruelty in terms of his pity. He is, concerned with death as he is, capable of that death of the self which Miss Murdoch values as a part of virtue; he does not pass the suffering on. He has qualities which become more central in terms of Ann in *An Unofficial Rose*, and Hannah in *The Unicorn*.

Of him Rainborough thinks that he has forgone the male 'right' to 'a certain brutality, a certain insensibility'. 'Here was a personality without frontiers. Saward did not defend himself by placing others. He did not defend himself.'[14] He has, that is, the passive freedom of being 'without frontiers'; he does not set up barriers between himself and the reality of other people by, as Jake Donaghue did, 'placing' them, and he is trained, as a historian, to look for truth.

To Rosa he represents 'the sweetness of sanity and work,

the gentleness of those whose ambitions are innocent, and the vulnerability of those who are incapable of contempt'.[15] But, although Mischa respects and honours him, he is a point of rest outside the action – like Max Lejour, Miss Murdoch's other half-contemplative scholar, he can partly afford to be, because he is dying. The violence at Mischa's party takes place after he has left, and Rosa cannot turn to him in her trouble, because, in his innocence, 'he would be unable to conceive of such a character as Stefan Lusiewicz.'

But Stefan and Stefan's world necessarily exist, and so, in the same way, does the violence unleashed by Mischa's action to protect Rosa. Peter is part of the picture, not an ideal. In work, as in personal relations, he is detached from the world of action; if he represents the 'sweetness of sanity and work' there is no guaranteeing that his work will bear fruit, and he too is subjected to the scholar's special form of enchantment, he 'had become the victim . . . of an absurd obsession' in the deciphering of the script.

It is worth noting, in the case of Peter's obsession, that the script is an Eastern script, and the East, in this book, represents the mystery which lies behind the civilization and the barbaric elements of a Europe, mechanized, uprooted, overrun by Hitler. Mischa seems to Peter to be able to read it, and Mischa predicts the finding of the bilingual.

> As he looked down at the writing, with his brown eye visible, and his sallow, hawk-like face, he seemed suddenly to Saward to be the very spirit of the Orient, that Orient which lay beyond the Greeks, barbarous and feral, Egypt, Assyria, Babylon.[16]

He bears, in this manifestation, a relation to Honor Klein, of *A Severed Head*, who is also preoccupied with the East, and reveals to the hero the 'barbarous and feral' elements of his own nature, which are the aspects of truth he is ignoring.

When we come to the personal enslavements in the book, the two characters whose fates are really at issue are again Rosa and Rainborough, and these are worth discussing at length. They are set, in their humanity, between the world of

Mischa Fox, with its mystery and barbarism, which has at its service the mechanical power and inhuman efficiency of Calvin Blick, and the ideal world of the Cockeyne family of which I shall write later. The forces which act upon them in the sex war are the Lusiewicz brothers and Miss Casement, who might be described as sub-enchanters.

Both Rosa and Rainborough are inheritors of the Liberal tradition of a world which seems to have died, and whose concepts of freedom and individuality seem to have lost power. At the beginning of the book we find Rosa in a faithless state which in many ways parallels that of Jake Donaghue. 'She had ceased to imagine that her life would ever consist of anything but a series of interludes'; she had tried to be a journalist, 'but had never recovered from the gloom and cynicism' which she brought to the trade. 'Where beauty and goodness were concerned, Rosa, had, of course, no particular expectations from her new life'.[17]

Rainborough is in a similar state; the hospital (another social force) is to encroach on his garden to the extent of destroying the grey stone wall on which grows the wistaria to which are attached both his childhood and 'all his deepest thoughts', the classic Romantic experience in which, contemplating the wistaria, he found 'the outer world had disappeared altogether, mingled with thought and transformed into an inner substance'.[18] But this is finally uprooted in a symbolic scene where Miss Casement, 'like Clytaemnestra', wields the axe which destroys the tree, and immediately afterwards, leads Rainborough away, captive, in her red M.G.

Rainborough's morals have the *ad hoc* solipsism of the liberal thinkers criticized by Miss Murdoch in *Against Dryness*.

> In moral matters, as in intellectual matters Rainborough took the view that to be mature was to realize that most human effort inevitably ends in mediocrity and that all our admirations lead us at last to the dreary knowledge that, such as we are, we ourselves represent the elite.[19]

There is some truth in this view, but like Rosa's it excludes beauty and goodness, and Miss Murdoch herself has warned us in another context against 'doctrines of necessity which show us (with professions of regret) the eminently desirable, the good, as being, alas the impossible'.[20] And this view makes him peculiarly vulnerable to the attacks of Miss Casement, whose mediocrity is aggressive and predatory.

It is significant that in the moment after the statement of this view of Rainborough's, he is described as having a moment of joy in the contemplation of some ants and a snail in his flower garden. He felt 'how little I know, and how little it is possible to know; and with this thought he experienced a moment of joy'. This moment of joy in mystery is associated with the arrival of Annette in his garden, and it is Annette, encased in plaster, who supervises the destruction of his wall, later on, when he has refused her appeal for help, in order to go off with Miss Casement.

Both Rosa and Rainborough are released from the power of their immediate enchanters by the power of greater enchanters; Mischa Fox and Marcia Cockeyne. Both are guilty of 'attacks' on Annette – Rainborough's a sexual attack, after which he traps her in a cupboard, whilst speaking to Mischa, Rosa's the outcome of rage at her attempt to attract Mischa. Annette is a sort of life-force, and although she cannot change Mischa, or, as Calvin who releases her from her plaster, puts it, 'liberate another soul from captivity', and although it is wrong in both Rosa and Rainborough to take no account of her moments of grief and bewilderment, she is not damaged. Of his clumsy attempt to grab her, Rainborough thinks in terms of the fish image:

> It was like hunting fish with an underwater gun ... At one moment, there is the fish, graceful, mysterious, desirable and free – and the next moment there is nothing but struggling and blood and confusion. If only, he thought, it were possible to combine the joys of contemplation and possession.[21]

This image of the impossibility of combining the joys of contemplation and possession, of respecting the mysterious 'freedom' of the other individual and not damaging or enslaving him or her, applies to all the relationships in the book; love and violence are closely interwoven, except in Peter Saward, coming to a culmination in Mischa, who can say 'I love all creatures' and mean it, but has been constrained to kill them for 'pity'. But Annette comes from a world to which this does not apply, and returns to it.

At Mischa's party, Rainborough apologizes to Annette for his grab, in these terms:

> . . . life has a great many random elements. One of the results of this is that there are a great many ways in which we can hurt and startle other people, to whom we wish only good. For beings like us, patience and tolerance are not virtues but necessities.[22]

Annette, characteristically, replies 'When I am patient, I'll be dead.' But this remark of Rainborough's, pompous though it is, touches a problem which Miss Murdoch raises again and again – the effect on a man's life and his freedom of seemingly random actions, moments of lack of insight at times when insight could hardly be expected of us, impulses which seem rationally to lead to no harm, and yet damage others. Michael's relationship with Toby – also 'young' in Miss Murdoch's sense – in *The Bell*, is such a random element, composed of Devon cider and good weather, at least on the surface. It is not, however, Rainborough whose involuntary weakness really damages others, but Rosa. And Rosa's freedom is, in the last resort, conditioned by these random elements; Mischa can free her of Stefan, but not of what she has done, inadvertently, to Nina.

It is significant that at moments of crisis for Rosa she is seen in the company of two people – Nina and Miss Foy, both of them innocent and subjugated – rather as Ann, in *An Unofficial Rose* sees Penn, another innocent sufferer, at moments of decision. Nina sees Rosa as someone who will help and understand, but is constantly frustrated by Rosa's involvement in her relationship with Mischa – first by the sight of the invitation to Mischa's party, and then by the fact that Rosa, when Nina comes with her final appeal for help to escape Mischa, is herself on her way to ask Mischa to rid her of Stefan.

Miss Foy appears as the bringer of a cake containing West Country cider, a gesture of normal human friendly contact that seems to come from a dead world.

> When I was a child my mother used to make cakes and send me out with them as presents to the neighbours. And the neighbours would give us presents too, and not only at Christmas time. Such a nice custom. In the towns nowadays you don't find it at all. But I'm told that on the Continent people still do that kind of thing. Perhaps [to Nina] in – er – your country, Miss er – .[23]

But Rosa ignores this gesture in her distress over Jan Lusiewicz's first appearance in her house and Mischa's invitation.

In the scene where Nina's final appeal to Rosa is ignored, she sees both of them again, and sees Nina as 'something . . . which seemed for a moment like her own shadow'. Later when she sees Mischa, she sees that she resembles him, too.

> 'How strange,' said Rosa. 'I never noticed before that we resembled each other.' 'It is an illusion of lovers,' said Mischa.[24]

That is, to state what is by now perhaps obvious, Rosa, in many ways the norm of the novel, contains in her nature elements of both victim and predator, enchanted and enchanter (consider her behaviour to Peter Saward, her initial feeling of pleasurable if frightening power over the Lusiewiczs). And the element of ruthlessness in her entails the destruction not only of Nina, but of Hunter, who resembles Nina and is reduced to a state of mysterious illness by his feelings of guilt and despair over the action he has not in fact taken, and is not in fact able to take, over Stefan. The terms in which he is described recall the description of Nina; 'he was an animal whose protection was not teeth but flight and camouflage'. And weighing the evil that Stefan in the house might do to Rosa, and the evil that might result for a lot of innocent people if he invokes the FPE line against Stefan, he feels 'hemmed in by evil'.

The brother and sister relationship is used here, as in other places in Miss Murdoch's work, as a symbol of some tie or understanding deeper than normal human contact. Annette is in Jan Lusiewicz's power because he threatens, quite at random, to kill her brother. Peter Saward, detached from life, preserves the photograph of his dead sister.* And Rosa at the beginning feels 'obscenely near' to Hunter. 'For him she had no exterior' which suggests an openness to other people, or another person, akin to Peter Saward's personality without frontiers. Rosa is afraid of her nearness to Hunter. 'One's closeness to oneself . . . is made tolerable by the fact that one can alter oneself, the structure is alive. But for this other proximity there was no remedy.'[25] And, for Rosa's enchantment, Hunter suffers.

Nina, Hunter and Miss Foy, then, are all in their different ways aspects of that transcendent reality that prevents Rosa from behaving as though she were Stuart Hampshire's 'lonely, self-contained individual'. She is not, and this is made clear to her in the scene where Calvin Blick persuades her to return from Mischa's house in Italy by showing her, first the photograph of herself in the arms of the Lusiewiczs with which he has blackmailed Hunter, and then the report of Nina's suicide. Rosa cannot enter Mischa's world, and returns to Peter Saward, whose world she cannot enter either.

She is decided by Calvin's emphasis that 'Someone ought to have explained things to (Nina) . . . As it was, she was just an incidental casualty.' Calvin then tells her

> You will never know the truth, and you will read the signs in accordance with your own deepest wishes. That is what we humans always have to do. Reality is a cipher with many solutions, all of them right ones.[26]

This is clearly not what Miss Murdoch thinks; it is indeed

---

* As Max Lejour, here again a similar case, preserves the photograph of his dead wife.

directly opposed to it. In Miss Murdoch's thought it is meaningful to say that there is a truth, a transcendent reality, and
therefore all the solutions are not tight. Rosa's return to
London is surely an acknowledgement of this. On her return,
Hunter recovers completely. And Rosa, recognizing her own
degree of freedom, her own personal involvement in and
responsibility for a world of other individuals, is freed of the
enchantment, the fantasy, the illusion, that she is subject to
Mischa's will entirely.

Leaving Mischa, and Calvin, looking at Mischa with 'a
tender predatory expression', Rosa tells him:

> I always felt that whether I went towards him or away from
> him, I was only doing his will. But it was all an illusion.'
> 'Who knows,' said Calvin, 'perhaps it is only now that it
> would be an illusion.'[27]

And this might be described as freeing from the Romantic
myth of necessity, which Miss Murdoch so mistrusts, for a
return to a world of 'a spread out substantial picture of the
manifold virtues of man and society',[28] which is a part of a
reality which, if we cannot ever completely comprehend it,
certainly has not 'many' 'right' solutions. And here, perhaps,
tentatively, we may connect Calvin's name with a belief in
necessary damnation.

Rainborough's fate parallels Rosa's in that he is released
from an interim enchantment by an enchanter, in this case a
female one, Annette's mother, Marcia Cockeyne, and taken
from the solid world of office and hospital wall to the warmth
and mystery of the south. The counter-spell consists of his
being made to recite the nastiest thing he can think of about
Miss Casement – her persecution of the little typist – and the
working on him of the female presence of Marcia. As far as
we see, he does not return; the last we see of him is that 'A
great wind was blowing through him . . . He was empty.'[29]
His moments of wisdom are the perception of flowers, or
insects, or the life in Annette or the wistaria; he is not,
like Rosa, someone involved willy-nilly in personal relations,
which make claims whatever we consciously *choose*, and

therefore it is perhaps right that he should be allowed a complete flight into the sun. But it is necessary to digress a little at this stage to discuss the Cockeyne family.

Marcia, it seems at least to me, represents something in Miss Murdoch's thought which is perhaps best compared with the Tintoretto painting of Susannah in *An Unofficial Rose* – 'Hugh's golden dream of another world' – or with Anna's song. She is not a 'natural' woman, who ages, like Anna, or Rosa here, or Ann. Nor is she artificial, in the sense in which Magdalen, with her perms and dyed hair, or Miss Casement with her powder, petticoats, lipstick-tipped cigarettes and perm are in this book. She is a woman who is a work of art and represents a permanent force of beauty – Platonic beauty – in the world; celestial Venus, as opposed to the earthly Venus perhaps best instanced by Lindsay Rimmer in *An Unofficial Rose*, who is specifically referred to as Venus Anadyomene. It is significant that Hunter, in his delirium, recognizes her presence as that of a 'film star'. In *Under the Net* Jake thought of the film star as indistinguishably similar to all women, a sort of refined essence of the female.

Marcia, like Mischa, has a mystery of foreignness:

> After the harsh sweetness which emanated from Miss Casement and Miss Perkins, the scent of Marcia was of a celestial subtlety . . . Sandalwood perhaps . . . It occurred to Rainborough suddenly that the whole extraordinary ensemble of powder, perfume and paint which gave so artificial a surface to Miss Casement, lay upon Marcia as a natural bloom. She was an exotic flower, like flowers which Rainborough had seen in southern countries, which were hardly flowers at all, and yet were undoubtedly products of nature. Rainborough's norm was still the wild rose, although he no longer even desired these simple blossoms.[30]

Here again the comparison with *An Unofficial Rose* obtrudes itself, and the comparison with Ann, coupled with the fact that Rainborough loves Rosa, suggests a reason for Rosa's name.

It is Marcia and her husband, in a description which surely deliberately invites comparison with the description of the relation between art, contemplation, love and possession in the *Ode to a Grecian Urn*, who provide the antithesis to the pursuit of the fish which inevitably ends in struggling and blood. This, we are to suppose, is love; but compared with the complexity of the relations of the other characters, it is precisely two-dimensional, perhaps deliberately, and seems imposed, in a not quite satisfactory way, upon the book as a novel. However, everything is here, mystery, pursuit, flight.

> He still hoped ... that he might read his answers in her eyes. Somewhere deep within, a light shone which could reassure him forever. But this reassurance was something which, deliberately or not, Marcia had always withheld from him ... So she escaped him, always evading the point of rest and contemplation towards which he always wished to draw her; and when at times he caught her head, violent almost with hunger for her gaze, she would move restlessly, tossing her hair, twisting her body, and turning away her eyes like an animal.[31]

In this scene we have our last glimpse of Annette, vitality completely restored, 'looking at the world', having made a recovery from her contact with the muddle and enslavement of human relations, comparable to that of Toby in *The Bell*. The fourth member of the family is the unseen Nicholas, who has followed Grahame and christened his parents 'the Olympians' – a reference which is to become more ambiguous in the later books, where to be 'Olympian' is to lack a proper respect for the contingency of things, to make myths.

Of Nicholas we know three things; he indulges in abstract philosophy, he lives in Paris, and he writes, when Annette needs help, to announce that he has joined the Communist Party and is interested in chess. He writes 'It is necessary, dearest Sis, to *have been* a Liberal'[32]; whereas it is clear from *Against Dryness* that Miss Murdoch thinks that we must return from the totalitarian myth of Marxism to a deepening of the Liberal idea of freedom, and a more complex Liberal theory of personality. Thus Nicholas is connected with the young Sartre, with an abstract and youthful world of pure thought and pure enthusiasm, ideals which seem impossible of achievement, or irrelevant when seen in the context of the human muddle of Rosa's world. Nicholas, like his mother, like his sister, like the relation between his mother and his father, lives in an ideal world where the savagery of Jan and Stefan, the real evil (which we have lost the sense of, Miss Murdoch says) brought about by Mischa, Rosa's openness to these, the bluntly *thwarting* nature of the mixture of cruelty in love, are not admitted. They are from a world where 'circles and melodies retain their pure and rigid contours'. It is perhaps proper that they should provide a retreat for Rainborough, the Romantic.

In *Against Dryness* Miss Murdoch speaks of 'the dream necessity of romanticism' and says

> This 'dryness' (smallness, clearness, self-containedness) is a nemesis of romanticism. Indeed it *is* Romanticism in a later phase.[33]

I have said that Rainborough is left feeling empty, a wind blowing through him; this state parallels that of Randall, in *An Unofficial Rose*, another romantic who engages in a search for the nemesis of Romanticism. Randall is clearly 'dry' and to be felt to be avoiding a reality he should admit and encounter to be really free. The same is not true of Rainborough – the whole idea of his fate and the presentation of it are lighter and more playful – nevertheless, I would tentatively suggest, he has, symbolically (and what a 'pure, clear, self-contained symbol' it is), accepted the consolation of art, which Miss Murdoch says is art's 'temptation'.

(I am by no means sure that I am not here criticizing Miss Murdoch in her own terms, rather than discovering her intention. It may be that Marcia is meant to have the permanent value of the pictures Dora sees in the National Gallery; or that it is here a *positive* value that Annette has as eternal youth, and not one of crystalline consolation – although it is tempting to see her collection of jewels as the 'crystals' with which fantasy-myth operates.[34] Nicholas's abstractions may be set against Annette rather than with her; I still find the concept of Annette, unlike Toby in *The Bell*, one that faintly cheats, or avoids an issue.)

Finally, we must consider the character of Mischa Fox himself, who is the spirit of the world where people age and are marked, suffer and are destroyed. Critics have generally seemed to find him rather a negative presence, an absence without an identity, and to have disliked him on these grounds. I think this is unfair, partly because he is to a certain extent meant to have this negative quality – he says to Annette 'I am not famous for anything in particular, I am just famous'[35] – and partly because the qualities in him that make him the enchanter are carefully mapped out.

The important thing about him is that he wields power. Michael in *The Bell* 'had always held the view that the good man is without power . . .' and 'felt himself compelled to remain in a region where power was evil and where he could not honourably find the means to strip himself of it completely'.[36] Calvin does most of Mischa's evil work, and the extent of Mischa's complicity in his evil is never certain, but the responsibility is there – paralleling perhaps Rosa's lack of knowledge about Nina's condition, for which she is nevertheless partially responsible.

For power exists and is there to be wielded, and, as Miss Murdoch says of political action, 'always falls into corruption'. Peter Saward thinks of Mischa 'how strangely close to each other in this man lay the springs of cruelty and of pity' and his power is seen as an inextricable combination of these. He asks Saward

> Do you ever feel as if everything in the world needed your – protection? It is a terrible feeling. Everything – even this matchbox.[37]

Saward says no, and means it, but for Mischa, who is intolerably conscious of suffering and weakness in things, the protective impulse is transformed into a necessity to kill. He killed a kitten in his childhood.

That was the only way to help it, to save it. So it is. If the gods kill us, it is not for their sport, but because we fill them with a sort of intolerable compassion, a sort of nausea.[38]

He sees Nina, we could thus argue, as she sees herself at the moment of her death, intolerably oppressed by the senseless blackness, better dead.

He is, as power is, very lonely – he is seen twice at the edge of the sea, of which Annette is aware that he is terrified. He is seen against a world where there has been the cataclysmic suffering and violence of the war (Hitler, mentioned only a few times, is a real presence in this book) and where love, human friendship, human contact, seem to be dead or dying. And he is aware of this.

Two things emphasize this. The first, the contrast of the Lusiewiczs' deliberate rejection of their childhood and roots with Mischa's attitude to his own childhood, which, in the form of photographs, he 'keeps' with Peter Saward. Peter was certain

that the pursuit here, of exactness and completeness was for him a terrible necessity.[39]

This childhood seems to be both innocence and, since we have the reminiscences of killing kittens and chickens and the weeping fish, the truth, the origins of his present power and its operations, at whose mercy he himself seems to be, as well as everyone else.

The other is the striking image of hands. Throughout the book one character attempts to 'imprison' another's hand (Rainborough and Annette, Mischa and Nina); this is connected with the image of helpless animals. Annette, after her suicide attempt, sees her hand as a dying animal she has killed without its permission. Peter sees Mischa's hand 'like some small and helpless creature'. Rosa feels the steel of her machine through the flesh of Jan's hand; an early image for the unease he generates before we are told why. Rosa at the end allows Calvin Blick to 'capture' her hand, but will not let him kiss it; Rainborough burns his on Miss Casement's stockings. There is a sense that the hand – which is what reaches out from one human being to another in friendship is also in this reaching out to be trapped, damaged, tortured. And Mischa's hands are of this kind, too.

And although he is seen as a rich mystery by the other characters, he, perhaps foreshadowing Hannah Crean-Smith in this, lives in a dry world. He tells Peter Saward that 'the surface of the world ought to be covered with dead animals', and his villa in Italy is not, as Rosa had imagined it, a 'tropical paradise' but in a landscape of which when Rosa praises it, Mischa says without reproach, 'It is a very poor landscape.' Together Mischa and Rosa study the insects which differ greatly from those which, earlier, Rainborough studied in his moment of joy.

> Rosa too looked down and saw that the gravel surface of the terrace was covered with living creatures. Ants passed by carrying heavy burdens. Poor dried-up beetles walked or staggered on their way . . . If she were to go away, all this would vanish too, and Mischa would be left, haggard and staring, in some place unimaginably stripped and denuded.[40]

Mischa's world, as I have said, is not a world in which Rosa can live. She cannot really belong, in the last resort, to a world which can *inevitably* kill Nina. Mischa's relations to other individuals are either those of pity, or those of destruction; he cannot *meet* them in love. But Rosa is, like Kafka's K, a character who must 'persist in believing that there is sense in the ordinary business of human communication'. She goes back to edit the *Artemis*, a 'little independent thing' which Mischa's impulse would be to grab (to 'protect' it) and destroy. She is last seen with Peter, contemplating the photographs of Mischa's vanished world of order and innocence. 'And here is the cathedral . . .'

This book marks an end of Miss Murdoch's writing of fantasy myth of this particular kind. It also marks an end of her attempt to present the 'complex virtues of man and society' in a God-like, symbolic way; from now on we have smaller canvasses, less philosophic patterning, more use of the microcosm of human affairs (a school, a religious community) to show us society and less attempt to give us, on a large scale, even fantastically, society as a whole.

Of the writer in our society Miss Murdoch has said that he felt

> A sense of the desperate rapidity of change, the responsibility of speech in an incomprehensible situation, a feeling of being 'left out', obscure guilt at the inhumanities of a materialistic society.[41]

In the effect of Mischa on the world of *The Flight from the Enchanter* we are shown, socially and sexually, the ingredients of this 'incomprehensible situation'. The direction in which Miss Murdoch's thought is leading is clear in the position of Rosa. Under the influence of Mischa she has been guilty of not apprehending the 'other', the individual people and their value. Here again, Sartre is apposite.

> The value of the person is detected by Sartre not in any patient study of the complexity of human relations, but simply in his experience of the pain of defeat and loss ... [The preciousness of the individual] is apprehended only in the emotional obscurity of a hopeless mourning. 'No human victory can efface this absolute of suffering.'[42]

The knowledge of absolute suffering is what Mischa has, and indeed Miss Murdoch uses her image of the hand, of Sartre as well as of the world of Mischa.

> The individual is a centre, but a solipsistic centre. He has a *dream* of human companionship, but never the experience. He touches others at the fingertips.[43]

But ordinary morals, which are involved in 'the complexity of human relations' are what, I would suggest, Rosa must return to come to grips with, and Miss Murdoch next turns to study. Miss Murdoch writes of Sartre that in *Les Chemins de la Liberté* he by-passes the complexity of the world of ordinary human relations which is also the world of ordinary moral virtues . . . Human life *begins*. But the complexity of the moral virtues, which must return, more deeply apprehended perhaps, with the task of 'going on from there', this we are not shown.[44]

We are not shown either how Rosa will 'go on from there' although it is clear she must. But in the next novel, *The Sandcastle*, things are seen much more in these terms.

4

THE SANDCASTLE

IT HAS BEEN remarked somewhere that *The Sandcastle* barely escapes being a woman's novelette (or perhaps an expansion of a story for a women's magazine, a slightly higher, because less remotely 'consoling' form of literature). I do not myself think that it does escape it, during considerable passages of the book – a failing I would attribute to the character of the artist, Rain Carter, who starts off hampered by a name, however symbolic, which comes straight from such a novelette. She is, that is, as Annette in another sense is, the sort of dream idealization of a young woman – beautiful, talented, rich, loving, intelligent – who has no right to appear in a 'solid' novel of this kind, since she is intended to be seen as something more than a symbolic personification of the needs of the protagonist, Mor; she is meant to be a person and a force in her own right, in which character, I would suggest, ultimately, she fails.

I would add that the book also suffers from fancifully imposed symbolism (the gypsy, the dog, Felicity's magic ritual) which hinder, rather than help, our apprehension of the novel as a 'real' action, with a 'real' meaning. Since I think it is a lesser work than its predecessors, or its naturalistic successor, *The Bell*, I propose to write much less about it. Nevertheless, to return to our original point, the comparison with the woman's story is helpful, at least to explain why Miss Murdoch turned from the highly polished complexity and wit (in all senses) of her earlier work, to this ordinary story, set in very humdrum and limited surroundings.

The function of the women's story is to console. A comparatively recent version in women's magazines of the story in which the girl rejects the romantic but basically nasty young man for the dull but honest young man from next door is the post-marital story, in which the protagonist (usually a woman) is tempted by a past lover, or glamorous next-door neighbour, to give up her obligations to the husband and children whom she has been finding increasingly limiting, exhausting, irritating, for a world of romance in which she can be herself, someone loved, important, beautiful. During the story, the romantic world is shown to be either basically nasty, or, more subtly, impossible to live in (thoughts of the unmade bed recur, perhaps) and a new and glamorous light is usually cast on the virtues of husband and children. In the end, the protagonist, and the reader, we suppose, return to their washing-machines, convinced of the solidity and value of their lives as they stand.

The Sandcastle misses this pattern by a hair's breadth. It is the story of the love of a middle-aged schoolmaster (Bill Mor) with a sarcastic wife (Nan) and two adolescent children, for a young and beautiful woman painter (Rain Carter) who has been invited to the school to paint the portrait of the retiring headmaster, Demoyte. At the beginning of the book, Mor is trying to persuade his wife to let him accept the invitation, organized by Tim Burke, the goldsmith, to become the candidate for the local 'safe' Labour seat. The rest of the story is simple; Mor decides to give up everything to go away with Rain, but is foiled, partly by the actions of his children (Felicity goes in for magic rituals; Don, desperate because he is being forced into university against his inclinations, and because of the knowledge he shares with Felicity of the relations between Mor, his wife and Rain, climbs the school tower, as a piece of bravado, with another boy, and nearly loses his life), partly by Rain's decision, when Nan reveals at a dinner party Mor's political ambitions which he had kept secret from Rain, to leave without him, and to continue her 'rootless' life as an artist alone. Nan has been rendered uncertain enough to have to reflect about her marriage as she has never done before; at the end of the book, the family is reconciled, Don, who had run away, has returned, Mor is now ready for Don to be apprenticed to Tim Burke, and Nan in her turn has accepted both that Felicity shall attempt to go to university and that Mor shall pursue his political career. There is no suggestion that the difficulties have all been replaced with radiant understanding, but some kind of insight has clearly been achieved by both partners to the marriage.

It is easy to see why this particular plot should appeal to Miss Murdoch at this stage precisely *because of* its ordinariness and triteness. It is, after all, a basic human problem – one of the problems of 'normal human intercourse', which Miss Murdoch considers we neglect at our peril, for abstract studies of the 'state of man'. It contains a problem which is a 'real moral issue' and involves 'ordinary moral virtue', which again, Miss Murdoch feels we neglect. It is an attempt to move, as I said earlier, from crystalline patterning to the naturalistic description of character; this is partly why the symbols seem tacked on. But its assertion that reality is more compelling than convulsive attempts to grab a freedom which denies the stuff of life comes dangerously close to being only a consolatory assertion. This is perhaps because the conflict is never made quite real to us.

The relationship between Mor and his children, on the one hand, which should be part of the stuff of his life, is asserted, rather than shown, to exist. The moment when he stands in the school courtyard and does not know what to say to Donald is a real moment, although other later ones are not, but his relationship with Felicity is barely sketched. Felicity's magical activities are no substitute for it, nor is the appearance of the gipsy,* associated with Felicity's magic, at the

---

* The gipsy, called up by Felicity's enchantment is, as well as being Felicity's familiar, an image for Rain's other 'gipsy' self, that which endangered her relationship with Mor. I had not quite understood this until Miss Murdoch pointed it out to me – but I do not think that to understand it disposes of my objection to such a symbolic figure appearing *as a substitute* for Felicity's relation with Mor, or even this apprehension of Rain's 'gipsy' quality.

moment when Mor has Rain in his house: these serve to cover a lack, in terms of the novel, of something real, solid, in which we can believe, and about which we can care.

And, on the other hand, Mor's relationship with Rain is too flimsy a substitute for an apprehension of people to give us any real moral trouble; the adolescent urgency of it is well drawn, but we feel its author to be too involved in it, too sure of the real power of her heroine's enchantments, which are again more asserted than shown, with constant references to the gamine, the boyish quality of her, and descriptions of her clothes of a kind which smack again of the romanticism of the women's magazine, rather than giving her being.

I have elaborated these criticisms because, particularly in the case of this book, and that of *An Unofficial Rose*, to show how its ideas on freedom are related and developed is to describe the structure of a better book than one actually feels oneself to be reading.

One feels that it is better and its action more interesting than it seems in itself because of Miss Murdoch's technique of pointing the conceptual content of the action by a series of neat and authentic little commentaries where abstract or philosophical terms would naturally be used: Mor's W.E.A. lecture on freedom, Bledyard's lecture, Everard's sermon to the school, Bledyard's private sermon to Mor. In the case of *The Bell* these commentaries are absorbed more naturally into an action which has more power to carry them; here, Bledyard has too much moral force for the events he is set against, and this diminishes him as well as them.

At the beginning of the book we have Mor involved in an apparently loveless marriage, and taking very seriously his responsibilities to wife and children, to what Nan calls 'our marriage'. We are told that he has been brought up as a Methodist and 'believed profoundly in complete truthfulness as the basis and condition of all virtue'.[1] The moral decisions which confront him are the decisions about the future of his children, and the decision whether to allow himself to become the candidate for the 'safe' Labour seat, which is seen as a kind of freedom to act, to be himself more fully, and of which Nan disapproves. There is a dog, Liffey, who represents the same kind of unreflecting, vital force as Mars in *Under the Net*, or the dogs in *The Bell* or *The Unicorn*. Liffey, however, is dead, and lives only in Felicity's imagination and in moments of contact between Nan and Mor.

> This animal had formed the bond between Nan and Mor which their children had been unable to form. Half unconsciously, whenever Mor wanted to placate his wife, he said something about Liffey.[2]

Again the existence of this symbol is a statement, an illustration, rather than a living part of the novel, and is, as the symbols in the earlier books were not, decorative, rather than a part of the action. (Compare Mischa Fox's fish and beetles.) However, it is a useful pointer; a vanished vitality, recalled by the imagination.

The first definition of 'freedom' in the book is Mor's own, during his W.E.A. class, when one of his pupils insists that freedom is a virtue. (The tone of pupil and teacher is here exactly caught; Miss Murdoch's arguments and sermons are almost always convincing.)

> If by freedom we mean absence of external restraint, then we may call a man lucky for being free – but why should we call him good? If on the other hand, by freedom we mean self-discipline, which dominates selfish desires, then indeed we may call a free man virtuous. But, as we know, this more refined conception of freedom can also play a dangerous role in politics. It may be used to justify the tyranny of people who think themselves to be the enlightened ones. Whereas the notion of freedom which I'm sure Mr Staveley has in mind, the freedom which inspired the great Liberal leaders of the last century, is political freedom, the absence of tyranny. This is the condition of virtue, and to strive for it is a virtue. But it is not in itself a virtue. To call mere absence of restraint or mere kicking over the traces and flouting conventions a virtue is to be simply romantic.[3]

This speech indicates both a right view of freedom, and a particular direction in which Mor's own striving for freedom should profitably lie; he is engaged in the strife for political freedom, the absence of tyranny. Indeed, although it is part of the story that during his enchantment his 'real' freedom becomes temporarily unimportant to him, the book would be better if his political beliefs and actions were more firmly established before they faded.

It is interesting to note that in this book, as in others, Demoyte, who is explicitly described as a 'tyrant', is made attractive, someone who 'draws love', whereas the character who most nearly corresponds to Mor's definition of freedom as a virtue, Mr Everard, who has no selfish desires, who, like Peter Saward, 'lived in the open, with simplicity, seeming to lack altogether the concepts of vanity or ambition, weaknesses which he was equally incapable of harbouring in himself or of recognizing in others'[4] is seen as a figure of fun, someone who is at a loss as to how to exercise the power he holds, someone perhaps, 'shapeless and awkward', like Ann in *An Unofficial Rose*.

When Mor embarks on his relationship with Rain, we have repeated the pattern of seemingly insignificant actions leading to acts of great moral importance. He goes out with her in her car, telephones Nan, automatically lies to her about where he is, and is immediately involved – he who believed that truthfulness is the basis and condition of all virtue – in a string of lies and deceits. His passion grows; he decides, as it seems to him he has the right to decide, to go away with Rain; walking with her in London, however, he feels that he is 'damned'. G. S. Fraser has pointed out that the episode of the car stuck in the mud, and finally overturned into the river, is a symbol for the intractability of matter, of the normal, against which one's efforts are unavailing, no matter how violent. But this applies most deeply to Mor. Rain is seen, by contrast, as a free creature, with the freedom of youth, money, and an absorbing talent; she is free in that she can concentrate entirely on her painting. It is here that Bledyard and his views, both on art and morals, becomes relevant to the argument.

Bledyard has much in common with Hugo Belfounder, even to the fact that both live in clinically simple bedrooms. He believes in an objectivity that does not classify, in a vision from which one's own desires and needs and patternings are purged.*

> When confronted with an object which is not a human being, we must of course treat it reverently. We must, if we paint it, attempt to show what it is like in itself and not treat it as a symbol of our own moods and wishes. The great painter the great painter is he who is humble enough in the presence of the object to attempt *merely* to show what the object is like. But this *merely*, in painting, is everything.[5]

He believes as an artist that our vision of other human beings is corrupted by our need to interpret them by what we are ourselves, and that to paint them at all is to lack reverence for God in them. He remarks (which may suggest a direction for an explanation of why Mor could love Demoyte and not the traditionally virtuous Everard)

> We cannot really observe really observe our betters. Vices and peculiarities are easy to portray. But who can look reverently enough upon another human face?[6]

Rain Carter feels of him, as Jake feels of Hugo, that what he says is 'so very abstract' or 'some colossal distortion'. But this view enables him to criticize Rain's painting in a way she accepts, when he says that it is 'a series of definitions' and 'does not look *mortal*'.[7]† And it is his view which, whilst we do not believe Nan when she tells Mor that he has 'no

---

* In the quotations I have made from Bledyard's speeches, it might be useful to point out that the repetitions of words are a reproduction of Bledyard's defect of speech.

† That is, it is something, like Roquentin's song as seen in *Under the Net*, which achieves a conceptual 'formed' necessity, at the expense of the individual particularity of the unique human being. It is a 'form', an 'idea' of a man, like the modern crystalline novel, not a living picture of a man, in the sense in which Miss Murdoch admires Tolstoi's characters.

choice', shows clearly that there are limitations to Mor's freedom which he is ignoring in deciding to go away with Rain. Bledyard himself is perhaps another of Miss Murdoch's victims of the theory that there should be no theory, which culminates in the ambiguous passivity of Hannah Crean-Smith: his ideal may be right, but it has stopped him painting people, and this, in Miss Murdoch's world, is not human in itself.

Bledyard's deciding speech to Mor is immediately preceded by a sermon from Everard to which Mor hardly listens because he is thinking of Rain. The sermon is, appositely, on the subject of 'God helps those who help themselves' – Everard explains that he does not mean thieves – and ends with the assurance that

> God is to be thought of as a distant point of unification: that point where all conflicts are reconciled, and all that is partial and, to our finite eyes, contradictory, is integrated and bound up.[8]

During this sermon Mor considers Nan; how telling Rain that she has 'frustrated him, breaking within him piece by piece the structure of his own desires', has released in him anger, and the certainty that he no longer loves her. And then he reflects.

> Of course he no longer loved her. But somehow to say this was not to say anything at all. He had lived with Nan for twenty years. That living together was a reality which made it frivolous, or so it seemed to him, even to ask whether or not he loved her.[9]

Earlier, we have been told that Mor, when their marriage began to fail, had discovered that 'he was tied for life to a being who could change, who could withdraw herself from him and become independent'.[10]

But his long relationship, love or no love, with this independent being, this 'other', is real, and cannot be destroyed merely by willing it. Everard's sermon, like other Christian statements of belief in Iris Murdoch's books – James Tayper

Pace's in *The Bell*, Donald Swann's in *An Unofficial Rose* – is both relevant to Mor's situation and somehow irrelevant because outside the scope of any way he can see it, or any way he can act. Voluntary crucifixion of his 'own desires'* is a very different process from Nan's deliberate breaking of them. It does not follow that Everard's sermon is to be taken as unrelated to Mor's predicament; it co-exists with it within the novel, a concept presented to us, even in the beautifully caught, largely lifeless language of the sermon, which, like the Abbess in *The Bell*, is a present force, whose existence we are aware of, even if its relevance to our situation is not clear.

Mor, however, has hardly heard him; he goes from the chapel to meet Rain, and finds instead Bledyard who has sent Rain away. Bledyard continues the theme of Everard's sermon – that there is 'one good thing' to do that is right, by telling Mor that he is 'deeply rooted' in his own life, and that 'if you break these bonds you destroy a part of the world'.[11]

Mor retorts that he might then build another part, but does not pursue this idea with any conviction (in another book, what he might build could have had a less flimsy power from the beginning, and this could have made the whole less of a foregone conclusion; in another book again the foregone conclusion might have had more real compelling necessity and less consolation about it). Bledyard then puts to Mor the idea that freedom consists of a respect for the limiting functions of reality; this is perhaps the most nakedly theoretical exposition we have of it in the seven novels under consideration.

> There is such a thing as respect for reality. You are living on dreams now, dreams of happiness, dreams of freedom. But in all this you consider only yourself. You do not truly apprehend the distinct being of either your wife or Miss Carter.[12]

* In so far as Everard's sermon recommends this 'voluntary crucifixion' it is an echo of Simone Weil's belief in the deliberate destruction of the self, and thus is related to Anna Quentin's 'philosophy of silence' at one extreme, and Hannah Crean-Smith's deliberate suffering at the other.

That is, Mor is 'placing' both Rain and Nan, he is not aware of them as 'real impenetrable human persons', he is deforming the nature of reality by fantasy.

> You imagine ... that to live in a state of extremity is necessarily to discover the truth about yourself. What you discover then is violence and emptiness. And of this you make a virtue ... You do not know even remotely what it would be like to set aside all consideration of your own satisfaction ... You live in a world of imagined things. But if you were to concern yourself truly with others and lay yourself open to any hurt that might come to you, you would be enriched in a way of which you cannot now even conceive. The gifts of the spirit do not appeal to the imagination.[13]

This contrast of the 'gifts of the spirit' with those of the imagination is the first mention of the conflict between these which is a central theme of *The Bell, The Unicorn* and *An Unofficial Rose*. It is a theme also in the work of Simone Weil, who regards the imagination, to which she usually refers as 'L'imagination, combleuse de vides', as something necessarily opposed to the spiritual path of self-effacement, acceptance of voids, acceptance of suffering which is not, in the manner of Até, passed on. She writes:

> Continuellement suspendre en soi-même le travail de l'imagination combleuse de vides. Si on accepte n'importe quel vide, quel coup du sort peut empêcher d'aimer l'univers?[14]

And she regards the imagination as essentially something which precludes an apprehension of reality in us.

> L'imagination combleuse de vides est essentiellement menteuse. Elle exclut la troisième dimension car ce sont seulement les objets réels qui sont dans les trois dimensions. Elle exclut les rapports multiples.[15]

This is here another angle on the particularity of reality.

The slight horror which Miss Murdoch allows us to feel at the *abstract* or apparently abstract quality of Bledyard's spirituality, and which we later feel about Ann and Hannah, is something which a reading of Simone Weil also inspires, and to have read Simone Weil illuminates for us Miss Murdoch's presentation of these characters. And Mor has our sympathy when he replies, as many of Miss Murdoch's characters reply to similar exhortations, 'Such an austerity would be beyond me.' It is something echoed in Dora's and Toby's reaction to what is at one point called the 'hideous purity and austerity' of the life of the nuns in the convent.

Mor then makes the standard assertion that would be made by the 'lonely self-contained individual' of *Thought and Action* as seen in *Against Dryness*. 'All I can say is that this is my situation and my life and I shall decide what to do about it.'

Bledyard uses against him the definition of freedom he has himself already offered to the W.E.A. class.

> 'You speak as if this were a sort of virtue,' said Bledyard, 'you speak as if to be a free man was just to get what you want regardless of convention. But real freedom is a total absence of concern about yourself.'

Mor, this time explicitly, says 'It doesn't manage to connect itself with my problems,' and Bledyard, finally, brings up the question of Rain; Mor, he argues, is 'diminishing' Rain by involving her in all this. 'A painter can only paint what he is. You will prevent her from being a great painter.'

Nevertheless it is not Mor but Rain who, by respecting the 'otherness' of the other partner, breaks the impossible fantasy. The crisis is precipitated by Nan's revelation of – and public acceptance of – Mor's political ambitions, at the dinner which marks the presentation of Rain's portrait of Demoyte to the school. Mor has not told Rain of these ambitions; when she learns of them, she too recognizes the limiting power of reality. She says (in novelette language)

> You are a growing tree. I am only a bird. You cannot break your roots and fly away with me. Where could we go where you wouldn't always be wanting the deep things that belong to you, your children, and this work which you know is your work? . . . I should die if I were prevented from painting.[16]

Mor brushes aside the connection here between his reality and hers, and makes the standard self-centred appeal.

> I began to be when I loved you, I saw the world for the first time, the beautiful world full of things and animals that I'd never seen before. What do you think will happen to me if you leave me now?

But Rain has decided, and turns away from him into her work. Later when she has left Demoyte's house, Mor who has gone to seek her there, tells Demoyte, 'It was inevitable'; Demoyte, who has been in favour of his convulsive bid for freedom, and whose dislike of Nan has made their married life more difficult, says 'Nothing was inevitable. You have made your own future.'[17]

To return again to Miss Murdoch's criticism of *Les Chemins*:

> In *Les Chemins* we constantly feel the violent swing from a total blindness to a total freedom, from the silence of unreason to an empty and alarming babble of reflexion. Human life *begins*. But the complexity of the moral virtues, which must return, more deeply apprehended perhaps, with the task of 'going on from there', this we are not shown.[18]

If Mor had felt that he 'began to be' when he loved Rain, he has now been pushed back into the moral virtues with the task of going on from there. The decision has not consciously been his, but Demoyte is surely right in that there is a sense in which it is the result of his life and his nature. And Nan has changed, sufficiently at least for it to seem possible for them both to apprehend the moral virtues more deeply.

Nan, it is clear, was at the beginning of the book in a state of *mauvaise foi*, which Miss Murdoch defines as:

> the more or less conscious refusal to reflect, the immersion in the unreflectively coloured awareness of the world, the persistence in an emotional judgment, or the willingness to inhabit cosily some other person's estimate of oneself.[19]

Miss Murdoch comments 'It is in terms of a dispersion of this gluey inertness that Sartre pictures freedom', and it is suggested in this book that Nan is moving towards this kind of freedom; the dual shock, first of her discovery of Mor with Rain in her house, and then of her coming to grips with what she has known but not admitted – that Tim Burke, the goldsmith, is in love with her – jolts her out of her refusal to reflect. For a moment she sees Tim as 'close, mysterious, other than herself, full to the brim of his own particular history;' she will not explore him, because she realizes (as Mor does not) 'the reality of her situation, the irresponsible silliness of her present conduct'.[20] But she has had to think. And her thoughts about Mor, when she has returned to Dorset, also move from the persistence in an emotional judgment to reflection. At first she believes that Mor will, as he has always done, do as she tells him.

> She was pleased that she had maintained throughout a civilized and rational demeanour. Fundamentally Nan grasped the situation at this time as a drama, and one which she was able to fashion to her own pattern. She felt the satisfaction of one who is in the right, able to impose his will, and doing so mercifully.[21]

But slowly she begins to see that she might really lose her husband, and to think – even to dream – about him. She 'thought about him more intensely than she had ever done since she had first been in love with him.' 'She began, though she did not let this become clear to herself, almost to desire him.'[22]

That is, she is aware again of Mor as another person, not an extension of herself, and her public acceptance of his political ambitions is not only what Mor thinks it is – a trap for him and for Rain, an attempt to destroy their relationship, as it does – it is an acceptance of him, as he is, his being. Nan achieves her freedom by a withdrawal from the normal.

> Her normal existence had not demanded, had even excluded reflection. It had contained her firmly like a shell with every cranny filled ... Now the pressure of reality upon her had been withdrawn and she was left alone in the centre of a void

> where she had suddenly to determine afresh the form and
> direction of her being.[23]

So, at the end of the book, having progressed in different directions away from normality, the two come together again, to make, we are told, wiser decisions about the future of their children.

I have already said why I find this book comparatively unsatisfactory; it is partly because it is too clear, too patterned, too much of a statement about complexity, with too little real complexity of feeling or action. In the first two books, the plotting and patterning is part of the artistic pleasure, because the patterning is so complex as to create a life of its own – a fantasy maybe, but a vital one. Here we have a slightly less than vital imitation of real life, where the tendency of art to impose its own shapes on the stuff of life, criticized by Bledyard from within the book, is too much apparent. But the much more leisurely exploration of naturalistic emotion in it leads directly to the book which has been called Miss Murdoch's best, and which is certainly the nearest, so far, to fulfilling the standards she sets for the naturalistic novelist in *Against Dryness*.

5
THE BELL

WITH THE BELL, as opposed to *The Sandcastle*, or indeed, to any of Miss Murdoch's other novels one has the sense that to attempt to expose a framework of thought is to diminish it in a certain way; this is because here we have a novel which has the solid life that Miss Murdoch praises in the great nineteenth-century novels. The characters are not tied up neatly at the end of the book; they have a life of their own which exists beyond it. What will happen to Michael Meade, or to Dora, is a matter for real concern and speculation, as what will happen to Rosa is not, because there is nothing more we can know, and what will happen to Randall and Ann is not, because we have never really learned to care, and these characters do not seem to be embedded in a life in whose continuance we can have any faith. But here Miss Murdoch has succeeded in writing a novel which, if it tends towards the crystaline, is more than that.

The Bell is the story of the happenings at an Anglican Lay Community, in the grounds of a house called Imber Court, in Oxfordshire, one summer. The story is seen through the eyes of Michael Meade, leader of the community, and owner of the house; Dora Greenfield, once an art student, and now, somewhat uncertainly, the wife of Paul Greenfield, who is studying some mediaeval manuscripts belonging to the Abbey, which is across the lake from the court; and Toby Gashe, a youth who has just left school, and is going up to Oxford in the autumn.

The events of the story are arranged, somewhat loosely,

around the bell itself. At the beginning of the story we learn that a new bell is to be hung in the Abbey tower, and will enter the gate like a postulant – here resembling Catherine Fawley, a member of the community who intends to enter the Abbey as a nun. Paul tells Dora the legend of the old bell, which flew out of the tower into the lake – this because the Bishop cursed the Abbey on an occasion when one of the nuns took a lover and would not confess; the guilty nun drowned herself in the lake when the bell was lost.

Toby finds this bell; he reveals its existence to Dora, having decided that Dora is the antidote to the emotional distress he feels after Michael involuntarily kisses him after a particularly happy expedition to Swindon to buy a mechanical cultivator. Dora decides, for her own purposes, to raise the old bell and substitute it for the new one at the Christening ceremony.

Dora feels that the community disapproves of her and judges her; her husband is unkind and unreasonable, but she can neither leave him, live with him, nor stay with her lover, a journalist called Noel Spens, in London. She sees the raising of the bell as 'a kind of rite of power and liberation'; this it is, in an ambiguous sense, since the bell embedded in the mud is a symbol for the involvement of spiritual energy in passion and ambiguous emotion.

Another member of the community is Nick Fawley, twin brother of Catherine, who once had a homosexual relationship with Michael, whilst he was a schoolboy under Michael's care. Nick has become dissolute and drunken; he has been sent to the community at Catherine's request, because he is in some kind of need, but seems to derive no benefit from his stay there, whilst the members of the community rather uneasily shun him.

It is he and Dora, the 'sinners', who between them precipitate the crisis. Nick forces Toby to confess to the upright James Tayper Pace both his relation with Michael and that with Dora, thus repeating Nick's own 'betrayal' of Michael; when at school Nick had made a 'confession' of a similar kind of his own relations with him. He also reveals to Noel

Dora's plan about the bell; Dora suddenly sees this as silly and nasty and rings the bell in the middle of the night, thus revealing its existence to the members of the community. The next day, at the Christening ceremony, in one of Miss Murdoch's most startling and effective series of apparent accidents, Paul makes a jealous scene, the new bell falls into the lake, Catherine attempts to drown herself, Dora, who cannot swim, attempts to rescue her, both are rescued by an 'aquatic nun', and Catherine, crazed, reveals her love for Michael, who is horrified. All this, through the agency of Noel and others, is reported in the newspapers, and the community dissolves in embarrassment, tragedy and lack of funds.

It is discovered that Nick was the agent of the bell's fall – presumably to interfere with his sister's vocation; Michael decides, at last, too late, to speak to him, but Nick commits suicide. Michael is overcome by grief. For some weeks he and Dora remain alone at Imber, before going off to begin their lives again. Michael is left responsible for Catherine, and Dora decides not to return to Paul, at least, not immediately, but to become an art teacher in Bath, and to attempt to become 'an independent, grown-up person'.

These two characters, Michael and Dora, are those with whom the book is most concerned, and whose fates are really in question. Toby Gashe, although he learns something during the action, is young enough, with the resilience Miss Murdoch attributes to extreme youth, not to have his liberty seriously impaired. Dora and Michael, however, are seen during the book to explore their limitations, their reality, and to make attempts to live a life which is their own; in this sense they are complementary and to be discussed at length.

But before beginning on this, I should like to look at the central symbol, the bell itself. With this, as with the magical symbolism in *The Sandcastle*, I have been uneasy for some time. It has seemed to me – both its legend, and the operations Toby and Dora engage in, subsequently, to raise it – much less interesting than the rest of the story, the relations between the characters in the religious community. It is something planted there, which one is surprised to be reminded of,* when occupied with more serious things. However, as planted symbols go, it is a good one, much more knit into the pattern of events and relationships than the excrescent gipsy, and much more complex. My criticism of it could perhaps best be expressed by saying that at the moment when Dora rings it – a symbolic sounding at night of 'the truth-telling voice that must not be silenced' – one has the feeling, while reading, that a symbolic action has been substituted for a real one, that the climax which is seen to occur is greater than the occurrence.

This is not to say that an action cannot be *both* symbolic *and* real (an example might be the relationship between Anna and Vronsky's riding, in *Anna Karenina* – or the relationship of Lear's madness to the storm – or perhaps the symbolic function of the Mass in one sense); it is only to say that in this case, the action is *largely* symbolic, and detracts a little from the greater reality of the rest of the novel. It is again an illustration, rather than an actual rendering of a state of mind.

This said, however, what does the bell symbolize? G. S. Fraser sees it both as a 'symbol of a lost order and faith' and, when it is dragged up from the mud, as something which, like the loss of Rain's car, 'creates a sense of intractability in things, sometimes ingeniously conquered, sometimes farcically or wretchedly triumphant'.[1]

I think that the bell certainly connects with the solidity of the normal, with the unutterably particular mystery; it is surely significant in this context that it is made, by a playful cross-reference not unique in Miss Murdoch's work, to have been built by 'a great craftsman at Gloucester, Hugh Belleyet-ere or Bellfounder' and it resembles Hugo, when it is dragged up from the depths in that it is seen as something 'enormous', 'monstrous', 'a thing from another world'. But the two bells, the old and the new, carry further associations in the novel.

* In this sense, of course, it is like the intractable normal; but there is a difference between reality, and the visible manipulations of the author.

James sees the bell as a symbol for purity, clarity, candour, and compares it explicitly with Catherine Fawley, who is seen as having these qualities by the other characters, and who, like the bell, will enter the Abbey as a postulant. But Catherine has her twin, Nicholas, whom James sees as a disruptive force, and the new bell has its twin, buried in the mud of the lake. The old bell is, through its history, associated with violent and disruptive passion, with sin and confession; its legend is, appropriately, *Vox ego Amoris sum* (as a medallion on Michael's house wears the legend *Amor via mea*). In this sense it helps to symbolize the ambiguity of love in the novel, where love is both a dangerous loss of purity and exercise of power, and a necessary part of humanity. And Nick's destruction of the second bell, the postulant, destroys his sister, who, like the nun, runs into the lake to drown herself, seeing herself as corrupt because she, as Nicholas has done, loves Michael.

Both Michael and James use the bell as a symbol for man's spiritual nature in their sermons; James is attracted by the idea of its simplicity, the way in which it must speak out clearly if moved; Michael uses it as a symbol for man's spiritual energy.

> The bell is subject to the force of gravity. The swing that takes it down must also take it up. So we too must learn to understand the mechanism of our spiritual energy, and find out where, for us, are the hiding places of our strength.

Here, the idea of gravity as a symbol for that which is simply mechanical in our lives is related to the thought of Simone Weil, who uses it in that sense, and opposes it to the supernatural grace; what Michael, with his bell image, is advocating, is a deliberate attempt to pay attention to the workings, and the sources, of our spiritual energy, so that by understanding it we may increase it. It is perhaps not impertinent to point out that the bell is somewhat forcibly yoked to this idea of energy by the concept of gravity – the equally powerful idea of 'the hiding places of our strength' is already in no way attached to the image of the bell. The association is a little too arbitrary.

The bell is also a part of the musical imagery which pervades the book, and which is, like the roses in *An Unofficial Rose*, or the physical appearance of the women in *The Flight from the Enchanter*, a reflection of the relation, in art and in life, of the natural to the artificial, the unutterably particular to the intellectually ordered and arranged, the simple to the complex form. There are all kinds of sounds in *The Bell*. There is bird-song, which Kant saw as the perfect example of 'free beauty'; he said, Miss Murdoch tells us, 'a bird's song, which we can reduce to no musical rôle, seems to have more freedom in it, and thus to be richer for taste, than the human voice singing in accordance with all the rules that the art of music prescribes'. There are Peter Topglass's 'artificial' imitations of bird-song. There is Catherine's singing of the madrigal, *The Silver Swan*, with its 'enchanting and slightly absurd precision'. There is the 'hideous purity and austerity' of the song of the nuns, unseen within their chapel. There is the jungle rhythm of the jazz records which Noel plays to Dora in London, which make a deliberate sexual appeal and contrast sharply with the note of the blackbird, which Dora hears over the telephone.

There is also Bach, whose music Dora finds too austere, although she comes finally to enjoy Mozart, and whose music, presumably, carrying with it the moral complexity of its subject-matter, and the conceptual complexity of its form, is open to Kant's criticism of being less beautiful than bird-song because less 'pure', less 'free'. Here we must remember that the over-simple 'dry' concept of the self-contained unitary work of art is said in *Against Dryness* to derive from Kant's theory of simplicity. Miss Murdoch criticizes his ideal of purity by comparing it to her own ideal of naturalistic study of character, of hard reality:

> Any attempt, for instance, to represent a certain kind of character mars the beauty of purity by the introduction of a

concept; and of course any concern with goodness or with a moral content is equally fatal.[2]

The musical imagery underpins, as it were, the moral themes of purity and complexity, freedom and deliberate restriction, either by a formal framework of concepts, or by a recognition of our limitations and lack of purity. Bach's formal complexity here resembles perhaps the formed beauty of the Tintoretto in *An Unofficial Rose*.

The bell unites the musical and spiritual themes curiously and very naturally when, during the Christening ceremony, the hymn, 'Raise it gently', is sung, against Father Bob's musical better judgment. It should, in these verses:

> There fulfil its daily mission
> Midway twixt the earth and sky

And

> As the birds sing daily matins
> To the god of Nature's praise
> This its nobler daily music
> To the God of Grace shall raise.[3]

Here the bell is like Bledyard's view of humanity 'incarnate incarnate creatures', earth-related and god-related. Dora rarely finds herself concerned beyond the birds and the God of Nature; Michael is intensely concerned with his relation with the God of grace; the bell, musical in the steeple, or 'much encrusted with watery growths and shell-like incrustations' in the mud below the lake is in this sense ambiguous too.

It is perhaps worth remarking before we leave the bell that it is the old bell which is covered with a pattern of living human beings, scenes from the life of Christ, which Dora sees in her moment of vision, before she rings the bell, as

> squat figures . . . solid, simple, beautiful, absurd, full to the brim with something which was to the artist not an object of speculation or imagination.[4]

It rep.esents in this sense, a unity of life, now lost, an area, as Christ's life properly should be to the Christian, where the unique individual and spiritual values are seen naturally to act together and to be one. But in our time, when human life and spiritual values are abstract 'objects of speculation or imagination', the new bell has a plain surface 'except for a band of arabesques which encircled it a little above the rim'.[5]

I shall discuss Dora first, if for no other reason than that she is established chronologically in the book before Michael. Dora is a refinement on the theme that we have met before – that of the freedom of youth – in that Dora, although still young, and not in possession of her own life, or sure of who she is or what she wants, has already around her a life – principally her marriage – from which she cannot simply, in order to discover herself, convulsively free herself. At the beginning of the book 'she vaguely thought of herself as past her prime', and when later, having left her husband and rejoined him at Imber, she sees Toby alone on the edge of the lake, from the window of the room where she is enclosed with Paul, he seems to her in his youth, to be 'the very image of freedom'.[6]

Dora is a character who does not judge, and lacks self-knowledge. She does not judge Paul, because, since she shares this quality of innocence at least with Peter Saward, 'A certain incapacity for "placing" others stood her here in lieu of virtue.' She has also no sense of the past. She has a deep need to 'assume her own being',[7] but as in the case of Mor, she is hampered in the pursuit of this by her marriage, and the nature of her husband, whose love is the exercise of a violent, restrictive and impinging power, which prevents her growth. 'She was at last disturbed by the violent and predatory gestures with which he destroyed the rhythms of her self-surrender.'[8] The pressure on her of the reality of this other person brings about a situation where 'although she conspicuously lacked self-knowledge, she became, in the face of this threatening personality, increasingly aware that she existed.' This awareness of her existence, and the threat to her self, causes her, 'obeying that conception of fatality which served her instead of a moral sense', to leave Paul. She is a creature, like those of *The Flight from the Enchanter*, whose chief weapon is flight – 'she depended, like some unprotesting but significantly mobile creature, upon the knowledge of her instant ability to whisk away'. But, even if she has no moral sense, conventional morals affect her use of her liberty; she feels guilty, and responsible to Paul; she finds that 'she could no longer be happy with her husband or without him'. So she returns, without reflecting, to Paul, and becomes part of the religious community at Imber.

Dora has an instinctive respect for life (consider her saving of the butterfly in the train) and an instinctive respect for, and interest in, other people; she attempts to make contact with both Mrs Mark and Catherine, and is, in fact, the only person to divine that Catherine's entry into the nunnery is not only a voluntary surrendering of selfish desires to a purer freedom, but in some sense an imposed trap.

With Mrs Mark, Dora's comical conversation throws into relief the petty and inhuman aspects of the rules of voluntary restrictions, which James Tayper Pace sees as a basis of the religious life. Dora's positive gesture of decorating her and Paul's room with wild flowers is quashed by Mrs Mark – 'It's a little austerity we practise' – and her attempt to make contact with Mrs Mark by asking about her life meets with the response that past lives are never discussed for fear of impure motives. 'That's another little religious rule that we try to follow. No gossip ... when people ask each other questions about their lives their motives are rarely pure, are they?'⁹ But Dora's motives are, in this sense, pure; she is without malice, and the restriction imposed upon her kills a natural warmth in human intercourse which is, in itself, good.

And Dora, at least initially, sees the religious structure, both of house and Abbey, as a trap, an unnecessary limitation of freedom, throughout. She feels that the moral side of Christianity merely draws the community together with Paul, as people who, unlike her, are prepared to judge, to treat

her as the conventional lost sheep, or erring wife. She sees
the nun as 'a shapeless pile of squatting black cloth', the
community's chapel as 'a shabby, derelict, pitiable, drawing-
room, harbouring an alien rite, half sinister, half ludicrous',
and the Abbey itself as a prison, its chapel, seen in contrast
to the park under the sun, as an 'annihilating' 'dark hole and
silence'.

She feels that Catherine's entry into the nunnery menaces
something inside herself with destruction. It is, in the early
part of the book, her own increasing awareness of herself as
a separate individual which gives her strength to fight against
the alien pressures brought to bear upon her. Before marching
to Paul's bed on her first night at Imber she sees herself in
the mirror.

> She continued to look at the person who was there, unknown
> to Paul. How very much, after all, she existed; she, Dora, and
> no one should destroy her.[10]

At Imber too, she cannot make a life with Paul, and is
driven, after a conversation in which she discusses Catherine
with him, to estimate

> with a devastating exactness which was usually alien to her
> just how much of sheer contempt there was in Paul's love;
> and always would be, she reflected, since she had few illusions
> about her ability to change herself.[11]

She feels that Paul's contempt is destroying her, and in this
state, with no real relationship with the outside world, or
any reality other than herself, has an almost pure experience
of what it is to live in a world of entirely self-centred fantasy.
She

> had the odd feeling that all this was inside her head. There
> was no way of breaking into this scene for it was all
> imaginary ... It was as if her consciousness had eaten up
> its surroundings. Everything was now subjective. Even, she
> remembered, Paul this morning, had been subjective. His love-
> making had been remote, like a half-waking fantasy, and not
> at all like an encounter with another human being.[12]

In this condition, Dora instinctively takes flight again and returns to London and the journalist, Noel Spens.

G. S. Fraser, in a mood of violent distaste which I cannot believe Miss Murdoch intended fully to inspire, refers to Noel as 'the journalist, who under a mask of tolerant hedonism is consumed by possessive lust and fanatical hatred of all religious experience'.[13] Whether his feeling for Dora is love or possessive lust I don't know – he is genuinely concerned with her moral well-being. But it is a little misleading to write that he hates *religious experience*; what Noel is, here, is the voice of the Stuart Hampshire Man, who is 'morally speaking, monarch of all he surveys', and the voice is raised, not specifically against religious experience but against Christian *morals*, the whole machinery of guilt, sin, repentance and judgment, the weapon which Nick Fawley uses to destroy Michael – and then himself – twice over. It is a voice which is necessary at this stage of the book, if only to say what the irreligious reader may have been feeling all along about the foundation of the life at Imber. Noel says:

> No good comes in the end of untrue beliefs. There is no God and there is no judgment, except the judgment that each one of us makes for himself; and what that is is a private matter.[14]

He then gives himself, and his self-centred view, away, by adding 'Sometimes of course one has to interfere with people to stop them doing things one dislikes,' an over-simplification which pushes us back into the realization that the moral life is more complex than Noel's solipsist view allows for, as it is perhaps more complex also than James Tayper Pace's adherence to rigid rules enjoined by a Church founded on a God and a Judgment which may or may not exist. Noel points out a partial truth; that it is wrong for the community simply to regard Dora as a 'miserable sinner' and Paul as 'an aggrieved and virtuous spouse'. But the fact that Dora *does* feel guilty, and that she does, without knowing him, love Paul, 'in a shy roundabout way', are in themselves enough to dispose of the simple solution Noel proposes, that she should fight for her freedom; although, later, she does fight, it is not with him, and not in his way.

At this point it might be as well to recall the *Against Dryness* picture of the transcendence of reality; it is to be 'non-metaphysical, non-totalitarian, and *non-religious*'.★[15] That is, Noel's dismissal of God and judgment as grounds for limiting Dora's freedom clear the ground. But when, after dancing with Noel to the primitive music of drum, clarinet and trumpet, Dora hears the 'clear, remote and strange' note of the blackbird over the telephone, behind Paul's voice, she feels Noel's flat to be unreal, the imposition of another alien organization. She leaves Noel too, and goes to the National Gallery, where at last she finds 'something real and something perfect'.

Dora's experience in the National Gallery is obviously connected with Jake Donaghue's sense of Jean-Pierre's 'good' book as something real, with Roquentin's experience of the tune. But it is not only an experience of the satisfaction of the beauty of forms; it is an experience of the kind Bledyard is describing when, in his lecture, he shows a slide of one of the later Rembrandt self-portraits and remarks

> here, if we ask what relates relates the painter to the sitter, if we ask what the painter is after, it is difficult to avoid answering – the truth.[16]

Dora thinks of the paintings as 'something which her consciousness could not wretchedly devour and by making it part of her fantasy make it worthless'. They are

> something real outside herself and good ... When the world had seemed to be subjective it had seemed to be without interest or value. But now there was something else in it after all.[17]

★ My italics.

It is worth remarking that the pictures she sees, as they are described, are pictures of human beings.

Dora feels that since, somewhere, something good exists, her problems are capable of solution after all. She returns to Imber.

Dora's plan, with the help of Toby, to raise the bell and substitute it for the new one is seen as a 'fight', 'a sort of rite of power and liberation',[18] and herself as a 'witch'; later this plot is seen as 'at best funny in a vulgar way, at worst thoroughly nasty', and Dora, left alone with the bell at night, is constrained to ring it; an act which compares perhaps with Jake's shaking of the thundersheet, an assertion of herself, as she is, and the bell as it is. It is something she has 'drawn out of the lake and lifted back to its own airy element'. Reality asserts itself. 'She had thought to be its master and make it her plaything, but now it was mastering her, and would have its will.' Her ringing of it is not a mere confession of guilt, although she has caused it to sound when embracing Toby in its mouth and disturbed Michael's dreams. 'If it was necessary to accuse herself the means were certainly at hand. But her need was deeper than this.'[19]

I have already said that I find this moment of truth unsatisfactory; I would add to what I have said the idea that what is missing from Dora's apprehension of reality is precisely an apprehension of Paul, who is her problem after all; Paul is never given space in the book to be a complete human being, and he is important enough for this to matter. It can be that some completely outside event can change one's relationship with another human being, but not, one feels, something of the nature of Dora's ringing of the bell.

At the end of the book, Dora, having attempted to rescue Catherine from drowning herself, and having herself been rescued by the 'aquatic nun', is left with Michael alone at Imber. At this point she does two things; she falls in love with Michael and learns to swim. Throughout the book, the water of the lake has been used as an image for the mystery, the depths outside the life which goes on in house and market-garden. The darkness of the nuns' chapel, Dora's 'black hole', reminds Toby of 'the obscurity of the lake, where the world was seen again in different colours'.[20] Murphy, the animal, swims naturally, paralleling the seal seen by Marian in *The Unicorn*, which swims in the killing sea which Marian ultimately fears too much. Mother Clare swims fearlessly and well. Catherine is afraid of the water; it is when she tells Dora this, that she is afraid of water and often dreams about drowning, that Dora senses her reluctance to enter the convent and speaks to her. Both Michael and Dora dream that the nuns are concerned with drowning someone in the lake; Michael has the sense that something in himself, 'in the depths of his mind', 'made him attribute something so terrible to these innocent and holy nuns'.[21] The lake is obscure and ambiguous, something that can destroy or support, if we can swim. Dora, at the end of the book, is capable of resting, as it were, on the mystery. 'She turned out to be a natural swimmer, buoyant and fearless in the water.'[22] One is reminded of Miss Murdoch's use of the same image for the same state of affairs at the end of *Under the Net*, where Jake says, 'Like a fish which swims calmly in deep water, I felt about me the secure supporting pressure of my own life. Ragged, inglorious and apparently purposeless, but my own.'[23]

In other ways, too, Dora's life is her own; she has learned to appreciate, if not the austere Bach, Mozart, and she is painting water colours of Imber. She helps Michael, whereas earlier she was useless in the house. She returns to her interrupted life as an art student, following her experience in the National Gallery, and not, or at least not immediately, to Paul. She destroys the two letters which Paul has left her, and with them, symbolically, his power to use the past as a weapon against her. She is to work out her freedom;

> She felt intensely the need, and somehow now the capacity to live and work on her own and become, what she had never been, an independent grown-up person.[24]

Her love for Michael indeed, if it is not 'understanding', shows a new capacity for the undemanding 'co-existence' which Jake Donaghue said was one of the guises of love.

She is also less instinctively horrified by the nuns and the religious life; she has three conversations with Mother Clare, although we are not told what is said, or what difference it makes. Michael feels that Dora's freedom is perhaps best not seen in conventional religious terms.

> He felt in the case of Dora too, that there was little point in forcing her willy-nilly into a machinery of sin and repentance which was alien to her nature. Perhaps Dora would repent after her own fashion; perhaps she would be saved after her own fashion.[25]

At least Dora has survived. 'Because of all the dreadful things that had passed there was more of her.' And our last view of Imber and of the book is through Dora's eyes.

'But in this moment, and it was its last moment, it belonged to her. She had survived.'

If Dora can work out her freedom and best use her spiritual energy without the 'machinery of sin and repentance', Michael Meade cannot. Michael is Miss Murdoch's first attempt to come to grips with the complex interrelations of religion and morals, freedom and restraint, from inside; Bledyard and Everard were Christians, but Christians used as pointers or landmarks. In Michael we have a study of the area where fantasy overlaps the spiritual world, as earlier we have seen fantasy overlapping the aesthetic world, and the world of love between human beings. Effingham Cooper, at the end of The Unicorn, thinks of the action of that book, which illuminates this one, as 'a fantasy of the spiritual life, a story, a tragedy', and thinks further, 'Only the spiritual life has no story and is not tragic.'[26] Michael's religious life, his founding of the community, are also a fantasy of the spiritual life, and become both story and tragedy.

The breaking up of the spiritual life of the community itself is perhaps best pointed to in the collapse of Catherine under the pressure brought to bear on her by the combination of the members' myth-making vision of her as 'their little saint', 'their' contemplative, and Nicholas's needs and passions. She is, in this sense, a forerunner of Hannah, the central figure in *The Unicorn* and it was not, indeed, until I had read *The Unicorn* that I came to see just how much weight of fantasy-making could be attached to Dora's perception, à propos of Catherine, that

> It's a sort of conspiracy against her. They've all been saying for so long that she's going in, and calling her their little saint, and so on, and now she can't get out of it.[27]

G. S. Fraser remarks that the breaking-up of the community is not tragic; 'it expires of unreality', and sets against the fantasy-spinning quality of the community's religious life, the religious life of the convent across the water. 'The convent across the lake has reality, its nuns are not playing a game.' But if the breaking-up of the community is not tragic, the death of Nicholas is, it is seen, too late, truly tragic. And between the lack of reality of this fantasy of the spiritual life, and the failure in human relations, the failure really to apprehend the reality of Nicholas as an individual, valuable human being, Michael's story is played out.

What seems to me really good in this novel, is the complexity with which Michael's situation is presented, the way in which the consequences of the moral decisions he must take are almost never clear to the reader in advance, the way in which Miss Murdoch has allowed herself to explore him slowly, without hurry or excessive neatness (which is different from economy). Thus, although one would not quarrel with G. S. Fraser's summing-up of the nature of Michael's religious fantasy:

> He also has to realize that what he thought was his religious vocation, the divinely ordained pattern of his life, was largely a matter of projection of a naïve self-importance and sublimation of homosexual impulses.[28]

one feels that the tone of this summing-up does violence to the subtlety of Miss Murdoch's imagination. She shows towards Michael, to an unusual extent in her work, the quality which, referring herself to the love the great novelist, such as Tolstoi, has for his characters, she calls 'tolerance', which she defines as 'a real apprehension of persons other than the author as having a right to exist and to have a separate mode of being which is important and interesting to themselves'.[29] She comments, 'We may decide later that "tolerance" is too mild a word for this capacity at its highest.' Thus, although both Miss Murdoch and Michael bring us to a sense of Michael's inadequacies, Miss Murdoch does not judge him coldly, as she judges the characters in *A Severed Head*, or do him the injustice of standing above and commenting on his blindness. It is significant here, I think, that whilst talking of Michael's sense of his vocation, which in this sense corresponds to Jake's view that he 'must' catch up with Anna in the Tuileries, she allows Michael partly to know what G. S. Fraser's summing-up baldly, might suggest him to be entirely blind to.

> It was an aspect of Michael's belief in God, and one which, although he knew it to be dangerous, he could never altogether reject, that he expected the emergence in his life of patterns and signs. He had always felt himself to be a man with a definite destiny, a man waiting for a call.[30]

This feeling that life and the world are apprehensibly patterned is something that goes against the sense that Miss Murdoch has of the world as something other, mysterious, unutterably particular (which is what makes it so hard to stomach the appearances of her symbolic gipsy in *The Sandcastle*; one feels that she, like Michael, has a taste that cannot be expurgated, for patterns and signs). This is not to say that one cannot come at truth, that the mystery is not graspable at all; Miss Murdoch has expressly dissociated herself[31] from Calvin Blick's 'Reality is a cipher with many solutions, all of them right ones.' But solutions, or rather the necessarily incomplete solution, are different from signs and patterns, and whereas one must seek truth, to look for patterns is to begin to indulge in fantasy. Michael's religious life is thus, from the start, suspect, an imposition of his own view and wishes concerning things and himself, on the unknown reality.

There are two other elements in Michael's religious inclinations which need to be mentioned. The first is his attempt to use religion unconsciously as an escape from power, or from the complexity and difficulty of life in a world inhabited by creatures like Mischa Fox who make it certain that human relations, love, work, are corrupted inevitably by the exercise of power, by the impingement of one man on another's freedom. Michael has believed that 'the good man is without power', and an extension of this idea has caused him to see his call to the priesthood in this sense as

> a loss of personality such as could perhaps come about through the named office of a servant, or the surrender of will in an unquestioning obedience.[32]

But this wish to avoid the 'region where power was evil' is seen, both in Michael, and in Rosa, as an escaping from reality, from responsibility, from other people. Miss Murdoch applies this judgment only to those who, like Michael, like, in one sense at least, Hannah, the unicorn, are seen as half-contemplatives. For the true contemplative, freedom can perhaps lie in the 'surrender of the will', the 'loss of personality' thought of by Simone Weil, a natural religious ascetic, as the highest way of life, which is an act too high for Michael, too 'hard' for Hannah, and the Abbess, who has, we must suppose, made this surrender, is seen by Michael as powerful in a different, and to him paradoxical and incomprehensible way. Miss Murdoch's definition of power, and its relation to the Good, is perhaps most clearly expressed in *The Unicorn*, in Max Lejour's Platonic speech to Effingham.

> Até is the name of the almost automatic transfer of suffering from one being to another. Power is a form of Até. The victims of power, and any power has its victims, are themselves infected. They have then to pass it on, to use the power on others. This is evil, and the crude image of the all-powerful God is a sacrilege. Good is not exactly powerless. For to be

96

powerless, to be a complete victim, may be another source of power. But Good is non-powerful. And it is in the Good that Até is finally quenched, when it encounters a pure being who only suffers and does not attempt to pass the suffering on.[33]

Michael's judgment of the nature of power is in accordance with this, but his retreat is not pure enough, too much a fantasy, to afford him any release at all from the world of power and suffering. He is merely refusing to look at his responsibility for it, to acknowledge his inevitable involvement in it, principally in so far as it concerns Nick. Thus Miss Murdoch comments on Michael's entry into the community

> Those who hope, by retiring from the world, to earn a holiday from human frailty, in themselves and others, are usually disappointed.[34]

Michael finds himself obliged to exercise power, that is authority, within the community, and this leads to his sins of omission, and commission, with regard both to Toby and Nick.

There is a character within the community who, like Peter Saward, like the reverend Everard, seems to have preserved a real innocence in that he does not exercise power; his innocence compared to the spiritual and moral innocence of youth of Toby, or even Catherine, seems to be durable as far as we can tell; his opaque presence on the circumference of the narrative gives it a dimension we feel it might otherwise lack. This is Peter Topglass of whom Michael

> marvelled at his detachment, his absorption in his beloved studies, his absence of competitive vanity. He lacked that dimension of the spirit which made James formidable as well as endearing; but he was a person who, like Chaucer's gentle knight, was remarkable for harming no one.[35]

The other fact in Michael's spiritual life which is most deeply involved in his attempts to retreat into contemplation is his homosexuality. I have already referred to G. S. Fraser's description of Michael's spiritual life as 'sublimation of homosexual impulses' and it is clear that Miss Murdoch means it to be seen in part in this way – although her reiterated descriptions of Michael's attempts to pray, of his own analyses of the relation between his sexual feelings and his religion, show more 'tolerance' in her sense, of his actual experiences, even if these are ultimately consoling or fantastic, than any such curt Freudian description of them.

The description of Michael's swing from homosexual love to religion and back follows three phases. The first is the factual description of his conversion at Cambridge, where he is awakened to a sense of guilt, gives up 'the practice of what he had come to regard as his vice', and 'certain' that he will never again gratify his tastes, leaves calmly for school-mastering, 'confident of a Love which lay deeper than the contortions of his egoistic and unenlightened guilt, and which worked patiently to set him free'.

The second phase is Michael's intense and overmastering love for the schoolboy, Nick Fawley – the inception of which is described with the same emotional compulsiveness which has characterized the description of Mor's love for Rain Carter. Here we have a concrete description of what seems to be a circle in a spiral of experience in which Michael is constantly engaged, and of which his involvement with Toby could be seen as yet a further stage – from sexual passion, to religious vocation, and round, without understanding the inevitability of the process, again. Michael is aware of the relation of the two forces in himself.

He began, hazily, to reflect on how he had formerly felt that his religion and his passions sprang from the same source, and how this has seemed to infect his religion with corruption. It now seemed to him that he could turn the argument about; why should his passions not rather be purified by this proximity? He could not believe that there was anything inherently evil in the great love which he bore to Nick: this love was something so strong, so radiant, it came from so deep it seemed of the very nature of goodness itself. Vaguely Michael had visions of himself as the boy's spiritual guardian, his passion slowly transformed into a lofty and more selfless attachment. He would watch Nick grow to manhood, cherishing his every step, ever present, yet with a self-effacement which would be the highest expression of love. Nick, who was his lover, would become his son; and indeed already, with a tact and imagination which removed from their relationship any suggestion of crudeness, the boy was playing both parts.[36]

This love is broken up after Nick's confession to the headmaster after the visit of an evangelical preacher to the school. It seems clear, from the description of Michael's emotions quoted above, that there is at least likely to be something illusory, something dreamed up, about it, something called into being by Michael's needs. And later, after the confession, he comes to see his love as 'that worst of offences, corrupting the young', and 'Whereas success and happiness had kept guilt at bay, ruin and grief brought it, almost automatically, with them.'[37]

The third clash between Michael's sexual feelings and his religion comes over Toby, whom he involuntarily and unexpectedly kisses, after drinking too much Devon cider. This incident follows a series of those apparently trivial and unimportant actions which we have already seen operating in the fate of Bill Mor. It unleashes in both Toby and Michael a gust of loose emotional power, and follows in Michael's case a feeling of protective security which we recognize, and Michael is in a position to recognize, as a parallel to his feelings over Nick. Watching Toby asleep, Michael felt

solemn now, responsible, still protective and still joyful, with a joy which, since he had taken a more conscious hold on himself, seemed deeper and more pure. He felt within him an infinite power to protect Toby from harm.

Michael experiences a recurrence of his feeling for Nick. Toby will be 'a long and profound responsibility, a task' and

It could not be that God intended such a spring of love to be quenched utterly. There must, there must, be a way in which

99

it could be made a power for good. Michael did not, in that instant, feel that it would be difficult to make it so.[38]

But the 'protective' and 'responsible' element in love appears so often in Miss Murdoch's novels as a guise for the destructive power which is inherent in earthly love. One recalls Mischa Fox asking Saward, 'Do you ever feel . . . as if everything in the world needed your – protection? It is a terrible feeling. Everything – even this matchbox?'*

Michael's passion and protectiveness, like Max Lejour's Até, are passed on from Michael to Toby, who in his turn begins to feel 'protective' about, and powerful towards, Michael. Toby, then, like Michael, and unlike James Tayper Pace, finds the moral muddle in which he now is ultimately 'interesting'.

> As he lay there in the darkness Toby found that after all what had happened had its interesting side. It certainly constituted an adventure, though a somewhat rebarbative one. And what he then experienced, although he did not at the time recognize it as such, was a feeling of pleasure at being suddenly in a position of power *vis-à-vis* someone whom he had so unquestioningly accepted as his spiritual superior . . . He felt, too, as he conjured up the image of that obviously rather complicated person, a new emotion about him. He found himself feeling, towards Michael, curiously protective. And with this thought at last he fell asleep.[39]

And Michael's decision to speak to Toby about the incident – a decision reached after much soul-searching, and a session of prayer in the visitors' chapel at the Abbey, after which he feels 'calmed, helped and supported', enmeshes them both further in this 'interesting' exercise of power and passion. It is clear that Michael's decision is not a result – or at least not *only* a result, of 'that *real* goodwill towards Toby' for which he has prayed; it is a need that is in himself which he does not exactly acknowledge, as well as in Toby, for a 'sequel'.

---

* See below p. 177 for Freud's description of this element of destructive impulse in 'protective' love.

> He felt dully and violently with a mixture of pain and pleasure
> which was not in itself unpleasurable, the desire to get it over.
> He needed above anything to rid himself of a craving which
> made all other activity impossible.[40]

When the cool apology ends in a handclasp of some power,
Michael has the sense of *deja-vu*; his prayers and good intentions, and reliance on the essential *goodness* of his love for
Toby, have ended in the same muddle and corruption as his
love for Nick. At this point it would be easy to dismiss
Michael's entwining of his homosexual impulses with his
sense of what comes from God and is good as merely neurotic
delusion on a large scale, repeated twice over, and likely,
since he cannot understand it enough to cure or evade it, to
recur again and again. The 'lofty' and 'pure' and remote
emotional language which is used in the descriptions of
Michael's preliminary religious musings over both his attachments, gives weight, by its dreamy vagueness, to this view.
But I hope to show that this view of Michael's moral predicament is too simple; the next stage in discovering what his
true relation to reality is might best be shown by an examination of the contrast between his moral views and those of
James Tayper Pace.

G. S. Fraser puts the conflict between Michael's views and
James's in these terms:

> There is no obvious Christian answer to the fundamental
> division between James Tayper Pace, who sees, in the manner
> of a military disciplinarian, the religious life as consisting
> fundamentally of rigid obedience to rules, and Michael, who
> sees it as a spontaneousness springing directly from self-
> knowledge (but he has not self-knowledge enough).[41]

James, a character for whom the modern 'neurotic' liberal
humanist reader feels automatically, perhaps, a certain distaste – we feel that we can 'place' him as pious, self-righteous,
bound by convention, lacking in vision – is treated by Miss
Murdoch with considerable respect. Michael likes and

respects him partly because 'some ingenuity would have been required to dislike him, he was a character of such transparent gentleness', and partly because he is rooted in a traditional, a 'normal' set of conventions which Michael finds 'at a moral level distinctly below that at which he aimed at present to live', nostalgically attractive and easy to communicate with.[42]

James, the 'younger son of an old military family', who has served in the Guards, has 'a deep and unquestioning spiritual life'. 'The custom whereby in certain families religious faith survived as part of the life of a country gentleman, deeply connected with all the rituals of living, was for James no empty form.' The fruit, in James's life of these roots and this faith is a morality very akin to that of Kant, as described by Miss Murdoch in the article 'The Sublime and the Good' (*Chicago Review*, Vol. 13, No. 3). Kant, says Miss Murdoch,

> does not tell us to respect whole tangled-up historical individuals, but to respect the universal reason in their breasts . . . Freedom is our ability to rise out of history and grasp a universal idea of order which we then apply to the sensible world . . . We are supposed to live by exceedingly simple and general rules . . . 'Always tell the truth,' etc. with no place for the morally complicated or eccentric.[43]

James, like Kant, like Dave in *Under the Net*, believes in truth-telling, and in living by clear and simple rules.

> James, it sometimes seemed to Michael, believed that truthfulness consisted in telling everybody everything whether it concerned them or not, and regardless of whether they wanted to know.[44]

Michael 'did not share James's view that *suppressio veri* was equal to *suggestio falsi*', or that privacy has a tendency to corrupt.

James's sermon puts very clearly the case for simple rules. He states, what Dora also, in the different context of the pictures in the National Gallery, considers herself to have seen: 'Where perfection is, reality is', and argues from there that, since perfection is God, who is 'so external and remote that we can get only now and then a distant hint of it', the Christian should look to 'God and His Law' for guidance, and not examine himself too closely (thus avoiding Michael's tendency, and Toby's under Michael's influence, to enmesh themselves in sin because they find it, to quote James again 'complicated', 'unique and interesting', 'something to be investigated').

He says:

> Truthfulness is enjoined, the relief of suffering is enjoined, adultery is forbidden, sodomy is forbidden. And I feel that we ought to think quite simply of these matters thus: truth is not glorious, it is just enjoined; sodomy is not disgusting, it is just forbidden. These are rules by which we should freely judge ourselves and others too.[45]

James, as I have said before, when considering Dave Gellman, is shown in action (which William James says is our only way of judging spiritual views or beliefs) to have been at least partially more right than Michael; at the end of the book, when Nick has forced Toby to 'confess' to James, James's simple action of sending Toby away immediately afterwards is seen to have been of more value in restoring Toby's lost innocence and peace of mind than Michael's instinctive and complicated impulse to 'talk' to Toby, to discuss and reopen the issue, would have been.

James, again like Dave, finds it easy to live with, and respect people to an extent which makes Michael's task of wielding power within the community more difficult.

> James, who believed that authority should melt in brotherly love, as would have been the case in a community composed of persons like himself, was careless of such matters.[46]

But what James is shown to lack, by implication, is the kind of love which Kant is also said to lack, in the article I have just quoted. Love, according to Miss Murdoch, is precisely the realization of the reality, the transcendent reality, of the 'whole, particular, tangled-up individuals', whom Kant does not tell us to respect. I want to come back to this – since this book, oddly, is the only one of Miss Murdoch's where one can be certain of observing anything like the operation of this love for individuals, however imperfectly, which is so highly to be desired – but first I want to outline the moral view which Michael opposes to that of James. All I would say for the moment is that the rock which shipwrecks both, James theoretically, Michael personally, is the individuality of Nicholas, which neither of them respects enough.

Michael's moral view derives from his mentor, the Abbess, who tells him at the beginning of the book that our duty

> is not necessarily to seek the highest regardless of the realities of our spiritual life as it in fact is, but to seek that place, that task, those people, which will make our spiritual life grow and flourish; and in this search, said the Abbess, we must make use of a divine cunning.[47]

Michael takes up this idea in his sermon. 'The chief requirement of the good life,' he says, 'is that one should have some conception of one's capacities' which he extends into the idea that self-knowledge is necessary and to be sought for. 'As spiritual beings in our imperfection, and also in the possibility of our perfection, we differ profoundly one from another.' He goes on to defend the 'second best act', in the sense that it is what the individual can in his individual apprehension of reality best perform, and ends

> This is the struggle, pleasing surely in the sight of God, to become more fully and deeply the person that we are; and by exploring and hallowing every corner of our being, to bring into existence that one and perfect individual which God in creating us entrusted to our care.[48]

In *Against Dryness* Miss Murdoch argues with some force against literary or philosophical forms where the 'idea of human nature was unitary and single'[49]; in so far as Michael's idea of self-knowledge is a realization of the individual who is necessarily unique and different from all others, it is something necessary, not provided for in James's view of things. Michael's view is an aspect of the truth which Miss Murdoch recognizes in Sartre, and with some qualifications, clearly approves of.

> True choice, according to Sartre, consists in the more long term attempt to *assume* our own being by a purifying reflexion. Liberty is not just the 'lighting up' of our own contingency, it is its comprehension and interiorization. Liberty, like the cure of the neurotic, lies at the level of a total understanding: an understanding which, I think Sartre would agree, we have no guarantee of reaching, or foolproof criterion for recognizing, although we know well enough in what direction it lies.[50]

Compare here Michael's 'one has, where God is concerned, a sense of direction, a sense that *here* is what is most real, most good, most true'.

Michael's reflections after his sermon deepen and illustrate the difference between his and James's view of the good life. He considers James's phrase 'sodomy is not disgusting; it is just forbidden', and thinks that 'He did not in fact believe that it was *just* forbidden', since men and women had been created with these tendencies and 'For himself, God had made him so, and he did not think that God had made him a monster.'

But if Michael's respect for the individual in himself, the complication of his being, cannot allow him to dismiss his nature with 'it is *just* forbidden', this respect and awareness of complexity can, on the other hand, lead him into finding himself too interesting, and thus becoming 'absorbed in the excitement of a spiritual drama for its own sake'.[51]

What is clearly wrong with Michael's in many ways admirable moral thinking at this stage is that it centres on Michael – he speaks and thinks, of respect for the individual, but the individual in question is himself, not the real contingent other people who are the objects of love. Miss Murdoch, in an article in the *Yale Review* speaks again of love as the apprehension of the reality of other people, and remarks that 'I take the general consciousness today to be ridden either by convention or by neurosis',[52] which she refers to elsewhere as 'the two enemies of understanding, one might say the enemies of love'.[53]

It is possible, whilst not losing sight of James and Michael as individuals, to see their moral views as tending towards convention and neurosis respectively. If James does not hold the logical empiricist views of the Ordinary Language Man whom Miss Murdoch takes in the *Yale Review* article as the type of convention, he has many things in common with him; a respect for society as it is, rules as they are – in his case Christian rules derived from the Biblical 'convention', but very similar to those of the Ordinary Language Man who derives, Miss Murdoch says, from Kant through the empiricists. Of him she writes

> the picture is conventional . . . the agent is seen as a being subject to rules, surrounded by a civilized society, surrounded in short by the network of ordinary language, that is, for these purposes, by the network of moral conceptual activity at its most common and universally accepted level.[54]

If James, then, has things in common with this man who represents the surrender to convention, Michael has things in common with his opposite, and equal, the Totalitarian Man of Sartre, who represents the surrender to neurosis. 'Sartre's man,' says Miss Murdoch, 'is like a neurotic who seeks to cure himself by unfolding a myth about himself.' This man is 'Hegel's man who is a clear-cut piece of drama rather than an individual' and who 'abhors the contingent or accidental'. 'According to Sartre,' Miss Murdoch says, 'a desire for our lives to have the form and clarity of something necessary and not accidental is a fundamental human urge.'[55] All these qualities are clearly present in Michael – the myth-making, the spiritual dramatizing, the need for finality, which connects with his call to the priesthood.

> His lot was rather the struggle from within, the day-to-day attempt to be impersonal and just, the continual mistakes and examinations of conscience. Perhaps this was after all his

road; it was certainly *a* road. But he was irked by a sense of the incomplete and ill-defined nature of his rôle. Thoughts of the priesthood returned to him more and more frequently.[56]

Miss Murdoch, commenting on Sartre's view of the relation between imagination and love, says that he

> presents love, even at its most vigorous, as a dilemma of the imagination ... Sartre's lovers are each engaged in perpetual speculation about the attitudes of each other ... Sartre's lovers are out of the world, their struggle is not an incarnate struggle. There is no suggestion in Sartre's account that love is connected with action and day-to-day living; that it is other than a battle between two hypnotists in a closed room.[57]

Here we have again the connection in Miss Murdoch's thought, of truth, moral truth and vision, which is love, with that reality which is normal – which is connected, like Bledyard's human beings and great paintings, with being 'incarnate' as opposed to imagined, inextricably involved in the *normal* being of 'action and day-to-day living'. Miss Murdoch's final comment on Sartre is

> It might seem clear in any case that the only way to regenerate the imagining spirit *is* to join it to the world of action. Love is not futile, not because we live it more imaginatively, but because we live it more externally.[58]

This last sentence seems to be directly relevant to Michael's case; what he comes, too late, to see, is that he should have loved Nicholas 'more externally', have abandoned his spiritual drama, in order, practically, not counting the cost, to have loved him.

The Abbess tells Michael, in an interview where at first Michael thinks she is talking of Toby, that he should 'go forward' to love Nick.

> Good is an overflow. Where we generously and sincerely intend it, we may be engaged in a work of creation which may be mysterious even to ourselves – and because it is

mysterious we may be afraid of it. But this should not make us draw back. God can always show us, if we will, a higher and a better way; and we can only learn to love by loving. Remember that all our failures are ultimately failures in love. Imperfect love must not be condemned and rejected, but made perfect. The way is always forward, never back.[59]

Michael, as usual, feels that this is 'too high' for him; 'her exhortations seemed to him a marvel, rather than a practical inspiration'. But, at the end of the book, after Nick has shot himself, Michael reassesses the situation and comes to the conclusion that

Nick had needed love, and he ought to have given him what he had to offer, without fears about its imperfection. If he had had more faith, he would have done so, without calculating either Nick's faults or his own.[60]

Love, says Miss Murdoch, is

the perception of individuals. Love is the extremely difficult realization that something other than oneself is real. Love, and so art and morals, is the discovery of reality. What stuns us into the realization of our supersensible destiny is not, as Kant imagined, the formlessness of nature, but rather its unutterable particularity; and most particular and individual of all things is the mind of man.[61]

One of the good things in this book is the way in which Nick, seen through the eyes of Michael, and to a lesser extent of Toby, with a sidelight thrown by our knowledge of his 'Byronic passion' for his sister, and close relationship with her, preserves this curious opacity, inexplicability, that real individuals have for us. This is to a certain extent obscured for us by the relation of his name to a more general symbolism for the disruptive force he is. But a careful reading of the first account of him as a boy, at the school where Michael teaches, impresses one with the skill with which Miss Murdoch leaves in doubt – an essential lasting doubt – the precise nature of his affection, impulses, motives. We are told that he 'was a master of the art of grimacing and in every way treated his face as a mask, alarming, amusing, seductive'. Michael, initially, thinks him 'essentially silly'. Later he stares at Michael 'with an appearance of fascination so bold and unconcealed as to be almost provocative', and later still he seems 'more sincere, and with that, more attractive'.[62].

The reader is left in considerable doubt as to whether his apparent change is a function of Michael's own desires, or a real view of him; it is, later, equally impossible to tell whether the misleading nature of his 'confession' is motivated by malice, real religious guilt, or unconscious resentment.

The individual in Sartre's *Chemins*, Miss Murdoch says, is 'Ivich, opaque, sinister, unintelligible, and irreducibly other; seen always from outside'[63]; these are qualities which the brother and sister of *The Bell*, Nick and Catherine, share with the brother and sister of *Les Chemins*, Boris and Ivich. It is only looking back that we see how skilfully Miss Murdoch has signposted Nick's feelings for Michael, or through him for the reader, if they care to see – the emotion Nick obviously shares when first meeting Michael after his arrival at Imber, which Michael, scared of Nick's sardonic behaviour and afraid to compromise his own morals, allows to degenerate into a state of apparent 'apathetic' non-communication, his half-appeals to Michael, which both Michael and the reader are uncertain whether to interpret as unpleasant jokes, or real appeals made by a man with whom a tremendous effort would be needed to break down defences and destroy masks. A clue to the reality of the situation is given by Michael's violent and irrational feeling, after having kissed Toby, that what *really* matters is whether Nick should think him unfaithful, or himself 'betrayed or abandoned' – Michael dismisses this, because he does not know what to do with it, and the reader too, is uncertain what weight to give to it, amongst the muddle of Michael's self-deceptions, desires and attempts to be morally as good as possible.

I have already pointed out how Michael's love for Nick is made suspect as a power for good both by the high-flown language in which we are offered it, and by its apparent repetition in Michael's love for Toby: the lesson nevertheless, here, as it is not with Toby, whom Michael does not love so much, and who does not need Michael's love, is as Michael reflects too late, that the way is, precisely, 'always forward'. Nick is in this sense analogous to Georgie Hands in *A Severed Head*, in that he is trapped by other people's – in this case, notably Michael's – desire to keep their hands clean. And he comes, like Dora, also trapped, to need, in his perverted way, a truth-telling that will clear the air; his revelation of the substitution of the bells to Noel is his dark version of Dora's bell-ringing.

> 'There are moments,' said Nick, 'when one wants to tell the truth, when one wants to shout it around, however much damage it does.'[64]

And his truth-telling precipitates the crisis.

After Nick's death, Michael comes to see these things.

> He forced himself to remember the occasions on which Nick had appealed to him since he came to Imber; and how on every occasion Michael had denied him. Michael had concerned himself with keeping his own hands clean, his own future secure, when instead he should have opened his heart: should impetuously and devotedly and beyond all reason have broken the alabaster cruse of very precious ointment.[65]

It is worth, perhaps, recalling here in connection with the idea of the alabaster cruse, the connection I have drawn between Dave Gellman of *Under the Net* and James Tayper Pace, since it is precisely here that both these in many ways admirable persons fall short of Miss Murdoch's standards. Dave is described as

> a Jew, a real dyed-in-the-wool Jew, who fasts, and believes that sin is unredeemable, and is shocked at the story about the woman who broke the alabaster vase of very precious ointment and at a lot of other stories in the New Testament ... There's no concept Dave hates so much as the concept of charity which seems to him equivalent to a sort of spiritual cheating.[66]

But charity, in its best sense, is not spiritual cheating, it is

110

love, which is greater than James's and Dave's rules. 'And indeed, it is of the nature of love to be something deeper than our conscious and more simply social morality, and to be sometimes destructive of it.'[67]

The idea of love as a force destructive of the normal (in the sense in which this tends towards the conventional) is developed, in a technically quite different way, in *A Severed Head*, which is the next novel to consider. But before that I should like, as a kind of tailpiece to this incomplete analysis of *The Bell*, to look a little at the universe in which the story is played out. If Michael's story – and the downfall of the community – can be seen as a failure in love, how does Miss Murdoch see this 'love' in relation for instance, to the spiritual life, which is not a story or tragedy, and the human freedom we began by discussing? It is worth sorting this out a little, here, since the religious universe does not really recur in the next two novels, which are more exclusively concerned with love, freedom and the normal; when it does recur, in *The Unicorn*, it will be useful to have the metaphysics sorted out already in terms of *The Bell*, which is a more complete, and in my opinion a better novel; and is not a fable.

René Micha (*Critique*, April 1960) would seem to deny this.

> Dans le cas de *The Bell* par exemple, une lumière heureuse baigne tous les accidents de la fable, nous la montre comme fable. Notre émotion demeure sur le plan esthétique.[68]

In so far as this remark is a criticism of Miss Murdoch as a novelist – in her sense – of her power to involve her audience in the story without allowing them to observe and take pleasure in observing, the logical arrangement of it, it is to a certain extent fair. The same critic has remarked also that 'chez Iris Murdoch la continuité même ne se développe pas sans quelque chose de mécanique, et le fer paraît toujours sous l'étoffe', which is also fair – but to imply that the death at the end of *The Bell* is not to be taken as tragic or moving is to criticize it very heavily on its own ground, and to a large extent unjustly. The revelation of the extremity to which both Fawleys have been driven is shocking in a tragic way, just because they have been so incompletely apprehended. In this context it is worth looking at Miss Murdoch's description of the universe of tragedy, in her two related articles, *The Sublime and the Beautiful Revisited* and *The Sublime and the Good*, and comparing it with Michael's state at the end of *The Bell*.

The article, *The Sublime and the Good*, from which I have already quoted Miss Murdoch's criticism of Kant's ethics, contains a broadening of her analysis of that desire for completeness which she remarks in Sartre and other existentialist thinkers. Kant's notion of the sublime (his own feeling on seeing the Alps is the instance given) is said to be a sense of the effort of reason to comprehend what is before it, and of its own simultaneous failure. Miss Murdoch suggests that we might find the idea of Kant himself looking at the Alps themselves rather small and ridiculous.

> With the theory of the sublime we have the distressing feeling of some vast and wonderful idea being attached to a trivial occasion. Who, one might say, cares what sort of emotions Kant experienced in the Alps?[69]

She sees Kant's concept of the sublime as something which just misses being a vision of the tragic, because it attaches itself only to nature and the Alps, and more importantly, because it springs from an unsatisfied and *inactive* demand of reason.

> The freedom of sublimity does not symbolize, but *is* moral freedom, only moral freedom *not practically active*, but only, as it were, intuiting itself in an exultant manner.[70]

And

> The sublime is an experience of freedom, but of an empty freedom, which is the fruitless aspiring demand for some sort of impossible total perceptual comprehension of nature. Hegel humanizes the demand of reason. Reason is now demanding a total understanding of a human social situation – but what

is unnerving is that, according to him, reason's demand is satisfied.[71]

Here, on a much larger scale, in Kant's aspiring to a reasoned complete comprehension, in Hegel's assurance that reality is a given 'totality', we have both James's feeling that to conform to given rules is to conform to a 'given' pattern, and Michael's ache for a clearly defined rôle, something complete. It is this need which has brought the community into being – a need which is perhaps also present in Catherine's devotion to Dame Julian of Norwich, who was assured by God that 'all shall be well, and all shall be well, and all manner of thing shall be well'. I am not saying that Dame Julian's sense of God as a mysterious unifying power is analogous to Hegel's sense of a totality (with which I am in any case only acquainted through Miss Murdoch's exposition of it): I am only saying that Catherine's yearning for completeness is analogous to that of Michael or even James, and that they all search for it in the half-contemplative life and fail to find it.

Their failure, in Miss Murdoch's universe is, I reiterate, because they have failed to recognize the unutterable and incomprehensible particularity of the individual human being, of the world of action, of the reality which we inhabit, in which, according to Miss Murdoch, we are 'sunk', 'benighted'. I have already quoted Miss Murdoch's dictum that love is the 'discovery of reality' in this sense. Love is the recognition that Hegel's totality is not there to comprehend, that reason's demand cannot, in this world, be satisfied.

> Kant's freedom is an aspiration to universal order consisting of pre-established harmony. Tragic freedom implied by love is this; that we all have an indefinitely extended capacity to imagine the being of others. *Tragic because there is no pre-fabricated harmony.*[72] (My italics.)

Love, the practical world, the incomplete, then, are the ingredients of tragedy, and seem to be the ingredients of the world in which we, and Michael, are left at the end of *The Bell*. Dora has her vision of reality and perfection together. James speaks of God as perfection and reality together, as something so external and remote that we get only now and then a distant hint of it. Everard, in the vein of Dame Julian, spoke of God as

> a distant point of unification; that point where all conflicts are reconciled, and all that is partial and to our finite eyes contradictory, is integrated and bound up.[73]

He continues, 'There is no situation of which we as Christians can truly say it is insoluble. There is always a solution and Love knows that solution.'

In a Christian universe, then, there is this unimaginably remote God, to whom love leads, the love the Abbess says is 'always forward', but desire for God can often become corrupted into the 'fantastic' desire for a rationally or emotionally satisfying total experience, or total understanding, and thus – the way of putting it is mine, not Miss Murdoch's – a corruption of Dame Julian's view into Hegel's.

I wrote of *The Sandcastle* that Everard's 'remote' God was juxtaposed with Mor's predicament: this is true of Michael's situation too, at the end of this book, where he has moved into a universe which is aware of tragedy, and has the freedom at least of knowing the reality this brings. Tragedy, Miss Murdoch says, 'leaves us in eternal doubt. It is the form of art where the exercise of love is most like its exercise in morals.'[74]

> The fact remains that love which is not art inhabits the world of practice, the world which is haunted by that incompleteness and lack of form which is abhorred by art, and where action cannot always be accompanied by radiant understanding, or by significant and consoling emotions. Tragedy in art is the attempt to overcome the defeat which human beings suffer in the practical world. It is, as Kant nearly said, as he ought to have said, the human spirit mourning and yet exulting in its strength. In the practical world there may be only mourning and the final acceptance of the incomplete. Form is the great consolation of love, but it is also its great temptation.[75]

In a description of Michael's feelings at the end of *The Bell*, the ideas are the same.

> After Nick's death, he was for a long time quite unable to pray. He felt indeed as if his belief in God had been broken at a single blow, or as if he had discovered that he had never believed. He absorbed himself so utterly, so desperately, in the thought of Nick that even to think about God seemed an intrusion, an absurdity ... He thought of religion as something far away, something into which he had never really penetrated at all. He vaguely remembered that he had had emotions, experiences, hopes; but real faith in God was something utterly remote from all that. He understood that at last, and felt, almost coldly, the remoteness. The pattern which he had seen in his life had existed only in his own romantic imagination. At the human level there was no pattern. 'For as the heavens are higher than the earth, so are my ways higher than your ways and my thoughts than your thoughts.' And as he felt, bitterly, the grimness of these words, he put it to himself: there is a God, but I do not believe in Him.[76]

To the relation between religion and tragedy I shall return when looking at *The Unicorn*; at the moment I want only to point to Michael's situation in these terms: his freedom is the tragic freedom which is the acceptance of the incomplete, and of the 'indefinitely extended capacity to imagine the being of others' (quoted on p. 113) which Miss Murdoch in almost the same words puts here.

> One day no doubt all this would seem charged with a vast significance, and he would try once more to find out the truth. One day, too, he would experience again, responding with his heart, that indefinitely extended requirement that one human being makes upon another.[77]

In the interim there remains, beside the incomplete, the symbol of the relation of the remote God to the world, the fact of the Mass.

> The Mass remained, not consoling, not uplifting, but in some

115

way factual. It contained for him no assurance that all would be made well that was not well. It simply existed as a kind of pure reality separate from the weaving of his own thoughts.[78]

In this, it is the analogue, in Michael's religious world, of Dora's vision in the National Gallery.

6

A SEVERED HEAD

The striking symbol of the petrifying Medusa is interpreted
by Freud as a castration fear (*Collected Papers*, Vol. V). Sartre
of course regards as its basic sense our fear of being observed.
(*L'Etre et le Néant*, p. 502). It is interesting to speculate on
how one would set about deciding which interpretation was
'correct'.[1]

THIS IS A a footnote from Miss Murdoch's book on Sartre,
appended to a passage whose ideas are by now familiar to us.

Sartre, like Freud, sees life as an egocentric drama; 'the world
is my world' in that it is shaped by my values, projects and
possibilities. Sartre wishes however, while attempting to lay
bare by a pure reflexion ... the nature of consciousness, to
preserve the sovereignty of the individual psyche as a source
of meaning. For him the psyche is co-extensive with consciousness. Whereas for Freud the deepest human impulse is
sexual, for Sartre it is the urge towards 'self-coincidence'
which is the key to our being.

A Severed Head could be seen as Miss Murdoch's attempt to
investigate the problem of which interpretation was 'correct',
among other things; by now it should be clear that no interpretation of events which can see life in terms of egocentric
drama, or the world as 'my world', is likely to do any character in one of Miss Murdoch's books very much good. And
the progress of this book, whose ideas are less startlingly
different from its predecessor than its style and story, can
best be seen as a comic and inexorable substituting of 'the
hard idea of truth' for the 'facile idea of sincerity' with which

both Freud and Sartre in Miss Murdoch's thinking are to a certain extent associated. The 'truths' are Freudian and Sartrean truths – the protagonist has to come to grips with his own sexual violence and fear, and with the 'urge towards self-coincidence', or whether his acts are his own – but these truths are only steps on the way to the discovery of a vaster and vaguer and more general truth, personified by Honor Klein, who combines in human form both Miss Murdoch's respect for the individual – 'I believe in people, Mr Lynch-Gibbon' – and that Love which we have discussed in terms of *The Bell*, and which is both inevitable and truth-seeking. 'El m'ha percosso in terra e stammi sopra.'

A Severed Head is recounted in the first person by Martin Lynch-Gibbon, a wine merchant and amateur historian who took the best first of his year in History at Oxford and always regretted in a way that he had not become a don. When the book opens he has a beautiful and civilized wife, Antonia, some years older than himself, and a young mistress, Georgie Hands, a lecturer at the L.S.E. He considers himself happy, although Antonia is childless and Georgie has had to have an abortion – something for which he feels obscurely that he has yet to 'pay'. His wife than announces that she has fallen in love with her psychoanalyst, Palmer Anderson, a person of great charm for whom Martin has felt a fleeting homosexual attraction. She asks Martin for a divorce, and Martin falls, or is pushed, rather uneasily, into an attitude of accepting the new relationship between the three of them in a 'civilized' and even 'loving' way. Matters are complicated by the arrival of Palmer's half-sister, Honor Klein, an anthropologist, who makes Martin uncomfortable by suggesting to him that he is 'letting them off' and that this is good neither for them nor for him. Martin takes Georgie to his house and is discovered there by Honor; in a panic he pushes Georgie out of the door, thinking Honor to be Antonia. Palmer and Antonia then discover (through Honor's agency) all about Georgie; they consider themselves wronged and deceived. Martin attacks Honor in the cellar of Palmer's house; after this he writes her a series of unsatisfactory apologetic letters;

Antonia insists on meeting Georgie; the meeting is most uncomfortable for all concerned.

At this point Martin realizes that he is in love with Honor, with an overwhelming urgency that he has never experienced before; he goes to Cambridge to see her and finds her in bed with her brother. This gives him a power over Palmer that he has not had earlier; when Antonia comes to him afraid of Palmer, he strikes Palmer and Antonia returns to live with him. At this point Georgie becomes engaged to Martin's brother Alexander, a sculptor, of whom Martin had said to Georgie that he Martin, left him all his girls when he had finished with them; Georgie however has divined that Alexander took them away. The news of this engagement distresses Antonia disproportionately. Later, Georgie attempts to commit suicide, cuts off her hair and sends it to Martin. Everyone visits her in hospital in a most 'civilized' way; Georgie enters Palmer's care and Antonia announces that she is going away with Alexander who has been her lover ever since she and Martin were married. Martin has become hardened; he wants to see neither Alexander nor Antonia. He does go, however, to London Airport to watch the departure of Honor and Palmer, having refused Palmer's invitation to accompany them to the East. He sees that Georgie is to depart with them, 'enslaved', he conjectures, by Palmer. He returns to his house alone, but is surprised by a knock on the door; Honor has, after all, returned to him; she tells him that he is 'privileged' because he saw her with her brother, as Gyges saw Candaules' wife. The two are left to face some kind of uncompromising future together.

Bearing in mind the Freudian and Sartrean significances of the central image, and my own suggestion of the way in which it is extended, let us now turn to analysing the action of the book in terms of the central ideas we have met before: freedom, love, the 'normal', power, truth. The first chapter, a conversation between Martin, and Georgie, his mistress, introduces, in a formal way, several of these.[2] The half-brother and sister, Palmer Anderson and Honor Klein, are spoken of, and 'real power' is ascribed to both of them.

Martin ascribes his present capacity to 'worry less about the rules', that is, about the conventional morality that is a value in Miss Murdoch's world, if not the ultimate one, to Palmer's influence; Palmer is 'good at setting people free'. Georgie retorts that she does not 'trust these professional liberators. Anyone who is good at setting people free is also good at enslaving them, if we are to believe Plato.' She adds, 'The trouble with you, Martin, is that you are always looking for a master', which is seen subsequently to be true. Thus Palmer is seen as to a certain extent responsible for the 'liberation' of Martin from the normal existence and obligations of his marriage; he is later seen as to a greater extent responsible for a similar 'liberation' of Martin's wife, Antonia, whom he takes over and intends to marry: later when Antonia has left Palmer to return to Martin, to leave him again for Alexander, Martin's brother, she ascribes this move too, to Palmer's 'liberating' activities: ' "Anderson woke me up," said Antonia, "he made me in some way more absolute." '[3] But Palmer's liberation of Martin is clearly also an enslavement in ways I shall discuss later.

The idea of truth as something consisting of a relation between individual human beings is also touched on here, when Martin defends his clandestine relationship with Georgie as something 'charming' because it is 'so utterly private'. Georgie, straightforwardly, calls it 'lies', and says that she fears that 'if it were exposed to the daylight it would crumble to pieces' (which in fact, after Honor Klein has exposed it, it does). Martin replies that

> Knowledge, other people's knowledge, does inevitably modify what it touches. Remember the legend of Psyche, whose child, if she told about her pregnancy, would be mortal, whereas if she kept silent, it would be a god.*

It is possibly worth remarking, in parenthesis, that to be a

---

* The same image is used of Hugo's 'philosophy of silence' (UTN, p. 93), although, of course, Martin's silence is a selfish mockery of Hugo's. Martin learns, as Jake does, that he *must* live more in the open, communicate, judge with concepts, be observed.

'god' is not anything of great value in Miss Murdoch's eyes
– Palmer and Antonia are seen as 'golden gods' 'who were
my oppressors' – whilst to be fully mortal and truthful is. But
what is important is the idea that other people's knowledge
modifies what it touches – and according to Miss Murdoch,
truth, and thus love and life, cannot be reached without
abandoning a state of 'egocentric drama' where other
people's knowledge has been rendered irrelevant. Psyche's
lover was Eros, and the action that follows in *A Severed
Head* is the unstripping, the making objective, of a series of
loves – Palmer and Antonia, Georgie and Martin, Honor and
Palmer, Alexander and Antonia – which renders them all, in
some way, human in the light of day. This process is set
in motion by Honor, who shares with Finn in *Under the Net*
'a capacity for making objective statements when these were
the last thing one wanted, like a bright light on one's headache.' It is significant that when Martin first meets her it is
this capacity that first impresses him in her; her reaction to
his running errands for his wife's lover is that of the outside
world, that in the 'civilized net' woven by Palmer and
Antonia he has been able to ignore.

> She said, 'This is an unexpected courtesy Mr Lynch-Gibbon.'
> It took me a moment to apprehend the scorn in this
> remark. It took me by surprise and I was surprised too how
> much it hurt. It occurred to me that this was the first judgment
> I had received from an outsider since I had officially
> taken up my position as a cuckold, and I was irritated to
> find that, for a second, I minded cutting a poor
> figure.[4]

The first part of the book is concerned with Martin's relation
with the couple, Palmer and Antonia. These two are 'civilized', and to a certain extent complementary. Antonia is
descended from Bloomsbury, her mother is 'something of a
minor poet and a remote relation of Virginia Woolf'. She has
many things in common with Anna of *Under the Net*,
although ultimately she is seen in a less friendly way; she has
the same look of ageing blonde beauty, a 'ravaged' look,

and the same belief in paramount personal relations, and in taking life 'intensely and very hard'. But where Anna's world, though impossible for Jake to attain, is seen to be something beautiful and desirable, Antonia's is a blurring of reality, a corruption of truth.

> 'She holds that all human beings should aspire towards ... and are within working distance of, a perfect communion of souls. This creed ... may best be described as a metaphysic of the drawing-room.' And, 'Antonia's undogmatic apprehension of an imminent spiritual interlocking where nothing is withheld and nothing hidden certainly makes up in zeal what it lacks in clarity.'[5]

One of the virtues of this book is the way in which the variations on the themes are offered and exposed – the way in which Georgie's 'youthful' insistence on scrupulous honesty to combat the 'lies' is seen to be an inadequate and helpless relation of Honor's truth, the way in which Palmer's way of liberating Martin is similar to Honor's and yet directly opposed to it, the way in which a state 'where nothing is withheld and nothing is hidden' where Antonia is concerned is an emotional muddle, whereas with Honor to tell the truth is a liberation (consider the opposed effects on the confessors of Martin's confession to Antonia, and Georgie's confession to Honor, of their liaison). Antonia's metaphysic of the drawing-room leads to a state of 'sincerity' as opposed to truth, since it conveniently refuses to allow for the facts – the violence, the ultimate opacity of persons, the transcendence of reality. She is brilliantly drawn – the way in which her values subserve her needs, in which she is the centre of her own universe and 'love' is what she exacts from the other characters as a kind of tribute, is part of a real novel, as is Martin's reaction of love and pity towards her when she is confronted with the ruthless young honesty of Georgie and he cannot bear that she should seem ridiculous to Georgie.

Palmer Anderson is, as it were, a demonic personification of the Stuart Hampshire free man, the man who is 'rational and totally free', of whom it is said that 'The only moral word he requires is "good" (or "right") the word which expresses decision.'[6] With his Scandinavian-American ancestry, and his looks – 'There was something abstract in his face. It was impossible to pin wickedness or corruption onto such an image'[7] – his power is precisely the imposition of this two-dimensional view of reality, this 'dreamlike facility' derived from 'our current view of freedom', whereas, again quoting *Against Dryness*, 'what we require is a renewed sense of the difficulty and complexity of the moral life and the opacity of persons'.[8]

He has Ordinary Language Man's power to raise ordinary good manners into virtue. 'Palmer conveys an immediate impression of gentleness and sweetness, almost, so far have good manners here assumed the air of a major virtue, of goodness.'[9] He does not respect the irreducible nature of the individual human being; he can say 'The psyche ... has its own mysterious methods of restoring a balance. It automatically seeks its advantages, its consolation. It is almost entirely a matter of mechanics, and mechanical models are the best to understand it with.'[10] He, again, sees sincerity as a fundamental virtue. 'We are civilized people ... We must try to be very lucid and very honest. We are civilized and intelligent people.'[11] The mythical shape of this drawing-room novel allows this complex of attitudes – this abstract sincerity with no consciousness of evil or limitations to understanding and freedom – to be seen as a naked force.

Martin's attitude of the complacent cuckold is an enslavement to Palmer and Antonia. He feels, in their desire to keep him in their 'loving net', or as Palmer calls it, 'the toils of love', that 'if I had any power I was already surrendering it' and that 'I felt the tender bond like a strangler's rope ... I was their prisoner and I choked with it. But I too much feared the darkness beyond.'[12]

'It was important to them that I should let them off morally, that I should spare them the necessity of being ruthless,' Martin remarks – as it was important to him that Georgie should 'let him off'. But he feels, whilst complying, that they are cheating him of his actions, of 'some special though perhaps fruitless movement of will and power; and for this at least I would never forgive them'.[13] Here we have both a Freudian and a Sartrean enslavement; Antonia and Palmer play the part of his parents suppressing with 'love' his feelings of antagonism towards the male and desire towards the female (Antonia is older than he, and addresses him constantly as 'My child'); and in Sartre's sense they are taking away his freedom to act from himself. Thus although he acquiesces in their praise of his 'civilization' and 'goodness' he is filled, when looking at Antonia with 'a spiritual nausea which made her look to me for a moment almost hideous'.[14]

But if Palmer and Antonia have enslaved Martin, it is arguable that he is also, by ignoring the impulse to violence, enslaving them. Georgie points this out to him.

> 'I suspect you of wanting to play the virtuous aggrieved husband so as to keep Palmer and Antonia in your power. But perhaps I underestimate your goodness.' 'In my power!' I said. 'I'm in *their* power, it seems.'[15]

I have already quoted the passage from *The Unicorn* where Max Lejour, discussing Até, remarks that 'to be powerless, to be a complete victim, may be another source of power', and from what I remember of a scene between Palmer and Martin in the staged version of the book, which uses the word 'suffering' in a way which I associate more with *The Unicorn* than *A Severed Head*, it is clear that Martin's position here is analogous to that of Hannah; Palmer and Antonia 'need' his scape-goat suffering for their freedom – but this kind of suffering and freedom are ambiguous and latently destructive.

Martin's first long encounter with Honor Klein conveys this precisely and puts squarely the clash between 'civilization' and the 'truth'.

> 'Truth has been lost long ago in this situation,' she said. 'In such matters you cannot have both truth and what you call civilization. You are a violent man, Mr Lynch-Gibbon. You cannot get away with this intimacy with your wife's seducer.'[16]

124

She also introduces the idea of payment – an idea related to an intractable environment, where things do not happen with a dreamlike facility. Martin, like Michael Meade, cannot opt out of a world where power is there and to be exercised.

'Everything in this life has to be paid for, and love too has to be paid for ... Without payment my brother's patients would be wretched. They would be captives ... By gentleness you only spare yourself and prolong this enchantment of untruth which they have woven about themselves and about you too. Sooner or later you will have to become a centaur and kick your way out.' And, 'if you want to let them steal your mind and organize you as if you were an infant, I suppose that is your affair. All I say is that only lies and evil come from letting people off.'[17]

At this point, before discussing the way in which through Honor's agency the net is broken and Martin released, it is necessary to look at the whole complex of images and associations that centre on the idea of the severed head. Before Honor Klein appears at all, the prophetic functions of the severed head are introduced in the scene in the studio of Alexander, Martin's sculptor brother, who is in the process of creating 'an imaginary realistic head', which, when Martin sees it, is at the stage when

the wire framework has been roughly filled out and then the clay laid over it in various directions in long strips until the semblance of a head appears. This particular moment has always seemed to me uncanny, when the faceless image acquires a quasi-human personality, and one is put in mind of the making of monsters.[18]

Alexander's remarks about it connect explicitly with the *Against Dryness* concept of naturalistic character, as opposed to 'dry' fables and symbols, as a means of apprehending reality.

'Why don't modern sculptors do them?' I asked. 'I don't know,' said Alexander. 'We don't believe in human nature in the old Greek way any more. There is nothing between schematized symbols and caricature. What I want here is some sort of impossible liberation.'

Here in the connection of 'liberation' with real 'human nature' we have something we can relate to Martin's feeling – much less clearly realized than Alexander's – just before the train bearing Honor Klein, whom he is waiting for, arrives. He thinks, with a selfish dissatisfaction, of Georgie, and that

> I wanted love, I wanted, to save me, some colossal and powerful love such as I had never known before.[19]

In Honor Klein are combined these 'saving' qualities of the 'human' vision of the reality of the head, and the colossal love.

For the moment, however, to return briefly to Alexander's head, there are two more points to be noted. Martin continues

> 'I envy you,' I said. 'You have a *technique* for discovering more about what is real.' 'So have you,' said Alexander. 'It is called morality.' I laughed. 'Rusted through lack of practice, brother.'

Here one recalls the dictum of *The Sublime and the Good*.

> Art and morals are, with certain provisos, ... one ... The essence of them both is love. Love is the perception of individuals. Love is the extremely difficult realization that something other than oneself is real. Love, and so art and morals, is the discovery of reality.[20]

But Martin's morals are rusty; he has been 'let off' paying for the abortion of Georgie's child, quite apart from his relation to Palmer and Antonia. He needs the revelation of the head.

The head, too, connects with the Freudian aspects of Martin's childhood and his relationship with his family, always present in the book, if never obtrusive. His family home, Rembers, is described, like many of Miss Murdoch's houses, as a kind of earthly paradise in a Jamesian way. It

> is in my thought of it perpetually clouded over with a romantic, almost a mediaeval, haze. It ought most probably to be surrounded by a thick forest of twining roses like the castle of the sleeping beauty.[21]

But behind the legend of the sleeping beauty lies violence, at least in Miss Murdoch's idea (this is implicit in the whole plot of *The Unicorn*) and here too is something accepted out of which Martin must kick his way. We are told of Martin's feeling for his mother, and of his identification of this with his feeling for Antonia – both are seen as *enclosing* him.

> I recalled [my mother] clearly, with a sad shudder of memory, and with that particular painful, guilty, thrilling sense of being both stifled and protected with which a return to my old home always afflicted me; and now it was as if my pain for Antonia had become the same pain, so closely was it blended in quality, though more intense, with the obscure *malaise* of my homecomings. Perhaps indeed it had always been the same pain, a mingled shadow cast forward and backward across my destiny.[22]

When Martin and Alexander look together at Alexander's sculpted head of Antonia, Martin refers to it as 'an unfair advantage, an illicit and incomplete relationship', and Alexander refers it explicitly to Freud. 'Yes. Perhaps an obsession. Freud on Medusa. The head can represent the female genitals, feared, not desired.'[23]

In this sense, presumably, Martin's relationship to his mother and Antonia can be seen – illicit and incomplete as it is – as a fear of emasculation, Oedipal in origin (it seems a little unfair to cross the t's and dot the i's of what Miss Murdoch conveys so delicately and so economically); he finds it protecting (Martin needs a master, sees himself as a child) and also stifling (he, like Alexander, needs a liberation from it). At the end of the chapter he realizes what the 'damp, grey, featureless face' of the unfinished head reminded him of.

127

When my mother had died Alexander had wanted to take a death mask, but my father had not let him. I recalled with a sudden vividness the scene in the bedroom with the still figure on the bed, its face covered with a sheet.[24]

And this too, the veiled last sight of his mother, another kind of sleeping beauty, is contained in the significance – for both brothers – of the head image – an image which 'works' far more subtly than that of the bell, throughout the book.

Once Honor Klein comes into the action, the significances of the head image cluster about her, although after Martin's first description of her, our next vivid picture is of her body, whilst her head is outside the car in the fog; her body 'sagged and jolted beside me like a headless sack'. He sees the seam on her stocking, which 'reminded me just for an instant that she was a woman' and establishes for her a strong physical presence in the book thereafter. This physical presence reinforces her connection with the Lawrentian 'dark gods', with whom she explicitly allies herself. Thus, her activities as a 'severed head' can be differentiated from the sense in which we see both Antonia and Georgie as part of a world where the 'head', our *conscious* activity, has been severed from the sexual impulses of which we are not fully conscious. She is related to the Freudian picture of the Medusa's head as 'the female genitals, feared, not desired'.

In the scene with the sword, which I find, in the way it is a set-piece, and the way it is too deliberately and portentously 'rich' less satisfactory than her other appearances, she is seen, having brought Martin's affair with Georgie into the open, as a judge, an executioner. She says that the use of the sword is 'a spiritual exercise', and further defines her 'truth'.

'Being a Christian you connect spirit with love. These people connect it with control, with power.'
'What do you connect it with?'
'I am a Jew.'
'But you believe in the dark gods.'

'I believe in people,' said Honor Klein. It was a rather unexpected reply.[25]

One is reminded of the continuing mystery of Dave Gellman's Jewishness, which is an irreducible human value in *Under the Net*; here, love and power are seen as aspects of a belief in 'people', in individual human beings who must be not only loved, but not 'let off', judged. 'People' is something beyond, say, James Tayper Pace's brotherly love, or Martin's inadequate attempt to be 'an angel of compassion', as it is also beyond the kind of power he and Palmer/Antonia exercise over each other.

This scene is followed immediately by the scene which Palmer says 'constitutes an apex' in which Martin brings wine to his wife and Palmer whilst they are in bed together. This is the last scene where they are seen as god-like; it is also the last scene where Martin is really involved in his rôle of 'angel of compassion'.

Martin's spilling of the wine on the bedroom floor is clearly a substitute for the act of violence he dare not perform or has been cheated of. Palmer's ordering him to carry the wine down to the cellar is sheerly funny in its preposterous quality; but when he comes to the cellar and wonders 'what the inside of a gas-chamber could be like', there is a sense that he is to be judged, that the punishment he has been 'let off' is to catch up with him. What happens is that he makes a violent attack upon Honor Klein, thus releasing the violence in him, a process that she herself has set in motion.

But it is clear that what has happened is something much larger than simply releasing the violence he feels towards Palmer and Antonia; the 'psychological' explanation of his first projected letter of apology to Honor which suggests that he attacked her as a symbol of Palmer's 'parental' dominance, which he unconsciously resented, is clearly inadequate, if true. The immediate result of this scene is that he feels unable to make any contact with Antonia or Georgie. 'A taboo seemed set upon the two women.'[26]

This brings us, having observed the way in which Honor

functions as Sartre's feared observer, to the 'taboo' quality in her, which she shares with Freud's Medusa.

'The strangest thing' about taboo, says Freud, is that anyone who transgresses a prohibition becomes prohibited. And Martin, from this point of contact with her onwards becomes in a sense, taboo to the other characters. They cease to concern him. He has left their world. Later he feels of Antonia 'She seemed, for such monstrous knowledge, too flimsy and too small,' and he thinks of his love for Georgie as a 'poor pathetic thing'. He feels, he says, like 'men who have slept with temple prostitutes and, visited by a goddess, cannot touch a woman after'.[27]

Honor's taboo quality is recognized already in Martin's touching of the sword and feeling it 'charged with electricity'. Freud says

> Persons or things which are regarded as taboo may be compared to objects charged with electricity; they are the seats of tremendous power, which may be liberated with destructive effect if the organisms which provoke its discharge are too weak to resist it; the result of a violation of a taboo depends partly on the strength of the magical influence inherent in the taboo object or person, partly on the strength of the opposing *mana* of the violator of the taboo.[28]

The book from this point onwards is the narration of how Martin develops the strength to oppose and equal the power of Honor as a taboo object; the real violation of the taboo is his seeing Honor in bed with her brother, but the power which impels him to Cambridge to make this discovery is released in him by the episode in the cellar – after which he feels that 'the decks are cleared for something, some drama or event'. He becomes obsessed with Honor, feels that, because of her 'extreme untouchability', he has not really touched her, and, peering about in a London mist (fog has characterized all his meetings with Honor so far), realizes together the contingency of the world, the solidity of things and the nature of his ailment. Here again the realization of

love and the realization of the solid contingency of the world
are set together.

> The task of peering through the mist was becoming exasperat-
> ing and painful. I cannot see, I cannot see, I said to myself:
> it was as if some inner blindness were being here tormentingly
> exteriorized. I saw shadows and hints of things, nothing
> clearly at all.

Then he notices a telephone box.

> I looked at the telephone box; and as I looked it seemed to
> take on a strange sudden glory, such as is said to invest the
> meanest object in the eyes of those who claim to experience
> the proof of the existence of God *e contingentia mundi*. Very
> dimly and distantly, but hugely, it began to dawn upon me
> what the nature of my ailment was. It was something new
> and something, as I even then at once apprehended, terrible.[29]

In the next chapter, driven by this love, he pursues Honor
to Cambridge, and discovers the incestuous relationship
between her and Palmer. He is now, in the old sense, enslaved;
the lack of freedom involved in this love is that of recognizing, and meeting, from oneself, the 'other' – the contingent
object of love. He feels this love to be deeper than his earlier
loves – 'a love out of such depths of self as monsters live in',
a love which has the complete authority and real power of
'the terrible figure of Love as pictured by Dante. *El m'ha
percosso in terra e stammi sopra*.' But his subjection to this
real force gives him the real freedom in Sartre's sense of self-
coincidence.

> Wherever it might lead, it was sufficiently what it seemed and
> had utterly to do with me; I would not, I could not, attempt
> to disown it or explain it away . . . I was doing what I had to
> do, and my actions were, with a richness, my own.[30]

What Martin sees in Honor's room is, as I have said, the
breaking of the taboo; it gives him power over Palmer, so
that he can hit and damage him later; it gives him, later,
privilege with regard to Honor, so that, in the final reference
to the tale of Gyges and Candaules, she can suggest that

what he saw privileges him to 'kill Candaules and become King himself'. There is also, I suppose, in the laying bare of an act of incest, a kind of cartharsis of Martin's own childhood impulses, which, unknown, have been strangling him; and the sleeping violence of these, too, is released, so that when he later discovers how Alexander, by making Antonia his mistress, has, in a kind of sibling rivalry which is at the same time a half incest, cheated him of both wife and mother, he can be ruthless and liberate himself, if painfully, from the whole complex of relations.

He says of Antonia at this time

> I could not forgive her and I wanted her out of my sight. I too had become harder and more absolute . . . The talent for a gentler world which Palmer had remarked upon was precisely what had now died in me. It had been at best no very saintly talent; merely a quieter mode of selfishness.[31]

The talent for a gentler world, that is, is a fantasy; an interpreting of the world in one's own way; in no other novel of Miss Murdoch's does reality obtrude itself with such absolute violence, make such uncompromising demands of its hero – although Martin's 'selfish' attempt at non-violence may perhaps be seen as a less ambiguous analogue of Hannah's non-violent and 'selfish' attempt at saintliness in *The Unicorn*. And the recognition of the hardness of real moral cause and effect is revealed in his attitude to Alexander.

> It was as if Alexander had done something to the whole of my past, to years which stretched far back, beyond my marriage, into the nursery, into the womb. That he in whom, more than in any other, my mother lived again should so quietly and so relentlessly have defrauded me cast a shadow that was like a scar upon an innocence of the past which I had believed to be impregnable.[32]

He remarks that 'It was not that I judged him morally' – that is, to give an instance of such a moral judgment, it was not a judgment, however right in its limited way, such as the members of the community passed on Dora in her capacity of erring wife, or Nicholas as homosexual and drunkard. But he is not tempted to try to let Alexander off, or to try to ignore the consequences of acts.

> My reaction to Alexander was something much more automatic than a judgment and much more relentless. It was odd that the pain of it felt so like loneliness. Through him so much of my past had been peopled, which was now a stricken solitude.[33]

He is thus stripped for his final encounter with Honor Klein, which occurs after a scene where he watches Palmer, Honor and Georgie at London Airport, a scene which he refers to variously as 'a waiting-room for the Last Judgment' as 'witnessing an execution', and as a murder at which he is not sure whether he will be victim or assassin. He notices Georgie and reflects that she is now, as she was not with him, 'enslaved' by Palmer – she had after all, been protected only by her own intelligence and solid youthful sincerity, which were not enough. But Honor is seen now as 'touchingly mortal' 'her demon splendour quenched'. When she returns unexpectedly to his house, their final encounter is one between equal human beings, no longer something merely daemonic, or monstrous, or totemistic, or mythical. Martin can, for instance, tell her that she is talking nonsense when she mentions the Gyges and Candaules myth. 'If I'm only privileged because I saw you embracing your brother.'

Martin, it is to be supposed, is now involved in that cataclysmic love – the image is significant, 'the little germ of some great joy, tiny still as the image of the whale far beneath the ship' – which is freedom and the apprehension of other people. 'I could not but experience her consciousness of me as a kind of ecstasy.' Mythically, this fits entirely satisfactorily, although the suggestion that we are to imagine it out into some 'real' future, is written, perhaps significantly, in Miss Murdoch's worst sloppy style.

> I said 'Well, we must hold hands tightly, and hope that we can keep hold of each other through the dream and out into the waking world.'[34]

I don't want to discuss the problems of Miss Murdoch's style at this stage – it is in any case not my primary purpose – but the only argument in favour of this sentence at this point is that it is what people do, at such times, say – and the book has not been constructed up to this point with much attention to naturalism of this particular kind. One wonders for a moment if it is intended to be funny,* but I think it is not; the whole scene, apart from the convincing irresistible smile which spreads over the faces of both participants is curiously stiff and awkward beside the sharply defined, amusing and sinister description of the previous one.

I spoke earlier of the way in which one form of action or pattern of thought is seen in this book constantly to parallel, parody or elaborate another; a final pointing of the 'degrees of freedom' available to Martin might be seen in comparing his position with that of Mor in *The Sandcastle*. Martin, like Mor, is embedded in a life composed partly of his own past acts, relations he has made, a reality of a kind; like Mor, he falls in love in a violent and compelling way which leads him to want to break up the structure of this reality – although here there are Georgie and Antonia's own vagaries of conduct, to say nothing of the partially neurotic foundation of the marriage, to complicate the issue, and make it clear that ultimately there was less to break up.

There is a point in the book at which Martin's situation is clearly analogous to Mor's in that he is offered a breaking-away, a violent snatch at freedom, that would clearly be destructive. This is when Palmer invites him to leave Antonia and to come away with himself and Honor. Palmer tells him

> 'You *want* to leave Antonia; and this is not a moment for placating your very abstract sense of duty. On the whole "do what you want" costs others less than "do what you ought".'

---

* I now think that it *was* intended to be funny and that I have underrated the simply preposterous quality of this love affair; but still feel the scene to be awkward – the mood difficult to place – as though Miss Murdoch found it difficult to find the tone of the requisite tying up of comedy and moral theme.

And

As a psycho-analyst, I don't of course imagine that freedom is to be won by convulsive movements of the will. All the same there are times of decision. You are not a man to be bound by ordinary rules. Only let your imagination encompass what your heart privately desires. Tell yourself: nothing is impossible.[35]

Martin comments, 'I had never heard speak more clearly the voice that says "all is permitted" '.

There is something in this attitude in common with that of that other 'demon', Calvin Blick, who, discussing not freedom but the related truth, says, 'You will never know the truth and you will read the signs in accordance with your own deepest wishes.' But reality is not a cipher with many solutions, all of them right ones, and freedom is not to be attained Palmer's way – only, one conjectures, a worse enslavement, involving Palmer and Honor. In his next encounter with Honor, who is instrumental in his refusing this invitation, she tells him to 'Return to reality' and 'You know that there are many ways in which your marriage is alive'. His love for her she sees at this stage as 'dreams' and she tells him that his fascination for her as a severed head is 'remote from love and remote from ordinary life. As real people we do not exist for each other.'[36]

We have already seen how this is reversed, and how they do come to exist for each other as 'real people' out of the world of gods and monsters. Thus his freedom is not, still, a breaking away from anything; it is something he has grown to fit, certainly, but something circumstances have, in the manner of Miss Murdoch's earlier novels, very conveniently put him in a position to be able to take. This brings us back to the curious feeling one has with the bell, that those things in the novel which represent both intractable reality and the normal are those which, after thought, are most clearly seen to be manipulated by the author. 'Le fer', indeed, 'paraît toujours sous l'étoffe'.

However, as far as freedom goes, the ways in which it is

permissible, necessary, or impossible, to 'break out' of the solidity of an existence, lead us directly to the consideration of the positions of Hugh, Randall and Ann in the next book, *An Unofficial Rose*. Martin Lynch-Gibbon has at least the distinction of being the only character in Miss Murdoch's canon to date who is seen permanently to have moved out of his normal life into a possibly freer world, and a certainly more absolute one. Dora's fate is in question, and Randall's move is much more dubiously a move to 'freedom' at all.

7

AN UNOFFICIAL ROSE

AN UNOFFICIAL ROSE might be said to centre around the
Tintoretto painting owned by Hugh Peronett, as *The Bell*
centred around the image of the bell itself. At the opening of
the book, Hugh is seen at the funeral of his wife, Fanny,
whose rich, art-dealer father had owned the Tintoretto, and
had left it to her. The themes of the book are two; the relation
of the idea of perfection to the reality we experience, and
the relationship between love and knowledge, freedom and
necessary lack of freedom in marriage. Hugh himself has
loved Emma Sands, now a famous detective-story writer, but
has finally, for some reason he cannot understand, decided
not to leave his wife for Emma. Hugh's son, Randall, is
married to Ann, in some ways the central character of the
book; together they run a rose nursery. There are two
children of the marriage, the dead Steve, and Miranda, who
is adolescent. When the book opens, Randall, a 'violent'
man, feels himself trapped in a loveless marriage; Ann, the
conventional, deliberately does not see the difficulties.
Randall has fallen in love with Lindsay Rimmer, the companion of Emma Sands, and is involved in an uneasy triangu-
lar relationship with Emma and Lindsay, vaguely reminiscent
of that between Martin, Antonia and Palmer.

The other family involved in the story is the Finch family;
Humphrey, a civil servant, whose career came to an end after
an 'incident in Marrakesh which even the British Foreign
Service with its wide tolerance of eccentricity could not over-
look', his wife, Mildred, who has cherished a romantic feeling

for Hugh since an isolated incident when he kissed her years ago, and Mildred's brother, Colonel Felix Meecham, a gentleman, in love with Ann and involved with a French girl, Marie-Laure Auboyer, who is in Delhi. Humphrey cherishes a hopeless and distant passion for the boy Penn, Hugh's other grandson, the child of his daughter Sarah who married an Australian; Penn is on a visit, having arrived in time for his grandmother's death. Penn, the innocent of this book, in his turn, bewildered by the English conventions and scenery, falls in love with his cousin Miranda, in a violent and distressing way which he has never experienced before.

Emma Sands appears at Fanny's funeral; Hugh is disturbed, and his old love is aroused. Mildred invites him to accompany her and Felix to India, but he has decided to renew his relationship with Emma, which turns out to be difficult. Randall engineers a row with Ann and leaves for London; there, Lindsay, who is 'unscrupulous', tells him that she will only leave Emma for him, if he can find money to support her richly. Randall asks Hugh bluntly to sell his beloved Tintoretto to enable him, Randall, to leave his wife and to go away with Lindsay Rimmer.

Hugh asks Mildred's advice; Mildred sees that, if Hugh sells the Tintoretto, she herself will lose Hugh, who will be able to comfort the deserted Emma, but her brother, Felix, will gain Ann, who would not leave Randall, but may feel free to love Felix if Randall removes himself. So she advises Hugh to sell the picture, and he does so, performing an act of 'vicarious violence' which he sees as redeeming his own passivity in the past over Emma.

Randall leaves with Lindsay; Ann falls in love with Felix, but for a variety of incompletely understood reasons, including the machinations of Miranda, who has herself been in love with Felix since the age of five, cannot accept the 'freedom' he offers her. Hugh finds that Emma will not redeem the past, and has simply replaced Lindsay with another companion, Jocelyn. He may visit, and love her in the imagination, but this is all. She reveals to him that she is in fact seriously ill, and contemplating death; she has left her money to Penn, who is to be their 'symbolic child'. Hugh is by this in another sense 'freed' in that he is now able to depart calmly on the trip to India after all, accompanied by Mildred, and by Felix, who, having failed with Ann, is returning to Marie-Laure. Hugh thus begins a new life in a sense; Ann simply returns to her old routines, not exactly waiting for Randall's return, but unable to live any other way.

The question which always strikes me about *An Unofficial Rose* is 'Why is it not a better book than it is?' This issue was raised by Angus Wilson in an early review in *The Guardian*, which made, though not in so many words, a point one would reiterate: any description of the plot, the interrelations of the characters, the ideas even, makes the whole seem a much more complex and significant structure than it appears to be when one is reading it. When one is reading it, there is something perfunctory, something lifeless about it, difficult to describe, and yet constantly irritating. Angus Wilson ascribes this partly to a kind of self-indulgent snobbery which has crept in, both in the matter of the roses, about which he feels strongly, and in the matter of social milieux. He also instances moments of bad writing; in this book one feels that Miss Murdoch often verges on unconscious parody, either of Iris Murdoch or of Henry James – what Jamesian tones there were in *A Severed Head* one could ascribe without much difficulty to the comic structure of that book.

My own feelings about the book is that it would have benefited from the slower pace, the more intricate and naturalistic description of detail which are naturally present in the three-volume novel. It needs filling out; there are too many characters here, simply, for the space which is allotted to them, as one did not feel, except perhaps in the case of Paul, with *The Bell*. There are loose ends, which are not the loose ends of life, are not those small mysteries at the edge of our consciousness of the action, which we feel open it up and indicate further complexities, but those loose ends which we feel are loose because we have not been given enough information about them to see how they function in the story at all.

Such a loose end is the dead son Steve, who is burdened somehow with a significance beyond that of being dead and a son, which never quite inhabits the action as it should – compared for instance with the Australian father of the other grandson, Penn. He, like the peripheral characters in *The Bell*, is present, economically, to be felt as a person and a point of view not sufficiently known or taken into account by the other characters; an opacity which enlarges the action.

The other, more serious, criticism I would make of the whole work is that, in so far as it consists of two opposed groups of characters – let us call them, for the moment, the 'rapacious' or 'violent' characters, and the 'conventional' or 'good' or more neutrally, 'normal' characters – it is only the second group who really have the life which the novel at its best demands, and this discrepancy is not a fruitful conflict, but a kind of grinding in the works which constantly brings one up short against an impatient disbelief one feels in the first group of characters which in turn vitiates one's faith in the springs of action of the second. In the second group I would put, obviously, Ann, Felix, Penn, Hugh, his dead wife, Fanny, and to a certain extent, Mildred; in the first, Randall, Lindsay, Emma Sands, the dead Steve, and the extraordinarily tiresome Miranda. These groupings may be seen to centre, as I intend to show more fully, around the ideas of the *Yale Review* article; the second group, with variations, are the Ordinary Language Men, whose danger is that they may fall from love into convention, and the first are the Sartrean totalitarian characters, who may fall into neurosis. Other ideas are at work here, too: this is Miss Murdoch's first sustained attempt to come to grips with the study of 'goodness' as opposed to 'freedom' as a primary term of value; she asks, not 'what is it to be free?' but 'what is it to be good?', and in so far as she is breaking new ground and her imagination is involved, the book has an exciting life.

But, to return to my criticism of the totalitarian characters, principally, of course, Randall, I mean this criticism to be much more damning than merely to say that Miss Murdoch has tried to show the interaction of a world where consciousness and freedom were supreme values with one where 'unknowing' and accepting and belief in the solidity of the normal were more powerful. This could have made a very good book indeed, and Miss Murdoch offers us enough pointers to how it would have done if it had worked, and they are worth observing. But what strikes me again and again is the *perfunctory* nature of her description of Randall, or Emma, or Miranda – one has the sense that she is here wearily covering old ground, not living anything new, and the irritating sense that one has had before that one is being *told* things, not shown them, not given them; we are constantly told, for instance that Emma is 'dark, perhaps twisted', that Randall 'needs forms' or 'is violent'; but in the novel these things have no life, as Ann's muddle or Hugh's moral problems have; they are manipulated counters only. That Randall's world should seem unreal beside Ann's is part of the purpose of the book, though not the whole purpose, but it should have had, say, for real power, the ultimate unreality of the community in *The Bell* – an unreality which springs from the real world – and not the fantastic conceptual unreality of – what it seems most like – the curious two-dimension 'free' characters in *The Flight from the Enchanter*, Marcia Cockeyne and her family, who 'free' the romantic Rainborough, much as Randall is freed by that other earthly Venus, Lindsay Rimmer.

For, after all, Ann is married to Randall, and for Ann's predicament to have the solidity it could have had, she needed a husband and an opponent who had life.

Let us deal first, then, with Randall and his freedom. He has things in common with the protagonists of *The Sandcastle* and *A Severed Head*; like Mor, he is trapped in a 'real' but to him meaningless marriage; like Martin he is violent, and needs to release his violence; like Martin, too, he is easily enslaved. The Emma Sands-Lindsay Rimmer ménage of which he makes a third takes the strength, the real love, out of him, as Palmer and Antonia sapped Martin's.

> Randall was well aware of the deliberation with which they weakened him, with which they turned his love-relation into a play-relation.[1]

He is looking for a master also, as Martin was; he allows Lindsay to 'dominate' him; he is helpless as a child before the 'real' power of Emma Sands.

His needs as he expresses them are those of the Sartrean existentialist. He tells Hugh, his father, that he needs 'form'.

> 'I need a different world, a formal world...' 'Form?' 'Yes, yes, form, structure, will, something to encounter, something to make me *be*.'[2]

As Miss Murdoch says:

> According to Sartre, a desire for our lives to have the form and clarity of something necessary, not accidental, is a fundamental human urge.[3]

And

> Virtue for total man is sincerity, courage, will: the unillusioned exercise of complete freedom.[4]

And again, from the aesthetic continuation of the same discussion

> An adoration of necessity, more or less concealed, has always been a characteristic of Romanticism, co-existing in the earlier days with the wilder, life-loving, more purely Rousseauesque elements, but in later times proving itself more powerful. What is feared is history, real beings and real change, whatever is contingent, messy, boundless, infinitely particular and endlessly still to be explained; what is desired is the timeless non-discursive whole which has its significance completely contained in itself.[5]

Randall has all these things: need for form, adoration of necessity – consider how he admires his love for Lindsay because it has 'that absolute authority which seems to put an act beyond the range of right and wrong'[6] – admiration of will and sincerity. He has also the symbolist hatred of 'messiness', which, in both article and book, Miss Murdoch associates with the infinitely particular and contingent individual. The symbolist dislike of 'mess' Miss Murdoch criticizes as a lack of tolerance and love, as a fear 'of the real existing messy modern world, full of real existing messy modern persons...' It is in this context that one should, partly at least, see Randall's hatred of Ann.

> [Form]. That's what Ann hasn't got. She's as messy and flabby and open as a bloody dogrose... That's what destroys all my imagination, all the bloody footholds... [7]

Ann I want to treat later; meanwhile Randall's need for form and necessity leads him into the curious relationship with Emma and Lindsay together which he feels to have precisely 'form', will and intelligence and freedom. Miss Murdoch here manipulates words like a curious code or shorthand: Emma is 'the darkness': or there are sentences like these, where one feels that something very abstract is being worked out which we are never to see *lived* or human in the novel at all.

> Only through intelligence could such a structure remain rigid; and at times he felt the sheer cleverness of Emma, Lindsay and himself, coiled like three great muscular snakes at the very centre of the edifice. Yet also love was its centre; and perhaps here cleverness *was* love. With the passion of the artist which he now increasingly felt himself to be he adored Lindsay's awareness, her exquisite sense of form, which was a sort of dignity of wit, a sense as it were of the movement and timing of life which made her like a great comedian. She was shapely and complete; and like a kaleidoscope, like a complex rose, her polychrome being fell into an authoritative pattern which proclaimed her free.[8]

This is not only pretentious writing; it relates to nothing in Lindsay which we see acted out which might support Randall's use of such high words of her, even seen ironically – we are *told, told, told,* what she is. It is writing which requires knowledge of Sartre, of Miss Murdoch's peculiar use of words such as 'love', 'free' 'form' to see what relevance it has at all. It is a substitute for an exploring of Randall's awareness of Lindsay, with love (on Miss Murdoch's part towards Randall, that is) that would have made this a good book.

However, it provides a convenient ground for discussing Randall as an artist, which is clearly related to his sense of form. He is an unproduced playwright at the beginning of the book; at the end it is clear that he will not be one at all. He is too afraid of the contingent and the individual, of love in the sense of tolerance. He gains Venus Anadyomene, the metallic, 'artificial' Lindsay, who is related surely to Madge and Sadie in *Under the Net;* but to gain her he causes the Tintoretto to be sold, and in this book, surely if ambiguously, the Tintoretto stands where Dora's experience in the National Gallery stood; a vision of perfection and reality united, seen with love.

Randall is self-centred, as the Sartrean existentialist is self-centred, to whom other people are 'organized menacing extensions of the consciousness of the subject'[9]; (he tells his father 'Ann is a hysterical woman . . .'), this does not lead, in Miss Murdoch's view to great art, which is not conscious of self, but only, as love at its most perfect, of others. Randall is too 'rapacious' to be a great artist, he has a 'rapacity such as is the mark of mediocrity in art'.[10] He has, in contradistinction to his bad novels, his good roses, but here too the man-made and imposed forms are inferior, another version of the pursuit of Lindsay rather than the Tintoretto, or perhaps Ann.

> What was it all for, the expulsion of the red, the expulsion of the blue, the pursuit of the lurid, the metallic, the startling and the new? The true rose, the miracle of nature, owed nothing to the hand of man.[11]

The roses are associated with Ann, whose capacity for always winning the local flower arrangement competitions is here not irrelevant – she has, on the other hand, not 'art' enough to be good at charades or make-believe, a quality she shares with Penn.

The great work of art, that is, like the rose, is in a sense free, because its form is particular, respects the individual, loves and includes the contingent – although it is here dangerous, as I hope to show later, in the way the religious love of God as a union of the real and the perfect is seen to be dangerous in *The Unicorn*. Emma Sands says, 'Randall may be saved in the end, because at least he loves *something*. Though I'm afraid Lindsay may be only the symbol of it'.[12] And his love, like that of the half-contemplative, is dangerous because it abhors the real world, 'that incompleteness and lack of form . . . where action cannot always be accompanied by radiant understanding or significant emotions'. 'Form,' Miss Murdoch finishes, 'is the great consolation of love, but it is also its great temptation'[13] and it is clear that Randall is 'tempted' by it into abandoning his real vision of the rose for something less.

What then does Randall gain, whose progress through the book is seen as a moral outburst (similar to the one Mor did not make) a gain of financial freedom (similar to the one Jake Donaghue refused) and a subjection to an overpowering necessity (similar at first sight to Martin's complete subjection to Honor Klein)? Money will buy spiritual goods, Mildred assures Felix, and she is of course right. What Randall buys is Lindsay, and to see what Lindsay is, it is necessary to look at chapter thirteen. In this chapter, discussing morals, Randall says to Lindsay

> 'I suppose we are rather unprincipled, aren't we?' 'We don't live by abstract rules,' said Lindsay. 'But our acts have their places. They belong to us.' 'Their places in a pattern,' said Randall. 'Yes. In a form. Our lives belong to us.'[14]

One remembers immediately Martin Lynch-Gibbon's 'my acts, were, with a richness, my own'. But Randall is not in Martin's position, and he thinks immediately afterwards 'I am talking nonsense. My life has not belonged to me for years. And then he thought, but it *will* belong to me, and he felt the shaft of light go through him.'

But if one is reminded of Martin's attempt to measure up to Honor, it is not Honor, with her respect for truth, to whom Lindsay is most closely related. When she remarks that morality is depressing, and Randall retorts that her morality is not – 'It invigorates, it inspires, it gives life. You have a marvellous moral toughness. You are so completely honest and genuine' – we see that she has, in her 'sincerity', much more in common with Stuart Hampshire's 'free' man, and with Palmer Anderson. (Again, I am not saying that this conversation is well-written, or 'real'; it has the perfunctory, ciphered air about it that I remarked earlier.) Like Palmer she is good at enslaving those she liberates.

> She was, he delighted to tell her, a demon, but an angel for him, heartless, but warm for him, a natural tyrant, but for him a liberator ...

But even in Randall's 'airy world of the imagination, the world above the mess of morality', into which he has 'risen', the forces of contingency and darkness and restriction are present. At the moment when he realizes his freedom, on receiving his cheque from Hugh, he feels completely alone, his father assassinated, 'Even the image of Lindsay was dissolved in a big golden consciousness, vast and annihilating as the beatific vision.'[15] Anything golden in this way in Miss Murdoch's novels is liable to be dangerous and fantastic – compare Honor's blackness against Palmer and Antonia's gold, or Denis's black face in *The Unicorn* with the gold of the family circle gathered together by Gerald Scottow. And Randall, proceeding through a 'Renoir landscape which is suddenly a heavenly version of Hyde Park' remembers Emma Sands.

> All the same, Emma existed, and with what authority, with what horrible contingent power, he suddenly felt as he neared the raucous whirlpool of Hyde Park Corner. He felt himself in the mood for another assassination.[16]

But Emma's 'contingency' destroys his freedom, almost at one blow. Emma exists and is individual and inscrutable. She manages to impinge on his view of his own acts; not only has she had an 'agreement' with Lindsay over him, but she has been to Grayhallock, 'leaving her snail's traces. She has even got hold of Ann, she has even stolen Grayhallock from me.' He cries to her, 'Don't pretend that it's you who have done this. It is I who have done it.' But the doubt is sown in his mind; Emma may have stolen his action; she is certainly a *fact*, influencing his life, outside his solipsist beatific consciousness. And at the end, when Randall is seen enjoying the fruits of his 'crime', it is clear, to labour a point that Miss Murdoch has already laboured for us, that his 'freedom' is at best an uneasy thing.

He sees Lindsay as Venus Anadyomene.

> For reality he made do with a vague shimmering apprehension of Lindsay's continual presence. She was indeed the Aphrodite of the world of sleep.[17]

His reality is a 'making do', his 'high up' region of perfect freedom, his 'paradise of the imagination' is something he cannot achieve because he has 'a little reckoned without his mind'.

All this is obvious and two-dimensional; we all know that to be financially free and in possession of the beloved is not freedom if the mind is not free; and the complications of Randall's mind have been so without depth that this truism is not clustered about with a complication of life as it could have been (consider Michael Meade). But in discussing the limitations present in Randall's 'freedom' Miss Murdoch, besides mentioning the fact that Randall is still worried about Emma and Lindsay, that he dreams constantly of Emma, Ann and Steve but never of Lindsay, introduces something more interesting.

> There was only one thing in the world that he was good at, and that he would never do again. He saw in a vision the sunny hillside at Grayhallock with its slight haze of green and

its myriad little coloured forms and he sighed. Ann. Through some mechanics of reality the figure of Ann remained steady.[18]

All this is clear enough and expected; Ann is, as Mor's wife, Nan, was, real to him, normal to him, in a way that cannot be rendered nothing by a violent action or crime – the 'connection' in a marriage which is a reality in itself. As he said to Lindsay

> I'm hideously – connected with her. It's odd how that *connection* survives any real relationship. And it seems to go out into everything. The roses. Even the bloody furniture.[19]

But Miss Murdoch complicates this issue further, and gives us a glimpse of something, not really achieved, a real conflict that could have lived in the novel.

> 'The figure of Ann remained steady,' she says, 'but somehow its power was broken . . . Ann's tyranny was broken, her dead hand was gone. Why had he fretted so in the old days when freedom was, after all, so easy? Perhaps this, and this only, was what Lindsay was for, to free him from Ann . . . Whereas Emma's awareness of him still seemed to hover over him like a cloud, Ann's awareness of him had vanished, it was nothing . . . And sometimes he imagined weirdly that this put them in a new and innocent relationship, as if they could set up house together like Christie and Old Mahon; and he would be the boss then.'

It is this idea of Ann's reality as a 'dead hand', a negative, something from which Randall's struggle to free himself could be seen as a real human need or even virtue, which is complex and interesting; this because Ann is clearly not only that, not only negative. One remembers again Max Lejour; 'to be powerless, to be a complete victim, may be another source of power', and from this angle we can see in Ann a foreshadowing of the central ambiguity of Hannah, the unicorn, who may be, as it were, a scapegoat, bearing other people's sin, or may be an enchantress, a destroyer, a denier of life. Ann herself comes at the end of the book to feel that she should 'free' Randall, that she has somehow damaged him.

> She was prepared moreover, and especially when she considered the wreck of her marriage with Randall and what she had somehow done *to* Randall, to see in her absence of straightforward operative desires something corrupting, something deadening. There was in her open formless life some dreadful lack of vigour, some lack of any hard surface to grasp or brace oneself against; and as she thus accused herself, ready almost to call her good an evil, she found herself again echoing some of Randall's words.[20]

Here, it seems to me, is where the real interest of the relationship lies – something which has already been suggested in, say, the contrast between the 'good' Everard and the 'imaginative' or 'interesting' Demoyte; something, also, inherent in the fact that Hugh, although he knows the 'good' thing would be to give the money from the sale of the Tintoretto to Famine Relief (as Everard gave part of his salary, which caused his food and his coffee to be bad), wants to do something violent and imaginative (and selfish). The question of goodness, and why it so often seems slightly repulsive, or uncomprehending, or unattractive, or dead, Miss Murdoch has excellently come to grips with in Ann, to whom we must now turn. But if the issue had not been prejudged so heavily – if Miss Murdoch had managed to put in the place of this abstract and fantastic Randall a real man, treated, to criticize her on her own ground, with love, whose need for freedom from deadness and convention she could treat with the tolerant agnosticism she herself requires, the book – and Ann – would have been better.

★ ★ ★

> This needful and homely finality would be ludicrous if it attempted a finely acted consciousness of its state. It is supremely undramatic and unselfregarding; it succeeds by taking for granted. And, homely or ludicrous or not, we receive the intimation that it is in this kind of relationship that love as a permanence must do its work.[21]

The conventional and the mysterious are closely allied, are indeed one and the same thing. It is the conventional act which challenges the imagination and produces mystery, not the daring and emancipated act: and mystery as James sees and presents it is the very stuff of life . . . For the convention of not-knowing . . . is allied with the moral impossibility of knowing completely.[22]

These two quotations are from John Bayley's book, *The Characters of Love*, from the chapter on *The Golden Bowl, Love and Knowledge*. Miss Murdoch acknowledges her debt to her husband's ideas in the issue of *Encounter* in which *Against Dryness* appeared; the values in this book, the love for whole, inscrutable, unpredictable *characters*, human beings, the sense of reality, are closely allied to those we have already been studying. The respect paid here to 'love' in the first paragraph, to mystery and 'the moral impossibility of knowing completely' in the second, are something we should recognize. And I would suggest that Miss Murdoch's depiction of Ann and the nature of her 'goodness' are closely related to her husband's concept of the nature of the goodness of Adam Verver and more particularly of Maggie, in *The Golden Bowl*.

Here is Maggie, according to John Bayley:

Maggie's resentment is muffled and yet attentive; she does not glory in it as she does not glory in any of the emotions; her lack of their kind of immediacy and spontaneity is the chief cause of her repelling so many readers. Yet it is an effect on which the author insists, and he will not temper her goodness with aesthetic vitality or a tendency to muddle. She *is* good, but her goodness is subject to the author's deliberate 'appeal to incalculability'; like that of the observed person in life, it remains incomplete and open to question.[23]

And

it makes her exceedingly human, not necessarily in the sense that is the opposite of 'inhuman', but in the sense in which we are actually surrounded in society by such human beings, the sense – oddly enough – in which to be human is to be virtually unknown.[24]

And

Maggie, on the other hand, rejects both her immediate impulses and the desire for knowledge, and finds in the refuge of convention and deliberate 'ignorance' salvation both for herself and for the others. She burrows back into the hallowed darkness of 'the forms', like an animal seeking shelter, and the ambiguity of appearance may make us wonder if there isn't resentment and cruelty in her action, or if she is not at least repressive, priggish, and narrow-minded. But however that may be, there is no ambiguity in the sense which James conveys to us that to support convention intelligently and savingly is at least as remarkable as to defy it.[25]

Mr Bayley points out that readers have seen the action of *The Golden Bowl* in two very different ways – as the triumph, in Maggie and her father, of innocence and unknowing over cleverness and duplicity, or as the trapping and 'collecting' by the 'monstrous' and 'dead' Ververs of the live Prince and Charlotte. Mr Bayley allows the ambiguity to stand, whilst making it clear that he considers Maggie and her father to be exercising real love and goodness; he is helped in this by his own belief that 'knowingness', as represented, say, in Iago, is the force opposed to 'love'. (Naturally, I simplify.) It is clear that this opposition between knowing and loving, or knowing and goodness, is also present in *An Unofficial Rose*; Randall's relation with Lindsay and Emma, like the Prince's with Charlotte, rests on a sense, we are told, of intelligent complicity. And Randall sees Ann's goodness as destructive.

'Ann lives by rules and her acts don't have places, they don't belong anywhere. It is a very depressing thing to witness . . . Ann is *abstract*.' He spoke with a sudden passion. What was it he so positively *hated* here?[26]

Ann's good is a state of unconsciousness; she refuses to imagine what Randall is doing away from her in London, she refuses to notice – until the end – how much his feeling for her is a positive hatred; she takes refuge in the ordering of house, garden, rose nursery, flower arrangements, from thinking about what she is doing.

Like Maggie

> She thought it better that her imagination should not entertain
> images of her husband's unfaithfulness: and in a way which
> was obviously incredible to Mildred she had not even felt
> curiosity about Randall's doings when he was away from
> home. How true her instinct had been she had occasion to
> know after Mildred had suddenly crystallized the situation
> by mentioning a name.[27]

And when Douglas Swann is interrogating her about
Randall's defection, she finds her strength in not-knowing
and convention.

> She could feel Swann's attention like a plucking of many
> strings. It was as if he wanted to break her down. Perhaps he
> did, even if unconsciously, want to break her down so that
> he could console her. There were a hundred things that she
> ought to be doing. She had promised Bowshott that she would
> help with the spraying. The proofs of the catalogue must be
> corrected. Miranda's clothes needed attention. She said, 'Well,
> I doubt if Randall has any love left for me by now. It doesn't
> matter.' But it did matter. What else mattered if this didn't?[28]

Allied to this accepting, loving, not thinking quality in Ann,
there is a refusal to blame, or hate, which makes a scapegoat
of her – a much less ambiguous scapegoat than Hannah
Crean-Smith – but one which results directly from her own
openness and lack of will in this direction.

> Something had been wrong, indeed, with her relations with
> Miranda since Steve died. The same was true of her relations
> with Randall. It was as if everyone blamed her for Steve's
> death. Or as if, she sometimes a little resentfully thought,
> since the others wanted to blame someone and she did not,
> she made a vacuum into which their blame ran.[29]

Hugh, at his wife's funeral, recalls Randall on this issue,
saying that 'Ann had never forgiven him' and comments to
himself, 'It was rather perhaps that he had never forgiven
Ann upon whom by some insane and fantastic logic he had
seemed to fix the blame of his bereavement'.[30]

But Ann, like Maggie here too, is human – 'in the sense in which to be human is to be virtually unknown'. Her goodness, like Maggie's, like that of 'the observed person in life', 'remains both incomplete and open to question'. In this she resembles Hugh too, whose goodness is not meaningful to him, and is incomplete. She remains 'in the world of practice, the world which is haunted by incompleteness and lack of form', to move to Miss Murdoch's terminology from Mr Bayley's. Like Maggie, she is capable of showing resentment – in the scene which Randall engineers to ensure his own departure from Grayhallock, Hugh is surprised by the readiness with which she produces anger, even petulance; so is the reader, but the surprise is an aesthetic pleasure in the reality of Ann as a woman.

Donald Swann in this novel serves fairly obviously the function of presenting the point of view of that ideal world I have mentioned before in connection with the sermons of Everard or James; he also throws into relief Ann's possible *human* goodness, as opposed to goodness seen in terms of the imagined and distinctly perfect God. Miss Murdoch has given him depth by suggesting his 'love' for Ann, 'in a way which was the tiniest bit more than pastoral', which causes his wanting to 'break her down' to be morally ambiguous, and himself to occupy a more than symbolic space. What he says is to be taken seriously; this is made clear by the description of him, seen through Hugh's eyes. Physically, he is described with a gentle mockery, but Miss Murdoch adds:

> He had, with his rather smart black suit, and crisp dog-collar, a professional air of slightly self-conscious benevolence, a sort, as it were, of clinically compassionate stoop. Yet, and this too Hugh had had occasion to remark, although the context for thinking him an ass was almost completely there, the judgment could not quite be made: the elusive but indubitable light of intelligence flickering in that mild visage forbade any too casual dismissal of its owner.[31]

In the conversation immediately preceding the departure of Randall, the moral tone of the three, Hugh, Ann, Swann –

is set by a reference to the innocence of the young – Penn in particular, the Toby of this book – and whether they should be taught to hate Hitler. Ann, who has thought about it, does not know. Swann argues that only love has clear vision, and that 'there can be, even for Hitler, a sort of intelligent compassion . . . The young have escaped the terrible compulsion to hate which is our lot. They should be left uncorrupted and judged lucky.' Hugh argues robustly, 'As the world runs, evil soon makes tools out of those who don't hate it. Hatred is our best protection',[32] and one feels again the pull between the practical world, where it is not certain that Hugh's view does not produce the best results, and the ideal world, where it may just be possible to purge inherent violence, but where, in practice, the attempt to love comes perilously near to fantasy. We are left with Ann's not-knowing again as a kind of touchstone of virtue.

In Ann's first conversation with Douglas it is he who puts forward, on the whole, Miss Murdoch's point of view. He pleads for 'love' which he says, here echoing Miss Murdoch in a passage I have already quoted, 'is a duty, and it is a matter much more genuinely subject to the will than is commonly supposed nowadays.[33]*

Ann, who has earlier felt that 'her long battle with Randall had seemed progressively to empty the certainties by which she lived, as if the real world were being quietly taken away grain by grain, and stored in some place of which she had no knowledge', now protests that her love for Randall is 'imperfect' and herself 'shapeless and awkward'. Douglas replies, stating neatly the positive side of Ann's goodness

> Shapeless and awkward. Precisely. We must not expect our lives to have a visible shape. They are invisibly shaped by God. Goodness accepts the contingent. Love accepts the contingent.

* I do not agree that only practical love can be commanded, and I cannot think why Kant, who attributes such majesty to the human soul, should hold that any aversion was strictly 'unconquerable'. Pathological love can be commanded too – indeed if love is a purification of the imagination, must be commanded. But the fact remains that the love which is not art inhabits the world of practice. (*The Sublime and the Good*, p. 55.)

Nothing is more fatal to love than to want everything to have form.[34]

Ann states that Randall needs form because he is an artist. 'He is a man before he is an artist,' said Douglas with magisterial severity. This is what we feel: this is, like James Tayper Pace's pronouncements, a judgment – Ann's real charity, real 'agnostic' love, become apparent when her answer to this judgment is to feel 'that she could not stand much more of this discussion. She hated this sense of their cornering Randall.' I say, 'agnostic' in the sense in which Miss Murdoch uses it, in the *Yale Review* article, to define the quality of the great novelist.

> The man I have in mind, faced by the manifold of humanity, may feel, as well as terror, delight, but not, if he really sees what is before him, superiority. He will suffer that undramatic, because un-self-centred, agnosticism which goes with tolerance.[35]

Ann will not 'corner' Randall, and this is better than to know why he is wrong.

Ann, unlike Maggie, does not finally and completely exercise power, nor does her unknowing lead to any obvious increase in understanding or love. She does not trap or master Randall, she does not entirely successfully refuse to know. Under pressure from Mildred and Emma Sands she is made to come out of her refuge of unknowing and to 'know' both that Randall has a mistress, who that mistress is, and that she herself and Felix Meecham are in love.

This is brought about by Mildred, who says 'You know that Felix is terribly in love with you?'. Ann reflects, along the lines of the Maggie-unconsciousness

> Mildred had led up to her moment of theatre, but she must be cheated of it and sent away empty. There must be no drama here, no possible foothold for the imagination. What Mildred was trying to conjure up must be made nonsense of, must be made not to exist. The thing must be laughed off briskly, Mildred must be clapped on the shoulder and taken to her coffee. There must be no admission of knowledge or

interest, no confused looks, nothing. Again it was no and nothing.

'Yes,' said Ann.[36]

Footholds for the imagination are what Randall craves and says that Ann destroys; but from this moment of admission she struggles in an unfamiliar world of consciousness and potential freedom, which centres around her love for Felix. Randall's removal, after Hugh's 'crime', upsets her pattern further; she has had 'a total grasp of his existence which was perhaps, after all, love',[37] but now she feels both jealous and more consciously passionate towards him. Here – although in this book Miss Murdoch seems to set a higher value on the lack of reflection in her unknowingness – her state parallels that of Nan in *The Sandcastle*, who feels, with the same shock of losing her husband, the same withdrawal of the pressure of the normal, of 'reality', the same new need to reflect where before 'her normal existence had not demanded, had even excluded, reflection'.

When discussing *The Sandcastle* I suggested that Nan was in a state of *mauvaise foi*, and that 'It is in terms of a dispersal of this gluey inertness that Sartre pictures freedom.' Miss Murdoch, in the Sartre book, describing the modern sense that

> meaning and purpose do not reside as objective facts in the world of things ... that personality is not a substance with which we are endowed by nature, but an inward integration which may be achieved only by decisive choice of oneself (Sartre).

comments, quoting Wittgenstein 'in the world everything is as it is and happens as it does happen. *In* it there is no value', that

> when purposes and values are knit comfortably into the great and small practical activities of life, thought and emotion move together. When this is no longer so, when action involves choosing between worlds, not moving in a world, loving and valuing, which were once the rhythm of our lives become problems. Emotions which were the aura of what we

treasured when what we treasured was what we unreflectively did, now glow feverishly like distant *feux follets*, or have the imminent glare of a volcanic threat.[38]

Ann, as a result of Hugh's 'crime', is thrown into precisely this stage of 'choosing between worlds' and, faced with the possible 'freedom' involved in loving Felix (a situation which does not confront Maggie's virtue), she finds herself in a position where her old emotions indeed 'glow feverishly like distant *feux follets*'.

For the fact was, that, keeping pace demonically with her love for Felix, there had developed in her a dark new passion for Randall. It was as if one were the infernal mirror image of the other ... Being in love with Randall in this way was something entirely painful with a brutality of its own ... It was quite unlike her old romantic love for the young Randall, or her steady married love for her husband. She was not sure indeed how she recognized it as love at all. It was a kind of mutual haunting.[39]

She is faced in fact by a kind of choice, a kind of act of will, which Sartre would approve, but which is quite alien to her way of life or love, and she finds it daunting. During her second moral conversation with Swann, concerning the nature of the marriage bond, Swann tells her that she must continue to love Randall, that 'If you can love him *now* and keep him in your heart that will be a joy that is better than happiness', and when Ann says, 'I don't know what I'm like any more. I feel now I've lived all my life in a state of unconsciousness', he tells her explicitly, 'Being good is a state of unconsciousness.'[40]

But Ann reflects that 'what she had to do with now was consciousness' and thinks further 'His words which in him were good words, were at her side of the picture temptation, almost corruption. Whatever she could do for Randall, she could not do *that*. A saint might do it, but she could not. She could not thus hold him; and as she imagined this "holding" she saw it almost as vindictive, revengeful, something to do with death.'

This prefigures one side of the myth of *The Unicorn*, in that Hannah's suffering and 'holding' might also be seen as a revenge; it also looks back to Hugh's act in abandoning Emma for his marriage – a saint's act, an act he feels 'too high' for him. Ann allows herself to wish for 'freedom' in Sartre's sense, even partially in Randall's sense, and to feel value in setting Randall free from her own negative power. She sees things with 'a sort of realism which she still hesitated to dignify with the name of truth'.[41]

But like Hugh, inexplicably, although wanting it, she does not break free. This is partly owing to the action of the predatory and powerful-willed Miranda; partly to the fact that both she and Felix, who is an officer and a gentleman, are bound by convention, and cannot in the last resort make movements of the will. Ann cannot love Felix because she wants him; a problem which recurs in Miss Murdoch's work – clearly it is good to renounce the self, to 'crucify our own selfish desires', but at what point does this become fantasy, retreat, a refusal to inhabit our own universe, our own reality? The problem recurs in *The Unicorn*; here, as in life, it is posed but not answered. Felix feels that there is something wrong in Ann's renunciation of himself.

> That he should be almost mechanically renounced with the renunciation of her own will seemed to him too cruel. He was to be destroyed, with her, by the sheer overbrimming existence of the absent Randall.[42]

(It is interesting in this context that the much more forceful Mildred feels much the same about Hugh; once she sees that to advise him to keep the Tintoretto would serve her own ends, she cannot do it; a curious moral truth which is both unexpected and real in the novel.) And Felix, although Ann is pleading with him silently to exert the necessary violence, cannot do it – here he is to be likened to Effingham, who, like him, hears and ignores a silent cry for help from his imprisoned lady.

At the end of the book Ann returns to a state of unconsciousness – a state not certainly morally preferable to love for Felix, to 'what was rational and beautiful and free',[43] but a state to which 'her whole life had compelled her'.[44]

She does not think that she has been moved by duty, or by selfish desire; she is less certain that she has not been moved by Miranda, but when she finds in the bonfire the pieces of torn photographs which are the evidence that Miranda has done what she has done out of love for Felix, she feels, and Miss Murdoch convinces us that she feels, no resentment. There is a real uncertainty about Ann's final state which does successfully echo the incompleteness, the lack of clarity, of understanding, of moral and spiritual certainty that one feels about life in the world as we meet it. It is not certain that in the strict, judged sense presented by Swann Ann is *good;* it is made abundantly clear that the feeling for Randall – even Miranda – which causes the act is 'more like some unrealistic haze of sentiment than the heavenly love desiderated by Douglas Swann'.[45] But Ann clearly *is*, even if her acts have been stolen from her by Miranda. Her reality is directly opposed to the 'inward integration which may be achieved only by decisive choice of oneself'. If she is not free to know and love Felix, she is abundantly aware of the transcendence of reality.

She cannot make, to quote John Bayley, 'acts of visibly analytic consciousness'.[46] 'She was not framed for recognizing, let alone grasping, her own felicity.' She does not try to understand. 'Felix would never understand either. But to be understood is not a human right. Even to understand oneself is not a human right.' She thinks of dead Fanny and dead Steve, and ends on a note Miss Murdoch's whole concept of reality goes along with.

> She had not known them. She did not know herself. It was not possible, it was not necessary, it was perhaps not even proper. Real compassion is agnosticism; and we must be compassionate to ourselves too. Tasks lay ahead, one after one, and the gradual return to an old simplicity. She would never know, and that would be her way of surviving.[47]

Between Randall's simple 'freedom' and Ann's complete lack

of it in any corresponding sense, there is the story of Hugh, like a variation on a theme, and perhaps as a pendent, to point the way in which Miss Murdoch has complicated the main issues, it is worth looking at him. There are also Penn and Miranda, whose situations I do not propose to examine at any length. They are, clearly, the young versions of predator and hunted animal – or, in another sense, neurotic and conventional. Penn at moments of crisis haunts Ann as Nina and Miss Foy, those other innocent victims, haunted Rosa. Their extreme first passions, Penn's love for Miranda, Miranda's for Felix, serve to throw into relief how embedded in life and history are the problems of their elders; the adolescent is, in Miss Murdoch's thought, 'the centre of an extreme decision', as she says of Sartre, as the historical individual with a life behind him cannot entirely be. Miranda I find unconvincing – fantastic and even chi-chi, with no depth to make these qualities, which undoubtedly exist in life, interesting or important. The shock revelation of her love for Felix – a moment which should be analogous to the very real and dramatically entirely successful shock of the revelation of Catherine's love for Michael Meade – falls, I am not quite sure why, quite flat. Penn is better; the innocence and freedom of his sense of his Australian nationality, corrupted by the English-novel Englishness of the setting, are good; socially, he enlarges one's concept of freedom by disliking even Ann for not treating the servants as equals; physically, his dream of a free Australia opens up spaces out of the English greenness, wetness and rose gardens which are like Hugh's and Mildred's projected voyage to the East. And the death of his imagined freedom under the power and violence of his love for Miranda is a real death which matters.

For a time the myth of his past seemed dead, the great image of the new free man, in the appallingly ancient land. They were far off now, the drooping myalls and the lordly kurrajongs and the crimson quondongs and the spotted leopard trees. The huge coloured country might have been a dream; and Penn apprehended with alarm a sort of failure within

160

him for the first time of his sense of nationality. It was no use, in the crisis which faced him, being, even, an Australian.[48]

Connected mainly with Penn and Miranda too, is the German dagger – a 'planted' symbol of Miss Murdoch's less impressive kind, like the samurai sword of *A Severed Head;* given by Felix to Steve, and passing through Ann's agency into Penn's possession, desired by Miranda, it bears with it in an artificial way the rash violence, the savagery, which is suggested in the conversation I have quoted about hating Hitler, and impinges really upon Penn in the scene where he attempts to return it to Miranda.

Miss Murdoch believes that violence is a power, an inescapable power in the world, but her moments of open violence are often artificial and mechanically symbolic; she is better at the muffled spiritual violence of the intellectual civilized world. There is something amateurish, something contrived, about Penn and Miranda.

Although, if one stops to think about Penn in his innocence loving the toy soldiers, the gentle Felix, developing from a boy who lived in 'a world of knives and ropes and things' into an officer and gentleman exercising a violent profession and bringing back the dagger as a trophy, compelling Miranda's love, the thing has a non-immediate complexity which puts it into the world of real and necessary savagery of *The Flight from the Enchanter,* and not that of *A Severed Head* (which is entirely intellectually contrived), a world again occupied with Hitler, where Nina's dream of a free Australia, like Penn's memory of it, is myth.

However, this point does not need expanding; let us return to Hugh, who, burdened neither with Randall's theoretical freedom nor Ann's slightly exalted virtue of not knowing, survives sheerly by virtue of taking life as it comes, and opens and closes the book. Hugh's position with regard to morals and freedom is half-way between those of Randall and Ann; like both of them he has been offered his moment to break loose from his 'normal' marriage and to choose a compelling love. Like Ann he rejects his 'freedom' for no very apparent reason, but he is able to tell both Emma and Randall, whose imagination has been at work on his father's past choices, that on the whole he regrets it. It is worth pointing out here that whilst the marriage Ann saves by her act of rejection is something which requires an act of faith to give it any reality, Hugh's marriage has been 'real' enough, worth saving, although Hugh cannot – as in life we cannot – see it usually, or with deep conviction in this way.

> No great store of spiritual energy had been liberated by his sacrifice; and his action, too high doubtless for any context he could sustain for it, appeared to have had merely a destructive effect. He had passed years in a resentment against his wife which had gradually deadened his tenderness into pity and his pity into a dull resigned companionship. Their marriage had become a hollow frame. It was for this solid but echoing framework, its painted exterior so bravely held up to the world, that he had given up the peril of a great love.[49]

This is what we are told of Hugh's thoughts during the funeral of his wife; at the end of the book, having attempted to remake the past and failed, Hugh can treat the idea of Fanny with a less demanding respect. He thinks of Emma, and that 'after all he had doubtless in the old days turned her down for some good reasons', and of Fanny, not as a resented wife, but as an individual.

> Poor Fanny! She had had, like Ann, her simplicities. He had indeed sometimes thought of her as a miniature Ann. Yet why miniature? Ann was not so large after all, nor Fanny so small. Fanny had had her life, she had been something ... It was as if at the end he had recognized in her a dignity she had had all along, but had kept humbly lowered, like a dipped flag or a crumpled crest. He was glad, after all, that he had stayed with her. He was glad that he had been good to her.[50]

The situation, of course, is not as simple as this; it is clear, for instance, that Emma has suffered and paid for Hugh's act – although not sufficiently clear since Emma is never fully realized. It is also clear that Hugh's 'crime' in selling the Tintoretto is not of the same order as Randall's 'crime' in leaving Ann. Mildred refers to it as 'violence' – 'a vicarious violence, a symbolic redemption of the past', but as Miss Murdoch remarks in connection with Penn's battle with Miranda, 'Between imagined violence and real violence there is a dimension of difference.'[51] And Hugh's violence is vicarious and, in this sense, imagined. This brings us back to the Tintoretto, for which Hugh thinks he may have married Fanny.

> Perhaps indeed he had married her for the Tintoretto, as in a curious muddled way it had sometimes seemed to him in his dreams when his poor wife and the picture became strangely identified with each other.[52]

Mildred, however, thinks of the picture that

> It was a picture which might well enslave a man, a picture round which crimes might be committed ... Fanny had wanted to sell it. Small Fanny had feared it perhaps: Hugh's golden dream of another world.[53]

Here it is clear that the picture is, as I said earlier, like Dora's vision in the National Gallery, the place where perfection and reality meet; Hugh wishes (like Randall) his marriage to have the beauty and necessity of the picture. But marriages are not like pictures, and art – like the contemplative life – is 'another world' where reality and apprehensible form coexist. Thus curiously, although Randall makes his father sell his 'golden dream' to further his own escape into the world of form, and loses his own vision of perfection and reality thereby (in the roses), Hugh, after his moment of imagined violence, is enabled to see reality more clearly for what it is; to respect Fanny not merged in the Tintoretto, to let the 'necessity' of his love for Emma go, to inhabit the world which is not consoled by form. He 'could now be demure with an untroubled heart. This crime squared him with the tipsy gods.' He leaves, with Mildred, for India. He too, with less resignation and suffering, with less self-effacement, and I would tentatively suggest with less fantasy mixed in with it – survives by virtue of not knowing, of recognizing and accepting the inscrutable nature of reality.

> Ann had forgotten the real Randall. Randall had forgotten the real Ann, probably by now. Hugh had rejected Emma for reasons and forgotten the reasons. His consciousness was a tenuous and dim receptacle and it would soon be extinct. But meanwhile there was now, the wind and starry night, and the great erasing sea ... Perhaps he had been confused, perhaps he had understood nothing, but he had certainly survived. He was free.[54]

This presentation, in Ann and Hugh, of the limitations of our attempts to understand what we have done or are doing, of the movement of our consciousness, not from blindness to enlightenment, but as it were, shuttling in and out of endless pathways, necessarily patient, is something achieved in this novel, something in precisely this form, new and exciting, however cramped in its action by the artiness or crystalline qualities of the rest of the story. It has – like much larger parts of *The Bell* – that quality which Miss Murdoch feels that we have lost since the great nineteenth-century novelists wrote, that respect for people as they are.

8

THE UNICORN

> There is a temptation for any novelist, and one to which if I
> am right modern novelists yield too readily, to imagine that
> the problem of a novel is solved and the difficulties overcome
> as soon as a form in the sense of a satisfactory myth has been
> evolved.[1]

THIS IS FROM the end of the *Yale Review* article; Miss
Murdoch's progress, which, from *Under the Net* to *The Bell*,
could be seen as a progressive moving away from fantasy
myth to naturalism and thickness of life, seems, in the four
novels which end with *The Unicorn*, to alternate between a
painstaking attempt at naturalistic complexity and an almost
joyful release into the more formal, more conceptual framework of myth – not fantastic now, in the light sense in which
Under the Net and *The Flight from the Enchanter* were
fantastic, but deliberate and rapid. *The Unicorn*, whilst it
retains many of the basic themes of *An Unofficial Rose*,
and re-introduces the problem of the religious contemplative,
which has been quiescent since *The Bell*, has the Freudian
mythical framework of *A Severed Head*, and in quite a different context, some of the bareness, the unashamedly contrived
necessity of that book. It is a good point at which to end
this study of Iris Murdoch's novels, if only because the problems of freedom or lack of it are here most starkly seen. I do
not wish here to attempt a judgment between the crystalline
and the 'real' novel; Miss Murdoch seems to me to be right
when she states in *Against Dryness* that most of the more

serious and better works of fiction written nowadays are crystalline, and, whilst it is clearly fair and accurate of the critics to point out that this book, seen as a novel, has a thinness, a lack of interesting life in the characters, these comments serve as much to point the real need we seem to feel for a novel that *has* life in the old sense, as to dismiss the myth we have, which has surely a right to stand or fall as a myth. And I do not propose to criticize the characters here, as one could legitimately criticize Randall, for being two-dimensional. They are occasionally boring, which is another matter, and more serious. But to say that the form is a lesser form than the solid novel is to open a large question outside the scope of an expository work of this kind: I think it is, and I think that this opens up an interesting train of thought about why it is necessary to write allegorical myth when it comes to dealing with metaphysical issues. It is easy to provide, from Miss Murdoch's own statements both in her critical writings and from within the novels themselves, including this one, sticks to beat her with. But the myth here I find coherent, and interesting, and illuminating as far as Miss Murdoch's own world goes, and I propose to discuss it in these terms.

Miss Murdoch herself has likened this book to the works of Sheridan Le Fanu, with which it has more in common than merely the Anglo-Irish background, or even the conventional framework of the mystery story, which takes its characters step by imperceptible step away from a carefully placed background of normality into a world of necessity and physical intractability (doors that will not open, seas that automatically kill) which are both part of the romantic 'myth' and acknowledgments of Miss Murdoch's sense of the finally irreducible reality which we cannot absorb or conquer.

This idea of physical necessity is also prominent in the work of Simone Weil, whose influence on Miss Murdoch's thought is particularly apparent in *The Unicorn*. She regards the 'mechanical' action of nature, for which she uses the law of gravity as a primary example, simply as *reality*, without the added supernatural 'light' of grace.

Tout ce que nous nommons le mal n'est que ce mécanisme.
Dieu a fait en sorte que sa grâce, quand elle pénètre au centre
même d'un homme, et de là illumine tout son être, lui permet,
sans violer les lois de la nature, de marcher sur les eaux. Mais
quand un homme se détourne de Dieu, il se livre à la pesanteur. Il croit ensuite vouloir et choisir, mais il n'est qu'une
chose, une pierre qui tombe. Si l'on regarde de près, d'un
regard vraiment attentif, les âmes et les sociétés humaines, on
voit que partout où la vertu de la lumière surnaturelle est
absente, tout obéit à des lois mécaniques aussi aveugles et
aussi précises que les lois de la chute des corps.[2]

Simone Weil, who has a naturally and fanatically religious
temperament, sees this necessity as in fact obedience to the
will of God, and thus both beautiful and to be loved.

Ce qui semblait nécéssite devient obéissance. La matière est
entière passivité et par suite entière obéissance à la volonté
de Dieu ... Dans la beauté du monde la nécessité du monde
devient objet d'amour. Rien n'est beau comme la pesanteur
dans les plis fugitifs des ondulations de la mer, ou les plis
presque éternels des montagnes.[3]

But if there are elements of this love of necessity, or obedience, present in Miss Murdoch's landscape, there are others
also – the landscape has a 'mythical' quality, a kind of
Romantic necessity, as I said earlier, a lack of messiness or
'give', which is something Miss Murdoch suspects. The use
of the landscape in this book in general is very powerful; it
is related both to our sense of that which is not human and
thus mysterious, and to the uncompromising, again, non-
messy, nature of the spiritual events which take place. And
on this level, Hannah's ambiguous passivity parallels the
ambiguity I have seen in Miss Murdoch's attitude to the
unusually intractable landscape.

The framework of the plot, too, would have pleased Le
Fanu; the story begins innocently enough with a governess
who comes to a remote part of a country which, although it
is not named, sufficiently resembles Ireland, in order, she
supposes, to teach the children at a decaying nineteenth-

century house or castle, and ends, after she has discovered
that there are no children, after two violent deaths and the
breaking of the decree which imprisons the lady of the house
in her own grounds, with three corpses, one of them muti-
lated in some indescribable way, covered with sheets and
dripping sea water in the lace-curtained drawing-room. It
would also, to a certain extent, no doubt, please V. S. Pritchett who, in his preface to Le Fanu's collection of stories *In a
Glass Darkly*, writes that with Le Fanu

> we progress ... not into fog or vagueness, not into a labori-
> ously created 'atmosphere' but into clearer and clearer par-
> ticularity. The sun shines more brightly, detail is more
> luminous, exact and terrible in its glitter, as the dread moves
> to its culmination.[4]

Miss Murdoch's story, intellectually as well as physically,
has this ambiguous clarity and definition; we always know
where we are, as well as what it is about; it is only not clear
what it *means*. But what is behind Miss Murdoch's horror
and haunting is also what V. S. Pritchett says is behind Le
Fanu's.

> Anglo-Irish society [he says], the most charming in the British
> Isles, was a guilty society. Insecurity and bad memories haun-
> ted it. Le Fanu's ghosts are the most disquieting of all ghosts:
> the ghosts that can be traced, blobs of the unconscious that
> have floated up to the surface of the mind. They are not
> irresponsible and perambulatory figments of family history.
> And the evil of the justified ghosts is not involuntary or
> extravagant. In Le Fanu, we are frightened at the sight of
> effect following cause; we get a glimpse of the iron of nature.
> Guilt is the ghost in Le Fanu. It is guilt that patters two-
> legged behind its victims in the street ... The secret doubt, the
> private shame, the unholy love, scratch away with malignant
> patience in the guarded mind. It is we who are the ghosts.
> Let illness, late nights and green tea weaken the catch we
> normally keep clamped so firmly down, and out slink all the
> hags and animals of moral or Freudian symbolism ... Self-
> destruction is the end of these stories; our guilt drives us to
> kill ourselves.[5]

Miss Murdoch introduces no hags or animals, no ghosts indeed, although the unnatural shading into the supernatural is sufficiently present. But guilt, and its relation to Freudian and Christian morality, allied to the idea of effect following cause, the 'iron of nature', which resembles the insistence in *A Severed Head* that we must not 'let people off', are clearly and very self-consciously central to the story. The difference is that Miss Murdoch's manipulation of the human beings involved against the 'iron of nature' involved is allegorical, whereas Le Fanu's is humanly mysterious. Not since *Under the Net* has there been so much philosophical talk, and if the 'real' nature of Hannah's predicament, suffering and relation with the other characters remains, as I think it does, ultimately mysterious, ultimately ambiguous, a fierce intellectual glare beats on all its aspects, which refers us again to Sartre or the modern fantasy builders rather than to Le Fanu.

Thus, here, 'what is it about?' is a relevant question. To answer it requires a summary of the plot to which we can refer back.

At the beginning of the book, Marian Taylor, the governess, arrives at Gaze Castle. The opening dialogue is masterly; so is the description of the landscape, which is called 'appalling' 'God-forsaken' (by Scottow) 'sublime' (also by Scottow, who tells Marian that he, as an inhabitant of the country, is 'too used' to it). This reminds one of Miss Murdoch's interest in Kant's theory of the sublime, and of what she thinks it ought to mean – it is 'an apprehension of the vast formless strength of the natural world' or 'a realization of a vast and varied reality outside ourselves which brings about a sense initially of terror and when properly understood, of exhilaration and spiritual power . . . and reminds us, to use Kant's words, of our supersensible destiny'.[6]

But this landscape – bog, cliffs, inky sea, lack of vegetation, the dolmen, 'a weird lop-sided structure, seemingly pointless, yet dreadfully significant', is hostile and remains terrible; Marian tries to swim in the sea later, but cannot – it is a 'sea that kills' – and if we remember what swimming means in terms of *The Bell*, or even of *Under the Net*, we know what it is that we have to deal with. Thus, the action takes place in a landscape symbolic indeed of 'our super-sensible destiny', but intractable and incomprehensible.

Marian finds that there are no children; she is to be 'companion' to the lady of the house, Hannah Crean-Smith, who is both beautiful and 'something very slightly unkempt, the hair tousled, the finger-nails not quite clean, the lovely face a little tired, a little sallow and greasy, like that of a person long ill'.[7] Marian feels an instinctive revulsion, which she later forgets, and that 'this person was harmless', an opinion she has later cause to revise.

This lady's story is gradually unfolded: married to her first cousin, who mistreats her and has a homosexual relationship with Gerald Scottow, she has committed adultery with Pip Lejour, son of Max Lejour, a Platonic scholar who is the head of the other household in the book, at Riders. Betrayed by Scottow, she has been 'dreadfully' punished by her husband; at one stage, having run away to the cliff edge, she has had an undefined struggle with him, during which he fell, but did not die. Her husband is in New York; she herself is confined to the house and grounds and apparently is under some compulsion to remain there. She is surrounded by those who 'love her'; her relations, the Evercreeches, Marian, Denis Nolan, the servant, Pip, who watches the house with binoculars, Effingham Cooper, the Lejours' visitor, who loves her with a kind of Platonic courtly love. The 'curse' is apparently to last seven years, which are almost out. Effingham and Marian, the two 'normal' human beings of the book, attempt to make her take her freedom by force; they are foiled by one of Miss Murdoch's apparent mechanical 'accidents' and Effingham in his distress is nearly drowned in the bog.

After this, Gerald, who is the wielder of power in this story, announces that the husband is to return from New York. All are appalled; all, in some sense, 'fail' Hannah, who is left to Gerald, who announces that he will himself 'rescue' her and apparently seduces her. At this stage, all the other attendant characters (except the Evercreeches, who are of Hannah's blood) feel that their freedom has been in some way restored to them, and form new relationships; Marian with Denis, Effingham with Alice Lejour; relationships which, however, do not survive Gerald's announcement that Hannah is not, after all, leaving.

After this, Hannah shoots Gerald with a shot-gun left by Pip, after the latter has unsuccessfully pleaded with her to go away with him. The husband, returning at last, is drowned by the good Denis, who has decided that evil must be fought with evil. In the interim, Marian has released Hannah, who is at last trying to leave her room, and Hannah has run over the cliff to her death. The house is left to Max Lejour, the Evercreeches are dispossessed, Denis goes away into the land, and Effingham and Marian return to real life.

I have already said that the book can in some sense be called allegorical; the best way I can think of to approach its meaning is to separate out strands of ideas, which is to a certain extent to do violence to it, since many of these ideas act at the same time and weigh equally. One thing does seem to me to need to be stated at the outset as well as at the end; we are dealing here, as in *The Bell*, with the spiritual values which pertain in the world of the half-contemplative, the sublunary world where perfection and reality do not automatically coincide and are not automatically apprehensible; if God is present in this book, the contemplative life, as an ideal, is merely juxtaposed with the events of the story, as the Abbey in *The Bell* was juxtaposed with the community. Effingham, at the end, sees the events as 'a fantasy of the spiritual life, a story, a tragedy', and the comment is made that 'the spiritual life has no story and is not tragic'. And in Marian's conversation with Denis (who believes that Hannah is good and that her confinement is related to the contemplative life) there is again the contrast between the true, the voluntary contemplative, and those who are forced into it initially by other needs or other pressures.

Marian says, 'I just can't imagine it. Staying so long in one small place. I'm surprised she hasn't run mad.'

'There are holy nuns in the convent at Blackport who live forever in smaller places.'

'But they have faith.'

'Perhaps Mrs. Crean-Smith has faith.'

'Yes, but she's wrong . . . It's morbid. And it's bad for him as well as for her.'[8]

Marian's cry is not the final comment, of course, on Hannah's spiritual state, but it is to be taken into account; it is at that stage of the action an 'uncorrupted' vision; and the idealized holy nuns must be supposed to represent that 'spiritual life which has no story and is not tragic' by contrast. Hannah has two obvious predecessors in Miss Murdoch's novels; Catherine Fawley in *The Bell*, driven to a contemplative life initially by other people's passions, and held there by her own sense of guilt and the community's need to see her as its pure centre, and Ann in *An Unofficial Rose*, with her passive acceptance of limitations, of waiting for the absent Randall, Ann whose goodness is partly ambiguous, who was, like Hannah, 'married in a church' and whose action may have been 'bad for him', for Randall, as Hannah's for Peter.

But before coming to the study of the good and evil involved in half-contemplation, it seems tidy to expose the 'simple' Freudian sub-structure of the myth. Effingham is the only character in the book who seems aware of Freud. He admires the Platonist Max – 'Max's oblivion of everything to do with Freud was one of the things that made Effingham love him'[9] – and his vision, when he is sinking in the bog, of the 'quite automatic' universal love which comes with the death of the self, brings him to cry to Hannah, 'It's not a bit like what Freud and Wagner think.'[10] But when Hannah betrays herself with Gerald, Effingham produces, like an incantation against his own failure to protect her, a Freudian explanation of his actions (which he dare not face telling Max). His courtly love, which the Platonist Max sees quite differently, has depended on Hannah's chastity.

The sin which Hannah was, through her own sinless suffering, redeeming for him, had been the sin of his own mother's betrayal of him with his own father . . . Because of his unconscious resentment of his own mother's sin of sex he had been, he explained, unable to establish any satisfactory relations with women other than those of Courtly Love. He would identify the woman he loved with his mother and then make her unapproachable and holy.[11]

Put like this, the whole set of concepts is allowed to seem over-simple, slightly ridiculous; Effingham here clearly has much in common with the initially paralysed, imprisoned Martin Lynch-Gibbon, who also suffered from an inability to treat women as anything other than mother or inferior (Effingham's relation with Marian has things in common with Martin's with Georgie). But, not made explicit in this way, and therefore working more thoroughly in the story, is what would be Freud's 'explanation' of Hannah Crean-Smith's own conduct. I cannot produce – as I suspect Miss Murdoch could – a case history of Hannah in purely Freudian terms. But I can try to indicate the lines along which such a history might proceed.

It might be maintained that a case of hysteria is a caricature of a work of art, that an obsessional neurosis is a caricature of a religion, and that a paranoic delusion is a caricature of a philosophical system.[12]

Freud makes this remark, paralleled in many places elsewhere in his work, at the end of the section of *Totem and Taboo* entitled *Taboo and Emotional Ambivalence*. There are pointers enough in *The Unicorn* for it to be certain that Hannah's passive suffering, her religion of guilt and withdrawal, can be seen, not as a 'real' religious act, but as an obsessional neurotic fantasy. Although what Miss Murdoch is studying here is partly the ways in which the one might shade into, or partake of, the other, so that to know what is 'real' in this area at all becomes almost impossible. But neurosis, Miss Murdoch has reiterated often enough, is one of the 'enemies of love' and the terms in which Freud continues his comparison of obsessional neurosis and religion are close enough to Miss Murdoch's own.

> The asocial nature of neuroses has its genetic origin in their most fundamental purpose, which is to take flight from an unsatisfying reality into a more pleasurable world of phantasy. The real world, which is avoided in this way by neurotics, is under the sway of human society and of the institutions collectively created by it. To turn away from reality is at the same time to withdraw from the community of man.[13]

There is clearly something which corresponds to Hannah's situation in Freud's description of obsessional prohibitions in neurotic patients.

> Having made their appearance at some unspecified moment, they are forcibly maintained by an irresistible fear. No external threat of punishment is required, for there is an internal certainty, a moral conviction, that any violation will lead to intolerable disaster. The most that an obsessional patient can say on this point is that he has an undefined feeling that some particular person in his environment will be injured as a result of the violation . . . [14]

> Obsessional prohibitions are extremely liable to displacement. They extend from one object to another along whatever paths the context may provide, and the new object then becomes, to use the apt expression of one of my patients 'impossible' – till at last the whole world lies under an embargo of impossibility.[15]

In the case of the first of these quotations it is clear that, although Peter Crean-Smith and Scottow represent 'an external threat of punishment' to a certain extent, Hannah is by now involved in feeling that she herself *must*, of her own will, stay within her own grounds or disaster will ensue. In the case of the second, it is apparent that Hannah, confined first to the domain, then to the garden, finally to her own room, is gradually putting the whole world under an embargo.

Freud also remarks, in the case of the Rat Man, that 'a relationship between love and hatred . . . is among the most

174

frequent, the most marked, and probably therefore the most important characteristics of obsessional neurosis'.[16] The result of the opposition and binding together of intense love and intense hatred in a neurotic is bound to be, he continues, 'a partial paralysis of the will and an incapacity for coming to a decision upon any of those actions for which love ought to provide the motive power . . . and gradually extends itself over the entire field of the patient's behaviour'.[17]

Again, Hannah exhibits symptoms which could be interpreted as showing this paralysis, this incapacity for love. Early in the book, she tells Effingham, 'Oh, I don't *feel* much any more, except about very immediate matters – what's for dinner, and Denis's fish and so on . . .'[18] which was a virtue in the case of Maggie and Ann, but here is ambiguous, surely; after her surrender to Gerald she tells Marian that 'I had no feelings, I was empty . . . I had no real suffering'.[19]

But if Hannah can be seen as suffering from the paralysis that results from the combination and opposition of love and hatred, what are the particular springs of her action? Her relationship to her husband is mysterious; they are first cousins in a very close Irish family, which brings with it at least a hint of the incest theme which has interested Miss Murdoch earlier, and if this is accepted, a reiteration of a situation which has recurred in various Protean forms throughout her work. Catherine, Hannah's nearest parallel, has had a relationship of 'Byronic passion' with her brother; attempting to retreat into the contemplative life, she becomes mentally ill, and obsessed with that brother's homosexual lover, Michael Meade. More remotely, Martin Lynch-Gibbon, who admits to slight homosexual feelings for that enslaver and liberator, Palmer Anderson, is irresistibly involved in a passionate relationship with Palmer's incestuously loved sister, Honor Klein, who is taboo, as Hannah is taboo. More remotely still, Hunter and Rosa, the brother and sister who figuratively share one skin, are somehow manipulated and enslaved by the powerful pair, Mischa Fox and Calvin Blick, the relationship between whom resembles, now Peter and Gerald, now Gerald and Jamesie Evercreech, who shares

Calvin's passion for trapping people with photographs. Hunter dreams of a loved figure who is indistinguishably Rosa and Mischa, as Martin dreams of Palmer and Honor until the two figures become one. I mention all this because the complex of brother, sister and homosexual outsider seems to carry in Miss Murdoch's work an emotional weight not always easy to grasp, or realize the power of – as I can't here. But in so far as Hannah is to be seen as an obsessional neurotic, the repressed feelings of love and hate which she ultimately can be seen to extend to all the community, and which paralyse her, are clearly involved in the relationship between the three of them – Gerald, Peter, herself – with Pip Lejour an unforeseen and ultimately helpless outsider.

> The obsessive acts [Freud says] are from one point of view evidence of remorse, efforts at expiation, and so on, whilst on the other hand they are at the same time substitutive acts to compensate the instinct for what has been prohibited. It is a law of neurotic illness that these obsessive acts fall more and more under the sway of the instinct and approach nearer and nearer to the activity which was originally prohibited.[20]

I do not know, in the case of Hannah, what was the activity that was originally prohibited – whether it was Pip or Peter or even Gerald, who was so ambiguously loved and hated, but it is anyway certain that, at the climax of the book, when Peter's return from New York is said to be imminent, Hannah breaks her long inaction to perform two violent acts; the first, her submission to Gerald Scottow, an act of a kind of love, and paralleling perhaps her earlier adultery which she is expiating – (she tells Marian 'I've always had, of course, a very special bond with Gerald, a mysterious bond'); the second, her killing Gerald, with Pip's shot-gun, which is certainly, if not only, the fulfilling of a death-wish towards him. Immediately before this incident, Denis tells Marian that Gerald has become Peter. 'He is no longer what keeps Peter away from her. Nothing keeps him off her now.' And her killing Gerald, after submitting to him, is, as it were, a successful repeat of her attempt to murder Peter. And Max's final judgment of her, although it cannot be seen only in this context, would square with Freud's.

> She could not really love the people she saw, she could not afford to, it would have made the limitations of her life too painful. She could not, for them, transform the idea of love into something manageable: it remained something destructive and fearful and she merely avoided it.[21]

But what Hannah's story has in common with a case history of an obsessional neurosis is not, even in Freudian terms, the whole of the story; she does not act alone, but is also acted upon, and her relationships with the other characters recall those of the king in Freud's description of the things which there are in common between primitive systems of taboo in kingship, and obsessional neurosis.

A ruler, Freud says, is isolated by his people, and is placed under taboo restrictions which are both to protect the people from contact with the magical power of the king, and to protect the king from outside danger.

> It need not be wondered at [he says] that a need was felt for isolating such dangerous persons as chiefs and priests from the rest of the community – to build a barrier around them that would make them inaccessible.[22]

He continues to explain the apparent paradox whereby a person whose power is infinite can be in need of protection by remarking that the primitive community never quite trusts its king to use his power for their benefit, and later, by remarking on the emotional ambivalence involved in 'excessive solicitude' or desire for protection. I have already discussed in terms of The Bell the ambiguous nature of the protective instinct in Miss Murdoch's world in any case; here, the wish of Hannah's 'lovers' to protect her is open to Freud's interpretation.

> It appears wherever, in addition to a predominant feeling of affection, there is also a contrary, but unconscious, current of hostility ... The hostility is then shouted down, as it were,

177

by an excessive intensification of the affection, which is expressed as solicitude and becomes compulsive, because it might otherwise be inadequate to perform its task of keeping the unconscious contrary current of feeling under repression . . . [23]

The resulting state of affairs in a primitive community is much the same as that at Gaze.

The sovereign in them exists only for the subjects . . . Worshipped as a god one day, he is killed as a criminal the next. But in this change of behaviour of the people there is nothing capricious or inconstant . . . If the king is their god he should also be their preserver; and if he will not preserve them, he must make room for another who will. So long, however, as he answers their expectations, there is no limit to the care which they take of him, and which they compel him to take of himself. A king of this sort lives hedged in by a ceremonious etiquette, a network of prohibitions and observances, of which the intention is not to contribute to his dignity, much less to his comfort, but to restrain him from conduct which, by disturbing the harmony of nature, might involve himself, his people and the universe in one common catastrophe. Far from adding to his comfort, these observances, by trammelling his every act, annihilate his freedom, and often render the very life, which it is their object to preserve, a burden and a sorrow to him.[24]

The parallels here, even if not exact ones, proliferate. Early, Denis tells Marian that Gaze is a prison, and the gaolers are 'Mr Scottow. Miss Evercréech. Jamesie. You. Me' and Effingham – ali of whom in different ways 'love' Hannah, and somehow – we must return to this in a different context – 'need' her suffering.

When Peter's return is forecast, Effingham feels that Hannah has power to keep the danger from him.

Hannah would make all well. She would swallow it all up, she would assimilate the evil news and make it not to be, she would suffer Peter internally as she had always done and there would no more be heard.[25]

But when this does not happen, when Hannah, through weakness or something else, violates the taboo by submitting to Gerald, both Effingham and Marian feel released from their allegiance to her, 'betray' her, and turn to Alice and Denis. As Freud says of the breaking of taboos: 'If one person succeeds in gratifying the repressed desire, the same desire is bound to be kindled in all the other members of the community'[26]; then it follows that sexual freedom is suddenly granted with Hannah's apparent departure from them – as perhaps the will to kill is released in Denis, and to a lesser extent in Marian and Jamesie, by Hannah's murder of Scottow.

Marian feels

> with her pity... almost a resentment against Hannah for having so entirely fascinated her. Then she thought again, I did not love her enough. Then she thought, she is gone into privacy, she is gone, and now we can all see each other again. She lifted her head and felt the giddy sense of her returning freedom.[27]

And Hannah, after the event, sees herself as a false God.

> The false God is a tyrant. Or rather he is a tyrannical dream and that is what I was. I have lived on my audience, on my worshippers, I have lived by their thoughts, by your thoughts – just as you have lived by what you thought were mine. And we have deceived each other.[28]

Freud says that 'some of the taboos laid upon barbarian kings remind one vividly of the restrictions imposed upon murderers', and Hannah, restricted to her house, like the primitive murderer, referred to by Violet as 'a murderous adulterous woman', has this quality too. And, in so far as Hannah is priestly ruler, surrounded by taboo restrictions and worship, Denis is her priest – this is made clear symbolically, in the scene where he cuts her hair, as in some communities only the priest could cut the king's hair, since only he could stand the contact with the taboo. And at the end, having murdered Peter, he goes away alone, her heir.

179

Marian had an eerie sense of it all beginning again, the whole
tangled business: the violence, the prison house, the guilt. It
all still existed. Yet Denis was taking it away with him. He
had wound it all inside himself and was taking it away.
Perhaps he was bringing it, for her, for the others, to an end.[29]

More precise parallels could be drawn between *Totem and
Taboo* and this book, but I hope I have made the general
pattern clear: Malcolm Bradbury, referring to *A Severed
Head* in his article on *Under the Net* compared that novel
to *Henderson the Rain King* in its interest in totemism and
taboo as a way of approaching the springs of human action,
and in some ways *The Unicorn* is closer to Bellow's book.
As Freud remarks, 'No one will be king because of the
danger', and this concept of suffering kingship could be
applied to Hannah and to Henderson, as well as, more obviously, to Christ. The unicorn is the type of Christ, as Max
Lejour points out, and, having suggested the ways in which
Hannah's religion, or religious function, could be seen as
neurotic manœuvres on the part of her or her worshippers,
it is now time to look at the more positive side of her doings.
If the 'love' and the 'suffering' involved in this action have
any positive value, of what nature are they?

I have thought that the two houses in the narrative –
Riders and Gaze Castle – are symbolically named, and stand
respectively for Platonic religion – Riders recalling the horses
of the *Phaedrus* – and Christian contemplation – Gaze sufficiently suggesting this – which is involved in the concepts
of guilt, sin and redemption; the division between the houses
is seen as something undesirable in the action, even, in the
flood, disastrous. The beautiful golden maids at Riders, and
the black maids at Gaze reinforce this allegorical feeling
about it, and it is at Riders that those are found who associate
Hannah's situation with aesthetic feelings, and with the joining of perfection and reality in beauty. Max is a pure Platonist; Pip Lejour, who loves and possesses Hannah, wished to
be an artist, a poet; Effingham loves Hannah because he finds
her situation 'somehow beautiful', and Max tells him that

beauty is a spiritual value. Alice is somehow outside this classification, I admit; she is concerned with nature and not with spiritual values at all; she and the seal are the only creatures who swim naturally in the sea, and she is a horticulturist – although she too has her own form of fantasy in her myth of hopeless love for Effingham, which depends on Effingham's Platonic hopeless love for Hannah.

Whereas at Gaze, there is Gerald, the avenger, 'the centre from which the furies came', Denis with his sense of the necessity of suffering, and his Christian sense of love as a power to overcome all, Violet Evercreech, with her Calvinist sense of sin and responsibility and all the imagery of the awaited bridegroom and the waited Day of Judgment. Those who express belief in the efficacy of Hannah's suffering are Max and Denis, and it is worth looking at their views of what is happening.

In obvious ways Max is a parallel to Hannah; a different kind of enclosed contemplative. It has always seemed to me likely that the scholar – particularly perhaps the philosopher, who is, as Dave Gellman was, as Max is, concerned with 'the central knot of being',[30] with 'ultimate things',[31] should be troubled by the problem of the half-contemplative. Effingham sees Max as 'a prisoner of books, age and ill-health', and speculates that Max might derive 'consolation from the spectacle, over there in the other house, of another captivity, a distorted mirror image of his own'.[32]

Max's statement about freedom is more extreme than Miss Murdoch's own pronouncements; she requires a concept of 'degrees of freedom' and asserts that freedom is the awareness of other people. Max, who has not gone to visit Hannah, has not attempted to study the individual she is, or to help her, says of freedom

> That rag freedom! Freedom may be a value in politics, but it's not a value in morals. Truth, yes. But not freedom. That's a flimsy idea, like happiness. In morals we are all prisoners but the name of our cure is not freedom.[33]

Max's view of Hannah's imprisonment is that she is 'our

image of the significance of suffering', that she is not Christ, but 'an ordinary guilty person' even if she feels no guilt – someone who is inevitably suffering because there was a crime – *whose* crime, with Max's view of the automatic transfer of suffering, does not particularly matter – but who may be the 'non-powerful' 'pure' being, who only suffers and does not attempt to pass the suffering on. Her significance for the others is then, for Peter, that she does not hate him or return the suffering to him, and for the others that she shows them that it is possible to suffer and neither to hate nor to damage others as a result of the suffering – that is, she does not make *them* suffer, although if they see her, and her suffering, and the guilt that causes it, as real forces (the 'iron of nature') they will suffer with her and in some way be purified.

This difficult idea of redemptive suffering derives clearly from the thought of Simone Weil, where it is the culmination of the idea of the transfer of evil which we have already seen at work in the uses of power in *The Flight from the Enchanter*, or the mixture of power in love in *The Bell*. She says:

Tout crime est un transfert du mal de celui qui agit sur celui qui subit. L'amour illégitime comme le meutre . . . Quand il y a transfert de mal, le mal n'est pas diminué, mais augmenté chez celui d'où il procède . . .

Alors où mettre le mal?

Il faut le transférer de la partie impure dans la partie pure de soi-même, le transmuant ainsi en souffrance pure. Le crime qu'on a en soi, il faut l'infliger à soi.[34]

And:

Le péché que nous avons en nous sort de nous et se propage au dehors en exerçant une contagion sous forme de péché. Ainsi, quand nous sommes irrités, notre entourage s'irrite. Ou encore, de supérieur à inférieur: la colère suscite la peur. Mais au contact d'un être parfaitement pur, il y a transmutation, et le péché devient souffrance. Telle est la fonction du juste d'Isaïe, de l'agneau de Dieu. Telle est la souffrance

rédemptrice. Toute la violence criminelle de l'Empire romain
s'est heurtée au Christ, et, en lui, est devenue pure souffrance.
Les êtres mauvais au contraire transforment la simple souffrance (par exemple la maladie) en péché.

Il s'ensuit peut-être que la douleur rédemptrice doit etre
d'origine sociale. Elle doit etre injustice, violence exercée par
des êtres humains.[35]

Simone Weil, then, sees the acceptance of injustice, the
acceptance of suffering, as an apprehension of reality, of a
kind – suffering simply *is*, and therefore we must pay attention to it. (Miss Murdoch in *Against Dryness* takes up
Simone Weil's word, attention, and emphasizes it. 'Simone
Weil said that morality was a matter of attention, not of will.
We need a new vocabulary of attention.')

L'esprit n'est forcé de croire à l'existence de rien. C'est pourquoi le seul organe du contact avec l'existence est l'acceptation, l'amour. C'est pourquoi beauté et realité sont
identiques. C'est pourquoi la joie et le sentiment de realité
sont identiques.[36]

Simone Weil's thought here, I would suggest, is our touchstone for the religious validity of Hannah's suffering –
although, as we shall see later, she was an acute and accurate
observer of states of suffering very different from the effective
redemptive suffering which Max at this stage ascribes to
Hannah. And from the last quotation it is clear that the
identity of beauty and reality in Simone Weil's thought, and
their relation to God, are related to Max's concept of these
things.

Effingham complains that Hannah does not love, although
she is made for love, and Max retorts

I think that must be what, in these last years, she has understood. If she were to give way to ordinary love in that situation she would be lost. The only being she can afford to love
now is God.[37]

God, Max defines Platonically, as the Good, that Good

which we have met before in the sermons of Everard and James Tayper Pace.

> The distant source of light, the unimaginable object of our desire. Our fallen nature knows only its name and its perfection. That is the idea which is vulgarized by existentialists and linguistic philosophers when they make good into a mere matter of personal choice. It cannot be defined, not because it is a function of our freedom, but because we do not know it.[38]

Leaving out for the moment the caveats that, in this chapter, so beautifully mix doubt with the assertions made, let us now turn from Max's view of Hannah's predicament to Denis's. Denis tells Marian that Hannah has 'claimed the act' of Peter's fall, and that 'there are acts which belong to people regardless of their will' (at moments like this it is sometimes very easy to feel that Miss Murdoch's language is so abstract that it is difficult to translate the ideas back into terms of any human action or relationship). And, whereas Max sees Hannah's suffering as a function of the transmission of Até, corrupting power, Denis sets it in Christian terms of sin.

> 'What is spiritual is unnatural. The soul under the burden of sin cannot flee. What is enacted here is enacted with all of us in one way or another. You cannot come between her and her suffering, it is too complicated, too precious.' And he says, 'She has found over these last years a great and deep peace of mind. As I think, she has made her peace with God'.[39]

Both Hannah and Denis share Max's vision of the creation divided from its creator, crying out for love, moved by desire towards God. Max tries to tell Effingham that desire of the true Good and possession of it are one – God is because I desire him – and Hannah, speaking of God, says, 'He desires our love so much, and a great desire for love can call love into being.' And, like Max, 'In a way, you can't love something that isn't there. I think, if you really love, then something *is* there. But I don't understand these things.'[40]

Again, this complex of ideas is present in Simone Weil, who

distinguishes sharply between the mechanical and random necessity of the natural, and the supernatural light of grace. She insists that we must accept a void (le vide) and that to be able to do that is to be able to do something *unnatural*, supernatural. The tendency to spread suffering, and also the use of the imagination (a force in Simone Weil's thought opposed to the passive *acceptance* of reality) fills up these 'voids' and this is a natural process. But the religious use of suffering is, precisely, unnatural. The following quotations clearly bear a relation to Hannah's spiritual activity as Denis sees it:

Mécanique humaine. Quiconque souffre cherche à communiquer sa souffrance – soit en maltraitant, soit en provoquant la pitié – afin de la diminuer, et il la diminue vraiment ainsi . . . Cela est impérieux comme la pesanteur. Comment s'en délivre-t-on? Comment se délivre-t-on de ce qui est comme la pesanteur?[41]

Ne pas exercer tout le pouvoir dont on dispose, c'est supporter le vide. Cela est contraire à tous les lois de la nature: la grâce seule le peut.[42]

Accepter un vide en soi-même, cela est surnaturel. Où trouver l'énergie pour un acte sans contre-partie? L'énergie doit venir d'ailleurs. Mais pourtant, il fait d'abord un attachement, quelque chose de désespéré, que d'abord un vide se produise. Vide: nuit obscure.

L'admiration, la pitié (le mélange des deux surtout) apportent une énergie réelle. Mais it faut s'en passer.[43]

L'homme n'échappe aux lois de ce monde que la durée d'un éclair. Instants d'arrêt, de contemplation, d'intuition pure, de vide mental, d'acceptation de vide moral. C'est par ces instants qu'il est capable de surnaturel.

Qui supporte un moment le vide, ou reçoit le pain surnaturel, ou tombe. Risque terrible, mais il faut le courir, et même un moment sans espérance. Mais il ne faut pas s'y jeter.[44]

Here we have both the 'unnatural' elements of Hannah's attempt at suffering, and the dangers – those of accepting the energy brought by admiration and pity, which she does, at least at first, those of falling, of finding the weight of the void too much – as again, perhaps, she does. I have quoted at such length, because I think an acquaintance with Simone Weil's terminology illuminates, and 'places' for us, Miss Murdoch's abstractions, if not, or not entirely, her story.

Max's and Denis's ideas of the nature of God and his relation to the universe also bear a relation to those of Simone Weil, who sees the creation as something put between God and God, between the love of God and the love of God. And our love towards God, she considers, since God can love only himself, must consist of 'de-creating' ourselves, consenting not to be, renouncing the 'I' in ourselves in order simply to be attentive to God.

> La création est un acte d'amour et elle est perpétuelle. A chaque instant notre existence est amour de Dieu pour nous. Mais Dieu ne peut aimer que soi-même. Son amour pour nous est amour pour soi a travers nous. Ainsi, lui qui nous donne l'être, il aime en nous le consentement à ne pas être.[45]

And:

> L'inflexible nécessité, la misère, la détresse, le poids écrasant du besoin et du travail qui épuise, la cruauté, les tortures, la mort violente, la contrainte, la terreur, les maladies – tout cela c'est l'amour divin. C'est Dieu qui par amour se retire de nous afin que nous puissions l'aimer. Car si nous étions exposés au rayonnement direct de son amour, sans la protection de l'espace, du temps et de la matière, nous serions évaporés comme l'eau au soleil; il n'y aurait pas assez de je en nous pour abandonner le je par amour. La nécessité est l'écran mis entre Dieu et nous pour que nous puissions être. C'est à nous de percer l'écran pour cesser d'être.

These metaphysical ideas, whatever we may think of them for ourselves, have an authenticity in Simone Weil's precise, worked, clearly contemplative aperçus which it would be difficult to give them in a novel, where they stand, a little stiff, a little lumpish, amongst the more conventional studies of the characters as such. The suitability of the form of *The Unicorn* to the study of ideas of this kind is discussed more fully in the next chapter. For the moment I would simply point out that this precision of Simone Weil's perceptions gives weight at least to our understanding of Miss Murdoch's intentions in presenting her universe.

And the idea of the light called into being by love, or desire, expressed by Hannah, left finally by an uncomprehending Effingham to the dying Max, is also excellently put by Simone Weil, about whose belief in the efficacy of such pure love and attention there is no question, no ambiguity.

This, as we never have it in *The Unicorn*, is the voice of faith.

> En dehors même de toute croyance religieuse explicite, toutes les fois qu'un être humain accomplit un effort d'attention avec le seul désir de devenir plus apte à saisir la verité, il acquiert cette aptitude plus grande, même si son effort n'a produit aucun fruit visible. Un conte esquimau explique ainsi l'origine de la lumière: 'Le corbeau qui dans la nuit éternelle ne pouvait pas trouver de nourriture, désira la lumière, et la terre s'éclaira.' S'il y a vraiment désir, si l'objet du désir est vraiment la lumière, le désir de lumière produit la lumière. Il y a vraiment désir quand il y a effort d'attention. C'est vraiment la lumière qui est désirée si tout autre mobile est absent. Quand même les efforts d'attention resteraient en apparence stériles pendant des années, un jour une lumière exactement proportionelle à ces efforts inondera l'âme.[46]

But the thing in the novel which most convinces one that Hannah's religion is at least related to something real is its connection with the salmon – something, unlike the idea of God crying out for love and brought into being by it, within the power of Miss Murdoch's artistic manipulation. At the beginning of the book Scottow tells Marian that the salmon have left after the great storm; 'now the moor is just another piece of bog and even the salmon have gone away'. So, when Hannah tells Marian 'They've come back. Only don't tell Mr Scottow,' there is already a sense of some secret good life going on, out of the eye of the wielder of power and violence, which reinforces Hannah's image for the leaping salmon. 'Such fantastic bravery, to enter another element like that.

Like souls approaching God.'[47] And Denis, showing Marian the salmon later, amplifies the image of their suffering leaps.

> Suffering is no scandal. It is natural. Nature appoints it. All creation suffers. It suffers from having been created, if nothing else. It suffers from being divided from God.'[48]

The salmon here have to be seen in the context of the wider fishing and hunting imagery of the book, which recalls strongly the dominant image of *The Flight from the Enchanter* – and also the related controversy in *The Bell*, as to whether the community should shoot squirrels, which is beautifully both cranky and serious. The unicorn image itself indeed occurs in *The Flight from the Enchanter*, where Mischa Fox talks generally of the illusion of the 'unicorn virgin' that she can conquer evil, and where Calvin Blick tells Annette, the unicorn virgin of this book, that 'The notion that one can liberate another soul from captivity is an illusion of the very young.' In *The Unicorn*, the virgin is 'Maid Marian' who begins by thinking that she can 'liberate' Hannah; 'I shall talk to her about freedom.'[49] And Marian, Denis thinks, may be like the virgin, some kind of trap for the unicorn. I don't want to make much of this point because I can't see that Miss Murdoch has really made it work within this novel – but I do think that the fact that there is such similarity between the themes and even the characters of these two very dissimilar books is worth pointing out. Mischa, helpless in the 'very poor landscape' full of suffering insects, where there is only the photographer, Calvin, whose soul is in his power, is, in his function as a transmitter of Até, very like Gerald, accompanied by his creature Jamesie, who says of himself 'Do you think that I myself am separated in any way from what goes on here, that I am free?'[50]

And the hunt in this book is very real, where the hunt in *The Flight from the Enchanter* was largely in the imagery. Scottow and Jamesie are seen as destroyers of life – hunters of hares – who rightly remind Marian that she herself feeds from the fruits of this 'necessary' violence. Denis protects goldfish from herons, showing an uncorrupted version of

Mischa's concern for all life, something he abandons momentarily when he decides to fight evil with evil, and kills Peter Crean-Smith, a deed which Miss Murdoch allows her novel to prove to have been unnecessary; he leaves carrying a plastic bag of goldfish and accompanied by yet another of Miss Murdoch's golden life-force dogs.

But the interesting hunter is Pip Lejour – showing in this, perhaps, the 'rapacity' that made Randall a poor artist. He meets Hannah when hunting with her husband; we see him poaching on her land, carrying hares that drip blood, bearing a gun that makes him appear to Effingham 'not as an absurd and insensitive youth but as some slim archaic Apollo, smiling, golden and dangerous'.[51] And, on the occasion when Effingham questions him about Gerald Scottow, he is seen playing and killing a trout, with artistry, with a fly made of hair resembling Hannah's. There is no question but that the death of the fish is something unpleasant – Effingham sees it as something 'dreadfully alive', Pip breaks its back, Effingham feels 'Such a rapid passage, such an appalling mystery'.[52]

Thus, although Pip complicates the issue by explaining that the big pike are female, and 'eat their husbands', when he comes to ask Hannah to go away with him, looking 'slim, elegant, feline, or . . . like a beautiful snake',[53] there is a sense, in spite of the dignity with which he behaves, in spite of the fact that Gerald's dismissal of him is seen as 'the defeat of a man by a beast', that he is an oppressor, a hunter, not one of the suffering innocent. This may be partly inevitable – in *The Flight from the Enchanter*, the majority of the women were seen as suffering fish, or as fish deprived of their freedom; there was only Miss Casement and possibly Mrs Wingfield who partook largely of the nature of the pike. And it is clearly possible for a man to be a man and have dignity, and still to exercise the inevitable power and cruelty that is part of male love. But we cannot take his statement that he has loved her and not used her quite at its face value – his long vigil with the binoculars has been a kind of using – and the way in which his love is seen to partake of Até is something which gives a real value to Hannah's refusal of him, her disposing of herself as a queen, an authority it would not otherwise have. When she tells him that in the beginning she thrust the suffering back at him in resentment, that she did not go on loving him, and that now he is, for her, a 'blackened image', one feels that the thing she has chosen instead of going away with him is something at least possibly valuable because it is at least an attempt to make a world where suffering is neither willingly inflicted, nor ultimately handed back. As with Ann's anger, the fact that Hannah is at this moment 'aggrieved and querulous', adds conviction to what goodness she has. What she has chosen may be impossible; it has at least a possible value.

That is, to return to the point I was originally making, the relationship of Hannah's and Denis's thought to the salmon relates their whole significance to a world where suffering is natural and inevitable,* something to be reckoned with, and the idea of Hannah as an innocent sufferer gains stature from our seeing not only Peter and Gerald as beasts, but even her lover as a hunter and destroyer. Although again, Hannah's feeling of affinity for the suffering bat, 'a mammal like us', is made ambiguously sinister by the fact that it dies, and that Denis brings her 'hedgehogs, snakes, toads, nice beasts'.[54]

This brings us back to the concept of Hannah, not as an innocent sleeping beauty, nor as a saint, but as a witch or vampire. And there is an interpretation of the events, and of Hannah's position which, in that it is moral rather than psycho-analytic, disposes of the value of Hannah's spirituality in its own terms. By this interpretation, her suffering, her good, are a fantasy, imposed upon reality by her will and unconscious needs, and by the need of the other characters

---

* Simone Weil, writing of the difference between the natural world, and the human world, says: 'Il y a toutes les gammes de distance entre la créature et Dieu. Une distance où l'amour de Dieu est impossible: matière, plantes, animaux. Le mal est si complet là qu'il se détruit; il n'y a plus de mal: miroir de l'innocence divine. Nous sommes au point où l'amour est tout juste possible.'

for drama, for meaning, for 'a story'. And this fantasy is destroying a real and valuable freedom in the other characters, the freedom to live and act in the real world, amongst 'real messy individuals', the freedom from romantic necessity, which in the case of Randall we saw to be a dangerous value – but here, Ann's passive suffering has become, in Hannah, a myth like Randall's freedom. It is not certain whether the myth has been woven by the others in spite of Hannah, or by Hannah in conjunction with, or even partially in spite of, the others, because of her own needs – although there is agreement that before Gerald 'awoke' her, that is what was happening. But here is perhaps the central ambiguity of the book.

At the moment when Effingham has just pledged himself to try and suffer with Hannah, he sees, through the window, Riders, a landscape with boats, a steamer, a silver aeroplane. Hannah tells him that he must learn to care for her with less 'imagination' and he thinks of this as a sort of death.

> Effingham saw it all with a sort of shock. There was life, indifferent life, beautiful free life going forward. But to what, in here, had he just pledged himself?[55]

(Hannah's suspicion of 'imagination' here resembles perhaps Simone Weil's, who opposes the imagination to the acceptance of the void, and sees it as something essentially exclusive of reality: it is something which invents objects of desire in order to avoid the pressure of reality. 'L'imagination combleuse de vides est essentiellement menteuse. Elle exclut la troisième dimension, car ce sont seulement les objets réels qui sont dans les trois dimensions.'[56] In this sense the 'death' which Effingham fears may be the spiritually desirable death of the self. But Hannah suffers perhaps from her own form of 'imagination'.)

Marian in those moments when she wants to 'free' Hannah, sees her as compelled into the spiritual life by her own need and those of others.

> She began, this is how I see it anyway, by simply being afraid

191

of that beastly man, just paralysed with fear. Then she became rather apathetic and miserable. Then she began to find her own situation sort of interesting, spiritually interesting. People have always got to survive and they'll invent some way of surviving, of seeing their situation as tolerable ... I've nothing against religion in general ... But if it's to be any good it's got to be taken to freely, out in the open as it were. Hannah took to the spiritual life, or whatever the hell it is, like someone taking to a drug. She had to ... She was becoming more and more hypnotized by the situation itself and by all those people ... murmuring into her ear in different tones, but all murmuring it: you're imprisoned ... She's psychologically paralysed. She's lost her sense of freedom.[57]

Simone Weil describes the process of becoming used to suffering in terms different from Freud's description of obsessional neurosis, but recognizably related to the same kind of behaviour.

Un autre effet du malheur est de rendre l'âme sa complice, peu à peu, en y injectant un poison d'inertie. En quiconque a été malheureux assez longtemps, il y a une complicité à l'égard de son propre malheur. Cette complicité entrave tous les efforts qu'il pourrait faire pour améliorer son sort; elle va jusqu'à l'empêcher de rechercher les moyens d'être delivré, parfois même jusqu'à l'empêcher de souhaiter la délivrance. Il est alors installé dans le malheur; et les gens peuvent croire qu'il est satisfait. Bien plus, cette complicité peut le pousser malgré lui à éviter, à fuir, les moyens de la délivrance; elle se voile alors sous de prétextes parfois ridicules.[58]

One remembers that Michael Meade had found his situation 'interesting', and had infected Toby with this too, as Catherine in the same book had taken to religion like a drug. And the result of this, in Hannah's case, has been a preying on others which again recalls the beautiful and complex vampire in Le Fanu's story *Carmilla*.

Carmilla has Hannah's physical weakness, and makes appeals to the frightened narrator of the story, who both loves and hates her, which are echoed by Hannah's approaches to Marian and Effingham; her vampirism,

Pritchett says, 'discloses the languid and yet insatiate sterility of Lesbian love',[59] and Hannah can be seen as preying in a 'languid and insatiate' way on the other characters (something like this may explain the importance attached to the fact that Violet and Jamesie are Hannah's relations; both are involved in homosexual and imperfect love; they are neither human like Marian and Effingham, nor of fair blood like Denis, but somehow human and dead, like vampires). Carmilla cries

> In the rapture of my enormous humiliation I live in your warm life, and you shall die – die, sweetly die – into mine. I cannot help it; and as I draw near to you, you, in your turn will draw near to others, and learn the rapture of that cruelty, which yet is love . . . [60]

And:

> I am under vows, no nun half so awfully . . . You will think me very cruel, very selfish, but love is always selfish . . . You must come with me, loving me, to death; or else hate me and still come with me, and *hating* me through death and after. There is no such word as indifference in my apathetic nature.[61]

Hannah seizes Marian's hand, as Carmilla seizes the narrator's and begs Marian to forgive her 'for so shamelessly crying out for love': Marian feels some 'vast claim'[62] is being made on her, and the reader is aware of some root of coercion in Marian's 'love' for Hannah. Earlier Hannah has said of Denis 'I think he would let me kill him slowly' with 'a startling possessive savagery'.[63] And when she tells Effingham that she ought to have made him suffer more, that she is 'a story for you. We remain on romantic terms,' and he replies 'You want me to be – resigned, with you – somehow, dead, with you',[64] the 'death' here is completely ambiguous, I think. It might be an unreal, fantastic death, a further twist of the romantic screw, a mythical death of the self which, avoiding the romantic drama of courtly love, makes an even more deadly drama out of resignation, of apparent lack of drama. Or it might be a really valuable death of the self, a possible form of goodness, such as that attributed to Ann, when she had found herself incapable of loving Felix in an 'ordinary way', or of knowing significantly what she had done. But it is perhaps significant that Ann's instinct is to dismiss Felix, even though she cries after him, as Hannah cries after Effingham when he leaves her on the eve of Peter's probable return.

Ann feels that to hang on to Randall is corruption; Hannah hangs on to everyone, Marian, Denis, Effingham, Violet, even Peter Crean-Smith – we must remember that 'to be completely powerless may be another source of power', that Marian thinks it is 'bad for' Peter to be allowed to punish her so; as Martin was exercising power over Palmer and Antonia, in the stage version at least, by giving them the suffering they needed. And in the scene when Max puts forward his view of Até, he also says 'she may be a sort of enchantress, a Circe, a spiritual Penelope, keeping her suitors spellbound and enslaved'.

All this is brought into the open when Hannah, after her submission to Scottow, takes this view herself. She says (like Michael Meade) that

> it is possible to go and on, and to suffer, and to pray and to meditate, to impose on oneself a discipline of the greatest austerity and for all this to be nothing, to be a dream.[65]

She has, she says, been playing God, has lived only as a story in their thoughts,

> I have battened upon you like a secret vampire, I have even battened upon Max Lejour . . . But it is the punishment of a false God to become unreal . . . You have made me unreal by thinking about me so much. You made me into an object of contemplation.[66]

And she intends, she says, in some way to begin again, really to suffer, not to live in unconsciousness.

Here, she completely parts company with Ann, the value of whose lack of resentment, lack of blame for Steve's death, was precisely its *unconscious* nature – and it is, of course, possible that Hannah, like Ann, like Hugh, has been good whilst feeling nothing, whilst not knowing what she was doing, and that, like Ann, she cannot be good consciously. The thing she is now to try to do – the martyrdom – is something Pip tells her she *cannot* do, she is 'too tired', and Marian sees her decision as 'a further turn of the screw ... if Hannah chose to suffer, she chose a suffering now for all of them which they could not avoid'.[67] And Marian feels that with this decision of Hannah's, when Gerald has 'become' Peter, 'the human world was at an end'.

Hannah's loss of innocence has reduced them all to animals, and Gerald is free to exercise power – a curious power, like that of Palmer Anderson. 'She feared and detested Gerald; yet something in her also said quite clearly: do what you will.'[68] I do not quite understand this stage of the action, but it is at least clear that the story has moved out of a world where the normal partakes of reality, where the rhythms of ordinary life have meaning. With the loss of Hannah's 'virtue', all morality and all forms are meaningless.

What happens at this point is perhaps illuminated by two remarks of Simone Weil:

> Ce que le mal viole, ce n'est pas le bien, car le bien est inviolable; on ne viole qu'un bien dégradé.[69]

That is, the power Gerald has over Hannah is over her as a 'false God', a wrongful, imagined, unreal object of contemplation. And, Simone Weil says, contrasting false and real Gods:

> Le faux Dieu change la souffrance en violence.
> Le vrai Dieu change la violence en souffrance.[70]

What happens, thus, is not that Hannah obviously suffers more, nor that Gerald is let loose to terrorize the others (unless that Hannah's suffering is the guilt she takes upon herself in keeping Gerald from the others and we are given to evidence to suppose this); it is just that the breaking of the taboo releases in Hannah the violence that Martin's breaking of the taboo releases in him. And whereas Martin, comically, strikes Palmer, Hannah kills Gerald – I use the analogy only because in Martin's case the violence was a kind of release, a kind of contact with reality, and it is not clear still whether Hannah's new state is better or worse than her old one. It may be that her waking up is a recognition of truth, in the existence of violence in herself, as Martin's was. Marian's new view of her would perhaps support this

> The change in her face now seemed to Marian to be this: the spiritual veil or haze, the strange light, had been taken away, to reveal the irregularities of the features beneath. But she was still beautiful.[71]

Here, there is at least the suggestion that Hannah has become an individual, a real person, and is acting now from herself. Marian thinks that 'Gerald had entered the landscape and made it real. But ... What *was* there, in that strange, desolate landscape?'[72]

Effingham reflects that

> he had never ... seen in her the violence which lay behind her apparent resignation ... He had had his own good reasons for suffering at her hands; she had doubtless had her own good reasons for suffering at Peter's. If it had been, for him, a psychological masquerade, so it had been for her something which had, in reality, little to do with the spiritual world whose light he had been pleased to see so purely shining all about her ... The change in Hannah's situation which had begun to effect his own liberation had let that violence loose.[73]

And, as the community in *The Bell* dissolved into violence, so does this community; Denis, 'driven mad by her actions', by her faithlessness, drowns Peter; Marian and Jamesie release Hannah, who now at last is trying to escape, to her death. And with her death, they are all, except Max, who inherits her death, and Denis, who inherits her guilt, released. Only she has taken with her those Effingham thinks of as her 'victims', Scottow, Peter, Pip, who shoots himself.

At the end of the book, the ambiguity is restated. When it is found that Hannah has left her goods to Max, Violet and Effingham see this as a last malicious act against those who have loved her. Jamesie makes a speech in which he compares, now, the others to vampires, battening on the lives of Hannah, Gerald and Peter, and Max draws all the threads together, suggesting that

> Hannah was like the rest of us. She loved what wasn't there, what was absent. This can be dangerous. Only she did not dare to love what was present too. Perhaps it would have been better if she had. She could not really love the people she saw, she could not afford to, it would have made the limitations of her life too painful. She could not, for them, transform the idea of love into something manageable: it remained something destructive and fearful and she simply avoided it.[74]

I have quoted this speech before, but now its whole meaning is clearer. Max, like Hannah, is a half-contemplative. He says of her that 'I've meant all my life to go on a spiritual pilgrimage. And here I am at the end – and I haven't even set out.' And 'Hannah is my experiment. I've always had a great theoretical knowledge of morals but practically speaking I've never done a hand's turn . . . I don't know the truth either. I just know about it.'[75]

That is, both of them have been concerned with the idea of the good, of the perfect, to the exclusion of Miss Murdoch's other good, which I have referred to elsewhere – the recognition of particular individuals, the love of other men as they are, the compassionate agnosticism. Max is old and dying, and Hannah has loved him, with his vision of God, as she dared not love the individuals around her – and they have been drawn into this remoteness from the normal, from day to day life, from ordinary human love. So that, now that Hannah has *become*, as Effingham sees it, 'that death which she had so much striven to emulate in life, which she had studied and practised and loved',[76] Effingham sees Max as 'the owner of her death, and she was waiting for you. You *are* her death and she loved you.'[77]

And Max, too, like perhaps Emma Sands, is waiting for death, 'a remote wizened sage who had long ago forgotten about life'. He is indeed concerned, as was said of him at the beginning of the book, 'with ultimate things'.

Here at last it is time to point out that our real glimpse of a vision of the good, of the perfect love which comes with the death of the self, is Effingham's vision, which comes to him when he is sinking into the bog, and fades again when he regains 'his old unregenerate being' and is rescued. This is 'the love which was the same as death', 'all that was not himself was filled to the brim with being and it was from this that the light streamed'.[78]

The expression of this idea again is very close to Simone Weil: 'Continuellement suspendre en soi-même le travail de l'imagination combleuse de vides. Si on accepte n'importe quel vide quel coup du sort peut empêcher d'aimer l'univers? On est assuré que, quoi qu'il arrive, *l'univers est plein*.'[79]

This expunging of the self is what Miss Murdoch values, both with regard to respect for the individual and with respect to the 'ultimate things'. If we return to the *Yale Review* article, where Miss Murdoch's definition of the good man and the great novelist are closely related, we find that she quotes T. S. Eliot 'The progress of an artist is a continual self-sacrifice, a continual extinction of personality' and comments 'Art is not an expression of personality, it is a question rather of the continued expelling of oneself from the matter in hand.' She continues

> Virtue is not essentially or immediately concerned with choosing between actions, or rules or reasons, nor with stripping the personality for a leap. It is concerned with really apprehending that other people exist. This too is what freedom really is; and it is impossible not to feel the creation of a work of art as a struggle for freedom. Freedom is not choosing; that is merely the move we make when all is already lost. Freedom is knowing and understanding and respecting things quite other than ourselves. Virtue is in this sense to be construed as knowledge, and connects us with reality ... The artist is indeed the analogon of the good man, and in a special sense he is the good man: the lover who, nothing himself, lets others be through him.[80]

Now, Max's ideal, the Good contemplated from his study, Hannah's ideal, the God she can afford to love when she dare not love ordinary, contingent, messy individuals, and Effingham's vision on the point of sinking into the bog, have this in common: they are all, ultimately, extinctions of the self in love, but they are all, also, ultimate, in that they are concerned with complete death, real death, mortality. They are, as Max said, love of what 'wasn't there'; Effingham's vision in his extremity, like Max's vision of Hannah, is curiously unefficacious when it comes to practically protecting, practically loving the individual Hannah in her fear. Max and the others, like Randall, are fascinated by the world of forms; the tale of Hannah's suffering is made into an object like, at best, Randall's rose, the Tintoretto, a vision of perfection dangerous to live by. And if Hannah is *not* the 'lover who, nothing himself, lets others be through him', this is because, partly, she does not, as the great artist does, enough respect the *contingency* of others, and partly because she (using her salmon image) construes virtue as 'stripping the personality for a leap'. And thus her whole story is a living of the 'Romantic adoration of necessity' and she makes of the concept of negative love a symbol, not a contingent and unknown reality with its transcendent quality. When she says of the landscape 'I have made it unreal by endlessly looking at it, instead of entering it',[81] she is expressing the sense we have elsewhere in Miss Murdoch's work, that to give form to, to contemplate, an idea, even the idea that one's surroundings are intractable, that reality is unknowable, that the way to virtue is to expunge the personality, is to make a symbol of the fact that a symbol cannot be made – like the bell.

One might say of the Symbol that it is an analagon of an individual but not a real individual. It has the uniqueness and separateness of an individual, but whereas the real individual is boundless and not totally definable, the symbol is known intuitively to be self-contained: it is a making sensible of the idea of individuality under the form of necessity, its contingency purged away.[82]

199

For individuality, substitute love, or suffering, and the remark applies; significantly Miss Murdoch comments 'the symbolists desired an art which would have pleased Plato'. The moment when Marian stops to grieve for the individual dead Gerald – hitherto seen as a power of evil, in a myth – is a moment in a real novel, a moment of real mystery, juxtaposed with all the meanings.

> Now in the black middle of the night it was the fact of death that mattered most, the translation of a big, healthy, powerful man into a piece of senseless, heavy stuff.[83]

This brings us back to death, and I would suggest that the vision of perfection and reality, the real love of God which is the love of a creation no longer divided from its creator, is seen to be a function of real death; something which we cannot hope to have more than fleetingly in real life, unless we are true contemplatives, although Miss Murdoch says of Effingham's vision 'And indeed he could always have known this, for the fact of death stretches the length of life. Since he was mortal he was nothing, and since he was nothing all that was not himself was filled to the brim with being and it was from this that the light streamed.'[84]* But even this knowledge is seen to be of doubtful validity as part of the whole, or when seen in terms not of death but of life. Hannah is dead, she has become her death. Effingham wonders 'Who knew if that was victory or defeat?' Max is dying: 'It was as if the funeral were Max's funeral and they were conveying him ceremonially out of the world, as if those others were dream deaths while Max wore the real garb of mortality.'[85]

And Effingham and Marian return to the real world, where truth cannot ever be completely known, where individuals

---

* This thought too is illuminated by Simone Weil, who, like Hannah, loved her death, saw it as the moment of supreme consciousness, both of the reality of suffering and of the power voluntarily not to be, for love of God. Death is 'l'instant où pour une fraction infinitésimale du temps la verité pure, nue, certaine, eternelle, entre dans l'âme'. 'La mort,' she says, 'est la norme et le but de la vie.' (A de D, p. 33.)

are boundless, where virtue is tolerant agnosticism. Marian, after Denis leaves her, taking the suffering with him,

> did not know whether the world in which she had been living was a world of good or evil, a world of significant suffering or a devil's shadow-play, a mere nightmare of violence.[86]

And Effingham thinks that they were waiting for Hannah's death.

> that was the most inevitable thing of all ... We were all attendants upon that ceremony, and we are all now dismissed. So we return to our real life and our real tasks: and God knows if we shall be the better for this dream of death, this enactment of last things.[87]

He too cannot tell whether this 'fantasy of the spiritual life' had been concerned with good and evil or not.

> If what was over had indeed been a fantasy of the spiritual life, it was its fantastic and not its spiritual quality which had touched him. He had, through egoism, through being in some sense too small, too trivial, to interest the powers of that world, escaped from evil. But he had not either been touched by good. That vision, true or false, he would leave to Max, of the good forced into being as the object of desire, as if one should compel God to be.[88]

Like the Mass in *The Bell* that 'real' symbol of the joining of the divided creation to its creator, the idea of the love for God, for the perfect, out of this world, is left to stand in the book beside the human mess made by the violence, the exercise of power, the imperfections of knowledge and love on a human or tragic level. Effingham goes back to his 'clever' Elizabeth (as Jake goes back to the clever Sadie from the beautiful and remote Anna) who has told him in purely Murdoch tones

> Art and psychoanalysis give shape and meaning to life and that is why we adore them, but life as it is lived has no shape and meaning and that is what I am experiencing just now.[89]

The story of Hannah has the 'form' of art, and the 'form' of psychoanalysis, but it is ultimately ambiguous, ultimately incomprehensible; it takes place in a world where form is felt to be significant, and form proves inadequate to unravel it. (However I may have weighted my arguments in favour of Hannah's religion being a myth, a fantasy, an illusion, it is not certain; her death may be Max's, but her suffering passes to the very positive Denis, whom we are not able easily to dismiss. Denis's feeling that if he had not repaid Peter with hate, and had stayed with Hannah, she would not have died, is convincing as well as Effingham's feeling that her death was inevitable.) So here, Miss Murdoch's myth – although it is a myth, it is ruled by necessity, and it is self-contained – none of the characters 'live' outside it – contains its own limitations. Like Kant's theory of the sublime, it contemplates the breakdown of its own attempt rationally to contain and understand itself.

And what of freedom? Max says that freedom is not a value in morals. Gerald Scottow says that 'freedom has perhaps no meaning.' Gerald too, insists on the concepts of destiny and pattern; 'There are great patterns in which we are all involved, and destinies which belong to us and which we love even in the moment when they destroy us . . . the pattern, that is what has authority here, and absolute authority.'[90] I remarked earlier how Michael Meade's sense of himself as a man of destiny, a man with a pattern, was a limitation of his freedom, because there is no pattern – except, again, under the ambiguous eye of God, which Donald Swann can vouch for, but we cannot. If Max sees no value in freedom, and Gerald thinks it does not exist, we are nevertheless left with Miss Murdoch's assertion that 'Freedom is knowing and understanding and respecting things quite other than ourselves. Virtue is in this sense to be construed as knowledge, and connects us so with reality.'[91] We return, then, to the concept we began with, that of 'degrees of freedom'.

It is here, perhaps, in some way I do not fully understand, significant that Gerald, the exponent of the romantic myth of necessity and destiny, should also be the voice of the modern man, monarch of all he surveys, whom Marian hears telling her, as Anderson, but not Honor, told Martin 'all is permitted'. All is not permitted, but neither are we not free at all. Reality limits us: other people limit us: there are facts, like marriage, which make our lives, and Hannah, like Ann, can feel 'her whole life had compelled her'. But to be compelled by one's whole life is not to be completely without freedom; one's life is something one has partly made oneself; to be completely without freedom is to have an inadequate view of reality, a myth which encourages a dream-like facility, to deform reality by fantasy.*

We are now back where we began; with the difference between Hugo's view of the world as entirely composed of 'unutterably particular' entities that we cannot understand, and Jake's view that concepts are necessary, that we need to think about truth and morals, and that truth needs words. Here Miss Murdoch is with Jake – and perhaps Max.

> The connection between art and the moral life has languished because we are losing our sense of form and structure in the moral world . . . It is natural that a Liberal democratic society will not be concerned with techniques of improvement, will deny that virtue is knowledge, will emphasise choice at the expense of vision . . . [92]

And

> our current picture of freedom encourages a dream-like facility; whereas what we require is a renewed sense of the difficulty and complexity of the moral life, and of the opacity of persons. We need more concepts in which to picture the substance of our being; it is through an enriching and deepening of concepts that moral progress takes place. Simone Weil

---

* Although, on the highest spiritual level, to be completely a slave, completely obedient to God and necessity, completely without room to move, is what is desired by Simone Weil. 'La plus belle vie possible m'a toujours paru être celle où tout est déterminé, soit par la contrainte des circonstances, soit par de telles impulsions et où il n'y a jamais place pour aucun choix.' But this is comparable to the nuns of *The Bell*.

said that morality was a matter of attention, not of will. We need a new vocabulary of attention.[93]

But, against this again, the Hugo warning:

Reality is not a given whole. An understanding of this, a respect for the contingent, is essential to imagination as opposed to fantasy. Our sense of form, which is an aspect of our desire for consolation, can be a danger to our sense of reality as a rich receding background.[94]

That is, the moral world *has* form and structure, it *has* concepts, it must have, and virtue is knowledge is attention to these things, and freedom is an attempt to realize them. But all the characters in *The Unicorn* – Hannah inside the prison, the rest outside – are tempted not only to 'pay attention' to reality, which is freedom, but to 'deform' it, by patterning it according to their own needs; here, Hannah's warning to Effingham to enjoy the 'story' less, with less dream-like facility, Marian's sense at the end that, if Hannah has not freedom of 'choice', she should have at least the right to dispose of herself with authority, are relevant, as is Hannah's turning of the landscape into a thing, instead of a 'rich, receding background': also Hannah's living on their 'image' of her, as they also live on what they *imagine* she feels (again we are back to *Under the Net*, to Jake's lack of knowledge of Anna and Sadie and Hugo, or *The Bell* and Michael's lack of knowledge of Nick and Catherine – knowledge which would be love and freedom).

It is Max – who knows *about* truth, not truth – who says that it doesn't matter whose crime it was; it is Effingham who says it doesn't matter what Hannah is if she has made saints of them all. But it clearly does matter, because what Hannah *is* is truth – Max says 'we must see her as real' but he himself uses her for his own ends, and none of them see each other as real enough, none of them exercise *this* freedom adequately, and therein perhaps lies the tragedy. And who has most restricted the freedom of the others is not clear; it is a network.

And all this, in Miss Murdoch's world, is inevitable; we

are free to know, we must use concepts – words like truth, like suffering, like unconsciousness – but we can never know completely, we are free to love, but we always fail. This, again, is like Miss Murdoch's interpretation of Kant's theory of the sublime: 'Tragic freedom, implied by love, is this; that we all have an indefinitely extended capacity to imagine the being of others. Tragic because there is no pre-fabricated harmony.'

> Tragedy in art is the attempt to overcome the defeat which human beings suffer in the practical world. It is, as Kant nearly said, as he ought to have said, the human spirit mourning and yet exulting in its strength. In the practical world there may be only mourning and the final acceptance of the incomplete. Form is the great consolation of love, but it is also its great temptation.[95]

And, with *The Unicorn*, the distinction between consolation and temptation is where the ambiguity of freedom rests, and the mystery. Perhaps here the conflict between Randall's need for 'form' and Ann's deliberate 'not-knowing' is more clearly balanced: in the Platonic world, concepts become myths, and disfigure reality: in the world where Ann naturally, and Hannah deliberately, choose not to know, not to feel, to accept only too well the incomprehensibly limiting nature of reality, the sense in which virtue is freedom is knowledge can in turn be lost, and reality can be lost with freedom: Ann cannot *see* Felix, because he is what she wants (but he is real) and dares not love him, through fear as well as virtue: Hannah cannot *see* anyone, dare not see anyone, as individual or particular or to be loved. We have moved, in one sense, a long way from Jake's problems of art and love in a hostile world, where Hugo, like the dolmen, was a sign and a portent set up before time, but in another we have not moved at all.

9

THE ART OF THE NOVELS

I

THIS BOOK IS not an attempt to make a critical survey, let
alone summing-up, of Miss Murdoch's work. It is clearly not
time to attempt this, both because we are still too close to
her work, and because she is an extremely rapid, various and
prolific writer, still in the middle of her career. I began this
book with a more precise and smaller intention; I began with
a very simple, nagging curiosity to know exactly what Miss
Murdoch was talking about, what sort of moral statement
she was making, what were the ideas behind her novels. They
presented themselves, it seemed to me, like puzzles out of
which a plan of ideas, a scheme of references could be
extracted for examination, with some effort. That effort was
required could, though not necessarily, be seen as a criticism
of Miss Murdoch as a novelist, depending on whether the
complication and occasional obscurity of her presentation of
her thought is to be seen as necessary or simply irritatingly
baffling. To have made the effort has increased my own
respect for her as a novelist – she seems to me to be dealing
honourably with real and important problems. I feel, too,
that to make the effort to understand her thought, to find
the statement of the abstract ideas behind her novels is in a
sense the best way to come at these, and ultimately to make
a critical judgment of them. There are good novelists now
writing whom one would not think of approaching initially
in this way; Angus Wilson, for instance, who seems to me to

be a real novelist in Miss Murdoch's sense, someone to whom the individual, morally and actually, is of highest importance: and others, such as William Golding, who, although he presents a 'crystalline' patterned narrative to explain in universal moral terms, is a much more 'poetic' writer than Miss Murdoch, and whose work would need a more literary elucidation of its symbols and style.

What I mean to do in this chapter is to look, briefly, at the novels as novels, to make an attempt at a critical judgment, however tentative and necessarily incomplete. Reviewers have talked a great deal about whether Miss Murdoch is or is not a 'philosophical novelist'; those who say she is not tend to describe her as a compulsive storyteller, which is not of course incompatible with being a philosophical novelist. She has proved difficult to place; when her books first came out they were automatically classed with those of the Young Angries, Wain and Amis, to whose rootless picaresque heroes Jake Donaghue bears a slight resemblance. Those who admired her for this reason were bewildered by *The Sandcastle* and *The Bell* and straightforwardly repelled by the snobbery they detected in the milieux, wine and roses, of *An Unofficial Rose* and *A Severed Head*. She has been castigated for whimsy, deliberate weirdness, wilful obscurity – there is something in these criticisms, although I feel that the whimsy and snobbery at least become less troubling if one realizes the seriousness of the underlying moral arguments; here again, the critic will condemn or excuse according to whether what he primarily values in Miss Murdoch's novels is the moral intent, the presentation of contemporary life which was important in *Under the Net* or her intermittent but very real capacity to involve her readers in the feelings of her characters.

About Miss Murdoch's tremendous narrative vigour and inventiveness there can be no question; all the novels from *Under the Net* to *A Severed Head* have a compelling power at the simplest level; we want to know what happens next. Half at least of *The Unicorn* has the same quality, and half of *An Unofficial Rose* has something as valuable – a real tension between the characters. She has great skill and accuracy in describing precise actions: the fall of Rain Carter's car, the raising of the bell – which are fascinating in themselves. She can create a narrative, if not always a real emotional tension.

I am uncertain about the real meaning of the term 'philosophical novelist', or even whether it is a term of praise or abuse. Miss Murdoch's own final criticism of Jean-Paul Sartre's novels comes, I think, to use it very judiciously as a term of abuse. She distinguishes between *The Castle*, which is a 'metaphysical tale' and *La Nausée*.

> Kafka's K is not himself a metaphysician; his actions show forth, but his thoughts do not analyse, the absurdity of his world. The hero of *La Nausée* is reflective and analytical; the book is not a metaphysical image so much as a philosophical analysis which makes use of a metaphysical image. This, its consistently reflective, self-consciously philosophical character, is what distinguishes it too from other novels which brood equally upon the senseless fragmentation of our experience or on the fabricated nature of its apparent sense ... Virginia Woolf, Proust, Joyce ... [1]
>
> Roquentin's problem is not the usual human problem. He is incurably metaphysical by temperament and lives totally without human relations. But nevertheless Sartre does, I think, intend to offer us here an image of the human situation in general. What he undoubtedly does succeed in displaying to us is the structure of his own thought. *La Nausée* is Sartre's philosophical myth.[2]

I have quoted earlier Miss Murdoch's comparison of Sartre's skills with those she considers the great novelist to have.

> Sartre describes the artist's 'evil' as the irreducibility of man and the world of thought. Sartre has an impatience, which is fatal to a novelist proper, with the *stuff* of human life. He has, on the one hand, a lively interest, often slightly morbid, in the details of contemporary living, and on the other a passionate desire to built intellectually pleasing schemes and patterns. But the feature which might enable these two talents

to fuse into the work of a great novelist is absent, namely an apprehension of the absurd irreducible uniqueness of people and their relations with each other. Sartre seems blind to the function of prose, not as an activity or an analytic tool, but as creative of a complete and unclassifiable image.[3]

And she ends her book:

His inability to write a great novel is a tragic symptom of a situation which afflicts us all. We know that the real lesson to be taught is that the human person is precious and unique; but we seem unable to set it forth except in terms of ideology and abstraction.[4]

Leaving aside for the moment the question of prose, either Sartre's or Miss Murdoch's, as creative of an image, it is clear that in general Miss Murdoch sees Sartre, the philosophical novelist, as someone who uses 'reflective, self-consciously philosophical' characters, and someone, moreover, who needs to build intellectually pleasing schemes and patterns. Sartre displays to us the structure of his own thought, but he does not give to us the *stuff* of human life. How far, loosely, does this critical attitude to the philosopher as novelist apply to Miss Murdoch herself?

It does seem to me that she has, naturally, much in common with Sartre as she sees him, and that she knows this. Particularly in the first and the last books under consideration, *Under the Net* and *The Unicorn*, the themes and the treatment of them are self-consciously philosophical, in the strictest sense, and of interest to those with a philosophical bent rather than to everyman. Dave Gellman, Jake's book, Hugo's ideas, Anna's theory of art; Max Lejour, Denis's expository Christianity, Hannah's fumbling explanations of her behaviour; these are philosophical quite purely, as problems to be studied and in the tone of the study. I would, myself, go further than this and say that I believe that some *idea*, which could well be called philosophical, provides much of the unifying framework for each of Miss Murdoch's novels – from the conceptual net (Wittgenstein) in *Under the Net*, to the Simone Weil suffering in *The Unicorn*, via the conceptual idea of power in *The Flight from the Enchanter* and the religious approach to the philosophical Hegelian totality in *The Bell*.

Miss Murdoch is, after all, a practising philosopher. It is unlikely that she would not think of the kind of moral and religious truth she is interested in in philosophical terms.

She did indeed say herself, in an interview in *The Times* (Feb. 13th, 1964): 'I suppose I have certain philosophical ideas about human life and character, and that these must somehow find expression in my novels: but for the most part I am not conscious of this process and I think it would be destructive if I were. Certainly I am not a philosophical novelist in the sense that Sartre or Simone de Beauvoir is.' But here she is disclaiming partly the didactic intention of which Sartre is proud; and in any case the result of the deliberate planning which she does not disclaim, is that the novels certainly *appear* to centre on the ideas, the variations on a theme, in terms of which we can analyse them without feeling that we are seriously distorting them. The characters are approached from the theme, whereas with other writers, Joyce Cary, Angus Wilson, one has the sense that character or action is where the novel began and that theme developed from there.

The next question then, is how we are to see Miss Murdoch's novels as works of art; what the fact that they are fictional narratives adds to their presentation of the ideas. Is there a sense in which she has introduced what Sartre, according to her, missed out, the stuff of human life? Is the art involved primarily the art of the novel proper as she sees it, or that of crystalline fantasy-myth? How far is she herself afflicted by 'the situation that afflicts us all . . . our inability to set forth [the value of the individual] except in terms of ideology and abstraction'?

La Nausée, Miss Murdoch says, is Sartre's philosophical *myth*. This word myth, as John Cruickshank points out in his book on Albert Camus, has become very popular as a critical term, in a rather vague way. Cruickshank describes the *roman-mythe* as follows:

> There has . . . existed, to some extent in the theatre but more
> strikingly in the novel, an attempt to create 'contemporary
> myths'. A great imaginative effort has been made to put into
> fiction situations and plots which do not simply deal with
> some universal human trait but are meant to express universal
> truth about man's situation in the world. The search for
> a myth is closely linked with the increasingly metaphysical
> aspirations of the French novel. The myth has provided a
> means whereby men of letters have taken over the rôle of
> commentators on human destiny – a rôle which professional
> philosophers once regarded as their own but now seem largely
> to have abandoned in favour of linguistics and logical
> analysis.[5]

Critically, Cruickshank adds, the term *roman-mythe* is used
variously and loosely; it 'will sometimes mean an allegorical
novel, sometimes a symbolist novel, sometimes any novel
which adds a metaphysical dimension to the temporal events
it describes'.

In some of these senses Miss Murdoch's books could certainly be called *romans-mythe*; none of them are precisely
allegorical, but all could in some sense be described as symbolist, and they tend increasingly to add a metaphysical
dimension to the events they describe.

Miss Murdoch, in her critical writings, has tended to value
the myth less than the naturalistic novel. In *Against Dryness*
she refers to it as 'fantasy-myth' and Cruickshank's neutral
description of it as something meant to 'express universal
truth about man's situation in the world' becomes, in Miss
Murdoch's description, 'crystalline', 'a small, quasi-allegorical
object portraying the human condition and not containing
"characters" in the nineteenth-century sense' as opposed to
the approval given to the nineteenth-century novel, *not* portraying the 'human condition' but 'concerned with real various individuals struggling in society'. Myths are 'small myths,
toys, crystals'. On the other hand she has told us that she
finds most of the better novels written at this time to be
crystalline.

I have quoted, in my chapter on *The Unicorn*, Miss Murdoch's remarks about the evolving of a 'satisfactory myth' and its relation to the problem of the novel as a whole.

I should like to quote this passage again, at greater length, and to set it against Cruickshank's picture of Camus' views on the use of myth and symbol in the novel. I think that this will give us a satisfactory framework within which to consider the structure of Miss Murdoch's novels in general and their use of symbolism in particular.

> we may turn at last to what finally differentiates art from life, the question of form. Form is the temptation of love and its peril, whether in art or life: to round off a situation, sum up a character. But the difference is that art has *got* to have form, whereas life need not. And any artist both dreads and longs for the approach of necessity, the moment at which form irrevocably crystallizes. There is a temptation for any novelist, and one to which, if I am right, modern novelists yield too readily, to imagine that the problem of a novel is solved and the difficulties overcome as soon as a form in the sense of a satisfactory myth has been evolved. But that is only the beginning. There is then the much more difficult battle to prevent that form from becoming rigid, by the free expansion against it of individual characters. Here above all, the contingency of the characters must be respected. Contingency must be defended for it is the essence of personality. And here is where it becomes so important to remember that the novel is written in words, to remember that 'eloquence of suggestion and rhythm' of which James spoke. A novel must be a house fit for free characters to live in; and to combine form with a respect for reality with all its odd contingent ways is the highest art of prose.[6]

Here, one supposes, Miss Murdoch is using the word 'myth' in the sense of a coherent narrative *pattern*, with its 'metaphysical dimension' related (probably by symbols) to its events. In the case of the philosophical myth, a set of events will have been found to illustrate the philosopher's abstract reflection on the 'human situation', or, in the case of *La Nausée*, 'the senseless fragmentation of our experience'.

It is interesting to consider Miss Murdoch's own novels in

terms of her own description of the ideal relation of form to free character. Perhaps, purely in terms of her work, it might be possible to distinguish 'fantasy-myth' from the symbolic novel – and to put the first two books in the category of fantasy-myth proper, *The Sandcastle*, *The Bell* and *An Unofficial Rose* certainly as symbolic novels, with *A Severed Head* and *The Unicorn* coming somewhere in between. Miss Murdoch's sense of the tension between the 'freedom' or 'contingent reality' of the characters and events in the novel, and the form, the myth, the symbols, the abstract statement, is expressed from another angle by Cruickshank's description of the theory of Camus, a writer whom Miss Murdoch seems greatly to admire. Cruickshank, describing *La Peste* says

> Perhaps it is not too great a generalization to say that whereas Malraux and Greene experience situations and then derive a philosophy from them, Camus, in *La Peste* has revised the process by imagining a series of events specifically designed to embody his prior metaphysic. The result is a more abstract novel, but one in which the literal and metaphorical levels are more closely combined.

Cruickshank defines the symbolist novel as one in which 'the relationship between two or more levels of meaning is not so completely sustained as in the allegory, yet is more complete and organic than in what might be called politico-metaphysical fiction.'

Here we have, according to him, a definition of the novel which allows us to write a 'real' novel, without losing the form and resonance of the metaphysical reference. Here is something clearly which would appeal to Miss Murdoch as a solution to her feeling that we need both form and reality in the sense of looseness and contingency. Camus' work is 'more abstract' but not pure fantasy, not simple myth-making, although it proceeds, as I have argued Miss Murdoch's does, from an idea.

> Camus [says Cruickshank] claims that the novel has tended, throughout its history, either towards increased naturalism or greater formalism. Particularity and abstraction are the two

poles by which it has been alternately attracted at different periods. But the novel has only been great, he claims, when it has been more or less equally attracted by both poles at once. Too ready a movement in either single direction has led to aesthetic heresy and a misunderstanding of the true nature of fiction. Camus then claims that the novel should take a middle path between the particular and the universal; that they will receive dimensional fullness only from a proper combination of both. Novels should hold the concrete and the abstract in a natural and closely knit proportion and balance. One would have to say, I think, that the symbolist novel is not the only way of obtaining this result, but it is also clear that the very nature of the symbol makes it one of the most obvious and natural means to such an end. The successful symbolist novel will combine the concrete and the abstract in an organically inevitable relationship. They will be as inseparable, and yet as distinguishable as the flower and its scent or the memento and its associations. In this way the symbolist novel achieves that reconciliation of the singular and the universal desired by Hegel and described by Camus as the essential activity of art.

Clearly, here, Miss Murdoch and Camus, as seen by Cruickshank, are talking about the same needs and the same formal problem in literature. What intrigues me is the difference in tone. Cruickshank's description of what Camus says achieves in the rhythm of the sentence, in the movement of the paragraph, that balance that Camus says we should seek, a kind of contentment with the symbolic novel as a combination of concrete and abstract (contingent and metaphysical) as a 'middle path between the particular and the universal'. He uses his good image of the memento and its associations and moves on to an acceptance of the Hegelian reconciliation of the singular and the universal as *the essential activity of art*.

I do not think that Miss Murdoch would argue with this, but her emphasis has been, throughout what I have read of her critical articles, especially when we consider the shape of her novels, startlingly different. She would accept, certainly, Camus' picture of the novel as moving alternately towards greater formalism or increased naturalism. But she does not rest so easily on the balance as Cruickshank/Camus. She feels, *in practice*, that we should rediscover naturalism (*not* journalism). We should learn again the freedom of character *as a primary object* (Tolstoi, Jane Austen).

When she says 'to combine form with a respect for reality with all its odd contingent ways is the highest art of prose', her emphasis is, as it has been throughout the article, on reality – we pay, she believes, in our time, quite enough respect to form.

And Miss Murdoch's descriptions of symbols and symbolism are not describing the same thing as 'the memento and its associations'; she considers the symbol to be essentially *self-contained*, to have a 'small, clean, resonant, self-contained' quality, to have 'the uniqueness and separateness of an individual' but 'whereas the real individual is boundless and not totally definable, the symbol is known intuitively to be self-contained'. And in *Against Dryness*, again, she sees the tension between naturalism and formalism, not, as Cruickshank does, *resolved* in the symbolic novel, but as a continuing *battle*. Here we have perhaps a clue to the uneasiness her symbols so often cause her readers.

> Reality is not a given whole. An understanding of this, a respect for the contingent, is essential to imagination as opposed to fantasy. Our sense of form, which is an aspect of our desire for consolation, can be a danger to our sense of reality as a rich receding background. Against the consolations of form, the clear crystalline work, the simplified fantasy-myth, we must pit the destructive power of the now so unfashionable naturalistic idea of character.
>
> Real people are destructive of myth, contingency is destructive of fantasy, and opens the way for imagination. Think of the Russians, those great masters of the contingent. Too much contingency of course may turn out into journalism. But since reality is incomplete, art must not be too afraid of incompleteness. Literature must always represent *a battle between real people and images* [my italics]; and what it requires now is a much stronger and more complex conception of the former.[7]

There are contradictions and points of emphasis here which for reasons of space I can't go into. It is clear – and the workings can be seen in *An Unofficial Rose* – that Miss Murdoch's aesthetic views are closely involved in her moral views; that her respect for the individual, who is boundless and cannot be summed up, as the centre of our moral thinking, is extended to her thinking about the form of the novel, about character, about any kind of abstract prior metaphysic shaping a novel to the detriment of that novel. It does seem to me that she has seized something extremely important here. There is a thinness about William Golding's excellently formed and framed *Free Fall* with its symbols so resonant and its message so startlingly similar to Miss Murdoch's own, that can best be located in her terms. Myth comes more easily to the Americans and the French than to us – this is why I think Camus' novels and *Henderson, the Rain King* are better, more vigorous, freer studies of human freedom than anything that either Miss Murdoch or William Golding have yet given us.*

But, if we do indeed accept that, say, *La Peste, La Chute, Henderson*, are both good novels and symbolic novels, what are we nevertheless to make of Miss Murdoch's own practice, so markedly opposed in many ways to her sense of what is wrong with our apprehension of reality, and our writing, today? What are we to say of her own use of character, abstraction, symbol, form?

I think that much of the uneasiness that her readers experience with her symbols in particular and patterning in general might well be attributed to the tension she herself seems to feel between her natural ability intellectually to organize, and her suspicion of the *tidying* function of the kind of literary form which now comes naturally to us. A novel, she says,

---

* There is something artificial, to take an obvious example, in Pasternak's 'poetic' use of rowan berries in Dr Zhivago, to point the relation of certain tragic scenes to his theme, which I find easier to describe in terms of Miss Murdoch's concept of symbol limiting, *tidying* reality, form *reducing* the frightening variety of our experience, than in terms of the symbol enlarging our knowledge or area of thought.

has *got* to have form; but she seems to feel a metaphysical regret about it. A close look at the narrative structure and symbolic patterning of the individual novels will illustrate what I believe to be the effects of this tension in her work.

II

Miss Murdoch's first two novels might be taken together here. Both could perhaps be described as 'fantasy-myth', the action of both is unreal, events happen with fantastic ease or suddenness; the settings are deliberately strange, the canvas large, and all the characters in each are related *as concepts*, to some central philosophic theme. Thus *Under the Net* is a philosophical myth – the question is, how do we experience reality, what is real in our experience? And the characters are grouped round this; Hugo with his simple nostalgia for the particular; Dave with his logical analysis of words and rigid, religious moral philosophy; Lefty with his subjection of everything to political expediency; Mars, our animal vitality; Anna, the experience of reality through 'pure' or 'impure' art; Sammy who wields money, Sadie who *uses* other people, herself; the contrasted worlds of business and art, silence and speech, isolation and society: all of these are patterned, introduced, reflected upon, and used in the story almost as dream allegory would use them.

And in *The Flight from the Enchanter*, too, the mythical framework is clear; around the figure of Mischa Fox, wielding power, cluster all the other characters, who are to varying degrees, wielders or victims of power themselves (except Annette, who evades it, and Peter Saward who is outside it). In both these books the planning, the deliberate arrangement, is apparent and unashamed. Indeed the discovery of it is a large part of the aesthetic pleasure we get from these books; I remember vividly that the first time I read *The Flight from the Enchanter* I was irritated by it, bewildered by the speed at which it moved, uncertain of what or whom to care about. But now I do see it as, if it can indeed be called fantasy-

217

myth, a powerful and bitterly amusing social myth of our times, containing its own historical terms and psychological explanations of our cruelty, our misunderstandings, our social insecurity. It is a complete and amusing and moving meditation on modern freedom and slavery.

One critic has complained generally that Miss Murdoch is a 'low-powered' novelist, and instanced the way in which we are not moved by the characters in *The Flight from the Enchanter*. Another, more precisely, said that if Mischa Fox was intended to be a newspaper magnate it was essential that we should see him in this capacity enough to believe in him. I don't think that either of these criticisms really touches the book as it stands – although they may be taken as statements that Miss Murdoch might have moved the reviewers more if she had written a different kind of book – because in its brilliant hurry, its intricacies of symbols and repeating actions it can move us *as a whole* without our being involved with any character, or even finding the world of the novel credible or inhabitable by us.

That this should be so depends, of course, on Miss Murdoch's narrative gifts; if her capacity to invent situations, twists of plot, vivid and violent action were not, in these two earliest books, apparently so inexhaustible, the whole would become a little stiff and dull.

But in both books, events are moving, both as part of the myth and in themselves. And of course, throughout *Under the Net* there is a great warmth and life in Jake himself – he involves us, emotionally, much more in my opinion, than the hero of *Hurry on Down*, a much less fantastic novel, because of the precision and enthusiasm with which he describes his reactions – to Anna in the theatre, to Lefty in the pub, to the problem of work, to Hugo's final revelations. The other characters, precisely enough drawn, vivid as near-caricatures, move like dream figures through the story, but Jake's apprehension of them gives them, within the myth, more than a mosaic reality. Consider how we *feel* the relationship between Jake and Dave, past and present, and how economically Miss Murdoch gives this feeling to us.

Another element of reality in *Under the Net* which prevents the fantasy from being simply brittle and clever is the realization of London as a whole city. This within the myth is deliberate; I have said that the contingent reality of London is set against the romantic unreality of Paris and the cinematic unreality of the plastic and Essexboard Eternal City at the studio. But London – mansions, pubs, buses, bridges, bombed churches, Thames – is sufficiently real and present in the book to anchor our feeling for it to something very real and experienced which enlarges our reaction to the theme.

And thus this book hangs felicitously together, as other later books do not. The balance between plan and reality has here, in one way, been achieved.

The Flight from the Enchanter also contains elements of 'reality' which hold us to it, and prevent us from enjoying it merely for the intellectual pleasure of apprehending the pattern. But the pattern here is arguably what is most real in a more exclusive sense than was the case with *Under the Net*. None of the characters has the reality of Jake, and many of them are not high-lit caricatures but real fantasy – Annette, Marcia, Calvin Blick. Nor are the settings and events so closely related to actuality; the London of this book lacks the vividness of that of *Under the Net*; Mischa's party, Rosa's affair with the Lusiewiczs, lack the dramatic solidity of the scene in the film studio, or the pub chase. Rosa's factory, SELIB, are slightly pale beside Dave's philosophical gatherings, Hugo's flat, the Mime Theatre. Moments are brilliantly funny – Rainborough's early arrival at Miss Casement's flat, the meeting of shareholders.

But there are failures in this book which make it less coherent than the first. Annette is fantasy, using the word in its derogatory sense. I do not know why Miss Murdoch is so unsuccessful with her portrayals of the romantic aspects of adolescence. Her sense of the indestructibility of youth seems to me to be an outside, comparatively elderly view of something which looks quite different from inside; and Annette's intense grief over Mischa is again done too much from outside – like her carefree *joie de vivre* it is ultimately unconvincing. I would apply the same criticism to Miranda in *An Unofficial Rose* – girls *do* feel such passions as Miss Murdoch attributes to Miranda, but not in this way; Miranda is romanticized from outside by her creator; her relations with Steve, Felix, Randall are perceived, not felt. Adolescence is not a simple state as Miss Murdoch sees it, nor are its complexities as romantically simple as Miss Murdoch sees them.

The funny moments in this book are more savagely, less happily funny than those in its predecessor – it is perhaps significant that we have no narrator. But even if we accept that Annette is a partial failure, the book has a controlled intensity of overall feeling which makes a direct non-intellectual appeal to us.

I would locate this in the cumulative effect of the repetition of fairly simple parallel situations. By itself Rosa's relation of enchanter/slave/master/victim with the Lusiewiczs might be said to be two-dimensional, rather coldly funny. But when it is seen as a variation on a theme of which all the other relationships in the book are equally variations (Rosa/Mischa, Calvin/Mischa, Agnes Casement/Rainborough, Mrs Wingfield/Miss Foy, Mischa/Nina, Rosa/Nina – this is not exhaustive) it gains in intensity. Coupled with the sense of Hitler, and all that entails, the sense the book conveys of our lost coherence of purpose and sense of rooted freedom in society since Rosa's mother lived, the meditation on inevitable ageing (Mrs Wingfield, Rosa, Miss Foy, the Lusiewiczs' mother) this heaping up of an insistent pattern of emotion, makes the novel a unified and finally emotionally intense picture of the state of mind of our society.

Within fantasy-myth, recurrent symbols are of course to be expected. The whole action is symbolic at its most important level. *Under the Net* is about the search for truth, social, moral and aesthetic. *Flight* is about the predatory aspects of power and love in society. And the symbols and the characters alike – Hugo, Mischa, the Lusiewiczs; the eyes in the mime theatre and the studio; the inhuman machinery in *Flight*; Hugo's fireworks; Mrs Wingfield's scars; the Artemis;

Jake's flight through Paris; Mars the dog; all these are simply part of the unity of the action, and Miss Murdoch can let her mechanical and elaborate imagination go on them because her main moral points are symbolic points – the book *is* the symbol. I think this is why I, at least, feel that Miss Murdoch was happiest when writing these first two books, and that in them form and subject matter, myth and ideas come most naturally together. The passions and the intellect do not always, as many people suppose, run in different directions. And Miss Murdoch seems to me to be a writer whose intellectual and emotional preoccupations must be running together before she can write at the highest pitch. With all the books after *The Flight from the Enchanter* there is a sense of the writer's being hampered by the battle between form and moral content, symbol and individual, theory of the novel and natural inclination. There is a sense of labour, of over-conscious effort not to pattern, which impedes our sense of the novels as novels. Miss Murdoch, like many of her characters, seems to me to be in the grip of the theory that there should be no theory; a theory that the novel is *not* a myth or a symbol, but 'a house fit for free characters to live in'.

It is arguable of course that a novelist could not sustain this kind of fantasy-myth for an indefinite period: and it is perhaps likely that Miss Murdoch would, quite apart from any theory on the matter, have moved naturally on to the more realistic novel. With *The Sandcastle* we come to a kind of fiction which cannot be called 'myth' at all and cannot, perhaps, even be seen as a symbolic novel. It is a naturalistic novel elaborated by symbols: Liffey, the dog, Felicity's gipsy and the sandcastle itself; the castle Rain kept building from dry sand on Mediterranean beaches, which were 'dirty and very dry. When I tried to make a sandcastle, the sand would just run away between my fingers. It was too dry to hold together. And even if I poured sea water over it, the sun would dry it up at once.'

This particular symbol clearly adds a kind of extra dimension to the novel. It is connected to Rain's name and, as

221

G. S. Fraser pointed out, to her feeling that she must find water when she drives Mor out in her car. The sandcastle image, since it reflects on Rain's illusory relationship with Mor, which dies of 'dryness' and also her life in a sense, and also connects her influence on Mor's dryness with that of the rain she symbolizes, could be said to work. It connects things which are not connected in any other way, and enlarges our sense of them – although not, I would suggest, very well, or very efficiently.

But what are we to make of dog and gipsy? Here, there is a difference of degree. The dog has elements of the 'natural' symbol; the sort of symbol, that is, that one finds working in one's own life. It does seem natural that Mor and his wife should remember this animal, which they had early in their marriage, as part of, or a symbol of, a vanished vitality in that marriage. Felicity's use of it – and of the gipsy – as part of her fantasy life and magic ritual is more suspect – an element of whimsy enters here, perhaps connected with Miss Murdoch's sentimental nostalgia about the intense feelings and imaginings of adolescence. And Felicity's asking Mor for a dog at the end of the book, *because of* the way the symbol has been used, adds a portentousness to what is in fact already being made, more delicately, clear by more simply narrative methods.

As for the gipsy: Miss Murdoch tells me that he 'is intended to relate Rain to Felicity (as rivals for Mor). The gipsy is Rain's unconscious "shadow" (she is a gipsy) and Felicity's "god" or help.'

There are several questions which it seems to me that a literary critic could ask here. Does the gipsy in fact relate these characters? If he does, is this the best way of doing it? And what does the introduction of this purely symbolic figure do to the unity of the book as a whole?

It seems to me that Miss Murdoch does have a limited success in relating Rain and Felicity through the gipsy, simply because his rather 'magical' appearances and reappearances do connect Felicity's emotions with Rain's since he is seen alternately with each. But, as I said in Chapter III, I do think that the use of the gipsy here does in fact avoid a problem the more consistently naturalistic novelist would have had to cope with; the making real and important of Felicity's relationship with Mor in the novel. Because of the gipsy we do not need a real confrontation of Mor with his daughter (or of Rain with Felicity) and thus the presence of the gipsy, far from intensifying the meaning or deepening our sense of complexity, produces a slackening of that emotional tension which is the great strength of the novel.

This point goes some way to answering my last question: the presence of the gipsy does, as perhaps Liffey does not, do violence to the unity of the book as a whole. Such a figure, appearing in *Under the Net* or *Flight* could have been taken as a sign or a portent, because we naturally expect in terms of fantasy-myth such odd appearances to be signs or portents. But here, where Miss Murdoch has tried so hard and in some ways so successfully to give the texture of life as we imagine we experience it, a 'sign' which appears, not to someone like Michael given by nature to see signs, but evidently with the weight of the author's idea of the book behind it, jars us because it is merely part of the author's conceptual mechanism, the ideas showing on the surface and not embedded in the story. We respond differently to signs of this kind in different textures of work and here it is incongruous.

There are good things in the book: Don's climb and flight, Mor's distress and most of the portrait of Nan who is very real and not too simple. The narrative tension is well constructed and the atmosphere of school and provincial society well sustained. I have picked on the gipsy because he is Miss Murdoch's first and crudest use of symbol in a naturalistic novel; he has been admired, by academic critics who admire a book for that kind of 'poetic' conceptual completeness which Miss Murdoch so suspects, and the discovery of which we feel as achievement, but should perhaps suspect too.

The Bell is in many ways Miss Murdoch's most complete achievement so far. It does combine, successfully, the complexity of theme and relation of characters to a central idea which is the strength of the first two books, with the straight-forward natural emotion and deepness of life which Miss Murdoch partially achieved in *The Sandcastle*. In *The Bell* both Michael and Dora are real and unexpected individuals; Michael as a type, ineffectual homosexual idealist, schoolmaster cum priest, we may have met often enough before, but such a character can rarely have been treated with the completely non-sentimental respect and the patient understanding which Miss Murdoch affords him. The same is true of Dora, who is a character less easy to stereotype absolutely, but possibly much easier to make into a fairly interesting variation on a stock theme – life-loving girl, not grown up, carelessly badly behaved. But Dora, too, cannot be so easily summed up, is treated with respect, has roundness and variety – consider the detail in which her feeling for Paul is presented, the 'rightness' with which her moments of self-consciousness are placed, and her sudden moments of wisdom.

And Miss Murdoch, by giving us unexpected peripheral detail – Peter Topglass, what information we have about the Straffords' marriage, Catherine as Michael sees her in London – has built up a solidity of real life around her community which does increase that pure pleasure in its reality which in a different context but for the same reasons we feel about a novel of Jane Austen's.

In *The Bell*, too, Miss Murdoch is more successful at integrating her symbolism and her imagery in general with the plot and characters at the simple narrative level. I am thinking here not so much of the bell itself, which I have discussed fairly fully in the chapter on the book, but of the other images, the symbolic, the metaphysical weights which attach themselves quite naturally to things which are part of the scenery; the lake, for instance, the birds, the music, the garden and the abbey. I think it might be useful here to make a distinction between a 'natural' symbol and what I have called a 'planted' symbol. The 'natural' symbol is something real in an action or a piece of fictional scenery, to which certain emotions quite naturally attach themselves, even in terms of the characters' own perception of them. I think in this instance particularly of Peter Topglass's trapped birds, where it is Michael who points out their symbolic relevance.

> 'Some birds will even enter an unbaited trap out of sheer curiosity.'
> 'Again, like human beings,' said Michael.

And it is Michael, in the same scene, who points the relevance of the imitated birdsong to the theme in Murdoch terms.

> 'It's as good as the real thing!' cried Dora.
> 'Nothing's as good as the real thing,' said Peter. 'It's odd that even a perfect imitation, as soon as you know it's an imitation, gives much less pleasure, I remember Kant says how disappointed your dinner guests are when they discover that the after-dinner nightingale is a small boy posted in a grove.'
> 'A case of the natural attractiveness of truth,' said Michael.[8]

Once we have these images of the birds and the birdsong in the novel, they reappear naturally enough and are reinforced by the associations they already have for us; the emotional weight in Dora's hearing the blackbird over the telephone from London would not be the same if we did not already know that the birds represent a particular aspect of the 'natural' purity of the country community. The same is true of the music imagery which interweaves with the bird imagery: Bach *is* austere, Mozart *is* an achievement for Dora, but these are more important because of the ways in which we see music related to the characters' spiritual states throughout the book.

Michael's thought about curiosity and traps both intensifies and directs the loose emotion the other characters feel about the ringing of the birds, because it does relate, precisely, Michael as we know him, to the action of ringing birds. And Paul laughing at Dora's distress over the trapped bird, while Michael laughs at Toby's, are supremely natural, Freudian if we like, symbols: the fear and laughter reflect, closely enough the attitudes of gentle predator and simple victim in the human relationships as in that between the man and the bird. And it is again, in a satisfactorily complicated way natural that we should see these attitudes to birds, symbolically and really, relevant to the community's controversy over whether shooting predatory squirrels and pigeons is permissible – the hunt, the decision, being human, not to hunt, the 'natural' killings of animals, the 'unnatural' aspirations of human beings, in Simone Weil's terms; all these are so contained in this idea that symbol and fictional reality work together. Liffey, and the more formal but delicately repeated hand imagery in *Flight* are natural images in this sense. They are all illustrative, intensifying, unifying symbols; they strengthen the frame and thematic structure of the novel.

But what of the bell itself? Is this natural or planted, or, if planted, does it work?

Miss Murdoch has certainly made a great effort to make it work. She has given it a vivid legend which relates it to the feeling that convents automatically arouse in many people; that they are traps, that they destroy love and turn passion into evil. She has made the raising of the bell mechanically entirely convincing and dramatic. J. Souvage, in what is in many ways a perceptive article, entitled *Symbol as Narrative Device*,[9] regards Miss Murdoch's use of the bell as something which affects the events in the narrative as a new and exciting technical achievement. I think myself that it is ultimately not successful, and for the same reasons as the gipsy is unsuccessful. Partly, Miss Murdoch fails simply to make us *see* the bell as a symbol for spiritual energy. James' and Michael's analogies between the bell and the spiritual events they are describing are a little far-fetched, a little too thought up in order to suit not their but their author's pattern. In the legend it is the sin and death of the nun which are moving and relevant; the bell here too is *decorative*, not an intrinsic part of the emotion; it is dragged in.

I am not splitting hairs here, I think. The only place where the bell is *naturally* symbolically involved in the real events is in the absurd hymn.

Some of the part it plays in the action, as I wrote earlier, could be more forcefully played realistically. If Dora is to have a 'rite of power and liberation' and later a 'truth-telling' then this *must* have force outside the associations of the bell as we have it. We understand Miss Murdoch's purpose at these moments, because we know that the bell is a symbol for spiritual energy, but we know it intellectually because she has decided that this shall be so, not because the bell works particularly well. And so we have a distressing feeling of being cheated of our climax, our moment of knowledge, as we were by the gipsy's appearance *instead* of a confrontation of Mor and his daughter. It is academically pleasurable to find that a symbol has been used, technically with success as a narrative device. But it is arguably less pleasurable than something more real would have been.

Although, with the drowning of the second bell the symbol is back in proportion and is not carrying too much moral or narrative weight; the reader's attention is focussed on Catherine, on Dora, on the Bishop and Paul, as it should be, and the bell is not troublesome.

I do not know whether I am here criticizing Miss Murdoch's achievement in using a symbol successfully as the narrative kingpin in a realistic novel, or whether I am making a more general statement that symbols in the symbolic novel can usefully intensify the narrative, as the birds do, and also broaden its terms of reference but cannot, successfully, take an essential part in the narrative without destroying its unity. I would agree with the critics who maintain that the golden bowl itself is almost irrelevant in a novel which achieves almost all that is said by its symbolic use better in other ways. In *Flight* we accept the arbitrary *Artemis*, another narrative device, because it amuses, and the whole framework is conceptual and fantastic. In *Henderson, The Rain King* the lions, frogs, Henderson's teeth, are both natural symbol, narrative device, and simply reality without any sense of jarring. But then, conversely, *Henderson*, vigorous though it is, and *achieved* in a way none of Miss Murdoch's books entirely is, does not have that sense of lived reality which is *The Bell's* greatest strength. Our reaction to

Henderson is intellectual and poetic, *not* primarily the sympathy one accords a good novel; it may well be that the bell would be more at home in a real myth of that kind.

This brings us of course, to *A Severed Head*, which Malcolm Bradbury specifically compared with *Henderson* in its use of mythical truth and myth as a method of approaching truth. I have already elaborated in Chapter V on the uses of the symbol of the severed head and I shall not go over that ground again. The symbol here, it could be argued, is in a way more successful than the bell since it does provide what one feels is the central unity of the book as a whole. The head image, more diffuse, more various, more elaborate (Georgie's severed hair, Alexander's realistic head, Martin's mother, Honor's references to it), is artistically a very different matter from the real bell stuck in the real mud and carrying planted overtones. *A Severed Head* in many ways returns to Miss Murdoch's earlier manner; the elaboration of repetitive situations around a central theme, her central image, to make a cumulative moral impression. It is a very 'finished' book; it all hangs together, it is worked through, nothing jars us. If it lacks the vitality, the intense feeling and movement of the first two novels, it has a certain subtlety to balance this.

It is not a realistic novel, nor even a novel which integrates symbol and action into myth, although is it worth remarking in passing that like *Under the Net* it has a reality that anchors its fantastic events to our experience; in this case a moral reality. Miss Murdoch has excellently caught the oddity of our behaviour when, faced with a moral and emotional crisis, we attempt to behave in a 'civilized' manner. Martin's contortions and manœuvres may be fantastic, but they grow from reality. It is not a book I like very much or take much pleasure in re-reading, in spite of this moral truth and in spite of the admiration I feel for the sheer ingenuity with which Miss Murdoch has worked her image into the very texture of her action, so that at every turn it deepens, reinforces, opens up the implications of her themes (sculpture and art; judgment; execution; body severed from mind; Freud; Sartre). She has indeed temporarily solved the problem of fitting intellectual symbolism into 'real' action, but at the price of returning partially to her old manner without her old intensity and warmth of feeling. There is a coldness, a contrived necessity about this book, which Miss Murdoch is not fighting against; it is damningly perceptive, but not, in Miss Murdoch's sense, tolerant or loving, and whilst one admires her inexorable pursuit of true judgment, it is simply amusing, simply vivid. The symbol here is not narrative device, nor does it grow naturally; it is illustrative and contrived – but contrivance does not jar for all is contrived.

And thus there is little room for warmth of character – Georgie who has it in her to be the muddle of intelligence and 'honesty' and emotion which is interesting in Dora and Jake, is edged out of the action before she has had any time to live, and at the end of the book the real sense we have of Martin's quite complex character – the mixture of weakness and a certain *inactive* intelligence – is sub-ordinated to the mythical and 'poetic' inevitability of the ending at that level. In fact if we look too closely we may even see that the study of Martin's *character* would lead us to require to explore a quite different situation from the one we are given to contemplate as the logical conclusion of the 'enslavement' and 'liberation' themes. But we do not look too closely for the book is too skilfully constructed, and too homogeneous in tone. It is indeed excellently constructed, but it seems to me a *jeu d'esprit* outside the line of Miss Murdoch's development.

An Unofficial Rose is Miss Murdoch's most ambitious book. In it she makes her most sustained attempt to integrate realism and symbolism, respect for the individual character and his individual fate with the 'metaphysical dimension' – the ideas of goodness and consciousness, or unconsciousness, 'form' and contingency with which she has been most concerned. Technically she has succeeded to a large extent, in that intellectually her patterning is coherent and acceptable. Both the Tintoretto and the roses are planted symbols but both, through the way in which Miss Murdoch has worked the story round them, take on the life of natural symbols more or less successfully. Hugh and the Tintoretto, that is,

Randall, Ann and the roses, and their different attitudes to them, illuminate each other, expand each other; Hugh's marriage and the Tintoretto are so naturally integrated to start with, that when the painting becomes part of the narrative mechanism it is much more deeply embedded in our consciousness of the characters than the bell which is isolated, planted on us. And the roses, although some of Randall's musings on them could be called 'fanciful', in a bad sense, are a datum, are part of the story even if Miss Murdoch's metallic grip can be seen manipulating the references to them to her own shape. As an *idea*, as the initial structure of a novel, the stringing of the themes and stories between the 'natural' perfection of the rose (Ann's dogrose, Lindsay's polychrome rose, 'his darling, the white rose, Miranda') and the artistic perfection of the individual Tintoretto painting is excellent.

I have discussed the German dagger earlier, and would only repeat now that it is a planted symbol of the gipsy kind, a mechanized statement of a dimension not fully realized and not integrated into the book. I mean that when I write that Iris Murdoch has put the whole German savagery into it and the savagery of Felix's profession, and the savagery of the relation of Penn and Miranda, I feel this is something she and I have *thought*, not something which works in itself; this because Penn and Miranda are not, as Felicity was not, present enough to be enlarged by the extra references of the symbol, and thus it becomes a substitute for their feeling and not a deepening of it. This point could perhaps be extended to a general thought about the place of the symbol in a novel in the naturalistic tradition: the symbol is almost never of use unless the emotions, or relationships, which it represents are already sufficiently realized by other means.

We could make out a good critical case for the novel having a reality of a naturalistic kind, selecting our material carefully. Most of Hugh (except parts of the scenes with Emma), a great deal of Mildred, especially her practical moral muddle over advising Hugh, and, most importantly, the extremely well-imagined, beautifully detailed, truly felt inarticulate relationships between Felix and Ann.

But in spite of these virtues I do not think the book does leave us with an impression either of complete complex reality or emotional power. I have offered some reasons for this in my chapter on it. Also it is, in parts, not well written; this is important, but to be discussed at a later point. But it can, perhaps, be seen, in terms of the symbolic novel, the tension between ideas, form and free characters, as the place where Miss Murdoch's theory has been most perfectly satisfied in its demands – to a certain extent at the expense of the novel. It is a realistic novel, but it has not the emotional atmosphere or depth of simpler structures – *Under the Net, The Bell* – and one feels that Miss Murdoch in some way *simulated* freedom in Hugh, in Penn, in Ann even, let alone Randall. It is in the last resort, an imitation – an excellent imitation – of a real novel.

To locate this feeling to explain it is difficult. If we take the more fantastic scenes – the scene where Randall seduces Lindsay, for instance – we feel there is something missing here which we have seen Miss Murdoch do in other places. If these scenes had been written in the first two books, one feels, Miss Murdoch would have *enjoyed* them more, and this would have been their justification. But their perfunctory nature here is partly a result of lack of pleasure and partly a result of their being subordinated to an over-rigid sense of what makes a good novel, what part they are to play in the pattern. This last criticism could be extended to the serious scenes in the book, too – it is as though the feeling had been over-digested at an earlier stage of the planning which we are not privileged to witness.

I am not here seriously comparing these scenes to the lively patterned ones of the earlier books, because Miss Murdoch is here attempting something different. Part of the theory behind *An Unofficial Rose* is that such rigid patterning is bad for the novel – but paradoxically, here, with the unashamed patterning some of the life departs and we are left with a carefully worked-in pattern dependent upon a theory of freedom of characters.

Miss Murdoch, it seems to me, like Simone Weil, in some fundamental way suspects the imagination. Whilst this may well be a virtue in a true ascetic, it is very dangerous for the novelist. Miss Murdoch has clearly a very lively and passionate imagination; we can see this when we consider both the vividness of events in *Under the Net* and the intensity of emotion as communicated to us, in both Mor and Michael Meade. But this imagination seems to work only intermittently.

In *Against Dryness* Miss Murdoch does contrast fantasy/imagination and connects 'imagination' with respect for contingency. Throughout *The Bell* however she is content to let the two words, as far as I can see, mean roughly the same thing; Dora thinks it was all in her imagination, and the word used here is derogatory. This is in a sense drawing a point too finely, but I think it is significant.

Fantasy, in Miss Murdoch's critical vocabulary, can mean anything from simple day-dreaming to making elaborate conceptual patterns from our experience which do not fit the brute and contingent reality they describe. *Under the Net* is an argument for the necessary use of Wittgenstein's conceptual net, *as a net*. Concepts, that is, we must have, whether we like it or not.

But day-dreaming, *enjoying* an imagined incident or emotion, I feel Miss Murdoch has come to fear. Thus *An Unofficial Rose* is bedevilled by the seriousness of its purpose, the moral *intention* of respect of the freedom of its characters, the novelist's gathering of material for characters 'other than herself'. It is not, or only patchily, informed by that sense of reality which we get from the novelist indulging in fantasy, in day-dreaming, in 'living amongst' her characters. Miss Murdoch is shy of them, because she respects them so; and when she rather deliberately tries not to be shy she is sometimes embarrassing.

It is very well and proper for Doctor Leavis to point out that George Eliot in Maggie Tulliver was paying back her own griefs – but part of Maggie's life came from that too; it was the excesses only that were uncomfortable, the *purely* wish-fulfilment day-dreaming. And I suppose there is an element of wish-fulfilment day-dreaming in the immense reality of the feeling in *Persuasion*. But Miss Murdoch here seems to me so obsessed with the expunging of the self from the work of art – what she calls the negative capability – that she does not, *as a writer*, inhabit her action with the vigour with which she should. And this, to a real novel, is fatal. We do not all have to be Brontës to take a pleasure in the life of our characters that comes from us; but if we, in Simone Weil's or any other *theoretical* sense, expunge ourselves completely from the matter in hand we shall hardly save the life. There is a unifying presence, in Shakespeare and Tolstoi, whom Miss Murdoch so admires, of a delighted imagination – a kind of pride, a kind of sense of life in perceiving – let alone in Keats who first said 'negative capability'. I believe Miss Murdoch (and I am not thereby comparing her with Tolstoi and Shakespeare in any other way) had this in *The Bell* and, through some excess of care and scrupulousness, lost much of it in *An Unofficial Rose*.

The Unicorn, like *A Severed Head*, makes no real attempt to come to terms with Miss Murdoch's idea of the novel proper. Indeed, it shares with that book both an interest in Freudian uses of mythology and a certain coldness, a certain ultimate impassivity towards its own story quite different from the unachieved feeling of *An Unofficial Rose*. It does not, with this book, matter as it mattered with *An Unofficial Rose* that the characters should seem unreal or uninteresting even; it is the events which must move us or fail to move us. It was the events that moved us in the two earliest books but the events here are of such a different kind that completely different formal questions become relevant in judging the novel. Both *Under the Net* and *The Unicorn* are fantasy-mythical pictures of the pursuit of truth: both *The Unicorn* and *The Flight from the Enchanter* are elaborate images of the workings of Até. But whereas the artificially various background and the unreally amusing events of the first two books were an excellent background for the high comic treatment of the metaphysical issues involved, the attitude to truth and to suffering in *The Unicorn* is not one which lends itself to a fantastic treatment with any ease – or at least, not one within Miss Murdoch's grasp.

It is significant, I think, that the beginning of the book is so much better than the end. Whilst Miss Murdoch is simply telling a story – communicating to us the sinister aspects of the landscape, Marian's unreasonable fear, the slight repulsion she feels from Hannah's oddity – she does so excellently, and the events have resonance outside themselves. The slow change in Scottow from pleasant burly countryman to something indefinably horrible and cruel is excellently done, too – the moment, for instance, when he touches Jamesie's cheek with his whip. The whole monotonous strangeness of country, house, society is something new and exciting.

But, the events cannot bear the weight of the spiritual significance they have, and this is because of something quite simple. We do not for a moment believe in Hannah's suffering, either in the earlier stages when she is a 'false God' or later when she has been awoken by Gerald. It all remains an *idea* – Miss Murdoch tells us that Hannah suffers and then proceeds to build philosophic patterns on the assumption that Hannah's suffering is, or might be thought to be, real in Simone Weil's sense. But we always know it is not real – and indeed unless we have read Simone Weil we do not know what it *is* enough to know the terms in which to think of its reality. This is partly a matter of Miss Murdoch's prose, which in *The Unicorn* is not only abstract but refers outside the novel for its meaning; it is a kind of shorthand to which we have the key only when we have read Simone Weil.

The Unicorn has, like *The Flight from the Enchanter*, a kind of crossword puzzle intellectual excitement; once one has as it were 'solved' the Freudian/mythical references of the behaviour of Hannah in particular and the community as a whole, the action becomes moving as we compare it to its interpretation. It has also the intellectual excitement present in *A Severed Head*; it is as though Miss Murdoch had set herself here the problem of seeing which interpretation was 'correct' in terms not of the Medusa's head as a symbol, but of actions which might ambiguously be called either obsessional neurosis or religious redemptive suffering.

There is a sense in which here to use a narrative, a novel, as our means of exploring the interpretations is less fantastic, less of a game than in *A Severed Head*. Religious activity is real, obsessional neurosis is real, the two overlap, and are something we can care about to a certain extent in a story, in a life as we see it, as we cannot care theoretically. It is also arguable that Miss Murdoch could not have studied this particular kind of religious activity except by describing it symbolically, from the outside, appealing to our imagination, as religion does, through the symbolic ambiguity and emotional force of myth.

To describe the spiritual progress of someone in terms in which it is to be assumed such progress takes place is something, as far as I know, only achieved successfully by Dostoievski, who had the advantage of a violent life in which his spiritual insights were also violent and easily translatable into narrative. Today we cannot write as he could, and in any case the contemplative life has, as Effingham observes, 'no story and is not tragic'. And it is with this and its peripheral activities that Miss Murdoch is concerned.

Granted, then, that *The Unicorn* is an attempt by means of the creation of a private myth, a private religious symbolism, to explore our attitudes, psychoanalytical and philosophic, to contemplation, to *religious* suffering, to evil and innocence, how far does it succeed and how far is it possible to succeed?

I think Miss Murdoch has a limited success in her creation of a significant set of surroundings for her myth. The whole scene: sea, cliffs, bog, vegetation, dolmen, villagers, the odd aeroplane, salmon, hares, pheasants, furniture, has indeed been invested with that curious *significance* the landscape has in a good fairy-tale, or in *Wuthering Heights*, even (although Iris Murdoch's precision of symbolic reference could with profit be compared to Emily Brontë's more general spiritual awareness of her *real* surroundings).

The echoes of Le Fanu are less fortunate. Strangeness for the sake of strangeness leads to a kind of fantasy in which it is easy to make subtle moral points or psychological points – that green tea releases the unconscious malevolent monkey in a clergyman's consciousness, that unconscious guilt can drive us to do violence to ourselves, apparently irrationally. But *spiritual* events are another matter.

Simone Weil's religious experience, if it has any validity, is uneasy seen in terms of the wealthy Anglo-Irish, or whatever they are, of vague 'distant' suffering, of magic garden and beautiful lady. Simone Weil wanted to study prostitutes and criminals; she herself worked in a factory and lived on the dole; she forced herself to eat too little and died partially of privation; her examples of the afflicted are always drawn from the outcasts, the refugees (like Nina), and part of the accuracy of her analysis of suffering depends on her seeing these conditions imaginatively and clearly. I am not saying that a rich and beautiful woman locked up by her husband does not suffer as Simone Weil and her outcasts suffered (however she *created* her own suffering to parallel theirs). I am only saying that as an image of suffering she is much less likely to do more than stir the fantasy in us. It is a point that Miss Murdoch could make but does not make that there is a difference between these kinds of suffering, particularly since the religious ideas without which we cannot understand Hannah's suffering at all are Simone Weil's and Simone Weil drew them from her experience of the real outcasts. Simone Weil's own self-created suffering is again different in *kind* from anything we can even attribute to Hannah. There is a touch of frivolity, a lack of seriousness in Hannah's story (not comic) which is uneasy when we realize how heavily the spiritual overtones are insisted on. Her death, Scottow's violation of her, her 'sick' suffering are moving in the wrong way. I am fully aware that part of Miss Murdoch's *point* is that they are moving in the wrong way. Effingham comes to see this sufficiently. But this does not still dispose of my point that there is a basic lack of balance, over and above what Miss Murdoch intended, between the religious 'reality' she is trying, however fantastically, to approach and the events she uses as symbols for that reality. This violates the unity of the book, produces artistic discomfort and uncertainty; *The Unicorn* is not sure what kind of a book it is.

So here we have again the tension between reality, freedom of characters, and the metaphysical dimension, the area of ideas created by the myth. Here, I think, it is the idea which is ultimately intractable; this is not to condemn the novel out of hand. It is all too easy to decide, with Miss Murdoch's novels, that something is wrong and forget what is right – Marian's bluntness, Denis's solidity, atmosphere, small moral and narrative twists. And it has extended the area in which Miss Murdoch can attack the relation of symbol to reality, even if it has partially failed on the way. The way in which the Freudian and religious interpretations of Hannah's behaviour reinforce and complicate each other is exciting technically, even if in the end the religious idea proves intractable.

We have now considered Miss Murdoch's first six novels in terms of their form, particularly the relationship of the symbols to the ideas and to the 'real' unity of the novel as a whole and Miss Murdoch's theory of the novel. It seems to me that many of the criticisms I have directed at the novels are partly a result of the developing complexity of Miss Murdoch's sense of the novel form; if the later books are less successful it is partly because Miss Murdoch is deliberately trying to extend the terms of reference of both her form and her ideas, and that this in itself is evidence of a continuing and powerful vitality. I know of no other novelist who sees the problem of form in the modern novel quite as she does; writers are, as she says, usually *simply* crystalline or simply naturalistic, and her attempt to explore the possibilities of a combination of the two seems to me intelligent and admirable, if at times a little nervous – because of the natural habit of her own mind, or because of a more general unease in the creation of sustained realistic narrative at this time, of which she is only more than usually conscious. It is a question, as always in art, of how to fuse the intellectual sense of order with a passionate sense of real complexity and solidity, and Miss Murdoch seems to me at her best to have the equipment to do this if she has never quite struck the balance in a sustained way yet.

III

At the end of *The Sublime and the Beautiful Revisited*, Miss Murdoch quotes Henry James from a letter about a novel by Pierre Loti.

> Perhaps you will find in it something of the same strange *eloquence* of suggestion and rhythm as I do: which is what literature gives when it is most exquisite and which constitutes its sovereign value and its resistance to devouring time.

She comments:

> This, which reads almost strangely now, comes to remind us that novels are after all written in words. I have suggested that we are still suffering from the Romantic attack on words. The novelist who is either poet or journalist is not using prose as he should.

And in *Against Dryness* she writes:

> Through literature we can rediscover a sense of the density of our lives. Literature can arm us against consolation and fantasy and can help us to recover from the ailments of Romanticism. If it can be said to have a task, now, that surely is its task. But if it is to perform it, prose must recover its former glory, eloquence and discourse must return. I would connect eloquence with the attempt to speak the truth. I think here of the work of Albert Camus. All his novels were *written*; but the last one, though less striking and successful than the first two seems to me to have been a more serious attempt upon the truth: and illustrates what I mean by eloquence.[10]

238

Miss Murdoch's novels have attempted increasingly to be eloquent in this sense. The first two are, one might say, more consistently well-written than the later ones and have fewer lapses into simply unsuccessful attempts on eloquence. It was fashionable in the early days to say that Miss Murdoch wrote beautifully; it is now fashionable to say that she is an interesting novelist but writes badly, is both too sloppy and too rhetorical now, and perhaps not careful enough. I think there is some justice in this criticism, but that it only becomes interesting or truly fair when it is elaborated out of its simplicity. There are ways in which Miss Murdoch writes extremely well, and there are ways in which she writes unsuccessfully, and these may coexist not only in the same book, but on the same page. As with the relation of naturalism to symbolism I find her own criteria of good prose apt and helpful. And again, in this case too, I think her sense of what prose *should be* has bedevilled her easy use of the kind of prose she naturally writes well. She is someone who is passionate or eloquent in bursts, and both when she is describing certain kinds of powerful feeling and when she is writing deliberately 'eloquent' descriptive prose, one senses a deliberate, almost devil-may-care bursting out of a natural restraint, a natural reluctance to write so, combined with a strong feeling that something is lost if this *kind* of thing cannot politely be done in prose. Here we should sympathize, and before we condemn look at the worst excesses of writers generally agreed to be good prose stylists – Lawrence, of course, and in our own time William Golding, whose descriptions of agony in *Free Fall* are much more worked up and sloppily 'poetic' than anything Miss Murdoch allows herself.

We are bedevilled in our time by a sense of humour – which Miss Murdoch excellently possesses – and prefer things said indirectly, or with understatement, or irony; Miss Murdoch's theory of eloquence could be made to argue perhaps that this is a limitation on what we can say. I would agree with this, and thus extend sympathy if not entire approval to Miss Murdoch's efforts to break the bonds of our mistrustful prose.

Miss Murdoch's use of the three terms, journalism, poetry and eloquence, to describe what prose can do, taken in conjunction with her feeling that Sartre is misled when he states simply that whereas poetry creates a thing 'outside language' prose is 'simply for communication', seems to me a good way of coming at the area in which a novel through its language moves us. It should, she says, 'create a complete and unclassifiable image'. And this image, within the novel, is necessarily diffuse; there is the eloquence created by someone with a natural ear for the banalities of ordinary conversation and ordinary thought, who can so 'place' these that they have a resonance beyond themselves; there is the eloquence of things vividly seen and accurately described (connected to our sense of the density of our lives); there is the eloquence of 'extra-ordinary' conversation and thought, precisely trapped and juxtaposed with each other; there is that deliberately serious, deliberately 'worked' description of high emotion or complex feeling, that most of us normally think of when we speak of eloquence of rhetoric. This is what we are most uneasy with, now; attempts at this are what we point to as faults in E. M. Forster or Lawrence. Our lack of this is why our sermons are now so bad, and our exhortations, since Churchill, so vulgar. It is maybe inevitable, but, within the novel, it is a significant loss. And it is, partly though not wholly, Miss Murdoch's attempt on this lost area of sensibility which has brought criticism upon her. It is easier in French; it is significant that it is Camus whom she singles out for praise.

A phrase like a 'complete and unclassifiable image' is vague enough when we come to look at it as a description of the whole effect of a novel. It is clearly associated with the literary idea of the 'organic whole' in poetry, although this is something which we may be able to admire by sleight of hand. The differences between 'self-contained crystal' (pejorative) and 'organically complete image, *sui generis*' (praise) may in practice be difficult to see, although the intellectual and emotional appeal of the ideas contained is easy enough to grasp. The 'complete image' in the poem is not the same as that in the novel; nevertheless we can discern a unity provided by the words in good novels, and can point out where that unity is broken. And if our criteria for judging what contributes to the unity and what disturbs it are different from those we apply to poetry, this is because the novel is more various and longer, and more diffuse – but the way in which a *poetic* novel resembles *symbolist* poetry to its detriment is not in the language so much as in its repetition of over-tidy symbols: Pasternak's berries, or William Golding's tying up of his themes in *Free Fall* with Kings of Egypt (who are in many ways successful) and mentally deficient girls who pee.

If we look at Miss Murdoch's first two books we see that they have largely a unity of tone, of style, which does flow evenly. Both are written in a dead-pan curt style with carefully controlled romantic undertones which rarely (more often in *Flight*) get out of hand. Jake himself is an excellent controlling device for Miss Murdoch's prose, because what we see, from her later novels, to be her natural fluctuations between washes of romantic feeling and a rather wry, rather dry wit, are naturally involved in his character. Because he is a kind of journalist and sees himself as an unscrupulous Bohemian, he indulges in amusing understatement and flat, effective jokes; because he is clearly, really and not through his creator, interested in purely philosophical problems, knows philosophers, and even goes as far as writing, apologetically, a philosophical book, the philosophical language used does not jar, but adds precision – and I would suggest that if we compare *Under the Net* with *The Unicorn* we shall find that the large difference between them is that with *Under the Net* the philosophical language can be understood in terms of what is in the book and refers to it, whereas with *The Unicorn* the language is too often a dead reference to some thought outside the book with which we are not properly in touch.

And Jake's moments of romantic prose strike us as entirely

in character, part of a picture, sudden bursts of not entirely successful lyricism which are rather touching, because he, as I have suggested Miss Murdoch is, without willing it, and we all are, is partially ashamed of them. 'On that day the city lets down its tumultuous hair which the high summer anoints with warmth and perfume.' More successfully, 'The twisting halls of falsehood never cease to appal me but I constantly enter them; possibly because I see them as short corridors which lead out again into the sun: though perhaps this is the only *fatal* lie.' This is evocative if grandiose and vague. Or

> What is urgent is not urgent forever but only ephemerally. All work and all love, the search for wealth and fame, the search for truth, life itself, are made up of moments which pass and become nothing. Yet through this shaft of nothings we drive onwards with that miraculous vitality which creates our precarious habitations in the past and the future. So we live; a spirit that broods and hovers over the continual death of time, the lost meaning, the unrecaptured moment, the un-remembered face, until the final chop that ends all our moments and plunges that spirit back into the void from which it came. So I reflected; and was reluctant to get off the bus.[11]

This is neither particularly original nor, although it has a good rhythm, particularly moving prose. The images are vague – 'shaft' 'habitations' neither vivid nor entirely neutral, giving the whole a slight air of pretentiousness. But it has caught, with precision, the language, the movement of language, of a romantic like Jake brooding on top of a bus. It contains an element of self-mockery, of poise, as well. It is part of the whole book, which hovers between the excellently vivid, idiosyncratic dialogue of thinkers, the description of events in themselves startling and economically told (Jake on the fire escape) and this kind of non-insistent Romantic brooding on Life.

In *The Flight from the Enchanter* apart from the scenes with Mrs Wingfield, there is less vivid exhilaration of dialogue; all is more mechanical. And odd moments of rhetoric stand out uneasily and break the mood; Annette and Mischa by the sea, Hunter's unconvincing illness. But Nina's death, told so flatly and without comment, is moving, and extends the book's terms of reference. Some attempts at eloquence let us down slightly: 'People whom she had known long ago came to her now, not clearly seen, but present in multitude, in a great community. She held out her hands to them across the recent past.'

But the final description of Nina singing and swaying on the windowsill, seeing her crucifix as 'a man hanging most painfully from his hands', is economic rhetoric and enlarges, as it should, our sense of the seriousness of the rest of the action.[12]

There are already traces, in Rosa's and Annette's relationships with Mischa particularly, of a certain embarrassed perfunctory use of emotional language, not so precise as Jake's self-conscious perceptions, which jars. 'Rosa inclined her head. She felt as if she was selling herself into captivity. But to be at his mercy was at that moment her most profound desire. If there had been a fire between them she would have leapt into it.' At these moments we feel that Miss Murdoch, by the use of a vaguely rhetorical style – derived perhaps from a philosopher's sense of what people 'do' say at times of crisis – is avoiding a more precise or vivid writing.

The Sandcastle creates a quite different image; Miss Murdoch lingers lovingly and on the whole successfully on the countryside, vividly on the boys' noise in the swimming-pool. She catches, as I said, the absurd tone of Mor's W.E.A. class excellently, and the gentle silliness of Everard. Here again her moments of intense feeling betray her. She allows herself to write of Rain's lovemaking 'It was like the moaning of a dove.' And I have already quoted the passage where Rain tells Mor that he is a tree and she is a bird (see p. 75).

Here one can only comment that Miss Murdoch, perhaps again because of a *philosopher's* concentration on 'usage', on what we do say, on whether our descriptions are recognizably accurate, has lost the purely literary sense that a cliché is a cliché; an outworn phrase, unless used deliberately to point the kind of emotion that arises from consciousness of its outwornness, arouses within literary writing primarily a consciousness of its outwornness and only afterwards a recognition of its accepted meaning. Both dove and tree/bird image are accurate enough, and not *simply* sloppy. Rosa's jumping into the fire might even be accurate too. Martin Lynch-Gibbon at the end of *A Severed Head* saying absurdly to Honor 'We must hold hands tightly and hope that we can keep hold of each other through the dream and out into the waking world' is using cliché absurdly and as we do use it. But in these cases neither usage nor aptness is the point – the verbal absurdity is not simply the one Miss Murdoch sees and either ignores (dove) or intends (tree/bird, dream/waking life) but jars us because the cliché on its own through our reaction to it, and unrelated to the characters, breaks the tension of the prose and the action. Martin is not, after all, inarticulate in the rest of this scene, which is in fact an example of how good and bad prose can occur on the same page.

Allied to this use of apparently sloppy cliché is Miss Murdoch's cheerful over-frequent use of certain key words which clearly move her in some evocative way – 'appalling' springs instantly to mind – with which she hopes equally vaguely to move the reader. Again, one feels, she thinks 'this word will *do* here' when in fact it detracts from the 'written' feel of her prose. This is partly why *The Bell* is better than *The Sandcastle* or *An Unofficial Rose*; it is simply more accurately, less loosely written; and Michael, like Jake, is an excellent focus for rather romantic brooding, for *self-conscious* eloquence about Life, about which the writer her-. self can be at the same time rather wry. Dora's language, Mrs Mark's idiocies, James's innocently pompous rhetoric and slightly unfeeling blurring of moral points reflected in his language 'Margaret is such a motherly soul and Dora seems to like her', 'tampering with the young's a serious matter': all these are excellently caught, various, reflecting on the central themes, making a composite prose out of diffuse elements. The dialogues between Nick and Michael are economical and moving. The descriptions are alive; lake, grass, butterfly. It is difficult to judge Miss Murdoch's prose because there is often a hairsbreadth only between her *right* use of cliché in Michael (who is shown complex in other ways; the cliché is a part of the complexity) and the wrong use I have just discussed.

It is only in the last two books that we get large passages of what I consider Miss Murdoch's worse faults: unsuccessful long rhetoric and philosophical shorthand. I have discussed the problem of Randall and 'form' earlier; in her use of the word here Miss Murdoch appeals, as she does in Max's discussion of Hannah's putative 'purity' 'suffering' 'goodness', to a knowledge we do not have and do not really obtain in the course of the book – the knowledge of an intellectual or incantatory meaning these words may have in her own thought. Even Marian's speech to Denis about Hannah, 'freedom', and 'the spiritual life or whatever-the-hell-it-is' is uneasy, because although Marian with the use of phrases like this suggests an unfamiliarity with the processes of thought behind the definition of Hannah's position, the word 'freedom' has non-fictional, non-practical connotations which we can feel Miss Murdoch manipulating – and this detracts from the reality of Marian, turns the novel into a kind of disquisition, and breaks the imaginative unity provided by the descriptive prose.

The passages of rhetoric I do not like are closely connected with these. I would instance Randall's vision of the roses, and Effingham's vision of the light streaming from everything that was not himself. These are vague, and they for their force depend, particularly Effingham's vision, on a philosophical knowledge we have not got. We have only to think of the accuracy with which a seventeenth-century writer could have built up a rhapsody on roses to see how embarrassed Miss Murdoch is with them; or, in comparison with Effingham, a seventeenth-century preacher on love and the extinction of the self.

There were moments when he knew that he loved nothing in

the world so much as he loved these roses; and that he loved them with a love of such transcendent purity that they made him for the moment like to themselves. He could have knelt before these flowers, wept before them, knowing them to be not only the most beautiful things in existence, but the most beautiful things conceivable. God in his dreams did not see anything lovelier. Indeed the roses were God and Randall worshipped.[13]

'Like to themselves' is significant; the archaism here sets the artificial tone of the whole passage, which has an artificial and worked up urgency. It is theoretical, derivative, literary, somehow finally unrelated to real or ideal roses in any concrete or written way.

But this said – and the vagueness is echoed in slightly less than clear-cut descriptions of Ann's emotions, Penn's emotions, too – there is much good writing left: the sustained accuracy of Ann's dialogue with Felix, the correctness of presentation in speech, of Mildred's *degree* of intelligence and insight, Hugh's trailing thoughts, the description of Ann's damp bonfire. I have thought that Miss Murdoch was being lazy in the last two books and writing too fast; but I now believe that some of the awkwardness is a result of a sustained attempt to extend her capacities, treat more directly, more truthfully, with powerful emotions; and that a combination of her own shyness, the state of written English prose at this time, and a kind of blunting of the sensibility which comes with the philosopher's awareness of what a word can 'normally' do, is hampering her. She can do what she did in *Under the Net* brilliantly; but her intention, her idea of the novel and indeed of prose seem to me important and her achievement seems so considerable, that we should consider seriously also the things she does with less complete success.

Walter Allen, in his book *Tradition and Dream* wrote that Miss Murdoch, alone of her generation, seemed to him to have the gifts that make a great novelist; but, he added, her use of these gifts was often 'baffling'. At the time I write there seems to be a critical tendency to emphasize her inadequacies at the expense of her gifts, partly simply out of reaction against the praise her earlier work received. She is accused of being too clever, too cerebral, too slick, too pretentious. I have argued that she is all these things but that this will not do as a summing-up, and she evades it even as it is made. *The Bell* is not cerebral, *Under the Net* is not pretentious, *An Unofficial Rose* is clumsy, not slick, when it does not work. She is a vivid, and generally accurate, if not always a fine writer; she is morally perceptive, inventive, and structurally skilfully enough to write a much better book than she has yet written.

If she is to be criticized it is not ultimately on these grounds, but because she has not yet measured up to the size of her purpose. The real inadequacies of her work as it stands derive from the conflict, which she sees only too clearly, between our literary ideals and natural bent at this time and her ideal of the novel as something wider in scope and more solidly 'real', and partly from the conflict between her own moral perceptiveness and her own ability too rapidly to make patterns of great complexity with it. If she has not balanced these yet, it may well be that she will. Her gifts are various and considerable; what she will make of them finally we cannot prophesy, but from what she has done already it is clear that it is of importance to us.

REVIEWS, LECTURES AND PAMPHLETS

10

THE TIME OF THE ANGELS

IRIS MURDOCH IS ONE of the very few novelists we now have who explores in any detail that area of life in which men are changed by thought. She knows that men are affected as moral and emotional agents both by muddled concepts and by intellectual passion, and presents these facts convincingly. *Under the Net* seems, in retrospect, to have been startling and refreshing partly because it presented a world in which characters were not only subjected to sexual or social pressure, nor were they simply puppets of their author's ideas: they *discussed* ideas and their actions and selves were changed by this discussion. Miss Murdoch wrote in 1961 that

> the connection between art and the moral life has languished because we are losing our sense of form and structure in the moral world ... It is natural that a liberal democratic society will not be concerned with techniques of improvement, will deny that virtue is knowledge, will emphasise choice at the expense of vision ... we need more concepts in which to picture the substance of our being; it is through an enriching and deepening of concepts that moral progress takes place.[1]

The Time of the Angels, like *Under the Net*, is a symbolic novel about the moral consequences of contemplating certain concepts. But between the first novel and the latest the concepts have become grimmer and larger and the emphasis has shifted from the process of ideas in the characters' minds to

251

the large and ritually significant actions the ideas elicit in them.

The Time of the Angels is concerned with the unrealized implications, psychological, moral, behavioural, of the concepts at work in the 'demythologizing' of the church, and the new 'death of God' theology. A recent article in *The Times* about this theology points out *en passant* that it has 'potentially at least a *para-comic* element' and it is clearly possible for second generation atheists, humanists and existentialists to dismiss the whole business with amusement. But anyone who has spent time talking to New Theologians about the New Morality and who shares Miss Murdoch's belief that a 'deepening and enriching of concepts' is possible and desirable may recognize the atmosphere of moral and intellectual panic confused, which pervades this novel. It *is* a frightening phenomenon, and most of its priests seem unaware of how frightening. The images of buzzing blackness and swirling fog that Miss Murdoch uses to evoke it seem to me appropriate.

Miss Murdoch's central character is a priest who says that God is dead and that 'people have often uttered the words but no one has believed them'. The most moving scene significantly is the one in which he lays out for his brother (a part-time philosopher who is writing a book demythologizing morals, a 'morality without Good') the intellectual structure of his despair. He argues that the rejection of the image of an external guarantor of order or goodness lays man open to the recognition that we are 'creatures of accident operated by forces we do not understand' and that *to know* this is very different from saying it. He argues that philosophers and theologians, with or without God, have always suffered from a facile optimism about human nature and the universe. 'It would be a consolation, it would be a beatitude, to think that with the death of God the era of the true spirit begins, while all that went before was a fake. But this too would be a lie, indeed it is the lie of modern theology ... Goodness is impossible to us.' 'Suppose the truth were awful, suppose it was just a black pit, or like birds huddled in the dust in a dark cupboard? Suppose only evil were real, only it was not evil since it had lost even its name?' In this scene Iris Murdoch evokes by flat statement that grim and perennial insight which is at the centre of Melville's 'wicked book'. 'Though in many of its aspects this visible world seems formed in love, the invisible spheres were formed in fright.' Christian love and liberal morality are inadequate to cope with the facts of existence. Carel, like Melville, appeals to Job.

> Any interpretation of the world is childish. Why is this not obvious? All philosophy is the prattling of a child. The Jews understood this a little. Theirs is the only religion with any real grimness in it. The author of the Book of Job understood it. Job asks for sense and justice. Jehovah replies that there is none. There is only power and the marvel of power, there is only chance and the terror of chance.[2]

This is a view of the nature of that Ground of our being to which *Honest to God* makes its appeal.

In a recent paper 'On "God" and "Good"' Iris Murdoch produced a metaphysical view very similar to her hero's. 'We require' she said,

> A realistic conception of natural psychology (about which almost all philosophers seem to me to have been too optimistic) and also an acceptance of the utter lack of finality in human life . . . 'All is vanity' is the beginning and the end of ethics. The only genuine way to be good is to be good 'for nothing' in the midst of a scene where every 'natural' thing, including one's own mind is subject to chance, that is, to necessity.[3]

She says that Freud's 'thoroughly pessimistic view of human nature' 'presents us with a realistic and detailed picture of fallen man.'

Freud sees the 'self' as

> an egocentric system of quasi-mechanical energy, largely determined by its own individual history, whose natural attachments are sexual, ambiguous and hard for the subject to understand or control. Introspection reveals only the deep tissue of ambivalent motive.[4]

Self-knowledge is thus impossible, and, as both she and her hero claim, 'all altruism only feeds the fat ego'. Carel her hero, also says that it is only in the infliction of pain and the use of power that human beings are directly related enough to be convinced of the existence of others. Good in this world is inextricably involved in egocentric fantasy: power and chance and fear are real. The effect of the contemplation of this idea on Carel is to cause him to withdraw into himself and the ritual exercise of sexual power over the three women of his household: black Pattie, his 'slave' whose love for him killed his wife, his daughter Muriel and his niece (later discovered to be also his daughter) Elizabeth, a blonde virgin with a spinal disease, immured with a surgical corset. His belief in goodness 'for nothing' leads him to require Pattie to perform the redeeming 'miracle' of continuing to love him after discovering his relations with Elizabeth. She cannot, and he kills himself.

Malcolm Bradbury pointed out last year that Iris Murdoch's novels could be seen as 'moral myths', the subject of which was Power. He said that *A Severed Head* 'takes us beyond the Christian liberal concept of love as understanding, as spirit, to love as something totemistic, violent and concerned with power'. His description of the function of the unrealistic sexual dance of her characters cannot be bettered.

> There are basic forces, definable in psychological or anthropological terms, which act in groups or communities and in the processes of love. The essential relationships of the Murdoch universe are not directly passionate ones; they are special groupings of men and women into fundamental rituals . . . Miss Murdoch's fiction is about love and power in groups of people and about the springs of experience which *in fact* lie behind our normal definition of our impulses. The moral speculations of the philosopher are allied to the sense of society of the anthropologist.

The structure of the 'moral myth' which centres around Carel's vision of a godless universe can perhaps best be examined by considering Nietzsche, who is invoked at moments of tension, both in the novel and in 'On "God" and "Good" '. Norah Shadox-Brown, a retired Fabian lady teacher, who represents common sense liberalism in the story, claims that the 'breakdown of Christianity' and 'this sort of twilight-of-the-gods atmosphere' is driving people mad: Nietzsche in *The Birth of Tragedy* makes much the same statement about the decline of the Greek myths. He claims, like Carel, that the rational 'inquiring mind' was 'simply the human mind terrified by pessimism and trying to escape from it' that 'Socratic dialectics, the temperance and cheerfulness of the pure scholar' were 'symptoms of decline, fatigue, distemper of instincts caught in anarchic dissolution'. There is, according to Nietzsche who feels an unholy joy about the situation which Miss Murdoch suspects, 'a *strong* pessimism. A penchant of the mind for what is terrible, hard, evil, dubious in existence arising from a plethora of healthy, plenitude of being.' His description of the fates of Hamlet and Oedipus as sages lies behind Carel's odd behaviour.

> What, both in the case of Hamlet and of Dionysiac man, overbalances any motive leading to action, is not reflection but understanding, the apprehension of truth and its terror. Now no comfort any longer avails, desire reaches beyond the transcendental world, beyond the gods themselves, and existence, together with its gulling reflection in the Gods and an immortal Beyond, is denied. The truth once seen, man is aware everywhere of the ghastly absurdity of existence, comprehends the symbolism of Ophelia's fate... nausea invades him.[5]

Critics have complained about Miss Murdoch's recurrent use of incest, as though she was simply out to shock and to shock repeatedly. I think the use of incest in her last few novels had not the full effect she intended; but let us be clear about what that effect was. Incest, for Freud, is the *ur-taboo*, the final social crime, the ultimate sexual disorder. Nietzsche moreover sees incest as a necessary accompaniment of true wisdom.

> Wherever soothsaying and magical powers have broken...

the magic circle of nature, extreme unnaturalness, in this case incest, is the necessary antecedent; for how should man force nature to yield up her secrets but by successfully resisting her, that is to say, by unnatural acts? This is the recognition I find expressed in the terrible triad of Oedipean fates: the same man who solved the riddle of nature (the ambiguous Sphinx) must also as murderer of his father and husband of his mother break the consecrated tables of the natural order. It is as though the myth whispered to us that wisdom, and especially Dionysiac wisdom, is an unnatural crime, and whoever, in pride of knowledge, hurls nature into the abyss of destruction, must also experience nature's disintegration.[6]

The myth of this novel could be said to centre on Miss Murdoch's critique of Carel as a Nietzschean sage, like his prototype maddened and destroyed by the power he evokes. He is called, without irony, a deeply religious man. But Iris Murdoch points out in 'On "God" and "Good" ' that

A chief enemy to clarity of vision is the system to which the technical name of sado-masochism has been given. It is the peculiar subtlety of this system that while constantly leading attention and energy back into the self it can produce, almost all the way as it were to the summit, plausible imitations of what is good ... Even suffering itself can play a demonic role here, and the ideas of guilt and punishment can be the most subtle tool of the ingenious self.[7]

She has examined the operations of sado-masochism in the contemplative in both *The Bell* and *The Unicorn* with shrewdness and ingenuity; in those books as in this it produced mental torture and actual suicide. 'On "God" and "Good" ' is a critique, amongst other things, of existentialist philosophies which Miss Murdoch calls 'Luciferian adventures of the will' and of which she remarks that 'contempt for the ordinary human condition, together with a conviction of personal salvation, save the writer from real pessimism. His gloom is superficial and conceals elation.' Carel says Nietzsche went mad because he saw the truth and failed to hold it in contemplation. His own 'wisdom' is perhaps converted by sado-masochistic playing with the idea of suf-

fering into a Luciferian parody of 'real pessimism'. He uses
and destroys others and is destroyed, not, as he says, he will
be, simply 'out of the boundless and impersonal justice of
the universe' but, being a Freudian fallen man, by himself.
The moral population of the novel is ritually related in various ways to this central figure. Carel's brother, Marcus, is a
neatly drawn study of the agnostic moralizing philosopher
who depends on being 'an amateur of Christianity' for his
thought. His intellectual panic on being offered by a New
Bishop with 'tolerant psychological small-talk and wordly
aphorisms' the view that morality and personality are irrelevant and that God is the 'God of the mystics' black and
empty, is comic, illuminating and moving. Muriel and the
mysterious Elizabeth have deliberately rejected God, are
'theoretical immoralists' who 'took it for granted that all was
permitted' and *know* that do-gooders are 'just gratifying a
sense of power'. A good and amusing thing is the way in
which this immoralism, by contact with real delinquency, is
shown to have an unacknowledged moral structure, just as
Marcus's agnosticism is shown, through contact with
religious unbelief, to have an unacknowledged religious
structure. Muriel learns through Leo Peshkov, who is
described as a 'natural delinquent'. His immorality was bred
in the transit camp where he was born and is a product of
the rootlessness and violence of the second war. (There is a
comic version of this theme in *The Flight from the
Enchanter*.) Leo tells Muriel:

> I want to train myself in immorality, really get all those old
> conventions out of my system, so whenever I have a chance
> to tell a lie I do so. Values are only relative anyway, there are
> no absolute values. And life's so short. And there's the Bomb.
> And one day you may wake up to find yourself getting lumpy
> and hey presto it's cancer.[8]

Many moral problems, comic and less comic, centre round
Leo's major 'crime', the theft of his father's icon – the beauti-
ful and impersonal image of the lost and no longer believed
God or Good. His father says to him 'It was a wrong thing

to do' and feels that the words are meaningless. 'One might as well have said them to Hitler or a hurricane.' But even Leo finds himself driven (utilizing Marcus's pleasure in moral sadism on the way) to restore the icon. The human incapacity to be thoroughly immoral, the validity of normal standards of honour, is the other side of the religious picture. There are degrees of immorality as there are degrees of freedom and the plot constantly opens and closes lights on to 'normal life' from unexpected angles.

The central scene, like those of *The Unicorn* and *A Severed Head*, is one where the ritual revelation of various sexual relationships breaks taboos and confers power on the onlookers. Muriel intends to introduce Leo, something 'noisy, unexpected, unpredictable and new' to her virginal and mentally drowsy cousin, procuring for all three of them a novel experience. What happens is that she herself overlooks her father's intercourse with Elizabeth through a spyhole; she uses the information to hurt Pattie, who hurt her mother; Pattie in turn reveals that Carel is Elizabeth's father; both of them now acquire power of life and death over father and master. Symbolically, this is a nice moment: the old immoralism introducing the new delinquency into the inner chamber in which the Nietzschean sage, knowing that all is vanity is incestuously engaged with a sleeping beauty (Ophelia? The Spirit?) who 'lives entirely in her mind'. But as fiction it is either too upsetting or not upsetting enough.

Miss Murdoch is as a writer burdened with the double gifts of a highly lucid capacity for forming social and moral patterns with the behaviour of what she calls the 'mechanism' of the psyche, and a real respect for, and at her best, a capacity to portray, the *unique* moral experience of the individual. I suggested at the beginning of this essay that her interests had shifted from the movement of the characters' ideas to the portrayal of ritual acts of increasingly stark and significant violence. One could wish this were not so. Even if we accept Malcolm Bradbury's view that her situations are not and need not be 'directly passionate' a myth must be either intellectually heavyweight enough, or fully enough embodied as story to stir the reader. The myth in *A Severed Head* seems to me more satisfactory than this one on both counts. Honor Klein is an anthropologist and talks *to* Martin Lynch-Gibbon about anthropology on a much more consistently real level than most of the theological conversation in this book. Moreover she is shown, in action, as Palmer's sister, before they are seen in bed together. One can use incest either way: Oedipus's marriage is embodied, and so the discovery of its incestuous nature is a shock. In *'Tis Pity she's a Whore* the incestuous love grows out of a close brother and sister relationship and is *seen* to do so. In this novel we have simply stark action, and it is not moving enough to bear the weight of representing the disintegration of nature or morals.

Miss Murdoch's last few books have been conjuring, it seems to me, with various mythical groupings which have not yet yielded a completely finished story or meaning. There are several unicorn virgins and several rapes or attempted rapes; the pairs of brothers and the power relationships in *A Severed Head*, *The Italian Girl* and this novel are startlingly similar. *The Italian Girl* has in common with this book not only two brothers, a Dostoyevskian mocking self-abasing delinquent, but also a suffering servant who is also a source of protective power – like the one in *The Unicorn*. It is as though Miss Murdoch is unable to work through certain images and free herself of them, even in order to use them differently.

I could wish, personally, that there was less ritual and more idiosyncrasy in Miss Murdoch's characterization. The best parts of the novel concern the love of the two 'deprived' characters, Eugene, the uprooted White Russian janitor whose patient presence in the basement is a counterweight to Carel's black power in the attic, and coloured Pattie whose loveless and confused childhood are described with loving detail. Their happiness is possible, and rendered impossible by Carel's sadism. But Carel and Elizabeth are too thin and fantastic to give theme or people the power they could have had. The cassock peeling off for sex is not as interesting as what is going on in the Bishop's head behind the psychological small talk. Miss Murdoch could, but doesn't tell us this. It is in the Bishop's head, and in that of the daffy psychiatric social worker, communist, *divorcée*, now 'a sort of Buddhist' that the death of God is taking place. The central story is a little too like Charles Williams. And High Anglican Gothic is finally too parochial a form for the complexity of Miss Murdoch's insights.

II

THE NICE AND THE GOOD

THE NICE AND THE GOOD is much more simply concerned with the pleasures and pains of sexual love than its immediate predecessors. It has a very large, intricately interrelated cast of characters, all more or less struggling to distinguish the nice – the pleasures of Freudian man which feed the fat relentless ego – from the good – that kind of objective and unselfish love which is not natural to human beings. Its aesthetic centre is perhaps Bronzino's painting of Venus, Folly Cupid and Time in which what one of the characters describes as 'the only real kiss ever represented in a picture' takes place amid a circle of curving and clutching limbs, where the beautifully sensual Venus and Cupid are surrounded by Despair, a prettily evil Deceit, two empty-eyed masks of youth and age, the whole unveiled by Time and Truth. Morally, like many of Iris Murdoch's other novels, it is about the inextricable relationship between love and power, and the almost automatic pain and damage this combination causes. In many novels, too, she is interested in the processes, useful and destructive, by which men make gods, or symbols of Good, out of other men. Here there are two: the 'nice' Kate, effortlessly holding together her court of dependents and worshippers in Dorset in the sun of her sensual hedonistic well-being, and the 'good' John Ducane, suddenly given power, through a suicide in his office, over various lives and careers, trying to be honourable with women and partially failing 'a man who unless he could think well of himself, became confused and weak of will'.

Kate's power is the power of benignant possessiveness: Ducane's the much more dangerous power of the good, the admired, the genuinely helpful man, whose failures can cause real tragedy.

I think this novel is formally more successful and much more rich and alive than many of Iris Murdoch's recent ones. It is a combination of lightly fantastic narrative patterning and realistic moral analysis that works very well. The tone is light and artificial – the book opens with a parody of a detective story and ends with a not unduly whimsical visit of a flying saucer – but also effortlessly serious. One of Iris Murdoch's great gifts as a realistic novelist, it seems to me, is a gift for analysing conscious thought in her characters as well as unconscious impulses and emotional states. Her characters *think* and what they think and how and how intensely they habitually think affects what they do, which is what we find in life more often than in novels. In her more remote and Gothic novels her powerful central characters are largely symbolic, rigidly contained in a philosophical myth designed by the author. This novel has no mythical centre and is the better for it. The ideas are worked out through the characters' reflections on them, like Michael Meade's painful religious and sexual tergiversations in *The Bell*. There is a dead character who practised Satanism in a cellar in Whitehall and saw himself as a god and ' "do what thou wilt" as the whole of the law'. In a bad Murdoch novel he would have been important; here his small evil is placed by Ducane's vision of it as empty and puerile. 'The great, the dreadful evil, that which made war and slavery and man's inhumanity to man lay in the cool self-justifying ruthless selfishness of quite ordinary people ... such as himself.' Ducane's attempts at moral self-control and self-analysis, the *degree* to which he is confused by his own sexual mechanism, and the *degree* to which he can control it, are excellently, realistically, patiently written. If he is never quite real as a sensual presence, and his sexual struggles seem a little like purely abstract case-histories, he is very real indeed as a moral consciousness; his struggles to be just and charitable and useful in public when he is confused and feels morally incapacitated by his failures of sympathy in private are beautifully described. Particularly good is the way he gets, with a combination of drifting and will-power, in and out of being blackmailed by a blackmailer he is chasing. His cast-off mistress, Jessica, is also, to a greater degree, not fully realized as a person – but the blow-by-blow particularity of Iris Murdoch's *abstract* description of what it feels like to contemplate the fact that your now unwanted love is a nuisance, is very moving.

The repetitive patterning of the sexual relationships is, in this novel, satisfying as it is not in some of the others. Several characters have been permanently changed by the effect of an act of violence in the past of which they were more or less guilty. Mary's husband was run over because she was quarrelling with him; Paula's lover's foot was amputated because her husband crushed it with a billiard table; Uncle Theo embraced a Buddhist novice who died in the Ganges; the refugee Willy carries an unmentionable guilt from Dachau. The repetitiveness of pain, like the apparently random sexual couplings, does act as a formal intensifier. This may be because the novel is partly about the contrast between the limited 'quasi-mechanical system of energy' which everyone has in common, and the individual ways in which this energy is expressed. Most of the characters feel desire and pain and the desire to cause pain. Most feel the pull between finding the universe random, meaningless and horrible and finding it multifariously beautiful. It is the contrast between the mechanical and repetitive inevitability of the abstract facts and the individual's complicated consciousness of them which creates the artistic tension. Sex repeated over and over and over is and is not the same each time. In this the novel is like the painting in which 'the only real kiss' which is so light that it is 'a kiss and not a kiss' is surrounded by formally similar, abstractly meaningful representative figures. The individual kiss is more and less than the meaning of the whole picture.

12

BRUNO'S DREAM

BRUNO IS VERY old and slowly dying, surrounded, like
Everyman, by the appurtenances of living he cannot take
with him: champagne, representing pleasure and society, the
£20,000 stamp collection he inherited, representing flimsy
worldly goods, his books on spiders which were his life-long
passion, which represent a meticulous particular interest in
the actual physical world and are also objects of contemplation which arouse thoughts about death, sex, propagation,
destruction and the life process generally. The novel is called
Bruno's Dream for various reasons. Bruno is like the Red
King in *Alice*. In his contracting world his consciousness
contains the life of the people he knows or knew, the dead
interacting with the living, all going through frenzied motions
which are snuffed out, artistically very neatly, for Bruno and
the reader at the inevitable end of the book and the dream.

The whole novel is in a sense a meditation on the effect of
the fact of death on our sense of the reality of our life. Bruno
is also like one of Beckett's desperate metaphysicians sans
everything, except that he lives in a Murdoch world of carefully differentiated streets, people with jobs, solid or fantastic, people who eat cream biscuits with mugs of Ovaltine in
dressing gowns, do slow foxtrots and talk metaphysics about
death. Hairless, monstrous, shrunken, smelly, almost and
then entirely immobile, human, Bruno broods about his own
ancient sexual misdemeanours and his long dead wife. He
tries to confront death, or anyway the thought of death,
'which is nothing to do with obelisks and angels'. What he

264

meets is the common metaphysical bewilderment we all feel, that life is slipping by, unrealized, like a dream – it is 'too *hard*' to realize, except when confronted by the urgency of imminent death when it is too late.

The other characters who attend Bruno's dying, like those in many of Irish Murdoch's other books, oscillate perpetually between living in the contingent muddle of incomprehensible and apparently pointless day to day life, and falling in love with each other with that sudden, compulsively violent love that inflicts itself, particularly on Murdoch characters, like a vision of necessity and meaningful reality. They include Bruno's son, Miles, whom Bruno rejected when he married an Indian girl, Parvati, who was killed in a plane crash; Miles's second wife, Diana, who married him out of a missionary need to devote herself to some sad man; Diana's sister, Lisa, a failed nun; Bruno's son-in-law, Danby, whose wife, Gwen, was drowned jumping from Battersea Bridge to save a child which then swam ashore on its own; Adelaide the maid who is sleeping with Danby and is afraid that she has no identity; and Adelaide's twin cousins, Will, the actor who is somewhat violent and wants to marry Adelaide and Nigel the male nurse. Nigel is a beautiful young man, given to tossing back his long black hair, lowering his eyes, smiling spiritual smiles, spying at everyone's windows, and meditation. He also makes it his business to inform everybody about everybody else's passions. Lisa reminds both Miles and Danby of Gwen. Danby flirts with Diana and falls desperately in love with Lisa. Miles discovers he loves Lisa passionately and that she has loved him since the day he married her sister. Nigel organizes a duel with pistols over Adelaide between Will and Danby on the shore of the Thames. The tangled web is sorted and the couples paired off in time for Bruno's dying.

The central theme of the novel could baldly be said to be the unity of Love and Death, a grand description which could mean everything or nothing. What it primarily means in terms of the human action of the story is that sudden passionate love is analogous to the apprehension of death in that it concentrates a man's mind wonderfully. It is also implied that the violence and intensity engendered by love are in a world of imperfect harmony at least as likely to destroy the loved object as to preserve it. The love which is death is perhaps one of those themes which has to be fully embodied in literature to be meaningful. It is the deflection of Othello's violent *love* for Desdemona into destruction which makes the play so peculiarly frightening, and gives precise point to the platitude that each man kills the thing he loves. In *The Bell* Michael Meade's passion for the doomed and destructive Nick, did, I think, embody the closeness of sexual savagery, intensity of vision, love and inevitable destruction. But in this novel the 'love' side of the equation is all a little remote, hinted with philosophical statements and the elegantly formalized, fantasied interlocking movements of the characters. Part of the remoteness is the effect of the dreamy quality of life the title implies, but even so it detracts from the effect.

Iris Murdoch has said herself that as a philosopher she 'inclines strangely towards monism' – towards believing that 'All is One' – and as a novelist too, both in the overt message of her books and in their aesthetic structure she is naturally monistic. She has also said that she alternates between writing 'free' books, in which the characters have more individuality and autonomy, and more tightly-constructed mythical ones. *Bruno's Dream* is one of the latter – the reader's attention is constantly deflected from the action, the physical world, loves and deaths, to the statements: God is Death, All is One. The characters merge into each other, the dead and the living bound up indistinguishably in a spider's web of relationships, similarities of temperament, repeated situations, so that there appear finally to be one man and one woman, both, like the Indian Deities, Shiva and Parvati, who are invoked throughout the book, waving innumerable arms in a dance of love and destruction. Shiva was a God of destruction who was placated like the Eumenides by being addressed as a lover and protector. Parvati, his loving child-wife, was in another incarnation Kali the destroyer who drank up all the blood of a demon to save her husband, and then in a drunken frenzy destroyed her husband too.

Other metaphors add to the stressed symbolic unity of the book. The spider, spinning its web, or trap of dreams endlessly out of itself, the eater whose love play ends in the female devouring the male, is seen by Bruno as God, creating and destroying. Nigel in his meditative fits sees himself as the slave of Shiva or of the spider, a black annihilating consciousness producing light and life. The Thames, real enough, is another undifferentiated life-force. It swallows Gwen, floods Bruno's house, Nigel sacrifices flowers to it as to the Ganges, and Danby, miraculously alive after the absurd duel swims up it under Battersea Bridge for *joie de vivre*.

The novel is saved from abstract rigidity by the precise rendering of Bruno's dying consciousness, his vague seeking after the sad, all-important small truths of his affair and his wife's vengeful fury, his fear of his dressing-gown and the doorknob, symbols of no more movement, even to the lavatory. Besides this, Nigel's youthful mysticism, his talk of death as a 'jet-black orgasm', his vision of light and dark and cosmic spaces, though recognizably part of the same problem seem reductively romantic in their desire for a whole statement. The abstractions are qualified.

I think it is because of Miss Murdoch's powerful urge to abstraction and monism that careful reading of her whole *oeuvre* lessens the impact of each individual novel as it does not necessarily do with other prolific writers. It is easier to trace analogies of themes and images – twins, suffering servants, sado-masochism – than to see how the books look on their own. *Bruno's Dream* is both unified, largely humane and moving. But, allowing for the reading difficulty imposed by the recurrence of persistent themes, I still feel some uneasiness about the mode of approach. The unity of love and death lends itself less easily to a mixture of metaphysics, fantasy and black comedy than did Jake's search for reality in *Under the Net* in terms of lesser abstractions – art, politics, the nature of language.

13

THE BLACK PRINCE

THE BLACK PRINCE is Iris Murdoch's fifteenth novel. Like her first novel, *Under the Net*, her fifth, *A Severed Head*, and recently *A Word Child*, it has a first-person, male narrator. It could be argued that Miss Murdoch uses this method of narration in stories where she is particularly concerned with illusion, partial understanding, and self-deception. All three of these narrator-heroes make a series of mistakes about the sexual and moral natures of the people around them which are more or less painfully corrected by the progress of the plot. The parallel between *The Black Prince* and *Under the Net* could be carried further since, although they are written in very different styles, the heroes of both novels, and those novels themselves, are profoundly concerned with the differences between good and bad art. Jake in *Under the Net* is a writer who finds it almost impossible to write. So is Bradley Pearson in *The Black Prince*. Both men have a relationship with another writer who is naturally prolific and who is, in their judgement, a bad or debased writer. Jake translates the 'bad, best-selling stuff' of the French Jean-Pierre Breteuil, who confounds him by suddenly winning the Prix Goncourt. Bradley Pearson judges Arnold Baffin, his 'protegé', of whose murder he is wrongly convicted at the end of the novel: 'Arnold Baffin's work was a congeries of amusing anecdotes, loosely garbled into "racy stories" with the help of half-baked unmeditated symbolism. The dark powers of imagination were conspicuous by their absence. Arnold Baffin wrote too much too fast. Arnold Baffin was really just a talented journalist"[1]. Both Jake and Bradley Pearson are drawn towards an aesthetics of silence, a belief that speech is necessarily impure, fictive, or egocentric. Both are driven, at the end of their respective novels, to end their silence and make an attempt at a 'good' book.

Iris Murdoch has always described herself as a 'realist' when talking about her own fiction. 'Realism' is for her a technique for discovering more about reality, for describing the world as it is, when not distorted by private fantasy or desire. *Under the Net* and *The Black Prince* are, however, not 'realistic' either in the way in which a novel by George Eliot, or Tolstoi is realistic, or even in the way in which some of Iris Murdoch's own novels – *The Bell, A Fairly Honourable Defeat* – are realistic. They have large elements of fantasy, improbable plotting, farcical invention and literary joke which, I would suggest, are partly connected to the fact that their subject-matter is so largely concerned with the nature of art. They could possibly be best described as fables *about* the moral value of realism, rather than as realistic novels in themselves.

The plot of *The Black Prince* is concerned with very large issues – the relationships between love and death, between art and life, between youth and age. The central events of the story – at least as that story is seen through Bradley Pearson's eyes – are to do with the complete shift in his vision of the world which is produced by his sudden, overwhelming experience of love for Arnold Baffin's daughter, Julian. The love of an old man for a girl is something which Bradley, from the outside, sees as 'ugly and pathetic' in his brother-in-law, Roger, and Roger's mistress Marigold – and also menacing in its immoral irresponsibility towards his sister, Priscilla's, unhappiness. At the beginning of the novel all the characters are much obsessed with approaching old age and decay. The women, Rachel, Priscilla, are particularly vulnerable, and Pearson's physical distaste for collapsing flesh and the smells associated with middle-aged distress are part both of his sexual isolation and of his vision of reality. He sees himself as an ascetic, and is repelled by Priscilla's distress,

Francis Marloe's seedy homosexual misery (and Marloe's affection for Bradley himself), and even Rachel Baffin's attempt to involve him in adultery. His passion for Julian (ambiguously male and female as she is) converts all these negatives to positives in the context of the passion itself. He assures her that he finds the smell of her sweaty feet delightful. He finds his own middle-aged body beautiful. He finds Roger and Marigold beautiful. He decides that he will re-read Arnold Baffin's books in order to find them beautiful. He lies to Julian about his age and finds Priscilla's agony so impossible to contemplate that he ignores it completely. He has a vision of cosmic order and a sense that he is face to face with the Good, the Real, and the True.

> Of course, the mind of the lover abhors accident . . . My love for Julian must have been figured before the world began. I realized now that my whole life had been travelling towards this moment. *Her* whole life had been travelling towards it . . . [2]

And

> This was no delirium. Those who have loved so will understand me. There was an overwhelming sense of reality, of being at last real and seeing the real. The tables, the chairs, the sherry glasses, the curls in the rug, the dust: real.[3]

Any character in a novel by Iris Murdoch who feels that his or her life has a necessary, non-accidental form, or that he or she has had a vision of truth or reality is almost certainly deluded. In her philosophical work Miss Murdoch has several times spoken of the human tendency to 'deform' reality by seeing it through egocentric fantasy. She likes to use an image of a 'machine' for the unconscious operations of the psyche, and has written of what she sees as 'true and important' in Freudian theory in her essay 'On "God" and "Good" '.*

Iris Murdoch is particularly interested in the psychological

* See p. 253.

'system to which the technical name of sado-masochism has been given'. She has described it as 'a chief enemy to clarity of vision, whether in art or morals' and sees a masochistic interest in suffering as a secret form of egoism masked as self-denial. In this context Bradley Pearson's own descriptions of himself as a masochist are interesting, as are Arnold Baffin's condemnations of him as one, and Francis Marloe's psychological portrait of him which appears among the postscripts to the novel. How far does Marloe's assessment of Pearson as a repressed homosexual, masochistic like 'all artists' coincide with Iris Murdoch's own understanding of her hero's inner machinery? How far is Marloe's description conditioned by Marloe's own homosexual masochism? The Black Prince, who is an object of love and terror, is a composite god-demon in the novel; he is Apollo, the god of light and art, but also the cruel god who punished the faun, Marsyas, by flaying him for daring to compete with him as an artist. He is Shakespeare and Hamlet, he is Love and Death, and Art. In this context it could be argued that Bradley's love for Julian is partly a love for Death. He can only make love to her successfully when she is clothed as Hamlet, a black prince, carrying a skull. The love-making hurts and distresses her. This is sado-masochism – is it anything more profound still? In the essay 'On "God" and "Good" ' in which Iris Murdoch discusses the relation between sado-masochism, art and morals, she comments that 'The idea of suffering confuses the mind and . . . can masquerade as a purification. It is rarely this, for unless it is very intense indeed it is far too interesting. Plato does not say that philosophy is the study of suffering, he says it is the study of death.'[4] Bradley, at the end of this novel, feels, during his trial, that he has been privileged enough to have an *ordeal* which is in some way a guarantee of true vision. Iris Murdoch feels that it is almost impossible to imagine death. Has Bradley been released to write a good novel by some *real* experience of death, Priscilla's or Arnold's? Or is he still enjoying a fantasy of suffering which secretly delights his ego? The knowledge of Priscilla's suicide contributes to Bradley's violent love-making to Julian dressed as Hamlet – but Bradley does not see that death clearly because of his involvement in his own desires.

Bradley Pearson's views on art, and on the relationship between art and morals are very like those expressed by Iris Murdoch herself in her philosophical essays.

> Art and morals are, with certain provisos, one. Their essence is the same. The essence of them both is love. Love is the perception of individuals. Love is the extremely difficult realization that something other than oneself is real.[5]

> I have always felt that art is an aspect of the good life, and so correspondingly difficult ('Bradley Pearson').

Iris Murdoch has commended, or endorsed, T S Eliot's view that the true artist should be impersonal, emptied of self, 'the lover who, nothing himself, lets all things be through him'. Bradley's 'silence', self-effacement, in morals and writing, are related to this ideal of impersonality – as is his preoccupation with the selflessness of Shakespeare's vision, which again has been expressed by Iris Murdoch herself on other occasions. Iris Murdoch has argued that the most difficult thing to see or represent truthfully or clearly is the distinct separate being of other people. Bradley Pearson in his apostrophes to his 'friend' about the difficulty of telling his story truthfully speaks in a tone and style remarkably similar to his creator's:

> How can one describe a human being 'justly'? How can one describe oneself? ... 'I am a puritan' and so on. Faugh! How can these statements not be false? Even 'I am tall' has a context ... Yet what can one do but try to lodge one's vision somehow inside this layered stuff of ironic sensibility, which, if I were a fictitious character, would be that much deeper and denser? How prejudiced is this image of Arnold, how superficial this picture of Priscilla! Emotions cloud the view, and so far from isolating the particular, draw generality and even theory in their train. When I write of Arnold my pen shakes with resentment, love, remorse and fear. It is as if I were building a barrier against him composed of words, hiding myself behind a mound of words. We defend ourselves

by descriptions and tame the world by generalizing. What does he fear? is usually the key to the artist's mind.[6]

It is worth pointing out, perhaps, that Iris Murdoch herself has said that 'What does he fear?' is the key to the philosopher's mind. Bradley Pearson's interpolated addresses to his 'friend', whilst they should alert the reader to question the style and emphasis of his narrative, are also, in their similarity both in style and in moral and aesthetic preoccupations to the author's own, a guarantee of his artistic integrity. He knows the difficulty of seeing people clearly. He allows Priscilla to die, out of a combination of fear and revulsion for her despair and decay, and obsession with his own self-renewal in his passion for Julian. But he is able to note, objectively, at the end of the passage just quoted that she 'was a brave woman. She endured unhappiness grimly, with dignity. She sat alone in the mornings manicuring her nails while tears came into her eyes for her wasted life.' In the same way, at the end of the book, his attitude to Julian has its ambivalences. There is a clear sense in which his 'work of art', the novel containing Julian, is *not* an impersonal objective vision of her, or of reality, but an act of domination and possession:

> She somehow was and is the book, the story of herself. This
> is her deification and incidentally her immortality. It is my
> gift to her and my final possession of her. From this embrace
> she can never now escape.[7]

But Bradley Pearson's narrative nevertheless ends on the contrary assertion, that he is aware, in a new kind of silence, that she is unknown and other than himself. His 'friend', P Loxias, has taught him, like Shakespeare's Prospero, to drown his books and 'abjure what you have made me see to be but a rough magic'. He can say to Julian, 'Art cannot assimilate you nor thought digest you.' Her separation guarantees her reality.

In her later novels Iris Murdoch has increasingly made use of Shakespearean plots and references to Shakespeare. This is partly because she is so concerned to identify the difference between good and great art – if one sees one's improvement, as man and artist, as a process of contemplating the truly good, the question of the nature of Shakespeare's gifts, of his vision of human beings, of reality, must arise. It is also partly because she sees him, with the great nineteenth-century novelists, as a high example of the 'realism', moral and aesthetic, that she wishes to understand and achieve. In other later novels she parodies his comic plots. *The Black Prince* is a complex artistic joke about the nature of *Hamlet* and *Hamlet's* relationship to its largely unknown and impersonal author. The crucial discussions between Bradley Pearson and Julian Baffin about *Hamlet* offer insights into the moral and dramatic problems of the whole novel.

Bradley Pearson's central observation about *Hamlet* is that it is the one Shakespearean tragedy in which the author can be felt to be identified with the hero, in which Shakespeare felt an 'urge to externalize himself as the most romantic of all romantic heroes'. 'Hamlet is Shakespeare, whereas Lear and Macbeth and Othello ... aren't.' *Hamlet* as a play has provoked Freudian interpretations, both of Hamlet's behaviour and of Shakespeare's own. It is the classic illustration of the Oedipus complex – Hamlet is in love with his mother, wants to murder his father, dare not, through guilt, kill the substitute father who *has* murdered his own father, and thus finds all sexual matters disproportionately revolting and his own existence problematic. Bradley Pearson endorses this Freudian view gaily, and also states that Shakespeare was 'of course' homosexual. Bradley's own sexual behaviour – and that of the other characters in the novel – is a kind of riddling parody of this 'vulgar' view of Shakespeare. In Shakespeare's plays women were boys dressed as women dressed as boys. In his sonnets his lover is addressed as 'the master-mistress of my passion'. Julian, with her name which is applicable to man or woman, *is* this master-mistress. What has this to do with Bradley's earlier love and rivalry for Julian's father, Arnold? For Julian's mother, Rachel? What provokes the murder of Arnold? After Arnold's murder Julian becomes much more like Ophelia, a daughter crazed by love of her dead father. In this context it is worth noting that Iris Murdoch's subplots in this novel are, like Shakespeare's, variations on a central theme. In *Hamlet*, Laertes and Ophelia have a murdered father as well as Hamlet. In *The Black Prince* Arnold's love for Christian reflects, with differences, Bradley's relationship with Arnold's daughter and wife. Priscilla's misery is a variation on Rachel's. Roger and Marigold are related to Bradley and Julian. Here Iris Murdoch seems to be deliberately exploiting what can be seen as a limitation on her, or any dramatic artist – the fact that, as Bradley tells Julian in the context of *Hamlet*, 'The unconscious mind delights in identifying people with each other. It has only a few characters to play with'. Julian says 'So lots of actors have to play the same part'. Iris Murdoch is playing a deliberate game with the fact that all characters can be reduced, at one level, to The Father, The Mother, The Lover, The Victim. Her novels have been criticized for repeating the same plots, relationships, sexual merry-go-rounds. Here she is, in terms of Shakespeare's great play, pointing out the artistic uses that can be made of such repetitions, their psychological inevitability at one level.

Francis Marloe's name is also a Shakespearean joke. Francis Bacon and Christopher Marlowe have both been claimed, by vehement advocates, to be the 'true' author of Shakespeare's work. This Marloe – homosexual like Christopher Marlowe – resembles, it seems to me, Mephistopheles in Marlowe's *Doctor Faustus*, a curiously attractive demon who knows only too well that the world is hell. 'Why this is hell, nor are we out of it.' Marloe's Freudian commentary on Bradley's work seems less distorted by personal fantasy or greed than the other commentaries, but nevertheless distorted – in this context it is interesting to reflect on the layers of biographical, critical and theoretical commentary beneath which the vulgar facts and the good art of Shakespeare are buried.

Bradley writes of *Hamlet* that Shakespeare

has here performed a supreme creative feat, a work endlessly reflecting upon itself, not discursively but in its very substance, a Chinese box of words as high as the tower of Babel, a meditation upon the bottomless trickery of consciousness and the redemptive role of words in the lives of those without identity, that is human beings. *Hamlet* is words and so is Hamlet. He is as witty as Jesus Christ, but whereas Christ speaks Hamlet is speech. He is the tormented empty sinful consciousness of man seated by the bright light of art, the god's flayed victim dancing the dance of creation . . .

Shakespeare here makes the crisis of his own identity into the very central stuff of his art. He transmutes his private obsessions into a rhetoric so public that it can be mumbled by any child. He enacts the purification of speech, and yet also this is something comic, a sort of trick, like a huge pun, like a long almost pointless joke.[8]

If this passage is compared with the definition of art offered by Apollo (P Loxias) at the end of the novel, it can help to clarify the subject-matter of *The Black Prince* and the central relationship, with which this essay began, between the prolific 'bad' novelist, Arnold Baffin, and the silent aesthetic perfectionist, Bradley Pearson. P Loxias tells Julian

To say that great art can be as vulgar and as pornographic as it pleases is to say but little. Art is to do with joy and play and the absurd. Mrs Baffin says Bradley was a figure of fun. All human beings are figures of fun. Art celebrates this. Art is adventure stories.[9]

And P Loxias ends with a pointed joke:

I hear it has even been suggested that Bradley and myself are both simply fictions, the inventions of a minor novelist. Fear will inspire any hypothesis.

Bradley protected himself from his fear of Baffin, with a barrier of words. Shakespeare exposed his own 'flaying' by 'the god' in a character whose being was words. Shakespeare was a great enough artist to transmute his own private agony into pure language, his personal vision into impersonal truth. But like the lovers and victims all the artists in this novel are in some sense one. Apollo killed Marsyas. Bradley killed Arnold. Bradley despised Arnold for using his friends as fictional matter, for being the hero of his own novels, for writing metaphysical adventure tales. But Bradley's tale of his love for Julian is an adventure tale, a comic murder story with metaphysical overtones, not so far from Arnold's own methods. The two men quarrel at the beginning of the novel because Bradley despises Arnold for being a prolific professional 'writer', whereas Arnold despises Bradley for the cowardice implicit in his perfectionism about good art, his inability to write at all. Bradley claims to be an 'artist'. Shakespeare, of course, was both prolific writer and major artist. Bradley's aesthetic embodies Iris Murdoch's own ideals, or some of them: Bradley's criticism of Baffin is a parody of the more disparaging current criticisms of the prolific Iris Murdoch. Much modern fiction is fiction about fiction, art about art, deliberately exploiting or displaying its own artificiality. *The Black Prince* is also a series of Chinese boxes, a game about the identity of writers and the sources of art, which requires a comic and ironic consideration of its own form and author.

14

HENRY AND CATO

THIS IS IRIS Murdoch's eighteenth novel in twenty-two years. During her extraordinarily prolific and consistently high-powered career her style has changed. Her early novels were witty, surreal fantasies, fast-moving and dreamlike, with large casts of rootless cosmopolitans. Then she turned deliberately to the leisured realism of the traditional English novel and tried to write with the social precision and density of Jane Austen in, for instance, *An Unofficial Rose*. Interspersed there was also the odd, half-mythical Gothic story like *The Unicorn*. Lately she has turned to fast-moving, melodramatic tales, learning from late Dickens and Robert Louis Stevenson. Both Miss Murdoch and her characters are for ever asserting 'art is adventure stories', meaning that novels should be plotted, and there should be action. But she uses her thriller plots for her own purposes of moral and philosophical exploration. What has not changed at the deepest level is the nature of the moral problems she explores.

She is interested in the complex relationship between love and the desire for power, realizing many people use love as a power game because they want to control the loved one's fate. For others, love is self-sacrifice, supposedly the highest Christian ideal, but in Iris Murdoch's world it usually contains elements of Freudian masochism. *Henry and Cato* explores these problems in an unusually stark, profoundly ironic and simple story. The two main characters are old childhood friends, Cato Forbes, a Catholic convert and a priest with doubts; and Henry Marshalson, an art historian in a third-rate American college. They are contrasted and related throughout the novel.

When it opens, Cato is disposing of a revolver over Hungerford Bridge; Henry is flying to England, full of glee at the death of his hated elder brother. Both are the children of bullying fathers. Cato is trying to help down-and-outs in a mission in Notting Hill, and is obsessed by love for a delinquent teenage charmer of a boy called beautiful Joe. Henry meets and takes under his wing a girl who says she is his brother's ex-mistress and an ex-prostitute. Cato is trying peaceably to rescue the uncivilized, taming the violence and power of the gangs with love. Henry, in a wild, purposeful mood, decides violently to destroy what he chooses to think is a corrupt civilization, but doesn't get much further than selling his own childhood home and land over his mother's head. Neither Cato or Henry has an easy passage. Neither is clear about what he is doing.

Other characters include Cato's lively, witty, wholesome, virginal and drop-out sister, Colette, who is in love with Henry; Lucius Lamb, a faded, beautiful boy of an ageing poet; Gerda, Henry's formidable, beautiful mother, grieving for her elder son, trying to deal with the fury of her younger son, manipulating and suffering. It is a small cast by Iris Murdoch's standards, and the novel does not explore even these characters with the delicacy and subtlety of the earlier *The Bell* or the more recent *A Fairly Honourable Defeat*. Cato, confused between his love for a vanishing God and his love for Beautiful Joe, is a descendant of Michael, also a failed priest, also a disastrous lover of boys, trying hard to do real good in *The Bell*. Like the liberal characters in *A Fairly Honourable Defeat* the thoughtful moralists of this novel do not know how to deal with real savagery and violence when they meet it.

Like most of Iris Murdoch's heroes, Henry and Cato are *intelligent* – they try to think out how they should act – and this capacity to present credible *thinking* beings is rare in modern novelists. But this novel depends peculiarly on its plot – which contains kidnapping, possible rape, movements of huge sums of money, violent death and a ridiculous, ironic and satisfying love story. It is one of the few novels where I found it almost impossible to predict the end. The result of the plotting and meditation is a tragi-comedy of the kind Iris Murdoch has lately made her own. In *The Black Prince* the god Apollo appeared briefly as a sort of impressario, assuring the readers that human life was essentially comic – human beings essentially figures of fun – and in *Henry and Cato* the ludicrous and blankly tragic become curiously intertwined.

I used to say jokingly of Iris Murdoch's earlier novels that they were imaginative recreations of the endless moral debates about what you would do if, say, you were a Quaker pacifist in an already overcrowded lifeboat and saw one man too many – a bad man at that – swimming desperately after you. This novel is very much one of these: what would you, or could you, do if . . . It puts you through it. And it is worth the struggle.

15

THE SEA, THE SEA

THE PLOT OF *The Sea, The Sea* concerns the tempest of passions aroused by Charles Arrowby, an impresario who has retired to a seaside retreat in order to abjure, like Prospero, the rough magic, illusion and power-games of the theatre and meditate on the end of life. He is a man who considers himself not highly-sexed, but attracts, voluntarily and involuntarily, two ex-mistresses, good, devoted Lizzie and witch-like Rosina, to disturb his retreat, as well as a series of wanted and unwanted male visitors – Rosina's ex-husband, an Irish actor, Peregrine, Lizzie's peaceable homosexual companion, Gilbert, his own mysterious cousin, General James Arrowby, expert on Tibet, Buddhism and Oriental lore and languages. He discovers in the village his childhood – and, he claims – only love, Mary Hartley Smith, now not a beautiful clean-limbed girl but an ageing, puffy 'bearded lady' as Rosina unkindly puts it. He attempts to 'rescue' her by abduction from what he deduces is an unhappy marriage, having enticed into his house her runaway adopted son Titus, who mistakenly believes Charles may be his father . . .

Like those of other first-person male narrators in Iris Murdoch's novels, Charles's very style is an indication that a major subject of this tale is illusion, self-delusion, wish-fulfilment, the impossibility of seeing truth. Indeed, he is more blatantly deluded than the heroes of *Under the Net, A Severed Head, A Word Child* and *The Black Prince,* and thus paradoxically more endearing: his precision about the details of daily life, from youth renewed through a woven hair piece to a series of recipes for cooking vegetable protein, boiled onions, kipper fillets and other such delicacies suggests a capacity for mundane attention to veracity and detail which in Murdoch is a virtue, in novelist or hero. When, as they must, both violence and comedy ensue, with more than hints of genuine magical or daemonic intervention, the novel becomes a curious patchwork of those of Iris Murdoch's novels which could be described as magical fables and those which are a sustained attempt on the style and virtues of the nineteenth-century 'realist' novels.

The title, I guess, derives from two sources. There is the cry of Xenophon's army in the *Anabasis* when, after struggling through cruel mountain passes the soldiers behold the end of their journey, the Euxine Sea, and cry 'the sea, the sea' in a moment of triumphant achievement. And there is the sea in Paul Valéry's poem, *Le Cimetière Marin*, the graveyard by the sea, in which Valéry meditates on death, eternity, and 'la mer, la mer, toujours recommencée' – the sea, the sea, always beginning again. Iris Murdoch seems to have a peculiar fondness for this poem – the four lines ending in 'la mer, la mer, toujours recommencée' are quoted in *The Unicorn*, and the aspiring poet, Muriel, in *Time of the Angels*, is writing a long philosophical poem in its stanzaic form. This is interesting, because both *The Unicorn* and *Time of the Angels* contain, in a much more stylised form, central situations in which a captive princess is kept in an inner room, intensely loved, but not allowed out, a sleeping beauty to be awakened by the kiss of reality and true love, so the other characters think, as Charles in this novel tries to persuade himself that his beloved Hartley will cease to drowse and snivel and wake to her old love for him. But both imprisoned princesses in earlier books have a chilly aspect, a kind of deadly touch in their passivity, and are referred to as *La Belle Dame Sans Merci*. Those earlier princesses are related at one level to the vampires and undines of fairytale: Charles's bearded lady is another fairytale motif, the old hag whose youth will be restored if he can only love well or wisely enough. It may seem to the reader of *The Sea, The Sea* that this is so hopeless an undertaking as to be ludicrous, even frighteningly pitiable; and in the management of the character, both as an unknown quantity and as a simple woman on whom the narrator projects his complex life's emotions, Iris Murdoch's hand is less sure than it can be. Hartley does not quite keep her distance enough, or come to life enough to be credible – though as I write this, I see it could have been what Miss Murdoch intended.

The sea, in a Murdoch novel, represents what the priest of no god in *The Time of the Angels* called 'power and the marvel of power, chance and the terror of chance'. It is beautiful, shifting, contains inhuman beasts friendly and alien (seals, in *The Unicorn* and in this book, a sea serpent in this book too). It kills, supports, entices, delights and terrifies, reminding one that those things exist, things that Wallace Stevens called 'inhuman, of the veritable ocean'. It is interesting that in both *The Unicorn, The Nice and the Good* and *The Sea, The Sea* death, or possible death by drowning give characters the nearest chance they have to a vision of the universe freed from their selfish desires. In *The Nice and the Good* John Ducane rescues a boy from the tide in an underwater cave, and wisely learns to love his own simple Mary in the real world, through a self-knowledge achieved as he is stripped of desire and illusion face to face with the sea. In *The Unicorn* Effingham Cooper, drowning in a bog, cannot hold on to the vision he has of 'the love that is the same as death' when he comes back to life, though he sees that 'since he was mortal he was nothing, and since he was nothing, all that was not himself was filled to the brim with being and from this the light streamed'. This is the saints' unsustainable vision, a recurrent Murdoch theme, voiced in Buddhist form by Cousin James in this novel. Charles, in this novel, is miraculously rescued from a fall into a boiling cauldron of waves but, like Effingham, returned to human petty concerns.

In *The Unicorn* Effingham explains his love of the imprisoned Hannah to himself as what Iris Murdoch would call a piece of Freudian 'machinery' – 'he would identity the

woman he loved with his mother and then make her unapproachable and holy'. I would argue that Charles has done
this with Hartley, who, though he never says so, resembles
his own mother closely (his father called his mother 'Maid
Marian'), in her preoccupation with quiet domesticity,
renunciation and duty. The women Charles has practically,
as opposed to idealistically loved, in the world of the theatre,
beginning with a considerably older ferocious, captious and
glamorous actress, Clement Makin, do not on the whole have
such preoccupations. They resemble his cousin's glamorous
mother, Aunt Estelle. He asks himself frequently 'Who is
one's first love?' But never answers: 'one's mother'. Another
Murdoch theme which is here played out with a difference
is the closely-netted workings of the desire for power and
the desire for self-abnegating love. Iris Murdoch wrote that
Freud's 'thoroughly pessimistic view of human nature' saw
the psyche as 'an egocentric system of quasi-mechanical
energy, largely determined by its individual history' and went
on: 'objectivity and unselfishness are not natural to human
beings'. This 'mechanism' is comically at work in *A Severed
Head* and many subsequent novels, where attempts at virtue,
clarity, love, lead back into the mazes of sado-masochism –
'a plausible imitation of the good' and a fascination with
master-and-slave relations.

Charles, the theatre director, was a 'cruel' master, exacting,
charismatic (by his own account), Prospero, or Oberon, king
of shadows. He manipulated people and events. Seeking not
to do this in life, he simply transforms his new hermitage to
another theatre. Set against Charles is James, who has the
antithetical virtues of soldier (unselfish obedience to rules),
aspiring saint (meditation, vision of empty 'clear light'),
truthfulness and in his case genuine magical powers, or what
he calls 'tricks', as Shakespeare's and Prospero's illusions are
'tricks'. Iris Murdoch once said that a major theme of all her
novels was the contrast between artist and saint, and one
can think of endless pairs of men who slightly resemble
Charles and James. Bradley Pearson and Arnold Baffin in
The Black Prince are artist as meditator (like Valéry on the

sea) and artist as trickster, though Pearson's 'illusions' turn
out to be more refined and dangerous than Baffin's. The
brothers in *A Severed Head*, sculptor and wine merchant,
are artist and moral being – to whom is granted a moment
of vision.

In *Under the Net*, Jake, narrator, failed artist, aspirant
epic poet, is contrasted with Hugo Belfounder, munitions
millionaire, trying to renounce power for the 'truthfulness'
of silence and particular moments of vision. Hugo's art forms
are the ephemeral firework 'set-piece' – honest because
momentary – and the mime. In that book Jake, like Charles
in this, is the self-deluding, egocentric 'artist' hopelessly cling-
ing to an unrequited love. Hugo the 'good man' is the almost-
saint, whose virtue has something apparently sinister in its
bareness. But Charles's plays in *The Sea, The Sea* are like
Belfounder's fireworks – ephemera, sound, light and dance,
with no aspirations to permanence. He is an illusionist. James
in *The Sea, The Sea* has much in common with the renunciat-
ory attractive soldier Felix, in *An Unofficial Rose*, who loses
his good domestic Anne behind her rose-garden to her dream
of her unfaithful 'artistic' husband Randall. He has also much
in common with James Tayper Pace in *The Bell*, who stands
for plain truth and rules of life as against the imaginative
inner life, or love, of the more 'interesting' Michael Meade.
In *The Sea, The Sea* both Charles and James turn out to find
it hard to renounce minor tricks of power, magical, or stage-
managerial, for true vision. As one might know, James turns
to the sea of death and the possible illusions or pure light of
the voyaging dead soul in the Tibetan Bardo Thodol or *Book
of the Dead*. Charles escapes death by drowning to return
to kipper and apricot recipes, intrigue, and a capacity to
remember the death of Clement, which he has avoided
throughout the tale.

One might ask, what is new in this novel – how far does
it simply echo themes – moral, Freudian, aesthetic, religious,
symbolic patterns and character groupings from earlier
works? I think what I ultimately most admired was Miss
Murdoch's extraordinary success, in this book, with one of

her expressed ambitions – to suggest, as Shakespeare and Dickens do – a world of people related to 'in' this fictive world – who are only sketched, or mentioned, or hinted at. A success with things unsaid, and people undescribed. Clement takes almost no page-space but is a huge presence. Another mistress, Jeanne, is a name, a few facts, also a presence. So is a dead actor and a live film producer. So also Titus, who is not Mary Hartley Smith's son by Charles. When Rosina learns of Titus she malevolently reveals that she caused Charles's child by her to be aborted. A careful reader notes – but Miss Murdoch never mentions – that Titus resembles Lizzie in having gingery corkscrew curls and that Lizzie mourns his eventual accidental death worst – which is in character anyway, but gives one to wonder . . .

And the magic? How do the daemons, sea-serpents, Tibetan magical 'tricks' and the careful realism of Charles's daily tidinesses and chaos fit? Not *quite*. Miss Murdoch has been searching for a way to combine Tolstoi's, or Jane Austen's, realism with the energy of a Shakespeare plot or an adventure story, for years. One has to change mental attitudes to read this book from time to time – as was not so with *The Unicorn*, fey and fabling – but the shifts and self-consciousness can produce pleasure in the 'made-up' story as well as irritation at breaks in the smooth flow of belief. It has a technical mastery of mimesis of human attention – bad tinned clams at moments of extremity take space that convention would decree should go to high sentiment – of which we also have enough. It ends on a series of random notes and further notes after the rounding vision of stars, seas and seals at the end – notes which reopen closed stories, change characters in two lines (foolish Peregrine is suddenly martyred by the IRA), introduces new people in the penultimate pages. As Valéry ended: 'Le vent se lève! . . . Il faut tenter de vivre! L'air immense ouvre et referme mon livre . . .'

La mer, la mer, toujours recommencée.

16

NUNS AND SOLDIERS

IRIS MURDOCH WRITES, as everybody knows, very complicated and convoluted love stories. She is also a philosopher who has meditated profoundly and elegantly upon both Freud's and Plato's concepts of love as a motive power in our universe. She would not, I take it, disagree with E. M. Forster's view of why there is more 'love' in novels than in 'life' perhaps. Forster wrote that 'The constant sensitiveness of characters for each other . . . is remarkable, and has no parallel in life, except among people who have plenty of leisure. Passion, intensity at moments – yes, but not this constant awareness, this endless readjusting, this ceaseless hunger. I believe that these are the reflections of the novelist's own state of mind while he composes . . .'[1] The glory of Iris Murdoch at her best – as she almost always is in *Nuns and Soldiers* – is that she can convey with total respect the awareness, readjusting and hunger, and at the same time 'place' it, with a severe but not savage irony, in a world which hints at quite different forces and priorities. The tramp of troops, genocide, pure perception, money, the absconded God, death.

The 'plot' of *Nuns and Soldiers* is simple but hard to summarize. Gertrude is married to Guy, who is Anglo-Jewish and approaching death, from cancer, at the age of forty-three. Anne Cavidge, Gertrude's old Cambridge friend, has just returned from an enclosed Catholic order of nuns to the mess of the real world, following some obscure religious compulsion to 'a kind of negative humility which did not aspire to the name of goodness'. Peter, known as the Count because he is Polish, is a solitary displaced person who rejected, and too late embraced, his parents' profound commitment to their country (as it no longer is), language (which he had refused to learn) and history (which the other characters don't know or understand). Peter is Guy's protegé and is in love with Gertrude. Then there are Tim Reede, a second-rate painter, Irish, feckless, untruthful, and his non-resident mistress, Daisy, another ex-Slade dropout, failed painter and failed novelist. They live, with increasing difficulty, from hand to mouth and haunt a pub called The Prince of Denmark. Most of the rest of the significant characters are part of Guy's large Anglo-Jewish collection of relations, protegés, doctors, lawyers . . .

Guy dies. Anne consoles, or appears or attempts to console Gertrude. The Count, who has overheard Guy asking Gertrude to remarry, possibly himself, decides to wait a year before proposing. Tim, driven by Daisy, comes to beg from Gertrude for money, is offered a summer as caretaker of her Provençal house in which he and Gertrude fall wholly and enchantedly in love . . . It has the fairytale quality of an innocent *Hamlet* where the Prince may marry the bereaved Queen and the childless woman may love a dependant and charmingly incomplete younger man . . . When it is no longer a secret, and when the existence of Daisy is no longer a secret, the fairytale passion is subject to the forces of moral judgment, social judgment, financial greed . . .

I shall not tell the plot, any further. But I should like to say something about Iris Murdoch's still increasing mastery of the unexpected shifts of pace, expansions and contractions of telling. Guy's death occupies the opening 97 pages of the book (which is 505 pages long). He wishes to die well, and his presence, both before and after his death, as the wisest and most thoughtful of the characters is powerful. Anne Cavidge and the Count are, like many characters in later Murdoch novels, most vividly alive in the synopsis of their history as they are first presented to us. Anne has had a greedy and wild sexual life at Cambridge, and a deliberately bare and deprived life in the convent. The Count, has tried, and failed, to be an 'English boy' and has learned Latin: he listens to the wireless perpetually in a characterless room, and is a Pole for no Poland as Anne is a nun for no God (as Iris Murdoch once said, we must learn to be 'good for nothing' since there is no God). Most of the narrative *space*, the loving detail, the wit and tension goes to the love affair between Tim and Gertrude – and its effect on the strong but apparently aimless tie between Tim and Daisy. More of the narrative space goes to the other characters' gossip and speculation about this tie – as though the private passion of love were not only the easiest object for novelists to display, but the most absorbing object for cousins, aunts and attendant lords at tea or cocktails. Indeed, one of the funniest and best moments is when Gerald, the astronomer, is led to admit that he has made 'a discovery' which might mean that 'something', 'a cosmic disaster', *could* happen, and the assembled company devote nine lines of six pages of furious amatory gossip to this topic before avoiding it as 'morbid'.

Anne, and the Count, although both fall passionately, obsessively in love, and both are apparently doomed to suffer love as a self-generating fantasy, not a reciprocity, are the nun and soldier, in a sense, of the title, those dedicated to concepts other than personal relationships. Tim is a parodic soldier-of-fortune, and Gertrude, like many of Iris Murdoch's glowing sexually self-confident ladies who attract love like magnetic fields, and like to 'draw people in' to their 'charmed circle' of personal affection, is a parodic dedicated courtly lady presiding over some medieval court of love where soldiers and knights are transformed, for better or worse, into *cavalieri servanti*. Or 'slaves', a bad word, with Hegelian overtones, in Murdoch.

But both Anne and the Count are *not good enough* at the virtues to which they aspire. In an article in 1970 on 'Existentialists and Mystics' Iris Murdoch divided recent novels into those which have reacted to a deep uncertainty about politics and religion by asserting either 'existential' virtues or a kind of godless mysticism. The 'existentialist hero' she says is 'the anxious man trying to impose or find or assert himself' whilst 'the mystical hero is an anxious man trying to discipline or purge or diminish himself.' 'The chief temptation of the former is egoism, of the latter masochism.'

I would argue that Gertrude and Tim are (naturally) cheerful egoists and existentialists whilst Anne and the Count are (naturally) self-diminishing masochists. Both Tim and Anne undergo near-drownings and face death differently both from each other and from Guy. Both, also have visions. Anne's is single and intense: a vision of Christ which owes much to Dame Julian of Norwich, much to Dostoevski, and yet is original, compulsive and strange. He shows her, amongst other things, the cosmos, 'all that is' as a small, grey, chipped pebble. Tim's vision is more diffuse – he may be a second-rate painter (as Gertrude is a second-rate goddess, Anne a second-rate mystic and the Count a second-rate soldier) but he has, and Iris Murdoch shows us he has 'a gift yearned for by sages, he was able simply to *perceive*! (He did not realize that this was exceptional, he thought everyone could do it.)' And at the end of the book, after his tragi-comic adventures, he has, and can paint, an intuition of some relation between geometric and organic forms which suggest, also a sense, however incomplete, of 'all that is', a cosmos full of inhuman and amazing things, as well as personal relations.

I have not mentioned those characters who see themselves as gods moving the others as puppets – though they are there – as are those who in their turn know 'more than' the god-figures 'suspect' about them. The novel is, like life, full of surprises, apparent captiousness about where it will direct its intention, and conveys a marvellous sense of underlying order and swarming randomness together.

17

THE GOOD APPRENTICE

THE GOOD APPRENTICE is a comedy, in places a fairy-tale, about horrible and unbearable things. It is like Shakespeare's *Winter's Tale*, a myth about death and rebirth, which resolves poetically moral torments it also renders with uncomfortable realism. It has two young heroes, brought up as brothers, both seen by Thomas McCaskerville, a benign psychoanalytic magician, as 'in pledge to death'. Edward is directly responsible for a fatal accident for which he cannot atone. He is the sorcerer's apprentice, purveyor of drugged vision, who becomes the prodigal son. Stuart, one of Iris Murdoch's embryonic saints looking for direction in a godless world, wants to be apprenticed to Good, to strip himself of desire and illusion, to find an ascesis. He is perceived by other characters, often, as deathly – inert, pallid, like a maggot. Both take symbolic and real journeys through the Underworld.

Edward goes in search of his real father, Jesse Baltram, a priapic painter he has never seen, who lives in a magical otherworld, a dangerous earthly paradise, guarded by three women who resemble the fading apples of eternal youth with 'fine blooming faces subtly wrinkled, wizened like apples lying long in store become golden and a little soft'. Jesse is a fertility God straight out of the Golden Bough – his first name recalls the biblical Tree of Jesse, his second the Beltane Fires. He has Dionysus' long hair and lives in one of Iris Murdoch's mysterious watery and wooded landscapes, in a house called Seegard, which has rooms jokingly called the

Interfectory and the Atrium, and a little Greek shrine to the *genius loci* with a phallic upright stone, the Lingam. There are 'tree men' who are both real and entirely mythical in this world of Dying Gods which is also a world of Arts and Crafts quaintness, the whimsy of William Morris or George Macdonald. They make comically execrable jewellery there, and have a religiosity Iris Murdoch has always parodied with sharp affection.

There is a large cast of students and doctors, *hommes et femmes moyens sensuels*, witches and seers, cranky and potent, who are driven by the desire to possess or manipulate others; also by a real wish to *help* each other which Thomas and Stuart see as both dangerous and necessary. In the end the moments of salvation are moments of clarity of particular vision. Seegard, like Gaze in *The Unicorn*, is a house of vision, of large religious contemplative vision, dangerous and compelling. But both Edward and Stuart have small moments of contact with the life of things which are saving. Edward reads a plain and beautiful sentence in Proust. Stuart sees a mouse living unperturbed in the underworld of the Tube rails. No one can do this like Iris Murdoch. At the end Edward sees his tale double – as a 'muddle, starting off with an accident . . . all sorts of things which happened by pure chance'. But is it also 'a whole complex thing, internally connected, like a dark globe, a dark world, as if we were part of a single drama, living inside a work of art'. Life, as well as art, *is* like that. There is order, or we see order, in mess and muddle, dramas have shapes, there is truth in fairy stories and fairy stories in truth. Iris Murdoch teases and illuminates us with these paradoxes.

18

THE BOOK AND THE BROTHERHOOD

HUMAN STORIES, IN Iris Murdoch's novels, have conflicting aspects. They are subject to ineluctable necessity, plotted, over-plotted, driven by superhuman Fates. They are also comic, ramshackle, patched together and surprising in their coincidental pleasures and little magic coincidences. In their determinist aspect the action is often conducted by an Enchanter, or daemonic figure, representing, since the very earliest novels, some necessary connection with the terrors of History and political power. Mischa Fox, in *The Flight from the Enchanter*, and Julius in *A Fairly Honourable Defeat* are both survivors of the concentration camps, who represent not only political necessity but also some allied sexual magnetism that goes with power. The Enchanter in the new novel, David Crimond, is no Jew but the son of a Scottish postman, who is first seen, pale, red-haired, freckled, dancing in a kilt at an Oxford Commem Ball. He is there compared to Shiva, the beautiful, the Destroyer. He is, or is believed to be, writing a large Marxist philosophical work which will offer a vision of the (not very agreeable) immediate future of the planet and a utopian vision of what *could* ensue.

This Book is being financed by the Brotherhood, a group of old Oxford friends who have not, as he has, kept up the purity of their socialist concerns, who are even afraid that he may represent all they have come to hate. He is said to believe in terrorism and a one-party state. He is possibly a charlatan. He is an ascetic and a marksman, with a predilection for Russian Roulette and other dangers. After the Ball the beautiful Jean Kowitz leaves her diplomat husband for Crimond – for the second time. Crimond's name ironically combines the Biblical David with the beautiful tune to which the 23rd Psalm is set, which trusts our human future to a benevolent Deity. 'The Lord's my shepherd: I'll not want.'

We never see, as readers, what Crimond thinks. Our way into the tale is through the Brotherhood, a well-meaning, well-off band of the chattering classes, or it might be the Treacherous Clerks. We feel an uneasy complicit sympathy and some irritation with these people. They were reared on the Classics. They still mourn Sinclair, young, beautiful, aristocratic, dead in his youthful prime. Sinclair's sister, Rose, has for thirty years stubbornly loved Sinclair's ex-lover, the handsome Gerard. They have beautiful ideals of friendship, derived from Oxford male bonding and perhaps the ideals of E. M. Forster and G. E. Moore. They believe in the value of the individual who Crimond says 'has withered into a little knot of egoism, even the concept stinks'. 'The bourgeois individual won't survive this tornado, he has already disintegrated, he has withered, he knows he's a fiction.' Gerard's way of running the Brotherhood is sharply described as 'a policy of calm, indecisive laissez-faire'. They collectively fail to notice the terrible tragedy which overtakes the girl Tamar, illegitimate daughter of an illegitimate and spitefully resentful mother (*beautifully* done) who tries and fails to be self-abnegating and self-effacing. They fail to prevent another act of random violence, provoked by Crimond.

Gerard, like earlier ineffectual Murdochian Platonists is in some sense a self-mocking self-portrait of his author. How can his confused ideas of bourgeois virtue stand against Crimond's Book of History, against the clear vision of a technological, bookless, politically violent future? The novel is full of real fear that we are at the *end* of some phase of civilization and can glimpse an incomprehensible world to come.

At one point in the novel someone remarks that the novel is now an outmoded impossible bourgeois form. This novel contemplated that possibility and proceeds, courageously to *be* a novel. Iris Murdoch has said that it is also essentially a *comic* form. The minor characters survive through a mixture of humility, minimal egoism and harmless minor magic. The world of *things* – essential to the true novel – persists; scratched tables, various carpets, tinned foods, carefully distinguished wallpapers. So does the human body – every possible variety of fading or vanishing human hair, efflorescence of unwanted flesh, veining, blurring, dying. And inhuman creatures live their own secret and important lives – snails, worms, a most beautiful grey parrot, the only true object of Gerard's love, who, in a daring vision, like Flaubert's transfigured Parrot, briefly reconciles Book and Brotherhood.

19

THE WRITER AND HER WORK

I

IRIS MURDOCH'S ACHIEVEMENT as a novelist has frequently seemed problematic to critics, reviewers and even readers, though her books have always sold extremely well, both in Britain and in other countries. When her first novels appeared in the mid 1950s she had, in common with writers like Kingsley Amis and John Wain, an interest in rapid comedy, and the long English tradition of the farcical episodic novel, though in fact, even then, her work was much more closely related to that of Beckett and the French existentialists and surrealists than to the eighteenth-century comic novels which Amis and Wain admired. Later, whilst she herself was claiming that she was 'a realist', and a novelist in the English realist tradition as exemplified by Jane Austen, George Eliot and E. M. Forster, academic critics were, with some justification, elucidating her novels as elaborate reconstructions of Celtic fertility myths (*A Severed Head*) or Freudian kingship (*The Unicorn*). There is a large and flourishing academic community of Iris Murdoch students, and there is a large number of suspicious reviewers and readers who find the elaborate, in some ways intensely artificial, world of her novels difficult to take. She is accused at once of being mandarin and sensational. She is described as the heir to the liberal humanism and technical subtlety of E. M. Forster, and at the same time compared, with some justice, to best-selling writers of melodrama (Daphne du Maurier), or detective stories for lady dons. (There is certainly something recognizably akin to the Murdoch world in the fantastic, busy, contrived, yet emotionally pleasing world of Margery Allingham's detective stories.) There is a perpetual debate about the probability, or improbability of Miss Murdoch's plots, centring largely on her characters' sexual behaviour. Her characters fall in love, fall in and out of bed, across barriers of age and sex normally assumed to be impassable, even break the incest taboo, with a kind of dance-like formalized frequency which some critics find fascinating, and indeed lifelike, some irritating, and some to have deep cultural or ritual symbolic meaning. (All three responses may, and do, occur at once in some readers.) I hope, at least, in what follows, to elucidate some of the ideas, about life and about fiction, behind the construction of this world, and then to return to the question of its success.

II

Iris Murdoch's philosophical work deals largely with the relations between art and morals, both of which she sees as, at their best, sustained attempts to distinguish truth from fantasy, particularly in the presentation of a sufficiently complex image of the human personality, and to find out what we mean by, what we really hold to be, 'Good'. It seems to me that the relationship between the kind of conceptual thought and the kind of fiction she writes has been unusually fruitful, very much part of the same search for ways of understanding, both historically and practically, the way human beings work. It seems therefore, a good way to begin a discussion of her novels by mapping out some of her ideas.

Perhaps her best-known piece of conceptual writing is 'Against Dryness', published in 1961 in *Encounter*, in which she argued that one of the major problems of the modern novel is that after two wars, and the philosophical debates of the Enlightenment, Romanticism and the Liberal tradition, 'we have been left with far too shallow and flimsy a view of human personality'. Briefly, she distinguishes between two archetypal modern ideas of man, Ordinary Language Man, as exemplified in the works of modern English linguistic philosophers[1] and Totalitarian Man, particularly exemplified in the works of Sartre and the French existentialists.* Miss Murdoch feels that both these images of the human self are profoundly inadequate, partly because they are egoistic, partly because they do not allow for the *variety* of experience, of men, of language, which human beings in practice encounter. She attempts to reassert the implicit and explicit values of the great nineteenth-century novelists who (partly because nineteenth-century society was dynamic and interesting) were more interested in the precise details of life, and the relation to these of complexities of thought. She writes, in 'Against Dryness', in prose of true eloquence:

> What have we lost here? And what have we perhaps never had? We have suffered a general loss of concepts, the loss of a moral and political vocabulary. We no longer use a spread-out substantial picture of the manifold virtues of man and society. We no longer see man against a background of values, of realities, which transcend him. We picture man as a brave naked will surrounded by an easily comprehended empirical world. For the hard idea of truth we have substituted a facile idea of sincerity. What we have never had, of course, is a satisfactory Liberal theory of personality, a theory of man as free and separate and related to a rich and complicated world from which, as a moral being, he has much to learn.[2]

In other philosophical essays, particularly 'The Sublime and the Beautiful Revisited' and 'The Sublime and the Good', Iris Murdoch attempts to be more precise about the processes by which we, historically and personally, arrive at experiences of freedom, or virtue, or beauty. She wrote in 1970 'When I was young I thought, as all young people do, that freedom was the thing. Later on I felt that virtue was the thing. Now I begin to suspect that freedom and virtue are concepts which ought to be pinned into place by some more fundamental

* See p. 4 and p. 106.

thinking about a proper quality of human life, which *begins* at the food and shelter level'[3]. In her book on Sartre she is much concerned with limiting and defining his notions of freedom, both in art and in politics. In 'The Sublime and the Beautiful Revisited' she comes to define freedom and virtue as in some ways identical – and they are related to beauty, too, because they are related to the kind of *formal* truth-seeking of the artist.*

One of the moral and aesthetic terms to which Iris Murdoch most frequently returns is 'attention'. 'Attention' is a word used by Simone Weil to describe the constantly renewed attempt to see things, objects, people, moral situations, truly as they are, uncoloured by our own personal fantasies or needs for consolation. Attention is in this sense a willed, thoughtful, selfless contemplation: Simone Weil remarks that those who *attend* properly to life make their moral decisions in terms of what their attention has made of them. They are not free to make random leaps of faith or violence; the freedom was in the choice of attending in the first place. In Miss Murdoch's thought, such attention is connected to Kant's concept of *Achtung* (attention) or respect for the moral law, which is 'a kind of suffering pride which accompanies, though it does not motivate, the recognition of duty. It is an actual experience of freedom (akin to the existentialist *Angst*), the realization that although swayed by passions we are also capable of rational conduct.' It is such attention which causes Miss Murdoch in 'On "God" and "Good"'[4] to be able to write 'Freedom is not strictly the exercise of the will, but rather the experience of accurate vision which, when this becomes appropriate, occasions action'.

The concept of attention in Miss Murdoch's terms is closely related to the concept of good, or goodness. Throughout her philosophical writings she returns to the question of perfection, of the nature of truth, of whether there can be said or seen to be any transcendent good outside human imperfections and vanities, in some way beyond the oper-

* See p. 198.

ations of time, chance and necessity, which can be a meaningful object of contemplation. In 'The Idea of Perfection' she criticizes the critics of G. E. Moore. Moore believed that 'good was a supersensible reality, that it was a mysterious quality . . . that it was an object of knowledge and (implicitly) that to be able to see it was in some sense to have it. He thought of the good upon the analogy of the beautiful . . . Moore's critics (especially Ordinary Language Man) thought 'good' was a subjective value-judgement, 'a movable label affixed to the world', not 'an object of insight or knowledge but a function of the will'. Miss Murdoch said she agreed almost entirely with Moore, and not with his critics.[5]

Miss Murdoch's own discussions of the process of attention to moral (and aesthetic) goodness are conducted with the assumption that such attention will bring with it a sense of where goodness and truth and reality *are*, that they are neither subjective nor arbitrarily open to the election of the will. Her most powerful discussions of the term 'attention' use in primary moral ways words which have become part of the technical language of literary criticism: realism, fantasy, naturalism. For instance:

> I would suggest that the authority of the Good seems to us something necessary because the realism (ability to perceive reality) required for goodness is a kind of intellectual ability to perceive what is true, which is automatically at the same time a suppression of self. *The necessity of the good is then an aspect of the kind of necessity involved in any technique for exhibiting fact.*[6]

Or, from the same essay, a little earlier:

> One might start from the assertion that morality, goodness, is a form of realism. The idea of a really good man living in a private dream world seems unacceptable. Of course a good man may be infinitely eccentric but he must know certain things about his surroundings, most obviously the existence of other people and their claims. The chief enemy of excellence in morality (and also in art) is personal fantasy: the tissue of self-aggrandizing and consoling wishes and dreams which

300

prevents one from seeing what is there outside one. Rilke said of Cézanne that he did not paint 'I like it', he painted 'There it is'. This is not easy and requires, in art or morals, a discipline. One might say here that art is an excellent analogy of morals, or indeed that it is in this respect a case of morals. We cease to be in order to attend to the existence of something else, a natural object, a person in need. We can see in mediocre art, where perhaps it is even more clearly seen than in mediocre conduct, the intrusion of fantasy, the assertion of self, the dimming of any reflection of the real world.[7]

In terms of the relationship between aesthetics and morals, Miss Murdoch's descriptions of the objects of fictional attention are instructive. She claims that true 'goodness', almost impossible to be clear about in life, can be discerned in art, that we can build an aesthetic, and a moral vision, from attempting to understand the precise nature of the excellence of Tolstoi, or, above all, Shakespeare. To these great writers she ascribes a quality which she initially names 'tolerance' or 'agnosticism' – related both to Simone Weil's impersonal 'attention' and to Keats's 'negative capability'.[8] To this quality she later gives the name, love. She writes

> Art and morals are, with certain provisos... one. Their essence is the same. The essence of both of them is love. Love is the perception of individuals. Love is the extremely difficult realisation that something other than oneself is real. Love, and so art and morals, is the discovery of reality. What stuns us into a realisation of our supersensible destiny is not, as Kant imagined, the formlessness of nature but rather its unutterable particularity; and most particular and individual of all natural things is the mind of man.[9]

The unutterable particularity, of experience in general, and of individual human beings in particular, is something to which, both as philosopher and novelist, she returns again and again. 'Against Dryness' ends with a plea to modern novelists, and modern Liberals of all kinds, to avoid simplified theories, Marxist or Existentialist, which assume that 'reality is a given whole', that there can be a theory which immutably describes our world. We must, she says, respect contingency and learn a new respect for the particularity of 'the now so unfashionable naturalistic idea of character'.* There is a great deal of tough thought behind these generalizations, these definitions of concepts. The same qualities of moral toughness and intellectual decisiveness have led Iris Murdoch to be able to make some precise and imaginative generalizations about the state of modern fiction, and its relation to the fiction of earlier times. It should by now be clear that Miss Murdoch prefers the major nineteenth-century novels, on grounds both moral and aesthetic, to twentieth-century ones. In 'Against Dryness' she offers her brilliant description of the modern novel as either 'crystalline'[10] or 'journalistic'; both of these relate to the impoverished images of human nature I described earlier.* Totalitarian Man is interested in the Human Condition, not the messy particular individual. His art is the crystalline work with himself as symbolic representative of mankind. Ordinary Language Man produces documents, concerned with social facts of behaviour, eschewing metaphysical depths.

In a later essay 'Existentialists and Mystics' Miss Murdoch created another dichotomy, between the existential novel and the mystical novel. The existential novel derives from Romanticism, like Totalitarian man: it believes in the individual will and vision, in a society where there are no longer political or religious certainties to give automatic depth to a picture. It is 'the story of the lonely brave man, defiant without optimism, proud without pretension, always an exposer of shams, whose mode of being is a deep criticism of society. He is an adventurer. He is godless. He does not suffer from guilt. He thinks of himself as free...' (D. H. Lawrence, Hemingway, Camus, Sartre). The mystical novel tries to return to the concept of God, or good, or virtue, and has to invent its own religious images in an empty situation (Greene, White, Bellow, Spark, Golding). Miss Murdoch

* See p. 215 and p. 216.
* See pp. 3–4.

claims that the new generation, concerned with human needs, now always present to our consciousness, for food, shelter, survival, is in fact utilitarian in that it works, morally, spiritually, up and out from biological survival. And this utilitarianism is a form of *naturalism*, she says, and implies that this naturalism could possibly create an aesthetic of its own, with stories in which goodness will be seen to be empirically necessary, particular, subject to chance and necessity, but valuable. The particularity of this new naturalism could not be the particularity of Tolstoi or George Eliot, because they were working and observing human beings in a world where there was a strong consensus about the nature of religion, society, politics, duty, whether one chose to elaborate or contradict this consensus. But, Miss Murdoch claims, art has always presented recognizable images of human value or virtue which survive social and metaphysical upheavals (the kindness of Patroclus or Alyosha, the truthfulness of Cordelia and Mr Knightley).[11]

One last word about Miss Murdoch's general ideas about art and life, before I proceed to a particular discussion of her fiction. She is a writer with a powerful sense of the difficulties entailed by any process of formulation in our attempts to attend to reality. She opens the essay 'Existentialists and Mystics' with a remark on this subject.

> Art represents a sort of paradox in human communication. In order to tell the truth, especially about anything complicated, we need a conceptual apparatus which partly has the effect of concealing what it attempts to reveal.[12]

In 'Against Dryness' she was pleading both for 'more concepts in terms of which to picture the substance of our being' and for a suspicion of the forms we *do* use to think, to perceive with. This sense runs through all her works, of a contrary tug of value between attempts at form and attempts to live with the knowledge that 'what *does* exist is brute and nameless, it escapes from the scheme of relations in which we imagine it to be rigidly enclosed, it escapes from language and science, it is more and other than our descriptions of it'.[13]

Her aesthetic remarks about this subject are, I think, both unusually clear and unusually subtle. She has, in her book *Sartre: Romantic Rationalist*, an excellent passage on the problems created by our modern attitude to language. This is impossible, in its admirable suggestiveness and precision, to summarize, but it is concerned with the effect on literature of our *self-consciousness* (historically exacerbated by the advent of scientific method, scientific symbolic languages), about the relationship between words and things. We know our language, both descriptive and emotive, creates the way we see things and also can be changed, is relative, if we use other concepts, other languages. So we think *about* words, as well as thinking *with* words. We are, says Miss Murdoch 'like people who for a long time looked out of a window without noticing the glass – and then one day began to notice this too'. We began to question the *nature* of referential language, which produced phenomena like Sartre's hero's nausea at the fact that the word *tree* bore no relation to the thing he saw, or, alternatively, Mallarmé's attempts to make language self-referring, abstract, like paint, like music.

As Miss Murdoch says, the novel is naturally 'referential' because it tells a story, and 'the telling of a story seems to demand a discursive referential use of language to describe one event after another. The novelist seemed to be, by profession, more deeply rooted in the ordinary world where things were still things and words were still their names.' But the novel, too, has become (in ways she defines in *Sartre*) linguistically self-conscious.[14]

Miss Murdoch's call for more and better defined moral concepts, on one hand, and her passionate belief in the importance of *stories*, of primitive human recounting of events, seem to me to be important ways of dealing with this problem. In 'The Idea of Perfection' she tells the story of the moral process whereby a mother-in-law comes to attend to the reality of a daughter-in-law she doesn't like, realizing that she is not 'vulgar' but 'refreshingly simple' and so on. This story is a novel in little: it also requires that reader and character *use* the conceptual words involved. Miss Murdoch says of this example 'I drew attention to the important part played by the normative-descriptive words, the specialized or secondary value words (such as "vulgar", "spontaneous" etc.). By means of these words there takes place what we might call "the siege of the individual by concepts". Uses of such words are both instruments and symptoms of learning.'

In an article on T. S. Eliot as moralist Iris Murdoch praises Eliot both for asserting the impersonality of the artist and for 'a continual concern, in the midst of difficulties, for the referential character of words'. T. S. Eliot has never 'made war upon language' and this is good.[15]

Shifting language, shifting concepts, never adequate, continually to be re-established and modified. Miss Murdoch makes Lawrentian claims for the importance of the novelist. 'The writer has always been important, and is now *essential*, as a truth-teller and as a defender of words. (There is only one culture and words are its basis.)' She sees the primitive force of stories, as a way of preserving, against our self-questioning, our culture and our language. 'The story is almost as fundamental a human concept as the thing, and however much novelists may try, for reasons of fashion or art, to stop telling stories, the story is always likely to break out again in a new form. Everything else may be done by pictures or computers, but stories about human beings are best told in words, and that "best" is a matter of a response to a deep and ordinary human need.'

Truth, the preservation of language, stories. But although *'the novelist is potentially the greatest truth-teller of them all*, he is also an expert fantasy-monger'.[16] Throughout Miss Murdoch's work runs a warning against the consolations of form.*

---

* See p. 114.

III

Iris Murdoch is now the author of seventeen novels. It is clearly not possible to discuss all of them in detail. What I propose to attempt is to group the novels in terms of the technical and philosophical preoccupations which seem to have been paramount in the writing of them.

The first two novels, *Under the Net* and *The Flight from the Enchanter* differ from all the later ones in various obvious ways. Formally, they could both be classified as 'fantasy-myth' in Miss Murdoch's own terms, and are akin to Beckett's *Murphy* and still more, Raymond Queneau's *Pierrot mon Ami*, a gentle surrealist picaresque fantasy. (Both *Murphy* and *Pierrot* are in Jake's library in *Under the Net*, which is dedicated to Queneau). Both are philosophical fables, using a proliferation of characters and dramatic incidents, farcical or tragic, to illustrate a central theme. In *Under the Net* that theme is the one to which I have just referred, the necessity and danger of concepts, forms, in thought and action, in the worlds of art, of politics, of work, of morals and of love. In *The Flight from the Enchanter* the theme is social, and concerns the proper and improper uses of power, personal and public, playing comic and bitter games with various forms of enslavement and emancipation, sexual, financial, bureaucratic, military. Both novels are close to Miss Murdoch's work on Sartre, in the sense that, lightly but profoundly, they take up the Sartrean issues, the relationship of the individual, and of art, to political structures and ideals, the nature of freedom, the nature of language. The central figures of both works, Jake Donaghue and Rosa Keepe are Sartrean in the sense that they 'move through a society which [Sartre's man] finds unreal and alien but without the consolation of a rational universe. His action seems not to lie *in* this social world; his freedom is a mysterious point which he is never sure of having reached. His virtue lies in understanding his own contingency in order to assume it, not the contingency of the world in order to alter it. It seems as if what 'justifies' him is just this precarious honesty, haunted as it is by a sense of the absolute. Sartre's heroes, Miss Murdoch says, are 'anti-totalitarian and anti-bourgeois'. Jake is certainly both – he won't write socialist propaganda for Lefty Todd, he won't, equally, attach himself more than peripherally to the capitalist world of bookmakers, film-makers and money-makers whom he occasionally cynically exploits. Rosa, aware of the faults of the Welfare State diagnosed in 'Against Dryness', aware that modern liberalism is not enough, although descended from a family of battling reformers and suffragettes, has retreated into a kind of stultified identification with the oppressed and is operating a mindless machine in a factory.

I want to leave consideration of *Under the Net* to a later point, but it might at this point be worth going in further detail into the relationship between thought and form in *The Flight from the Enchanter*. This novel puzzled reviewers and irritated critics, who tended pompously to castigate it for failures in realism of a kind it was not attempting, or like F. R. Karl for 'creating characters who are suitable only for the comic situations but for little else'.[17] In fact the power of this novel lies in the intricate patterning of its variations on a theme which, however comically treated, is shown to the *mind* to have tragic implications.

It is a novel about the rootlessness caused by the Second World War, and is full of refugees and persons without political identity – from Nina, the dressmaker, the archetypal victim first of violence, then of bureaucracy, finally of Rosa's obsession with her own fantasies of enchantment, to Annette who is rich, young, emotional and in a sense untouchable. Miss Murdoch, besides her interest in the fate of Liberalism, is an admirer of Simone Weil, whose studies of 'affliction', in communities or individuals, contributed much to the depth of this book. Simone Weil was interested in the mechanical way in which the suffering was transferred from person to person, a blow was passed on, the damaged attracted violence and in their turn inflicted damage. Uprooted central European refugees, the Lusiewicz brothers, Mischa Fox, provide the daemonic forces of enslavement, loose unconnected power, both in the fairytale, in the sexual, and in the social areas of this work. The novel is pervaded by images of traps and hunts, machines which savage their slaves (Nina's sewing-machine, Calvin Blick's camera), fish and underwater guns. Sexuality is seen largely in terms of enchantment, pursuit of a free creature, enslavement of a free creature. (Rainborough has fantasies of Annette as a smooth little fish, 'graceful, mysterious, desirable and free – and the next moment there is only struggling and blood and confusion. If only, he thought, it were possible to combine the joys of contemplation and possession.')

Mischa Fox, at a much more extreme point, is caught in the same paradox. Obsessed by suffering, caught in its machinery, he sees power as protection, and protection paradoxically leads to destruction; he is compelled to destroy what he protects, from chickens, to 'slaves', to women. His battle to gain possession of the suffragette periodical, the *Artemis* (named itself after the virgin huntress, edited by Rosa's brother, Hunter Keepe, his name the paradox of pursuit and possession in little) typifies both political and sexual themes.*

If these early novels ask Sartrean questions, they do not offer Sartrean answers. Sartre's heroes agonize and contemplate in a lucidly tortured solitude. Miss Murdoch points out that Sartre claimed that 'the mode of self-awareness of the modern novelist is the internal monologue', which is not primarily concerned with 'character' and 'individuality' in either the narrating consciousness or the other people reflected through it. She criticizes his novels, further, for not presenting individuals in the world of action.

> Sartre's individual is neither the socially integrated hero of Marxism nor the full-blooded romantic hero who believes in the reality and importance of his personal struggle. For Sartre the 'I' is always unreal. The real individual is Ivich [the silent sister in *Les Chemins de la Liberté*] opaque, sinister, unintelligible and irreducibly other; seen always from

* See p. 42–3.

outside ... Sartre, like Freud, sees life as an egocentric drama.[18]

There is a sense in which the comic and densely populated worlds of Iris Murdoch's first two fantasies are a kind of meaningful game with the Sartrean universe. Jake tries an internal monologue, but discovers that the world is full of other people whose views he has misinterpreted but *can learn*. Rosa fails to observe properly the individual life and needs of Nina, but they are there to be *observed*, and Rosa can learn. No single view of the world, no one vision, is shown to be adequate, in a form of novel where everyone is always offering epigrammatic views on the nature of society or reality or suffering. No one is right, but everyone – Dave Gellman, the linguistic philosopher, Lefty Todd, the socialist, Rainborough, the mediocre modern élite bureaucrat – is there, and the reader and other characters must take them into account. I have described elsewhere how I think the last scene of *Under the Net* is a comic parody of the end of *La Nausée*.* Both Jake and Roquentin are saved from a sense of futility and drudgery by a vision of their future induced by hearing a song. But Roquentin turns *from* the nauseating horrors of the world and society to the pure necessity of art. Jake finds a way into curiosity about, and delight in, the endless differences of people and proliferation of things. It is the villain of *The Flight from the Enchanter*, Calvin Blick, who offers the solipsist view, to Rosa, that 'You will never know the truth and you will read the signs in accordance with your own deepest wishes. That is what we human beings always have to do. Reality is a cipher with many solutions, all of them right ones'.

This is not so: no solution is complete, but some are wrong, and freedom consists in *not* reading the signs according to personal fantasy or desire. And this can be done. The sense that the characters in these books have reached new insights and new beginnings is worked for, and valuable.

* See p. 22.

Her next book, *The Sandcastle*, is dedicated to her husband, John Bayley, and her work from *The Sandcastle* onwards shows an increasing concern with the moral and critical principles explored in his book, *The Characters of Love*, and later in *Tolstoy and the Novel*. John Bayley argues that the contemporary impatience with the idea of 'character' as an attempt to create a unique individual is a sign both of a literary and of a moral failing. Both he and Iris Murdoch quote with approval Henry James on Balzac's characters – 'it was by loving them that he knew them, not by knowing them that he loved'. Both see it as a function of the English novel at its greatest that the writers, and thus the readers, *loved* the characters and felt them to be free agents, in some sense. Both are troubled at the erosion of the sense of reality of characters created by insistent aesthetic symbolism in novels, or by the attempt to write allegories of the Human Condition.* Iris Murdoch's technical interest in nineteenth-century 'realism' is an interest in the recreation of a fictional world in which separate individuals meet, change, communicate. A good novel is 'a house fit for free characters to live in'. Before *The Sandcastle* Miss Murdoch's models were French, or Irish; now she makes a sustained effort, in *The Sandcastle, The Bell, An Unofficial Rose*, to learn from Jane Austen, George Eliot, Henry James.

The Sandcastle is a not entirely successful attempt at a description of a 'normal' but difficult moral problem – the attempt by Mor, a middle-aged schoolmaster, to break out of a largely dead marriage when he falls in love with a young woman painter, Rain Carter. It contains a character – Bledyard, the art master – who combines T. S. Eliot's view of the impersonality of the artist, with John Bayley's sense that the individual human being is a mystery, a compelling moral object, incredibly difficult to comprehend. He argues that the true artist 'is humble enough in the presence of the object to attempt *merely* to show what the object is like. But

* See p. 7 and p. 208–9.

310

this *merely*, in painting, is everything.' And he asks 'who can look reverently enough upon another human face?'

Bledyard argues further that Mor, planning a violent bid for freedom, is indulging in fantasy. 'You do not truly apprehend the distinct being of either your wife or Miss Carter.' In *The Bell* and in *An Unofficial Rose* Iris Murdoch makes much more successful and sustained attempts at showing efforts, failures, partial failures, to apprehend the distinct being of other people.

Both *The Bell* and *An Unofficial Rose* are concerned with the relationships between freedom and virtue, and also between beauty and truth. Both could be described, as *Howard's End* or *A Passage to India* could be described, as English symbolic novels, in which a powerful formal element is provided by the relationship of plot and characters to certain symbolic objects.

In *The Bell* the central episodes of the plot concern the substitution of the medieval bell (legendarily supposed to have flown from the Abbey belfry into the lake when a nun had a lover) for the new bell, decked to enter the Abbey as a bride, or postulant, and open a new kind of speech between the enclosed, silent religious order and the outside world. The bell represents art.[19] As art, it is related to all the other music in the novel, jazz records (primitive sexual urgency), Bach, the 'hideous purity' of the nuns' plainsong, birdsong which to Kant was the only pure because the only free music, natural without concepts. It is also related to the other works of art seen by Dora in a vision in the National Gallery, a moment of truth where Gainsborough's portrait of his children is an image of Iris Murdoch's idea of the *recognizable* authority of the Good. The central symbols in *An Unofficial Rose* are analogous. They are, first, the Tintoretto portrait of Susannah, golden, serene, authoritative, a source of power and value, both moral, aesthetic and social (it is sold, for a large sum, to purchase a fantasy of freedom for Randall, a freedom in itself an enslavement to a factitious beauty). And second, the rose itself, like the birdsong a *natural* beauty, with a *natural* form, also, on a rose farm, a source of value, vision, or even money. Both novels are about the intermittent human attempts to reach perfection, vision, a life which shall seem to have a sense of form or destiny. Both describe a large number of patterned, related, individual successes and failures. Both, also, like *Under the Net* and some later books, are about the pull between silence as purity, and the use of language as a necessary means to discovery of truth and complexity. What is most impressive about both is the degree to which Miss Murdoch succeeds in her aim of creating free and individual characters, whose experience is diverse and not to be summed up.

In 'The Sublime and the Beautiful Revisited' Iris Murdoch makes her very useful distinction between 'convention', the force which drives Ordinary Language Man, and 'neurosis' which drives Totalitarian man.* In the delicate and detailed descriptions of the moral decisions of the principal characters in *The Bell* and *An Unofficial Rose* we can see the effort, reasoned or instinctive, to understand and love, falling away constantly into one or the other. Neurosis drives Randall, who leaves his wife in order to suffer enslavement at the hands of Lindsay Rimmer; while Lindsay herself, an earthly Venus, not a heavenly one, is the slave of Emma Sands who writes detective stories with structured plots, and whom Randall's father, Hugh, rejected, for no clear reason, in order to stay with his wife. Randall leaves the natural roses to be 'a writer', for form – and ends up living off his father's sale of the Tintoretto in an empty freedom designed, he suspects, as part of Emma's vengeance. Convention drives his father, Hugh, who could not leave his wife. It drives, supremely, Randall's wife, Ann, the 'unofficial rose' of the title, who is in love with Felix, a soldier and a gentleman, also held by convention, and who is unable to distress her daughter, or abandon the faithless Randall, for happiness against duty.

In *The Bell* it is Michael Meade, homosexual schoolmaster, who – with his sense of destiny in his call to the priesthood, his sense of patterns and portents in his life, his imaginative

* See p. 4 and p. 106.

312

vision of moral situations when he falls in love with Nick as a boy, or impulsively kisses Toby – is tempted towards a neurotic vision (although he ironically fails Nick by a contrary recoil into self-protective convention). Convention is represented by James Tayper Pace who finds it easy to say that some things are *simply* forbidden, and to close a moral argument. There is not space here to describe the patience with which Miss Murdoch explores the fluctuations between vision, convention, neurosis, fantasy in these characters. But it is worth remarking that the fates of the most important – Hugh and Ann in *An Unofficial Rose*, Michael and Dora in *The Bell* are unpredictable precisely because several outcomes are possible to their dilemmas; they are, in other words, 'free' characters. And this is no mean achievement.

One recalls *The Characters of Love*, in which John Bayley, analysing James's *The Golden Bowl*, describes Maggie's love of the Prince as a saving use of convention – she avoids drama, avoids knowledge even, she 'finds in the refuge of convention and deliberate "ignorance" salvation both for herself and for the others'. I have always felt that Ann in *An Unofficial Rose*, whom Randall hates for 'living by rules', who seems to attract suffering, who feels herself 'shapeless and awkward', is related to Maggie, who is mysterious in the way in which 'to be human is to be virtually unknown' and of whom it might be said 'the conventional and the mysterious are closely allied, are indeed one and the same thing'.[20] She is also related to Lionel Trilling's description of Fanny Price in *Mansfield Park* as one who is 'poor in spirit' and thus blessed.[21] One feels, with these early 'realistic' novels of Miss Murdoch, that much of her hope of combining a well-formed novel with a sense of the mystery and formlessness of people's lives has been fulfilled. And it has partly been fulfilled by a profoundly intelligent use of concepts such as convention and neurosis, not as total patterning devices, but as instruments for exploration of character and motive.

Malcolm Bradbury, one of Miss Murdoch's most intelligent

critics,[22] has argued that her practice as a novelist in many ways runs counter to her theoretical beliefs. She claims, he says, that life has finally no pattern, no meaning, that we are ruled by necessity and chance, yet one of the strengths of both her plotting and her symbolism is that it explores fully the sense in which we feel that our lives *are* gripped by formative forces which function below our conscious knowledge or choice. She describes those aspects of sexual and social behaviour in which men are remarkably similar to each other and meaningful patterns and generalizations can be drawn, whose power can be felt. I refer particularly to the ideas of psychoanalysts and of students of myth, where they are interested not in the individual whole person, but in the machinery of behaviour.

Miss Murdoch frequently uses the word 'machinery' to describe recognizable patterns of human behaviour. In *A Severed Head*, Palmer Anderson, the psychoanalyst, claims that 'The psyche ... has its own mysterious methods of restoring a balance. It automatically seeks its advantage, its consolation. It is almost entirely a matter of mechanics, and mechanical models are the best to understand it with' (Chapter Four). In this context, I used to think that this was simply an indication that Palmer was a totalitarian man, unaware of the irreducibly unique individual. I now see that his remark is a statement of a partial truth which interests Iris Murdoch very much. Only unremitting attention to what lies outside the mechanism can save human beings from being entirely controlled by this psychic machinery. Thus Michael Meade is caught in the (excellently described) *machinery* of guilt and repentance. The title of *The Sacred and Profane Love Machine* itself indicates the strength of that novel, which is its exploration of the automatic elements involved in most love, most efforts at virtue, which, imperfectly understood, can grip and destroy. In 'On "God" and "Good" ' Miss Murdoch claims that Freud made an important discovery about the human mind which 'might be called a doctrine of original sin'.* Later in the same essay she specifically describes a psychic mechanism, sado-masochism, which has certainly affected her own understanding of behaviour, and played a major part in the plots of her novels.

> Refined sado-masochism can ruin art which is too good to be ruined by the cruder vulgarities of self-indulgence ... Fascinating too is the alleged relation of master to slave, of the good self to the bad self ... [23]

There are several novels which one could call 'mythical' novels in which Miss Murdoch's interest in these mechanisms, in parodies of good, in patterning, leads to the structure seeming to hold more aesthetic power than the individual characters – even though the morality of these novels continues to assert the paramount imperative of observing the free individual. Such novels include *A Severed Head, The Unicorn*, and *The Time of the Angels*.

The first of these is slightly different from the others, in that it is not concerned with overall metaphysics, but with patterns of social and sexual behaviour. Its cool elegance, its 'dream-like facility' to quote Miss Murdoch on crystalline fantasy-myth, has a bite which comes from observing human helplessness before human incomprehension of the machinery. The central image – the severed head, image of the petrifying Medusa, the dark (female) Celtic gods, the sooth-saying Orpheus – has a poetic force that the delicate imagery of Venus and Mars in *Under the Net* for instance, is not required to carry. Alexander, the sculptor of that novel, making a portrait head swathed in bandages, like a death's-head, talks as Bledyard in *The Sandcastle* talks, of the use of portraiture as a means to truth. But the associations are those of magic, myth, and ritual. At the same time, Miss Murdoch's technical, cool interest in the sado-masochism of a man who tries to love his wife's lover, is reinforced by her use of the contrasting Freudian and Sartrean concepts of what the ancient image of the severed head, the Medusa, meant. Freud

* See p. 253.

saw the head as a symbol of male fear of castration, 'the female genitals, feared not desired'. Sartre saw it as an image of the basic fear of being observed. Miss Murdoch plays one off against the other. In this novel it is woolly, greedy, selfish Antonia who holds a watered-down version of the Bloomsbury ethic of loving individuals, which is crushed by the powers of sexual violence as easily as Martin's assumed 'tolerance' of her behaviour. Castration, the voyeuristic witnessing of secret sex, including incest, underlie the plot of this drawing-room comedy, and contribute to its ambiguous elegance. The sexual shifts, the changes of partners, which annoy many of Miss Murdoch's readers, are here part of a stylized fictional representation of the ways in which we are all puppets of blind and incomprehensible forces.

The Unicorn and *The Time of the Angels* are both, as is made explicit in *The Unicorn* itself, 'fantasies of the spiritual life'. The good man, the saint or artist, 'nothing himself, lets all things be through him'. Hannah Crean-Smith, the guilty, enclosed 'princess' of *The Unicorn*, attempts a kind of renunciation of the ego – and ends maybe, with a monstrous sado-masochistic parody of such a renunciation. Carel, the priest of no god, in *The Time of the Angels* sets out to destroy the fantasies of religion which persist from the days when Christianity was alive: he tries to be 'good for nothing', which not only he, but Miss Murdoch in 'On "God" and "Good"', claim is all that is morally possible in a world where God is dead, and Good an undefinable sense of direction only. He is aware, like his creator, that at the human level life is random and horrible, subject to chance and necessity, without form, without consolation. He creates, therefore for himself, the Nietzschean drama, a high version of the existentialist drama of the lonely, defiant hero. He commits incest with his daughter out of a compulsion which might be part of a Gothic novel, or might be related to Nietzsche's description of Oedipus as the man who had seen the secret of life, 'the horror of nature',[24] the reality of death and the meaninglessness of existence, and who thus knew that all was permitted because all was equally valuable and valueless.

In any case, his behaviour, in his attempt to annihilate his ego, is a reinforcement of the sado-masochistic mechanism again. Miss Murdoch is concerned with religious terrors. She is aware, in a way I think no other English novelist is aware, of the importance for our cultural life of the decay of believed Christianity, the loss of a sense of central authority, believed in or opposed. She is aware of the importance of spiritual experience. Various of her characters make sustained attempts at the spiritual life which, with its selflessness, as she says both in *The Bell* and in *The Unicorn*, is not dramatic, and has no story. People have moments of true vision – Effingham, on the point of death in *The Unicorn* sees that love and death are the same, sees the universe flooded with light and meaning because he himself has for a moment been expunged. Carel in *The Time of the Angels* offers the contrary vision, in fact the same, of the true Chaos and Old Night, the vision of the Book of Job that 'there is only power and the marvel of power, there is only chance and the terror of chance'. But neither they, nor the other characters, can live by these visions, and the moment story, drama, action are resumed, so are the psychic mechanisms that pattern them. It is not possible not to have a story. Hannah Crean-Smith's 'religious' behaviour in *The Unicorn* is profoundly ambiguous, but it bears a close resemblance to Freud's description of obsessional neurosis,* as the behaviour of her dependents and retainers bears a close resemblance to Freud's quotations in *Totem and Taboo* from Sir James Frazer about the treatment of kings as gods in primitive communities. It is a poetic image, an intellectual game, expressing general truths about human habits and fantasies. (It might be added that the elements of high Gothic[25] in both these novels are part of the same human interest in primitive forces and the forms in which they can be described.)

It might, in this context, also be worth quoting a remark which Iris Murdoch made about the relations of life and myth in a review of Elias Canetti's *Crowds and Power.*

* See pp. 174–5.

'Canetti has ... shown, in ways which seem to me entirely fresh, the interaction of the "mythical" with the ordinary stuff of human life. The mythical is not something "extra"; we live in myth and symbol all the time.'[26]

Literature, Miss Murdoch said, was 'a battle between real people and images'. In an interview with Frank Kermode she remarked that she felt her novels 'oscillate rather between attempts to portray a lot of people and giving in to a powerful plot or story'.[27] In those of her later novels where she is attempting psychological realism, free characters, the portraiture of 'a lot of people', she has come to be able to make a very sophisticated use of Shakespeare, both as matter for allusion, and as a source of reference, depth, a real myth of our culture himself. The plots of *The Nice and the Good, A Fairly Honourable Defeat, The Black Prince*, among others, owe much to him, and what they owe is fascinating and valuable.

There are two excellent reasons for Miss Murdoch's interest in Shakespearean plotting. The first is that she seems to understand, instinctively or as a matter of intellectual decision, that it is a way out of the rather arid English debate about the preservation of the values of nineteenth-century realism against the need to be modern, flexible, innovating, not to say experimental. Nathalie Sarraute once remarked that what crushes modern writers is less the sense that their society and situation is incomprehensible than the sense of the weight of their predecessors' achievement, the *use* and exhaustion of the art form by the great writers of the past and the immediate past. In a sense Shakespeare, an eternal part of our culture and mythology, and yet a great technician, is available to learn from in a way that neither George Eliot, nor Forster are. Reading him can be formally exhilarating.

The second reason is an intrinsic part of Iris Murdoch's aesthetic. Shakespeare is the Good, and contemplation of the best is always to be desired.

What Iris Murdoch seems to me technically to have learned

from Shakespeare is, again, two things. The first is, as a matter of plotting, that you can have intense realism of character portrayal without having to suppose that this entails *average probability* as part of your structure. Real people may, do, dance in the formal figures of a Shakespearean plot (or indeed, a grotesque Dickensian one) without the sanction of the sense that one is studying a *probable* developing person in a *probable* developing society, which is so necessary to the scientific and sociological beliefs of a George Eliot.

The second is that a very large cast, including a number of peripheral people who are felt to have a life outside the plot, makes for the desiderated 'spread-out substantial picture of the manifold virtues of man and society'. In two radio interviews I had with Iris Murdoch, she returned to Shakespeare's comic people, to Shallow and Silence and the *particularity* of their life, as an example of a moral and aesthetic achievement beyond most of us. In the thirties and forties novelists such as Elizabeth Bowen were placing immense stress on 'relevance' – to plot, to novel-as-a-whole – as a criterion for inclusion in a story. Iris Murdoch has rediscovered the richness of adding apparently gratuitously interesting people and events. These indicate worlds outside the book they are in. (A good example is the strange letters from non-participating people which chatteringly punctuate *An Accidental Man*, offering passion, tragedy, comedy, somewhere between Waugh, Shakespeare and Dickens; these letters are outside the central plot, but enrich our vision of it.)

In these Shakespearean novels with their huge casts, the central enchanter figures, representing metaphysical powers or truths, are less powerful. Radeechy, whose death and courting of evil in *The Nice and the Good* is a little thing beside the Shakespearean dance of paired lovers, moral mistakes and discoveries, is a poor relation of Carel in *The Time of the Angels*. Julius King, the enchanter, the Prospero, the master of ceremonies in *A Fairly Honourable Defeat* enchants and manipulates both more and less, depending on the moral powers of the people whose lives he touches. He

319

is related to Mischa Fox, in that his rootless violence (he is a germ-war scientist) has its roots in his experiences in Dachau, but his power is less than Mischa's, and the people he meets are denser. He is, like Carel, Nietzschean in his compelling vision of life as a formless joke. Indeed, his relationship with his victim, Rupert, is very like that of Carel with his brother Marcus. Both Rupert and Marcus are writing ethical treatises on Good, on morality in a godless world. Both are unaware of their true dependence on the power of the vanished religion to sustain their hierarchies of value and discrimination. Both are vulnerable to the ruthlessness and violence which mock their morality. But Julius, unlike Carel, does not behave like a Frazerian mythical god-man. He copies the plot of *Much Ado about Nothing*, and like a naturalistic Mephistopheles uses Rupert's own moral blindness and secret complacence to destroy him.

The reason why this novel is in many ways my favourite of Miss Murdoch's later works is because I think, in it, both reader and characters are drawn through the experience of *attention* to the being of others which Miss Murdoch sees as the heart of morality. Julius destroys Rupert. He does not destroy the homosexual marriage of Simon and Axel because, as we are shown, as we experience, they know each other too well. They love each other, talk to each other, consider each other, and reach a breaking-point when they automatically discuss Julius's lies and manipulations for what they are. Just as, in the scene where the black man is being beaten in the restaurant, the characters react typically, morally, entirely convincingly – one is amused (Julius), one intervenes incompetently (Simon), one makes a moral generalization (Axel) and Tallis, who represents Miss Murdoch's new vision of starting from real human needs, as well as the self-denying gentleness that can seem repellent or abstract – Tallis knocks the thugs down. This is a novel in which a patterned plot, the thoughts of the characters, the multiplicity of people, the events, add up to a moral and aesthetic experience both unexpected, delightful and distressing.

At this point it might be worth returning to the critical doubts and debates I have discussed briefly in my opening paragraphs. As I hope I have to some extent shown, much of the trouble readers and critics have in responding to, and evaluating Iris Murdoch's novels, is a result of a tension between 'realism' and other more deliberately artificial, even 'experimental' ways of writing in her work. Robert Scholes, in his book *The Fabulators*, includes *The Unicorn* as an example of a new kind of narrative art which returns to older forms of 'fable' rather than following the realist tradition of the novel proper. His other examples are mostly American, and critics who admire the work of such modern American fantasists, or parable writers, as Vonnegut, Hawkes, and Pyncheon have found Iris Murdoch timid or old-fashioned by comparison. Such critics tend to see *Under the Net* as her most successful work, as well as her most original, and her painstaking efforts at creating a fuller and more realistic world in her later books as an aberration, or a retreat into English bourgeois complacencies. Political criticisms have been levelled at her for the increasingly narrow scope of her social world – criticisms that on moral grounds she herself does not feel to be valid. If you are interested in unique individuals, she argues, they can as well be located in the English *haute bourgeoisie* as anywhere.

I would agree, in many ways, that *Under the Net* is aesthetically Iris Murdoch's most satisfying novel: the balance of lucid philosophical debate, lightly but subtly handled emotional pace, and just surrealist fantastic action is new in the English novel and beautifully controlled. *A Severed Head* has the same qualities of delicate control and fusion of several styles and subject matters; drawing-room comedy, shading into French bedroom farce, combined with Jungian psychoanalytic myth and cool philosophical wit.[28] At the other end of the scale, *The Bell* seems to me arguably Miss Murdoch's most successful attempt at realism, emotional and social – the tones of voice of the members of the religious community are beautifully caught, the sexual, aesthetic and religious passions and confusions of the three main characters, Dora,

Michael, and, to a lesser extent, Toby, are delicately analysed with the combination of intellectual grasp and sensuous immediacy of George Eliot.

It is, as I have tried to suggest, with those novels in which Iris Murdoch has tried to combine widely differing techniques and narrative methods that confusions arise, sometimes because readers are insufficiently alert and flexible, and sometimes because the writer herself creates jarring effects or difficulties for them. I have suggested, for instance, that *The Time of the Angels* is best read as a mannered philosophical myth, or fantasy, playing games with Nietzsche's *The Birth of Tragedy* and the new school of 'Death of God' theology. The introductory description of the character of Pattie O'Rourke, half-black, half-Irish, however, is written with a clarity, sympathy, density and lack of irony which involve the reader in a way that suggests that the rest of the story will have the emotional immediacy of *The Bell*. Pattie's actions are in fact almost entirely part of Carel's religio-sexual myth (she has to be the Black Madonna to balance the White Virgin Princess, his incestuously seduced daughter Elizabeth). The reader who had responded to that initial description has a right to feel, I think, that the author has promised something she has not performed, whatever the illumination provided by the myth.

In general, Iris Murdoch's careful introductions and histories of her characters are among her best passages of prose, thoughtful, clear, compact – I think of Michael and Dora again, in *The Bell*, of Simon and Axel in *A Fairly Honourable Defeat*, of Hilary Burde in *A Word Child*. Hilary Burde, like Pattie, is a case of a character where a change in both prose style and plotting jars a reader prepared for emotional density and realism. He is, as initially seen, a character created by education, a man made civilized by learning grammar and language to a level of high proficiency, a man of clear mind on a limited front, and violent and ill-comprehended passions. His story, though dramatic, and cleverly related to the story of *Peter Pan*, a recurrent preoccupation of Miss Murdoch's, is not the story of the man we first meet. It is an

adventure story, with two accidental deaths and very contrived repeated relationships: it is a Freudian game with
incest, with the compulsion to repeat the actions which trap
and terrify us. It is rapid, perplexing, funny and terrible. It
does not satisfy the realistic expectations aroused by the
patient and delicate introductory analysis of the main
character.

There is also a problem about Iris Murdoch's use of symbolism,* which she herself mocks in *The Black Prince*.[29] The
English have arguably never handled the symbolic novel as
well as the French, Germans or Americans – Proust's symbols,
Thomas Mann's symbols, are woven into the very texture of
their prose in a way that neither Lawrence's, Forster's, nor
Iris Murdoch's exactly are. In *A Passage to India* Forster
made his landscape symbolic and real together: Iris Murdoch
attempts such a fusion in *The Bell*, with wood, water and
abbey. In *Howard's End* and *The Longest Journey* Forster's
symbols are rather too deliberately *pointed at* as symbols of
England, or social truths (including Howard's End itself). I
would argue that this is the case with the roses and painting
in that nevertheless excellent novel, *An Unofficial Rose*.

The critic approaching Iris Murdoch's later novels for the
first time needs to do so, I think, in the awareness that many
serious English novelists are technically moving away from
simple realism, from social analysis and precise delineation
of the motives and emotions of individuals, to forms much
more overtly and deliberately 'unreal'. Not only Iris Murdoch, but Angus Wilson and others are taking an interest in
the fairy stories buried in Dickens's plots, in the grotesque
caricatures, so like fairytale characters, who move amongst
Dickens's more 'real' characters. If *The Black Prince* is overtly
artificial, drawing attention to its own fictive nature, and to
other works of literature in a parodic manner, so are Angus
Wilson's two latest novels, *No Laughing Matter* and *As If
By Magic*. So, also, are the excellent series of brief novels
recently written by Muriel Spark, which call constant

---

* See pp. 81–2 and pp. 226–7.

attention to the fact that they are just 'stories', fictions, and that that is what is interesting about them. Both Angus Wilson and Iris Murdoch have deep roots in, and strong moral attachments to, the English realist tradition. Both are writing novels which combine old realist morals, and old realist techniques, with a new kind of literary playfulness of which the reader needs to be aware.

I want to end by suggesting that a comparison between Iris Murdoch's first novel, *Under the Net* (1954) and *The Black Prince*, published in 1973, shows a remarkable consistency of themes. These two novels are interesting because both are first-person accounts by men who want to be, or to see themselves as, serious artists, and who are, in this capacity and as lovers, bedevilled by the problems I discussed earlier in this essay – the tension between the attempt to tell, or see, the truth, and the inevitability of fantasy, the need for concepts and form and the recognition that all speech is in a sense distortion, that novelists are fantasy-mongers, and that, as Hugo says in *Under the Net* 'The whole language is a machine for making falsehoods'.

In the book that he is writing, Jake casts Hugo as the character Annandine, with his central view that 'all theorizing is flight. We must be ruled by the situation itself and this is unutterably particular. Indeed, it is something to which we can never get close enough, however hard we may try, as it were, to creep under the net.' (The image of the net comes from Wittgenstein's *Tractatus Logico-Philosophicus* in which he likens our descriptive languages to a mesh put over reality, to map it, and continues that 'Laws, like the law of causation, etc., treat of the network and not what the network describes'.)

In *The Black Prince*, Bradley Pearson, trying to write his *magnum opus*, the story of his love for the daughter of a rival novelist, despairs frequently in the manner of Bledyard in *The Sandcastle* about the impossibility of precise description:

> How can one describe a human being 'justly'? How can one
> describe oneself? With what an air of false coy humility, with
> what an assumed confiding simplicity one sets about it! 'I am
> a puritan', and so on. Faugh! How can these statements not
> be false? Even 'I am tall' has a context.[30]

Jake as a high sense of difficulty – 'nothing is more paralysing
than a sense of historical perspective, especially in literary
matters'; Bradley, also has a crippling sense of difficulty and
the requirements of true excellence. But both are prepared
to feel gripped and driven by a sense of destiny, of direction,
of a source of power, ambivalent to the last, art, love, or
fantasy.*

In *Under the Net* it is Jake's experience of his own mis-
prision of people and situations, his own undervaluing of
their difference from himself, their complexity, that makes
him use concepts, makes him write. Bradley Pearson is invig-
orated by a contact with the Black Prince, Apollo Loxias,
Hamlet, the Love that is the same as Death, the Nietzschean
vision which insists that Apollo the Lord of the Muses and
Dionysos the god of drunkenness, destruction and chaos are
both necessary to art. Bradley is wise and witty in a Murdochian manner about the sado-masochism involved in this
vision of art, as he is about his own shortcomings. The fact
that these narratives are first-person accounts by intelligent
men makes the reading hard, since the narrator's illusions
are refined illusions. In *The Black Prince*, Miss Murdoch
comically layers this difficulty with references to Bradley's
own fictionality, to the idea that both he and Apollo might
be 'the invention of a minor novelist', and with other, partial,
accounts of the plot by other characters. Yet Bradley says
much that she has said herself, *in propria persona*, and is
clearly, among other things, an authorial joke about the
relations of author and character. It is in this context that
Bradley's description of Shakespeare's achievement in *Hamlet*
becomes fascinating from the point of view of Miss Murdoch's work. She believes, she has said, that the self of the

* See p. 268.

artist should be expunged from this work, that Shakespeare's greatness is his anonymity. Yet she recognizes, in the Sonnets and in *Hamlet* a kind of 'self' which Bradley discusses in a speech which I quote again here.

Shakespeare, he says 'is speaking as few artists can speak, in the first person and yet at the pinnacle of artifice ... Shakespeare here makes the crisis of his own identity into the very central stuff of his art. He transmutes his private obsessions into a rhetoric so public that it can be mumbled by any child. He enacts the purification of speech, and yet this is something comic, a sort of trick, like a huge pun, like a long almost pointless joke.'

'*Hamlet* is words, and so is Hamlet.'[31]

In a sense, here, we have another version of Miss Murdoch's 'Good' which is virtually impossible to attain – the complete creation of a character in *words*, using the writer, but *for* the language. It is an extraordinary example of one of the high moments of art where there is no contradiction between words and things, between men and the images of men. But it is also, as Miss Murdoch and *her* character point out, endlessly comic. And Miss Murdoch's novel conducts a comic joke, itself, around the vision of *Hamlet*. 'All novels' she once claimed, 'are necessarily comic', just as her Apollo claims, in his epilogue, 'all human beings are figures of fun. Art celebrates this. Art is adventure stories'. Another thing for which one increasingly admires Miss Murdoch is aesthetic courage: knowing, better than most writers, the historical difficulties of writing good novels now, the moral difficulties of writing good novels at all, she continues to produce comic metaphysical adventures of a high order. What Arnold Baffin did not say, but might have said, in his quarrel with Bradley Pearson about being an 'artist' and being a 'professional writer' is that Shakespeare was both of these, too.

POSTSCRIPT 1986

SINCE 1976, WHEN this essay was first published, Miss Murdoch has written four more novels and the important and beautiful essay *The Fire and the Sun: Why Plato Banished the Artists* (1977), which continues and extends her study of the conflict or tension between the artist and the saint. If there have been no violent changes in her preoccupations or forms, there are nevertheless various shifts in emphasis and changes in technique that can be remarked on.

The most striking formal change is an increase in length and in apparent looseness of structure, as though the novelist was exploring more seriously the nineteenth-century fictional model that Henry James called 'loose, baggy monsters'. Favourable reviewers of *The Good Apprentice* (1985) have remarked on a kind of deliberate roughness in her style, which more than one has connected to a fear of the seductions of art. Stephen Medcalf calls this 'a deliberately throwaway style, a piling up of wanton expression, as if she fears the temptations and magic which a perfect style would offer'. Her characters certainly communicate increasingly in long, rushing, self-revelatory outpourings of thought about themselves and the nature of things, with words heavily italicized for emphasis, concepts grasped at rather than thought through. In this they are reminiscent of Dostoevski's endlessly fascinating, endlessly maddening self-revealed casuists and pleaders. In a communication at a conference in the University of Caen, Miss Murdoch made a statement about her ideal novel that is illuminating both about the novel she had then just finished (*The Sea, The Sea*), and about the conjunction of moral and aesthetic principles that guide her later work:

> The advantages of writing in the first person are obvious. In a way they are enormous because you can then ramble around endlessly, you can address your reader, and you can produce a tremendous amount of verbiage which has got a sense in relation to the speaker ... On the other hand, the danger of this is that it's harder then to create other characters who can

stand up to the narrator, because they're being seen through his eyes. And I think my ideal novel – I mean, the novel I would like to write and haven't yet written – would not be written in the first person, because I'd rather write a novel which is more scattered, with many different centres. I've often thought that the best way to write a novel would be to invent the story, and then to remove the hero and the heroine and write about the peripheral people – because one wants to extend one's sympathy and divide one's interests.[32]

The witty and often startling use of the 'peripheral people' in her later novels is worthy of comment. Many of them contain long passages of formalized social chatter, full of news and views, spoken by a kind of drawing-room chorus of minor characters, which have been excellently analyzed by Barbara Hardy in an essay in her book *Tellers and Listeners*, on the uses of talk in fiction.

An example I would offer here is the chorus of family and friends in *Nuns and Soldiers* (1980) who wait, in the early chapters, for Guy Openshaw to die, and whose discussions punctuate, half shape, and permeate his widow's subsequent remarriage to one of their number, the painter and hanger-on Tim Reede. Guy refers to them as 'les cousins et les tantes': Murdoch takes pleasure in giving us glimpses into their private hells and passions, outside their public choric function. Two of this chorus, Manfred and Mrs Mount (a kind of earthly Venus, with Tannhäuser associations), turn out in the penultimate chapter to have manipulated quite a lot of the plot of this novel, but are no hidden gods: a very minor character indeed then makes his only appearance, and, we are told, knows 'more about them than they imagined'.

Another example might be the density of Miss Murdoch's creation of the small spa town of Ennistone in *The Philosopher's Pupil* (1983), with its streets, housing, old families, varying religions, and of course its network of talk and gossip, centring on the public baths, a most imposingly *concrete* imaginary structure and institution, a natural force, the hot spray, contained in buildings and decor, utility and frivolity, of various decades. Connected to this specificity is the strange and almost fanatical gourmet regime of Charles Arrowby, the highly unsuccessful Prospero of *The Sea, The Sea* with his kippers and Cox's Orange Pippins, a saving grace in his fantastic world. Murdoch's new, shifting, and leisurely pace means that her work can contain, without apparent furious shaping (which would be 'magic'), a multiplicity of things and voices that embody the variety and strangeness of the known world. There are ways of looking *out* from all the private dramas of her protagonists and other vantage points from which to look in.

The idea of the danger and seduction of 'magic' is not new in Murdoch, although she continues to explore both magic and magicians with subtlety and invention. In *The Fire and the Sun* she writes that Plato 'always feared magic', and locates his disapproval of art in a fear of its unconscious sources and its indulgence of the human desire for power and fantasy. Plato's objections to theatrical illusion stand, lightly and comically, behind her choice of Charles Arrowby, a retired theatre director, as the hero-narrator of *The Sea, The Sea*, who incarcerates his childhood beloved in order to *make* her accept freedom and love at his hands. Art, according to Plato, according to Miss Murdoch,

> is dangerous chiefly because it apes the spiritual and subtly disguises and trivializes it ... Art delights in unsavoury trivia and in the endless proliferation of senseless images (television). Art is playful in a sinister sense, full of (φθόνος) a spiteful amused acceptance of evil, and through buffoonery and mockery weakens moral discrimination. The artist cannot represent or celebrate the good, but only what is daemonic and fantastic and extreme; whereas truth is quiet and sober and confined.

There are enchanter-artists in these later books, dangerous manipulators related to Mischa Fox and Julius King, but there is also an increased interest in a 'natural magic', in forces in the earth not part of our moral system or urgently related to it. There is much good magic in *The Sea, The Sea*, partly connected with Charles's Buddhist and military cousin

James, a self-disciplined saint who keeps demons in boxes and can descend into a churning sea-cave to rescue his cousin from death. There is a sea-serpent and there are seals, whose strangeness and yet human appeal has always seemed magical to us. In *The Good Apprentice* the prodigal son, Edward, who has killed his best friend by mistake, is sent by a Prospero figure, a lay analyst of unusual scrupulousness in Murdoch, in search of his natural father, Jesse Baltram, a painter who lives with his beautiful wife and two daughters in an enchanted castle, which is also an absurd ad hoc religious community called Seegard. Jesse's name suggests Frazer's dying gods: he is the progenitor, as Jesse at the foot of the Tree of Jesse in church windows led to Christ through David. Baltram suggests Beltane fires and religions of vegetation. He has a sickness like the Fisher King of the Grail legend, and is almost animal in his intense sexuality, in his hairy body and huge eyes, in his mute dying. Animals in Murdoch are always innocent and alive, from spiders to the 'papillon' dog whose consciousness she briefly inhabits in *The Philosopher's Pupil*. Edward's quest for his father brings him into contact with a mysterious natural world of women like withered golden apples and threatening 'tree men'; I think we are not meant to read these events as a bad fantasy but as a healing brush with old myths. Miss Murdoch has said that in writing of Jesse she was thinking of *Sir Gawaine and the Grene Knight*, of magical powers in the world that have nothing to do with Christianity and our system of ethics. Jesse has named his environment for sex and death: there is a 'lingam stone' in a forest glade, and the dining room is not the refectory but the Interfectory (killing place).

This increase in magic connects with a considerably increased urgency in Miss Murdoch's concern with Christianity, with what she sees as a contemporary need for a religion, albeit a religion without a God, for a new Christianity, centering on the acceptance of a mythical Christ who is Goodness, or the good man. In the colloquy at Caen she spoke of the difference between nineteenth- and twentieth-century novels in terms of religion. The nineteenth-century novel was, she said,

> a major product of religion, and one could say that the most important change we have experienced during this century has been the disappearance of religion as something that goes without saying, in the sense in which all the great nineteenth-century writers were, to a remarkable degree, religious thinkers – however they defined themselves – for whom the religious background went without saying.

She goes on to claim that in England the demythologizing of religion, the new consideration of dogmas as myths, could 'bring religion back into the realm of the believable'. Here art would be religious in the Tolstoyan sense, would *make* religion.

I believe this hope for a revitalized, demythologized religion is central in all these later novels. It takes a Buddhist form in *The Sea, The Sea*, inventing supernatural events to endorse the moral insight of the selfless James. In *The Good Apprentice* Edward the prodigal son is counterbalanced by his brother (by upbringing, not parentage), Stuart, who apprentices himself to Good and has the lack of charm often associated with good people in Miss Murdoch's work – for example, Ann, in *An Unofficial Rose*, or Tallis, in *A Fairly Honourable Defeat*, an explicit Christ-figure. Stuart practises celibacy, meditation, and a kind of disciplined annihilation of the ego. (He is interesting because his ego is powerful and determined.) He is perceived by others as a 'white maggot' and by Jesse, when they encounter each other, as death itself. He makes innocent and purposeful interventions in the complicated lives of others, resembling in this Dostoevski's innocent, occasionally disastrous, not quite human Prince Myshkin, the Idiot who imitates Christ and shares Christ's apparent ignorance of sexual life. Some of Stuart's acts produce good, some are more doubtful, but the *ideal* of virtue is credible and attractive (if that is not a dangerous word). Edward has too much myth, Stuart none. He is explicitly *not* the Sorcerer's Apprentice, but the elder brother in the parable of the Prodigal Son, who, Miss Murdoch feels, has had a rough deal, morally.

If Stuart represents a possible and credible modern religious stance, both *The Philosopher's Pupil* and *Nuns and Soldiers* offer us moments of myth, or art, where Christ is present. In *The Philosopher's Pupil* it is a whole scene, a beach picnic, where the innocent young man, Tom, is overcome by his discovery of Christ's legendary visit to Britain with Joseph of Arimathea; and where the daemonic George braves the Murdochian rite of passage of near drowning to rescue the papillon dog, which is subsequently nestled between his sister-in-law's breasts, watched by his nephew, Adam, who loves the dog. The papillon is, in its way, the soul (papillon = butterfly in French = Psyche, in Greek). George harrows hell to fetch it back to Adam, who has named it Zed, because he and it are Alpha and Omega, the beginning and the end. In this scene, which I can only adumbrate and took several readings to understand, *everyone* is Christ, contributes to Christ as part of the community, even George, and despite the usual Murdochian tensions, bickering, life of chatter and triviality, power struggles and pain. In this novel, too, is Father Bernard, a successor to Carel in *Time of the Angels*, a priest of no God, who celebrates masses and prays to a Christ he knows to be dead and not risen. 'And it is essential that he did not rise. If he be risen, then is our faith vain.' At the end of this book, which opens with a near-murder and is in many ways blacker in its vision of human nature than many of Murdoch's novels, Father Bernard defines religion:

'Metaphysics and the human sciences are made impossible by the *penetration of morality into the moment-by-moment of ordinary life*: the understanding of this fact is *religion*. . . .

'There is no beyond, there is only here, the infinitely small, infinitely great and utterly demanding present. This too I tell my flock, demolishing their dreams of a supernatural elsewhere. So you see, I have abandoned every kind of magic and preach a charmless holiness. This and only this can be the religion of the future, this and only this can save the planet.'

In *Nuns and Soldiers* Anne Cavidge, who has given up being a nun because she has lost her faith in God, has the most direct and startling experience of Christ, when she is visited by him in her kitchen and told 'almost carelessly' that there is salvation, but 'you must do it all yourself, you know'. Also: 'I am not a magician, I never was. You know what to do. Do right, refrain from wrong.' This Christ is very real and somewhat inconsequential; interestingly, he shares with all Miss Murdoch's 'good' people a blanched look: 'He had a strangely elongated head and a strange pallor, a pallor of something which had long been deprived of light, a shadowed leaf, a deep sea fish, a grub inside a fruit.'

It is Anne, another of the community of religious godless, who says something that connects this religious morality to the form of Miss Murdoch's novels:

'Your life doesn't belong to you,' said Anne. 'Who can tell where his life ends? Our being spreads far out beyond us and mingles with the being of others. We live in other people's thoughts, in their plans, in their dreams. This is as if there were God. We have an infinite responsibility.'

For this reason the peripheral characters spin their half-glimpsed stories. Edward, at the end of *The Good Apprentice*, has a familiar vision of life as both particular and accidental and intensely ordered, like art:

'In a way it's all a muddle starting off with an accident: my breakdown, drugs, telepathy, my father's illness, cloistered neurotic women, people arriving unexpectedly, all sorts of things which happen by pure chance ... In another way it's a whole complex thing, internally connected, like a dark globe, a dark world, as if we were all parts of a simple drama, living inside a work of art. Perhaps important things are always like that, so that you can think of them both ways.'

Miss Murdoch's novels think of life in both ways, accidentally and as a complex order. If the drive to represent particularity, the accidental, the unknown, the unfinished is at present even more powerful, the artist has found new ways of dealing with, representing, and ordering that drive. There is no other English novelist whose understanding of the patterns and lapses in our thought and attention is so careful and so morally exacting.

ESSAY:
THE RELIGION OF FICTION

By Michael Levenson

ANGELS & INSECTS: TWO NOVELLAS
BY A. S. BYATT

SUPPOSE THAT OUR modernizing century has been, on the whole, a mistake. Suppose that what it called liberation – in the arts, but also in politics in religion, in philosophy – was only a new confinement; that its craving for revolution, with all its ferocities and its ambitions made this modernity cruelly unjust to those who came before. Suppose, finally, that the older, nearly forgotten path of slower (call it revolutionary) growth, interrupted by our great-grandparents, the whooping young modernists, remains for us to resume.

A. S. Byatt frequently gets called a postmodernist. Fine. She does go in for smart parodies of earlier narrative forms; she enjoys literary gamesmanship; and like many teasing contemporaries, she breaks up her stories with stories about her stories. But you miss a good deal of what is most interesting in Byatt, and what is most significant in the movement of which she is a part, if you ignore the way her postmodernity finds its ground in something else, something older, namely an earnest attempt to get back before the moderns and revive a Victorian project that has never been allowed to come to completion. What you have in Byatt is an odd-sounding but perfectly intelligible creature, the postmodern Victorian. She knows where we live and when; she knows her Joyce and Woolf and Beckett; but she is undeterred in the belief that the road into the twenty-first century winds exactly through the middle of the nineteenth.

337

Just over thirty years ago, Iris Murdoch published an essay called 'Against Dryness', which built an image of the modern novel as diminished, depleted and thin, failing badly in two opposed ways: through an excessively tight formalism, which produced overly polished jewels of authorial control; and through loose journalistic rambles, the lazy, loopy meander through anything crossing the path of reverie. Different as they were, the two forms shared a cult of the brave, lonely ego – solitary, adventurous, free – aiming to fulfil its private destiny. Lost was the older, thicker sense of the ego in community, of a novel full of many separate beings, of a world beyond the self. Authenticity, sincerity, self-assertion: these were for Murdoch the meagre modern legacy, bequeathed by a philosophy of subjectivity and a politics of happiness. Against this dryness, this fetish for the lonely, authentic self spreading the feathers of its 'brave naked will', Murdoch invoked Jane Austen, Leo Tolstoi and George Eliot, who produced thick social fictions that never forgot 'that other people exist'.

In a formulation that Byatt calls 'electrifying', Murdoch praised the 'hard idea of truth' at the expense of the 'facile idea of sincerity'. Byatt, who wrote a critical study of Murdoch early in her own career, returns frequently, even obsessively, to 'Against Dryness', citing her favourite phrases as if to remind herself of what she believes. Murdoch has been her literary mother. The two of them alone are enough to count as a distinct contemporary lineage, nourished on the conviction that, our modernist complacencies aside, our Victorian origins are unresolved, unsurpassed.

Three years ago *Possession* gave Byatt big international success. It not only brought her fame, it gave her career a new roundness. Much of the earlier fiction was quickly and finely reprinted. Scattered essays were collected. Translations, introductions and interviews crowded her life. After two decades of writing, her work assumed a more vivid shape for her readers, and still more interestingly, it seemed to assume a more vivid shape for Byatt herself. Now, in the long middle of her career, her intentions seem sharper, her future more interesting than it has been before.

The two novellas that make up *Angels & Insects* are not yet that future, but they are signposts. Taken together, they show the reach and the promise of the Byattian project of resuming the incomplete work of the past. In the first of them, 'Morpho Eugenia', the Victorian scientist William Adamson, a student of ants, beetles and butterflies, comes home to England after years in the rain-forests of South America. Most of his specimens having been lost in a shipwreck, Adamson, estranged and friendless, faces personal catastrophe. But then the Reverend Harold Alabaster, a wealthy baronet and an amateur naturalist, invites Adamson into his grand mansion, where the shattered scientist is given free rein first to rethink his studies and then to marry Eugenia, the beautiful daughter of the house.

Adamson finds himself back inside the mid-Victorian matrix with its class rigidities, its religious panic, its moral agitation. He looks for solace in the insects. Turning his practised eye to a colony of ants living on the grounds of the estate, he initially finds an alternative to his tense family life, but the longer he looks the more clearly he sees his own world reflected in the mirror held up by the little bugs. Adamson fights those analogies. He doesn't want to know himself as a drone recruited to serve his more powerful conquerors, the country-house aristocracy with its endless appetite for blood, money and horsemanship.

But his denials aside, 'Morpho Eugenia' is intent on forcing the thought that seen from a height, watched across centuries, we humans creep and crawl, scratch and burrow like any other low creature moving close to the surface of the planet. Are we little more, too little more, than the insects? When we watch the ants, making war, making love, carrying crumbs, building ant cities, stealing ant babies, can we keep from growing dizzy? The old shudder of Darwinism is what Byatt's story wants to give.

And why shouldn't we still shudder? What have we become that we have forgotten the shock of our origins? Byatt has accepted from Murdoch, who accepted it from George Eliot, the urgent literary imperative to make struggle against fantasy. This is Byatt's version of their realist credo: 'That there is a hard reality, not ourselves, which is not amenable to our planning, plotting and power-strategies.' So 'Morpho Eugenia' thrashes Adamson's self-deceptions, his blindness to class and domestic violence, his cult of innocence and beauty, forcing him into the rude perception that what we call civilization is a fancy name for our animal contrivances.

A natural history of the ant colonies is what Adamson writes, but Byatt makes clear that a 'natural history' of humanity is what any strong novel must be. It must disregard the fantasies of species-pride that we use to cheer ourselves up. It must face up to the Darwinian nightmare, well expressed by Tennyson when he enters the second novella, 'The Conjugial Angel', as a shambling, frightened old man:

> Men now saw what he saw, the earth heaped and stacked with dead things, broken bright feathers and shrivelled moths, worms stretched and sliced and swallowed, stinking shoals of once bright fish, dried parrots and tigerskins limply and glassily snarling on hearths, mountains of human skulls mixed with monkey skulls and snake skulls and asses' jawbones and butterfly wings, mashed into humus and dust, fed on, regurgitated, blown in the wind, soaked in the rain, absorbed.

If that were all, it would be bad to be alive. But it is a first principle of the natural history of humanity, as Byatt inherits it from Eliot, that you must tell all, where 'all' includes not only the bad moments when we know ourselves to be beasts among the beastly, but also the moments of shivering insight when we feel that we float like angels under the eye of a winking mystery.

If it were only a matter of finding an open space between the Angels and the Insects, being human would be easy. What makes it hard in Byatt's world is that we are hybrid beings who go wrong when we seek purity of any kind. In 'Morpho Eugenia', Adamson must free himself from class indignity and sexual humiliation by seeing the insect in the human, where this means understanding the natural cruelties beneath the myth of Victorian family harmony. Only if we know ourselves as partly animal can we be fully human. This implies, among other things that to exaggerate our creepy crawliness is as dangerous as to ignore it, and further along this line of thought, that our human chances depend on knowing that we two-legged insects are also fallen angels.

Thus the perspective in the second novella turns upward, not to transcend this world but to bring higher visions down into the earthly mix. The events of 'The Conjugial Angel' take place in the mid-1870s, a little more than ten years after the time of 'Morpho Eugenia'. Byatt the precise Victorianist knows that the brief period saw some large changes, including, for instance, the great vogue of drawing-room spiritualism, with its séances and mediums, its dark closets and mumbled voices and apparitions. She has described this as 'the religion of a materialist age', part of a craving to confirm a threatened faith through visible proof of the life immortal. Bowing under the worldly pressures of science and industry, Darwin and advertising, a more desperate band of seekers looked to find spirits as material as any other commodity in the new commercial age.

They fought death with all means available, with 'animal magnetism' and 'aethereal telegraphy' – and then also with poetry. No Victorian death was more extravagantly resisted, not even the death of Prince Albert, than that of Arthur Henry Hallam. In 1833 he was gone at twenty-two. Seventeen years later Tennyson published 'In Memoriam', the more than 100 lyrics of his long mourning for this friend. From this point, Hallam's untimely death became the type for all inexplicable suffering and for the fragility of faith under the heavy tramp of science. 'Next to the Bible,' said Queen Victoria. 'In Memoriam' is my comfort.

But of course Hallam's death caused other, less literary, less public, griefs. The conceit of 'The Conjugial Angel' is to ponder the case of Tennyson's sister Emily, engaged to marry Hallam after knowing him just four weeks, and condemned to represent the Bereaved Lover frozen into a pose of 'perpetual maidenhood' (her brother's phrase). After nine years of mourning for Hallam, she married a Captain Jesse, and 'The Conjugial Angel' imagines what it must have been for Emily Tennyson Jesse to endure the sniffy opinion that she should never have married, but should have burned always for the young god Hallam. What must it have been to be married to another when 'In Memoriam' appeared with all its steadfast, untainted fidelity? What must it have been to age with the memory of an absurdly short romance, longing to settle emotional accounts with the ghost of the young lover?

Building on the fact that the aging Emily Tennyson Jesse attended séances and dallied with the spiritualists, Byatt imagines her way into this spiritually edgy world. She invents a circle of initiates who yearn really to see what they hope they believe. A second leading character in 'The Conjugial Angel', Mrs Lilias Papagay, has drifted into the séance business, looking first for word on her lost husband and then finding a tidy profit in hosting respectable sessions with the ghosts. Byatt neatly tags her as 'an intelligent, questioning kind of woman, the kind who, in an earlier age, would have been a theologically minded nun, and in a later one would have had a university training in philosophy or psychology or medicine'. But Byatt, I suspect, rather likes Mrs Papagay just where she is, neither devout nun nor rational psychologist, caught in the twisted branches of sex and money, even as she yearns to see an angel in the sunset.

For Byatt, those twisted branches, this yearning, are ours, too. She has described late Victorian spiritualism as 'part of a whole shift in religious feeling', and she sees us in our own late century as living in the same spiritual swamp. But this perception is entirely without scorn. Byatt may not believe in the truths of religion, but she unquestionably believes in the belief. And so she takes pleasure in recalling George Eliot's religious progress from 'evangelical Anglican' to 'resolutely anti-Christian' rationalist and then finally to the larger, more generous humanism that 'saw Christian belief and morality as forms of human experience that must be studied and valued as part of our natural history'. This is what Byatt appears to want for herself: she wants to be the natural historian of a post-Christian spiritual life.

All through Byatt's writing life, she has reflected on the way we earthly beings dream of spirit. She is a Realist, a post-Christian, a sometime academic living in sceptical times. These may seem heavy drags on the religious turn, but for Byatt these are simply the latest natural conditions for our spirit-hunger. It's no use whining. Her point is not to confirm religious truth, but to enlarge the religious sense, which locates value not in the infinite but in the yearning for the infinite, not in God but in the search for God. In a more than clever analogy, Byatt has drawn a connection between the 'afterlife' of the Bible and the 'afterlife' of the nineteenth-century novel. We live in the shadow of both. But the task, as she sees it, is not to get out from under the shadow into the white modern light. It is to respect and to love our old shadowy needs, to keep faith with faith, and with realist fiction.

The insight – you might even call it the revelation – that seems to have clarified for Byatt through the writing of *Possession* is that a novel might not only be about the act of faith; it can itself be the act. Soon after *Possession* appeared she wrote a long essay on the persistence of belief in nineteenth-century culture, in which she took the French historian Michelet as a beautiful instance, beautiful because in choosing a name for his history, Michelet rejected 'Narrative' and 'Analysis' in favour of 'Resurrection'. To write history (or, by extension, historical fiction) is to resurrect the dead, it is to raise Lazarus: this thought is made for Byatt. It leads quickly to her own elevated vision for the contemporary novelist, who through strenuous imagining might herself raise the dead, and it encourages her in the proud thought that what religion was, literature can now be.

At the end of 'The Conjugial Angel', when the ghost of Hallam appears to appear, Byatt's reader must experience an unnerving double response. The first instinctive mockery of those who see ghosts gives way to a second, less cosy recognition that we novel readers are always seeing ghosts. Every character is an apparition. Whenever we lend solidity to the stories we follow, we are living proof of a visionary capacity almost always undervalued. Byatt's purpose is to push this fact about fiction into the foreground of consciousness, so that reading novels becomes the training of vision.

She asks no one to believe in God, and she doesn't tell us to pray. But lately she wants to remind us at every turn that our species has an entrenched habit of looking into the sky, and however little that may tell us about the sky and beyond, it tells us a good deal about our believing, hoping, fearing selves. We do want thicker characters alive in many dimensions. We do want to summon the fading impalpable past. Many of our most disbelieving friends call certain things 'sacred.' Some of the most worldly among us throw embarrassed upward glances at the highest blue.

MICHAEL LEVENSON teaches English at the University of Virginia.

SELECTED BIBLIOGRAPHY

I. BIBLIOGRAPHY

Thomas T. Tominaga, *Iris Murdoch and Murial Spark: A Bibliography* (USA, 1976); C. K. Bove and John Fletcher, *Iris Murdoch: A Descriptive Primary and Annotated Secondary Bibliography* (New York and London, 1994).

II. NOVELS

Under the Net (1954); *The Flight from the Enchanter* (1956); *The Sandcastle* (1957); *The Bell* (1958); *A Severed Head* (1961); *An Unofficial Rose* (1962); *The Unicorn* (1963); *The Italian Girl* (1964); *The Red and the Green* (1965); *The Time of the Angels* (1966); *The Nice and the Good* (1968); *Bruno's Dream* (1969); *A Fairly Honourable Defeat* (1970); *An Accidental Man* (1971); *The Black Prince* (1973); *The Sacred and Profane Love Machine* (1974); *A Word Child* (1975); *Henry and Cato* (1976); *The Sea, The Sea* (1978); *Nuns and Soldiers* (1980); *The Philosopher's Pupil* (1983); *The Good Apprentice* (1985); *The Book and the Brotherhood* (1987); *The Message to the Planet* (1989); *The Green Knight* (1993)

III. SEPARATE WORKS

Sartre, Romantic Rationalist (London, 1953, reissued with new introduction by Miss Murdoch, 1987), philosophy and literary criticism; *A Severed Head* (London 1964), a play, with J. B. Priestley; *The Sovereignty of Good* (London, 1970), philosophy, contains three previously pub. philosophical papers: 'The Idea of Perfection,' in the *Yale Review* (Spring, 1964), 'The Sovereignty of Good over Other Concepts,' Leslie Stephen Lecture (in 1967), 'On "God" and "Good," ' in *The Anatomy of Knowledge* (New York, 1969); *The Italian Girl*, (London 1969), a play with James Saunders; *Three Arrows and the Servants in the Snow* (London, 1973), plays; *The Fire and the Sun: Why Plato Banished the Artists* (London, 1977), based on the Rorranes Lecture (1976), philosophy; *A Year of Birds* (Wiltshire, 1978; rev. ed. London, 1984), poems with engravings by R. Stone; *The Servants* (London 1980), libretto for an opera by William Mathias; *Acastos: Two Platonic Dialogues* (London, 1986), philosophy; *The Black Prince* (1987), a play; *The Existentialist Political Myth* (London, 1989), philosophy; *Metaphysics as a Guide to Morals* (London, 1992), philosophy.

IV. ARTICLES

'Rebirth of Christianity,' in *Adelphi* (July-September 1943); 'Worship and Common Life,' in *Adelphi* (July-September 1944); 'The Novelist as Metaphysician,' in the *Listener* (16 March 1950); 'The Existentialist Hero,' in the *Listener* (23 March 1950); 'The Existentialist Political Myth,' in *Socratic*, 5 (1952); 'Nostalgia for the Particular,' in Proceedings of the Aristotelian Society, supp. vol. 30, *Dreams and Self-Knowledge* (London, 1956); 'Knowing the Void,' in the *Spectator* (2 November 1956); 'Important Things,' in the *Sunday Times* (17 February 1957), review of S. de Beauvoir, *The Mandarins*, repr. in *Encore: A Sunday Times Anthology* (London, 1963); 'Metaphysics and Ethics,' in D. F. Pears, *The Nature of Metaphysics* (London, 1957); 'Hegel in Modern Dress,' in the *New Statesman* (25 May 1957); 'Existentialist Bite,' in the *Spectator* (12 July 1957); 'T. S. Eliot as a Moralist,' in N. Braybrooke, ed., *T. S. Eliot: A Symposium for His Seventieth Birthday* (London, 1958); 'A House of Theory,' in N. Mackenzie, ed. *Conviction* (London, 1958), repr. in *Partisan Review*, 26 (1959); 'The Sublime and the Beautiful Revisited,' in *Yale Review*, 49 (1959); 'The Sublime and the Good,' in *Chicago Review*, 13 (Autumn 1959); 'Negative Capability,' in *Adam*, 284–286 (1960); 'Against Dryness,' in *Encounter*, 16 (January 1961); 'Mass, Might and Myth,' in the *Spectator* (7 September 1962); 'Speaking of Writing,' in *The Times* (13 February 1964); 'The Darkness of Practical

Reason,' in *Encounter*, 27 (July 1966); 'Existentialists and Mystics,' in W. W Robson, ed., *Essays and Poems Presented to Lord David Cecil* (London, 1970); 'Salvation by Words,' in *The New York Review of Books* (15 June 1972); 'Socialism and Selection,' in C. B. Cox and R. Boyson, *Black Paper* (London, 1975), 3rd ed.; 'Epistolary Dialogues,' in *Soviet Literature* (London, 1977), pt. 2, with V. Ivasheva; 'Art Is the Imitation of Nature,' in *Cahiers du Centre de recherches sur les pays du nord ed du nord-ouest*, no. 1. (Caen, 1978).

V. INTERVIEWS

F. Kermode, 'House of Fiction: Interviews with Seven English Novelists,' in *Partisan Review*, 30 (1963); P. Orr, interview recorded 27 May 1965, the British Council, London: F. Dillistone, 'Christ and Myth,' in *Frontier* (Autumn 1965); S. Nettell, 'An Exclusive Interview,' in *Books and Bookmen*, 11 (September 1966); W. K. Rose, 'An Interview with Iris Murdoch,' in *London Magazine*, 8 (June 1968), also in *Shenandoah*, 19 (Winter 1968); R. Bryden and A. S. Byatt, interview recorded March 1968, partly reproduced in the *Listener* (4 April 1968): A. S. Byatt, 'Talking to Iris Murdoch,' forty-minute interview recorded 26 October 1971, BBC Archives; 'Iris Murdoch in Conversation with Malcolm Bradbury,' recorded 27 February 1976, British Council tape no. RS 2001; M. Jarrett-Kerr, 'Good, Evil and Morality,' in CR *Quarterly Review of the Community of the Resurrection* no. 265 (Michaelmas 1969); J. L. Chevalier, ed., 'Recontres avec Iris Murdoch,' Centre de recherches de littérature et linguistique des pays de langue anglaise, Université de Caen (Caen, 1978); B. Magee, *Men of Ideas: Some Creators of Contemporary Philosophy* (London, 1978); A. S. Byatt reviews *Nuns and Soldiers* with Sheridan Morley, Kaleidoscope, BBC (September 1980); H. Ziegler and C. W. E. Bigsby, eds., *The Radical Imagination and the Liberal Tradition: Interviews with English and American Novelists* (London, 1982); J. Haffenden, 'John Haffenden Talks to Iris Murdoch,' in the *Literary Review*, 48 (April 1983); A. S. Byatt with Iris Murdoch, *Writers Talk: Ideas of Our Time*, Series No. 9, ICA Video *Guardian Conversations* (London, 1984); A. S. Byatt reviews *The Message to the Planet*, Kaleidoscope, BBC (October 1989).

VI. CRITICAL STUDIES

K. Allsopp, *The Angry Decade: A Survey of the Cultural Revolt of the Nineteen-Fifties* (London, 1958); G. S. Fraser, 'Iris Murdoch: The Solidity of the Normal,' in J. Wain, ed., *International Literary Annual II* (1959); James Gindin, 'Images of Illusion in the Work of Iris Murdoch,' *Texas Studies in Language and Literature* (Summer 1960); Marvin Fellheim, 'Symbolic Characterisation in the Novels of Iris Murdoch,' *Texas Studies in Language and Literature* (Summer 1960); René Micha, 'Les Romans à Machine d'Iris Murdoch', *Critique* (April 1960); Olga McDonald Meidner, 'Reviewer's Bane, *Flight From the Enchanter*,' *Essays in Criticism*, II (October 1961); G. Pearson, 'Iris Murdoch and the Romantic Novel,' in *New Left Review*, 13–14 (January-April 1962); M. Badbury, 'Iris Murdoch's *Under the Net*,' in *Critical Quarterly*, no. 4 (Spring 1962); J. Souvage, 'Symbol as Narrative Device,' in *English Studies* (2 April 1962); W. Van O'Connor, *The New University Wits and the End of Modernism* (London, 1963) contains an essay on 'Iris Murdoch: The Formal and the Contingent'; M. Graham, 'Iris Murdoch and the Symbolist Novel,' in *British Journal of Aesthetics*, 5 (July 1965); P. Wolfe, *The Disciplined Heart* (London, 1966), contains useful information but some very odd interpretations of the moral structure of the novels; R. Scholes, *The Fabulators* (London, 1967), contains an essay on *The Unicorn* as fable; R. Rabinovitz, *Iris Murdoch* (New York, 1968), Columbia Essays on Modern Writers, no. 34; J. Bayley, *The Characters of Love: A Study in the Literature of Personality* (London, 1968); H. German, 'Allusions in the Early Novels of Iris Murdoch,' in *Modern Fiction Studies*, 15 (Autumn 1969), special issue on Iris Murdoch; P. Kemp, 'The Fight Against Fantasy': Iris Murdoch's *The Red and the Green*,' in *Modern Fiction Studies*, 15 (Autumn 1969); A. P. Kenney, 'The Mythic History of *A Severed Head*,' in *Modern Fiction Studies* 15 (Autumn 1969); H. German, 'The Range of Allusion in the Novels of Iris Murdoch,' in *Journal of Modern Literature* (1971); F. Kermode, *Modern Essays* (London, 1971); R. Hoskins, 'Iris Murdoch's Midsummer Nightmare,' in *Twentieth Century Literature*, 19 (January-October 1972); R. Haskins, 'Shakespearean Allusions in *A Fairly Honourable Defeat*,' in *Twentieth Century Literature*, 19 (January-October 1971); M. Bradbury, *Possibilities: Essays on the State of the Novel* (London, 1973), a very illuminating essay, extending his earlier work on *Under the Net*; P. Swinden, *Unofficial*

Selves (London, 1973), pursuing Murdoch's ideas about character, esp. good on *A Fairly Honourable Defeat;* B. Hardy, *Tellers and Listeners* (London, 1975); M. Bradbury, ed., *The Post-War English Novel* (Stratford-upon-Avon studies, London, 1977); L. Sage, 'No Trespassers,' in the *New Review* (September, 1977); L. Sage, 'The Pursuit of Imperfection,' in *Critical Quarterly,* 19 (Summer 1977); M. Scanlan, 'The Machinery of Pain: Romantic Suffering in Three Works of Iris Murdoch's,' in *Renascence,* 29 (Winter 1977); Z. T. Sullivan, 'The Contracting Universe of Iris Murdoch's Gothic Novels,' in *Modern Fiction Studies,* 23 (Winter 1977–1978); Z. T. Sullivan, 'Iris Murdoch's Self-Conscious Gothicism: *The Time of the Angels,*' in *Arizona Quarterly* (1977); R. Scholes, *Fabulation and Metafiction* (Urbana, Ill., and London, 1978); M. Bradbury and D. Palmer, eds., *The Contemporary English Novel* (London, 1979), contains L. Sage, 'Female Fictions' and A. S. Byatt, 'People in Paper Houses: Attitudes to "Realism" and Experiment in English Postwar Fiction'; R. Todd, *Iris Murdoch, The Shakespearean Interest* (New York, 1979); M. Weldhem, 'Morality and the Metaphor,' in *New Universities Quarterly* (Spring 1980); P. J. Conradi, 'The Metaphysical Hostess,' in *English Library History,* 48 (Summer 1981); P. J. Conradi, 'Useful Fictions,' in *Critical Quarterly,* 23 (Autumn 1981); N. Vance, 'Iris Murdoch's Serious Fun,' in *Theology* (November 1981); E. Dipple, *Iris Murdoch: Work for the Spirit* (London, 1982); A. MacIntyre, 'Good for Nothing,' in the *London Review of Books* (3–16 June 1982); R. Todd, *Iris Murdoch* (New York and London, 1984); S. Medcalf, 'Towards Respect for Reality,' in the *Times Literary Supplement* (27 September 1985); P. J. Conradi, *Iris Murdoch: The Saint and the Artist* (London, 1986, revised 1989); C. K. Bove, *Character Index and Guide to the Fiction of Iris Murdoch* (New York, 1986); D. Johnson, *Iris Murdoch* (London, 1987); R. C. Kane, *Iris Murdoch, Muriel Spark and John Fowles, Didactic Demons* (London, 1988); R. Todd, *Encounters with Irish Murdoch* (Amsterdam, 1988); P. O'Connor, 'Iris Murdoch: Philosophical Novelist', *New Comparison: A Journal of Comparative and General Literary Studies* 8 (Autumn 1989); A. N. Wilson, 'On The Novel's Far Horizons', *Weekend Guardian* (Sept 30–Oct 1 1989); D. Dezure, 'The Perceiving Self as Gatekeeper: Choice in Iris Murdoch's "Something Special",' *Studies in Short fiction* 27.2 (Spring 1990); J. Fletcher, 'Iris Murdoch, Novelist of London', *International Fiction Review* 17.1 (Winter 1990); D. J. Gordon 'Iris Murdoch's Comedies of Unselfing', *Twentieth-Century Literature* 36.2

(Summer 1990); D. Phillips, 'The Challenge of the Past'. Iris Murdoch and the Legacy of the Great Nineteenth-Century Novelists', *Caliban* 27 (1990); S. Ramanathan, *Iris Murdoch: Figures of Good* (London, 1990); J. Turner, 'Murdoch vs. Freud in *A Severed Head* and Other Novels', *Literature and Psychology* 36.1–2 (1990); M. Wheeler, 'The Limits of Hell: Lodge, Murdoch, Burgess, Golding', *Literature and Theology: An Interdisciplinary Journal of Theory and Criticism* 4.1. (Glasgow, 1990); J. Fletcher, 'Rough Magic and Moral Toughness: Iris Murdoch's Fictional Universe' in *The British and Irish Novel Since 1960*, ed. by J. Achesan (New York, 1991); D. D. Mettler, *Sound and Sense, Musical Allusion and Imagery in the Novels of Iris Murdoch* (London, 1991); L. Tucker, ed., *Critical Essays on Irish Murdoch* (New York, 1992); C. K. Bove, *Understanding Iris Murdoch* (Columbia, 1993); G. Griffin, *The Influence of the Writings of Simone Weil on the Fiction of Iris Murdoch* (London, 1993); P. P. Punja, *The Novels of Iris Murdoch: A Critical Study* (1993); D. Scott Arnold, *Liminal Readings: Forms of Otherness in Melville, Joyce and Murdoch* (1993); P. Conradi, 'Platonism in Iris Murdoch' in *Platonism and the English Literary Imagination*, ed. by A. Baldwin, S. Hutton (Cambridge, 1994); P. Conradi, 'Iris Murdoch and the Sea' in Études britanniques contemporaines, *Revue de la Société d'Études Anglaisés Contemporaines*, no. 4 (June 1994); P. Conradi, 'Iris Murdoch and Dostoevsky' in *Dostoevskii and Britain*, ed. by W. Leatherbarrow (forthcoming); A. S. Byatt and I. Sodré, *Imagining Characters: In Conversation about Literature* (London, 1995), will contain a discussion of *An Unofficial Rose*.

Note: The author wishes to thank Peter Conradi for help in the preparation of this bibliography.

VII. IRIS MURDOCH NEWSLETTER

Europe: c/o Prof. Peter Conradi, Dept. of Humanities, Kingston University, Peurhyn Road, Kingston-on-Thames, Surrey KT1 2EE; USA: c/o Dr Cheryl Bove, Iris Murdoch Society, Dept. of English, Ball State University, Muncie, Indiana 47306–0460.

NOTES

CHAPTER 1 Introduction

1. 'Against Dryness' (AD), p. 19.
2. AD, p. 17.
3. AD, p. 17.
4. AD, p. 18.
5. AD, p. 20.
6. AD, p. 20.
7. AD, p. 18.
8. *Sartre, Romantic Rationalist* (*Sartre*), p. 13.
9. *Sartre*, p. 75.
10. 'The Sublime and the Beautiful Revisited' (S&BR), p. 255.
11. See Bibliography.
12. *The Characters of Love*, p. 239.

CHAPTER 2 Under the Net

1. 'Iris Murdoch and the Solidity of the Normal'. p. 38.
2. 'Iris Murdoch's *Under the Net*', *Critical Quarterly*, No. 4, Spring 1962, p. 49.
3. *Under the Net* (UTN), p. 69.
4. UTN, p. 92.
5. Ibid.
6. Ibid.
7. AD, p. 20.
8. Op. cit. p. 39.
9. UTN, p. 23.
10. UTN, p. 13.
11. UTN, p. 34.
12. UTN, p. 14.
13. UTN, p. 22.
14. UTN, p. 21.
15. UTN, p. 29.
16. UTN, p. 27.
17. UTN, p. 26.
18. UTN, p. 24.
19. Ibid.
20. UTN, p. 29.
21. UTN, p. 30.
22. UTN, p. 9.
23. Ibid.
24. UTN, p. 24.
25. UTN, p. 279.
26. UTN, p. 26.
27. UTN, p. 32.
28. UTN, p. 42.
29. UTN, p. 201.
30. Op. cit. p. 51.
31. UTN, p. 259.
32. UTN, p. 61.
33. UTN, p. 48.
34. *Sartre*, p. 12.
35. Ibid.

36. UTN, pp. 283–4.
37. *Sartre*, p. 67.
38. *Sartre*, p. 14.
39. *Sartre*, p. 17.
40. Ibid.
41. *Sartre*, p. 35.
42. UTN, p. 158.
43. UTN, p. 159.
44. UTN, p. 162.
45. *Sartre*, p. 69.
46. UTN, p. 110.
47. *The Bell*, (B), p. 82.
48. UTN, p. 113.
49. *Sartre*, p. 54.

50. *Sartre*, p. 55.
51. UTN, p. 277.
52. *Critical Quarterly*, op cit. p. 47.
53. UTN, p. 236.
54. UTN, p. 194.
55. UTN, p. 207.
56. Ibid.
57. UTN, p. 219.
58. *Critical Quarterly*, op. cit. p. 51.
59. UTN, p. 269.
60. UTN, p. 45.
61. UTN, p. 269.

CHAPTER 3 The Flight from the Enchanter

1. AD, p. 18.
2. *The Flight from the Enchanter* (FFTE) p. 187.
3. FFTE, p. 47.
4. FFTE, p. 45.
5. *The Unicorn*, (U), p. 116.
6. Simone Weil, *Attente de Dieu* (A de D), p. 85, Paris 1950.
7. FFTE, p. 106.
8. FFTE, p. 7.
9. FFTE, p. 155.
10. FFTE, p. 82.
11. FFTE, p. 289.
12. FFTE, p. 291.
13. A de D, p. 88.
14. FFTE, p. 34.
15. FFTE, p. 256.
16. FFTE, p. 226.
17. FFTE, pp. 47–8.
18. FFTE, pp. 129–30.
19. FFTE, p. 131.
20. S&BR, p. 258.

21. FFTE, p. 135.
22. FFTE, p. 204.
23. FFTE, p. 163.
24. FFTE, p. 262.
25. FFTE, p. 48.
26. FFTE, p. 305.
27. FFTE, p. 308.
28. AD, p. 18.
30. FFTE, pp. 276–7.
31. FFTE, p. 309.
32. FFTE, p. 236.
33. AD, p. 19.
34. Ibid.
35. FFTE, p. 87.
36. B, p. 86.
37. FFTE, p. 226.
38. Ibid.
39. FFTE, p. 224.
40. FFTE, p. 299.
41. *Sartre*, p. 26.
42. *Sartre*, p. 53.
43. *Sartre*, p. 25.
44. *Sartre*, p. 24.

CHAPTER 4 The Sandcastle

1. *The Sandcastle* (S), p. 8.
2. S, p. 9.
3. S, pp. 54–5.

4. S, p. 69.
5. S, p. 77.
6. S, p. 78.

7. S, p. 172.
8. S, p. 209.
9. S, p. 208.
10. S, p. 11.
11. S, p. 215.
12. S, p. 216.
13. Ibid.
14. Simone Weil, *La Pesanteur et la Grace* (P et G), p. 21, Paris, 1948.
15. P et G, p. 19.
16. S, p. 304.
17. S, p. 312.
18. *Sartre*, p. 24.
19. *Sartre*, p. 42.
20. S, p. 198.
21. S, p. 228.
22. Ibid.
23. S, p. 226.

CHAPTER 5 The Bell

1. See Bibliography.
2. 'The Sublime and the Good' (S&G), pp. 43 et seq.
3. B, p. 276.
4. B, p. 270.
5. B, p. 242.
6. B. p. 44.
7. *Sartre*, p. 62.
8. B, p. 11.
9. B, p. 63
10. B, p. 45.
11. B, p. 182.
12. B, p. 183.
13. See Bibliography.
14. B, p. 187.
15. AD, p. 19.
16. S, p. 255.
17. B, p. 192.
18. B, p. 213.
19. B, p. 270.
20. B, p. 173.
21. B, p. 80.
22. B, p. 303.
23. UTN, p. 283.
24. B, p. 305.
25. B, p. 307.
26. U, p. 317.
27. B, p. 139.
28. See Bibliography.
29. S&BR, p. 257.
30. B, p. 83.
31. See article by Olga McDonald Meidner, 'Reviewer's Bane', *Essays in Criticism*, II, October 1961.
32. B, p. 86.
33. U, p. 116.
34. B, p. 86.
35. B, p. 124.
36. B, p. 106.
37. B. p. 108.
38. B, p. 158.
39. B, p. 163.
40. B, p. 168.
41. See Bibliography.
42. B, p. 85.
43. S&G, p. 51.
44. B, p. 89.
45. B, p. 133.
46. B, p. 87.
47. B, p. 82.
48. B, pp. 205–6.
49. AD, p. 18.
50. *Sartre*, p. 62.
51. B, p. 207.
52. S&BR, p. 256.
53. S&G, p. 52 and passim.
54. S&BR, p. 254.
55. S&BR, p. 255.
56. B, p. 87.
57. *Sartre*, p. 65.
58. *Sartre*, p. 67.
59. B, p. 237.
60. B, p. 311.
61. S&G, p. 51.
62. B, p. 102.

63. *Sartre*, p. 52.
64. B, p. 267.
65. B, p. 311.
66. UTN, p. 24.
67. S&G, p. 54.
68. See Bibliography.
69. S&BR, p. 250.
70. S&G, p. 46.

71. S&G, p. 50.
72. S&G, p. 52.
73. S, p. 209.
74. S&G, p. 55.
75. S&G, p. 55.
76. B, p. 312.
77. B, p. 313.
78. Ibid.

CHAPTER 6 A Severed Head

1. *Sartre*, p. 62.
2. *A Severed Head* (ASH), pp. 8 et seq.
3. ASH, p. 232.
4. ASH, p. 69.
5. ASH, p. 22.
6. AD, p. 17.
7. ASH, p. 37.
8. AD, p. 20.
9. ASH, p. 24.
10. ASH, p. 39.
11. ASH, p. 35.
12. ASH, p. 67.
13. ASH, p. 42.
14. ASH, pp. 64–5.
15. ASH, p. 83.
16. ASH, p. 81.
17. Ibid.
18. ASH, p. 52.

19. ASH, p. 68.
20. S&G, p. 51.
21. ASH, p. 40.
22. ASH, p. 49.
23. ASH, p. 54.
24. ASH, p. 56.
25. ASH, p. 120.
26. ASH, p. 147.
27. ASH, p. 171.
28. Freud, *Collected Works*, Vol. XIII, p. 20.
29. ASH, p. 152.
30. ASH, pp. 156–7.
31. ASH, p. 241.
32. Ibid.
33. Ibid.
34. ASH, p. 252.
35. ASH, pp. 205–6.
36. ASH, p. 225.

CHAPTER 7 An Unofficial Rose

1. *An Unofficial Rose* (UR), p. 74.
2. UR, p. 39.
3. S&BR, p. 255.
4. Ibid.
5. S&BR, p. 260.
6. UR, p. 72.
7. UR, p. 39.
8. UR, p. 75.
9. S&BR, p. 255.
10. UR, p. 316.
11. UR, p. 218.

12. UR, p. 228.
13. S&G, p. 55.
14. UR, p. 123.
15. UR, p. 203.
16. Ibid.
17. UR, p. 312.
18. UR, p. 317.
19. UR, p. 122.
20. UR, p. 290.
21. *The Characters of Love*, p. 235.
22. Op. cit. p. 239.

23. Op. cit. p. 237.
24. Op. cit. p. 238.
25. Op. cit. p. 239.
26. UR, p. 123.
27. UR, p. 155.
28. UR, p. 132.
29. UR, p. 131.
30. UR, p. 16.
31. UR, p. 61.
32. UR, p. 62.
33. UR, p. 132.
34. UR, p. 134.
35. S&BR, p. 269.
36. UR, p. 138.
37. UR, p. 156.
38. *Sartre*, p. 33.

39. UR, p. 270.
40. UR, p. 274.
41. UR, p. 276.
42. UR, p. 301.
43. UR, p. 339.
44. UR, p. 333.
45. UR, p. 335.
46. *The Characters of Love*, p. 236.
47. UR, p. 340.
48. UR, pp. 279–80.
49. UR, p. 18.
50. UR, p. 347.
51. UR, p. 288.
52. UR, p. 13.
53. UR, p. 98.
54. UR, p. 348.

CHAPTER 8 The Unicorn

1. S&BR, p. 271.
2. A de D, p. 90.
3. A de D, p. 91.
4. Sheridan Le Fanu *In a Glass Darkly*, Ed. 1947, preface by V. S. Pritchett, p. 9, The Chiltern Library.
5. Ibid.
6. S&BR, p. 268.
7. U, p. 30.
8. U, p. 75
9. U, p. 115.
10. U, p. 203.
11. U, p. 275.
12. Freud, *Totem and Taboo*, p. 73.
13. *Totem and Taboo*, p. 74.
14. *Totem and Taboo*, p. 27.
15. Ibid.
16. Freud, *Collected Works*, Vol. X, pp. 239 et seq.
17. Ibid.
18. U, p. 109.
19. U, p. 259.
20. Freud, *Totem and Taboo*, p. 30.

21. U, p. 301.
22. Freud, *Totem and Taboo*, p. 43.
23. *Totem and Taboo*, p. 49.
24. *Totem and Taboo*, (quoting Frazer) p. 44.
25. U, p. 209.
26. Freud, *Totem and Taboo*, p. 72.
27. U, p. 237.
28. U, p. 258.
29. U, p. 311.
30. UTN, p. 26.
31. U, p. 95.
32. U, p. 114.
33. Ibid.
34. P et G, p. 85.
35. P et G, p. 84.
36. P et G, p. 73.
37. U, p. 117.
38. Ibid.
39. U, p. 76.
40. U, p. 64.
41. P et G, p. 6.
42. P et G, p. 72.
43. P et G, p. 13.

44. Ibid.
45. P et G, p. 36.
46. A de D, p. 73.
47. U, p. 51.
48. U, p. 235.
49. U, p. 76.
50. U, p. 177.
51. U, p. 98.
52. U, p. 128.
53. U, p. 261.
54. U, p. 48.
55. U, p. 110.
56. P et G, p. 19.
57. U, p. 138.
58. A de D, p. 86.
59. *In a Glass Darkly*, p. 10.
60. Op. cit. p. 240.
61. Op. cit. p. 251.
62. U, p. 63.
63. U, p. 52.
64. U, p. 109.
65. U, p. 257.
66. U, p. 258.
67. U, p. 268.
68. U, p. 269.
69. P et G, p. 81.

70. P et G, p. 84.
71. U, p. 257.
72. U, p. 259.
73. U, p. 276.
74. U, p. 301.
75. U, p. 118.
76. U, p. 303.
77. U, p. 302.
78. U, p. 198.
79. P et G, p. 21.
80. S&BR, pp. 269–70.
81. U, p. 258.
82. S&BR, p. 260.
83. U, p. 284.
84. U, p. 198.
85. U, p. 316.
86. U, pp. 311–12.
87. U, p. 316.
88. U, p. 318.
89. U, p. 120.
90. U, p. 177.
91. S&BR, p. 270.
92. AD, p. 19.
93. AD, p. 20.
94. Ibid.
95. S&G, p. 55.

CHAPTER 9 The Art of the Novels

1. *Sartre*, p. 16.
2. *Sartre*, p. 17.
3. *Sartre*, p. 75.
4. *Sartre*, p. 76.
5. *Albert Camus and the Literature of Revolt*, pp. 164 et seq.
6. S&BR, p. 271.

7. AD, p. 20.
8. B, p. 129.
9. See Bibliography.
10. AD, p. 20.
11. UTN, p. 275.
12. FFTE, pp. 290–1.
13. UR, p. 219.

CHAPTER 10 The Time of the Angels

1. AD.
2. *The Time of the Angels* (TOA), p. 184.
3. 'On "God" and "Good"' (OG&G), p. 71.
4. OG&G. p. 51.

5. Nietzsche, *The Birth of Tragedy*, Section VII.
6. Ibid. Section IX.
7. OG&G, p. 68.
8. TOA, p. 73.

CHAPTER 12 The Black Prince

1. *The Black Prince*, (BP), p. 27.
2. BP, p. 170.
3. BP, p. 173.
4. BP, p. 68.
5. S&G, p. 51.
6. BP, pp. 55–6.
7. BP, Postscript by Bradley Pearson.
8. BP, pp. 163–4.
9. BP, pp. 362–3.

CHAPTER 16 Nuns and Soldiers

1. E. M. Forster, Ch. 3 'People', *Aspects of the Novel*, Edward Arnold, 1927.

CHAPTER 19 The Writer and her Work

1. I take these to be the philosophers who have learned from Wittgenstein, such as Gilbert Ryle, and the Logical Positives, such as A. J. Ayer. The particular example Miss Murdoch offers in 'Against Dryness' is drawn from Stuart Hampshire's *Thought and Action*.
2. AD, p. 18.
3. E&M, p. 179.
4. OG&G, p. 67.
5. OG&G, pp. 3–4.
6. OG&G, p. 66.
7. OG&G, p. 59.
8. 'Negative Capability' is a phrase used by Keats in a letter to describe the particular quality of Shakespeare's imagination – the capacity not to formulate ideas of patterns but to be 'capable of being in uncertainties, mysteries, doubts, without any irritable reaching after fact and reason'.
9. S&G, p. 51.
10. Examples of the crystalline novel might be French philosophical myths like Sartre's *La Nausée* or Camus' *La Chute (The Fall)*, or in English some of the elegant, beautifully shaped late fables of Muriel Spark – *The Driver's Seat, The Public Image* – or William Golding's *Pincher Martin*, an allegorized vision of a man coming to grips with his death. Much good recent American fiction, such as that of Thomas Pyncheon, is also 'crystalline' in form.
11. Patroclus in Homer's *Iliad*; Alyosha in Dostoevski's *The Brothers Karamazov*; Cordelia in Shakespeare's *King Lear*; Mr Knightley in Jane Austen's *Emma*.
12. E&M, p. 169.
13. *Sartre*, Ch. I.
14. *Sartre*, Ch. III.
15. 'T. S. Eliot as a Moralist', p. 156.
16. E&M, p. 182.
17. F. R. Karl, *The Contemporary English Novel*, London, 1963, p. 261.
18. *Sartre*, Ch. VII, VIII.
19. See Ch. V, 'The Bell', for a

fuller discussion of the symbolism of the bell.

20. John Bayley, *The Characters of Love: A Study in the Literature of Personality*, Ch. IV.

21. Lionel Trilling, 'Mansfield Park', in *The Opposing Self*, New York, 1955.

22. See his essay on Iris Murdoch in *Possibilities: Essays on the State of the Novel*, Oxford University, 1973.

23. OG&G, p. 68.

24. See Nietzsche, *The Birth of Tragedy*, and see p. 251, my review of *The Time of the Angels*.

25. High Gothic – a literary mode, originally very popular in the eighteenth century, which relied on some, or all, of the following constituents: a reference to medieval times, an element of the supernatural, horror, mystery, ruins and haunted castles. It was satirized by Jane Austen in *Northanger Abbey* but has been used, especially by American writers, as a framework for metaphysical speculation and spiritual explanation.

26. In *The Spectator*, 7 September 1962, pp. 337–8.

27. Frank Kermode, 'The House of Fiction', p. 64.

28. See Ch. IX, 'The Art of the Novels', p. 228–9, for my earlier opinion of *The Severed Head*.

29. BP, p. 37, and Ch. V, 'The Bell' and Ch. IX, 'The Art of the Novels'.

30. BP, pp. 55–6.

31. BP, pp. 161 et seq.

32. 'Recontres avec Iris Murdoch', 1978.